Praise for this book

"Richard provides real Scrum guidance for real teams. If yo[...], this book is a great resource."

—Aaron Bjork, Principal Group Program Manager, Team Foundation Server, Microsoft

"Richard successfully marries the best tools for .NET developers to the most effective practices without sacrificing the people."

—David Starr, Senior Program Manager, Visual Studio, Microsoft

"Finally, a book about Scrum from the Development Team's point of view; Richard's description of the best and worst ways to implement Scrum is priceless. The first chapter alone is one of the best descriptions of 'Scrum done well' that I've ever seen."

—Charles Bradley, Scrum Coach & Professional Scrum Master

"The very first book on Team Foundation Server that I read was written by Richard, and he's done it again this time with another fantastic read."

—Brian Keller, Principal Technical Evangelist for Microsoft Visual Studio

"Richard does a fantastic job of blending theory, practice, and tools in one easy to read book! This book will surely be a staple for many of our Scrum coaching engagements."

—Chad Albrecht, VP Centare, PST

"As an encore to helping introduce the industry shaking Professional Scrum Developer program, Richard reminds us in this book why he's a leading voice in Scrum and Visual Studio ALM."

—Ryan Cromwell, Professional Scrum Trainer, MVP

"I've known Richard a long time and it's been great to follow his progression towards becoming a Scrum 'white robe.' I'm so happy the community now has the ultimate resource on understanding the marriage of Scrum and TFS."

—Adam Cogan, Microsoft Regional Director, Visual Studio ALM MVP [of the year 2011]

"If you're new to Scrum or even if you've been doing it for a while, this book will help you get the big picture."

—*Benjamin Day, Professional Scrum Trainer, MVP*

"If you're using Scrum and TFS and you haven't read this book, then you're probably doing it wrong."

—*Brian Randell, MCW Technologies, Visual Studio ALM MVP*

"In this book, Richard uses the core values of Scrum to describe how to get the best Scrum adoption of Visual Studio 2012. This is a superb combination of principles and mechanics that should be on all teams' bookshelves."

—*Simon Reindl Professional Scrum Developer Trainer*

"I don't keep a lot of technology books on my bookshelf due to the pace at which developer tools evolve but this book, with its focus on people and processes, is definitely a keeper. Richard's book is to Scrum development as Petzold's was to Windows development."

—*Charles Sterling, Visual Studio Senior Program Manager, Microsoft*

"Among the plethora of Scrum literature out there, Richard's book makes a difference by bringing Scrum closer to where it belongs: the day-to-day work in the context of a team, supported by suitable practices, and the state-of-the-art Visual Studio toolset. You'll benefit from most of the advice it contains, even if you don't use Visual Studio!"

—*Jose Luis Soria, Plain Concepts ALM Team Lead, PST*

"Scrum, Visual Studio, and Team Foundation Server are just tools, and they will not make you better by themselves. If you really want to improve you need to understand the tools and learn how to improve, and definitively, Richard's book will help you to get there"

—*Luis Fraile, Visual Studio ALM MVP, Globe ALM Division Manager*

"A masterpiece which distills the world of Scrum in a Visual Studio environment; anyone who is using Scrum will recognize many of the 'smells' and appreciate the sharing of real-world experience and guidance."

—*Willy-Peter Schaub, Program Manager, Visual Studio ALM Rangers*

"This book should be required reading for everyone on your team. It will help you bring people, processes, and technology together quickly with Scrum."

—*Mike Vincent, Professional Scrum Developer Trainer, Visual Studio ALM MVP*

Professional Scrum Development with Microsoft® Visual Studio® 2012

Richard Hundhausen

PUBLISHED BY
Microsoft Press
A Division of Microsoft Corporation
One Microsoft Way
Redmond, Washington 98052-6399

Library of Congress Control Number: 2012948863
ISBN: 978-0-7356-5798-4

Printed and bound in the United States of America.

First Printing

Microsoft Press books are available through booksellers and distributors worldwide. If you need support related to this book, email Microsoft Press Book Support at mspinput@microsoft.com. Please tell us what you think of this book at *http://www.microsoft.com/learning/booksurvey*.

Microsoft and the trademarks listed at *http://www.microsoft.com/about/legal/en/us/ IntellectualProperty/Trademarks/EN-US.aspx* are trademarks of the Microsoft group of companies. All other marks are property of their respective owners.

The example companies, organizations, products, domain names, email addresses, logos, people, places, and events depicted herein are fictitious. No association with any real company, organization, product, domain name, email address, logo, person, place, or event is intended or should be inferred.

Acquisitions and Developmental Editor: Devon Musgrave
Project Editor: Rosemary Caperton
Editorial Production: Christian Holdener, S4Carlisle Publishing Services
Copyeditor: Andrew Jones
Indexer: Jean Skipp
Cover: Twist Creative · Seattle

This book is dedicated to my Scrum Team: Esmay, Isla, Berlin, Blaize, Sawyer, and Kristen.

Contents at a Glance

Contents

Chapter 7   Acceptance test-driven development   197

Chapter 8   Effective collaboration   227

PART III IMPROVING

Chapter 9 Continuous improvement   275

Foreword

By 2001, the software industry was in trouble—more projects were failing than succeeding. Customers began demanding contracts with penalties, and increasingly sending work offshore. Some software developers, though, had increasing success with a development process known as "lightweight." Almost uniformly, these processes were based on the well-known iterative, incremental process.

In February of 2001, these developers issued a manifesto—the Agile Manifesto. The Manifesto called for Agile software development based on 4 principle values and 12 underlying principles. Two of the principles were 1.) to satisfy customers through early and continuous delivery of working software, and 2). to deliver working software frequently, from a couple of weeks to a couple of months, with a preference to the shorter timescale.

By 2008, the Scrum Agile process was used predominantly. A simple framework, it provided an easily adopted iterative incremental framework for software development. It also incorporated the Agile Manifesto's values and principles. The two authors of Scrum, Jeff Sutherland and myself, also were among the authors of the Agile Manifesto.

I had anticipated some of the difficulties organizations (and even teams) would face when they adopted Scrum. However, I believed that developers would bloom in a Scrum environment. Stifled and choked by waterfall, developers would stand tall, employing development practices, collaboration, and tooling that nobody had time to use in waterfall projects.

Much to my surprise, this was only true for perhaps 20 percent of all software developers.

Note In 2007, Martin Fowler characterized most Agile software development as "flaccid." He stated: There's a mess I've heard about with quite a few projects recently. It works out like this:

- They want to use an Agile process, and pick Scrum.

- They adopt the Scrum practices, and maybe even the principles.

- After a while, progress is slow because the code base is a mess.

> What's happened is that they haven't paid enough attention to the internal quality of their software. If you make that mistake you'll soon find your productivity dragged down because it's much harder to add new features than you'd like. You've taken on a crippling Technical Debt and your Scrum has gone weak at the knees. (And if you've been in a real scrum, you'll know that's a Bad Thing.) *http://martinfowler.com/bliki/FlaccidScrum.html*

Martin's description of flaccid Scrum resonated with our experience. Most developers were skilled, but not adequately skilled in the three dimensions required to rapidly build complete increments of usable functionality. These dimensions are:

People   The ability to work in a small, cross-functional, self-organizing team.

Practices   The knowledge of and ability to apply modern engineering practices that short cycle development mandates.

Tooling   Tools that integrated and automated these practices so that successive increments could be rapidly integrated without the drag of exponentially accruing artifacts that must be handled manually.

We put our business on hold while we worked through 2008 to create what has become known as the Professional Scrum Developer program. Offered in both a three- and five-day format, we formulated a workshop. The input was developers whose knowledge and capabilities produced flaccid increments. The output were teams of developers who had developed solid increments of software called for by the Agile Manifesto and demanded by the modern, competitive organization.

Richard has been there since the beginning. His book, *Professional Scrum Development with Microsoft® Visual Studio® 2012* continues his participation in the movement started by us few in 2009.

When you read Richard's book, you can learn the three dimensions needed for Agile software development: people, process, and tools. Just like the course, Richard intertwines them into something you can absorb. If you are on a Scrum team, read Richard's book. List the called-for practices. Identify which practices pose challenges to your team. Order them by their greatest impact. Then remediate them, one by one.

Many people spend money going to Agile conferences. Save the money and more by buying this book, discussing it with others, and going to Code Camps, the "un-conference" for the serious.

Richard and I look forward to your increased skill. Our industry and our society need it. Software is the last great scalable resource needed by our increasingly complex society. The effective, productive teamwork of Agile teams is the basis of problem solving that our society also needs.

Scrum on!

Ken Schwaber
co-creator of Scrum
September, 2012

In 2009, Richard took on a daunting task. Ken Schwaber and I came together because we lamented the impediment facing software teams trying to improve their ability to deliver customer value on frequent, short cadence. They could learn about practices, they could learn about tools, or they could engage coaching, but putting it all together was an exercise left to the readers.

That's when Richard Hundhausen stepped into the breach. He put together Professional Scrum Developer in a whirlwind. Quite literally, he toured the world delivering beta courses, relentlessly receiving feedback, and inspecting and adapting. The result was the first highly scalable training program that combined modern software engineering practices and readily available tooling at the global scale. Richard has been improving the course for three years through a dedicated community of certified trainers and has now distilled the basics into an easily accessible book.

If you're new to Scrum and want to get better at delivering high-quality software that your customers want quickly, Professional Scrum Developer is a great place to start.

Sam Guckenheimer
Product Owner, Visual Studio Product Line
Microsoft Corporation
September, 2012

Introduction

Scrum is a framework for developing and sustaining complex products, such as software. Scrum is just a set of rules, as defined in the *Scrum Guide* (*www.scrum .org/Scrum-Guides*), and it describes the roles, events, and artifacts, as well as the rules that bind them together. When used correctly, this framework enables a team to address complex problems while productively and creatively delivering products of the highest possible value. Scrum is an Agile method. In fact, it is the most popular Agile method in use today.

Scrum employs an iterative and incremental approach to optimizing predictability and controlling risk. This is due to the empirical process control nature of Scrum. Through proper use of inspection, adaptation, and transparency, a Scrum Team can try a new way of doing something (an experiment) and gauge its usefulness after a short iteration. They can then collectively decide to embrace, extend, or drop the practice. This includes the tools a team uses and how they use them.

Combining Scrum with the application lifecycle management (ALM) tools found in Microsoft Visual Studio 2012 is a powerful combination. It is the purpose of this book to establish a baseline understanding of Scrum, as well as how Scrum is supported in Visual Studio 2012. I will also illustrate which practices provide more value when executed *without* the use of tools. In addition, I will point out those tools which have been erroneously marketed as healthy when used by a collocated, collaborative Scrum Team.

In software development, anything and everything can change in a moment's notice. Healthy teams know this. They also know that continuously inspecting and adapting the way things are done is a way of life. High-performance Scrum Development Teams take it a step further. They know that within every dysfunction or impediment identified is an opportunity to learn and improve. Reading this book is a great first step.

Who should read this book

This book will be of value to any members of a software development team using Scrum. I primarily focus on the responsibilities and tasks of the developer (which in Scrum includes designers, architects, coders, testers, technical writers, etc.). Product Owners and Scrum Masters will also derive value from this book, as they will be using many of the same Visual Studio tools to plan and manage their work and assess progress. Stakeholders, including customers, users, and managers, will also gain value from this book, especially when they learn what they can and cannot do according to the rules of Scrum and which tools in Visual Studio support this.

Who should not read this book

This book is intended for teams using Scrum and Visual Studio 2012 together. It won't provide *as much* value for teams executing Agile (non-Scrum) software development and won't provide *any* value for teams running more formal "waterfall" software development projects, although Chapter 1 may hopefully change the minds of such proponents. Likewise, if a team is using Scrum, but not yet using Visual Studio 2012, the bulk of the book won't be very interesting. This is also the case for teams using Visual Studio 2012 *Express* or *Professional* editions, which don't contain the high-value, team-based tools for planning and managing the backlogs and team collaboration.

Organization of this book

This book is divided into three sections, each of which focuses on a different aspect of the marriage of Scrum and Visual Studio. Part I, "Fundamentals," sets a baseline understanding of the Scrum framework, Visual Studio 2012 editions and their interesting ALM features, as well as the Visual Studio Scrum 2.0 process template. Part II, "Using Scrum," provides several chapters detailing the practical application of how a Scrum Team would use the relevant features of Visual Studio 2012. Part III, "Improving," includes a chapter on identifying common challenges and dysfunctions in order to remove them, as well as techniques to continually improve your game of Scrum. By reading all sections sequentially, you will see how Visual Studio and Scrum can be used together in an effective way and how a team can become high-performance in the way it develops software.

Finding your best starting point in this book

The different sections of *Professional Scrum Development with Microsoft Visual Studio 2012* cover a range of topics. Depending on your needs and your existing understanding of Scrum, Visual Studio, and the related development practices, you may wish to focus on specific areas of the book. Use the following table to determine how best to proceed through the book.

If you are	Follow these steps
New to Scrum or have never heard of it	Read Chapter 1
New to Visual Studio 2012 or its ALM tools	Read Chapter 2
New to the Visual Studio Scrum process template or want to know what's new in version 2.0	Read Chapter 3
Familiar with Scrum and Visual Studio and only want to learn how to setup and manage a Product Backlog.	Read Chapters 4 and 5
Familiar with Scrum and Visual Studio and only want guidance on overcoming common challenges and dysfunctions.	Read Chapter 9

Conventions and features in this book

This book presents information using conventions designed to make the information readable and easy to follow.

- Screenshots from relevant Visual Studio 2012 features are provided for your reference.

- Boxed elements with labels such as "Note" or "Tip" provide additional information and guidance related to the subject.

- Some notes and tips are practical guidance provided by fellow Professional Scrum Developers who have helped review this book.

In addition, I have included two additional boxed elements, one labeled "Smells" and the other labeled "Tailspin Toys Case Study.". These are discussed in the following sections.

Smells Throughout this book, I point out specific situations and traps that a Scrum Team should avoid. I refer to these as *smells*. These smells typically indicate an underlying dysfunction or other unhealthy behavior. For teams new to Scrum, these smells may be hard to identify. Once they are brought to light, however, they should be used as learning opportunities. As a team improves, it should be able to recognize dysfunction on its own, as well as remove it. High-performance Scrum Teams reach the ability to identify potential waste, evaluate the risks, and even decide to opt-in to specific behaviors, including those that may be a smell to the uneducated.

Tailspin Toys case study As you flip through the pages, you will read about Tailspin Toys as a case study. This is a fictitious organization and team that is building an online retail website that sells model aircraft and accessories. The team has been using Scrum for some time and is moving to Visual Studio 2012. My opinions on healthy and unhealthy behaviors are made evident through the choices made by the Tailspin Toys team.

Code samples

Although this book contains almost no code samples, I did build a utility application to help create and manage the Product Backlog and Sprint Backlog. This helped me prepare the data seen in the various screen captures in this book. I affectionately named this utility the *Scrum Robot*. The source code is yours if you think it can be helpful. If nothing else, it demonstrates how to connect to a Team Foundation Server 2012 instance and manipulate basic team project data. The Scrum Robot can be downloaded from the book's companion content page:

http://go.microsoft.com/FWLink/?Linkid=267484

Note You will need to have Visual Studio 2012 with Team Explorer installed in order to use the Scrum Robot.

Installing and using the Scrum Robot

Follow these steps to install the Scrum Robot on your computer so that you can programmatically access Team Foundation Server and manipulate a team project's areas, iterations, Product Backlog, and Sprint Backlog.

1. Unzip the *ScrumRobot.zip* file that you downloaded from the book's website (name a specific directory along with directions to create it, if necessary).

2. If prompted, review the displayed end user license agreement. If you accept the terms, select the accept option, and then click Next.

Note If the license agreement doesn't appear, you can access it from the same webpage from which you downloaded the *ScrumRobot.zip* file.

3. Once unzipped, you can open the *ScrumRobot.sln* solution and review the code. Press F5 to run the utility after changing any variables or constants, such as the name and address of your Team Foundation Server.

Acknowledgments

There are several people who helped me write this book: Christian Holdener, for his infinite patience. Devon Musgrave and Rosemary Caperton, for yet another opportunity to write for Microsoft Press. Fellow Professional Scrum Developers: Mike Vincent, Simon Reindl, Jose Luis Soria, David Starr, Jeroen van Menen, Chad Albrecht, Ryan Cromwell, Luis Fraile, Rob Maher, and Peter Gfader for helping me sharpen the message. Fellow Scrum and Visual Studio practitioners: Charles Bradley, Bob Hardister, Graham Barry, Anna Russo, Christofer Löf, Willy-Peter Schaub, and Peter Provost for providing great ideas and reviews. Thank you everyone.

Errata & book support

We've made every effort to ensure the accuracy of this book and its companion content. Any errors that have been reported since this book was published are listed on our Microsoft Press site at oreilly.com:

> *http://go.microsoft.com/FWLink/?Linkid=267483*

If you find an error that is not already listed, you can report it to us through the same page.

If you need additional support, email Microsoft Press Book Support at *mspinput@microsoft.com.*

Please note that product support for Microsoft software is not offered through the addresses above.

We want to hear from you

At Microsoft Press, your satisfaction is our top priority, and your feedback our most valuable asset. Please tell us what you think of this book at:

http://www.microsoft.com/learning/booksurvey

The survey is short, and we read every one of your comments and ideas. Thanks in advance for your input!

Stay in touch

Let's keep the conversation going! We're on Twitter: *http://twitter.com/MicrosoftPress*

Fundamentals

The chapters in this section will establish a baseline understanding of the three areas that every professional Scrum developer using the Microsoft tools platform must know:

- Scrum

- The Microsoft Visual Studio 2012 Application Lifecycle Management (ALM) tools

- The Visual Studio Scrum process template

We will begin by looking at Scrum and the rules of Scrum from the developer's perspective. The focus will be on how and when the Development Team interacts with the Product Owner and Scrum Master, participates in the various Scrum events, and uses the various Scrum artifacts. Remember that in Scrum, the term *developer* equates to a Development Team member. This does not necessarily equate to programmer or coder. In fact, Scrum recognizes testers, coders, designers, architects, analysts, and database administrators (DBAs) as developers. It's important for all developers to understand the rules of Scrum, and what's expected of them and their team, as well as when and how they can interact with the Product Owner, the Scrum Master, and the various artifacts.

The remaining chapters will be more technical in nature and cover the ALM tools found in Visual Studio 2012, including Team Foundation Server and its Scrum process template. This is Microsoft's fourth release of these tools and a lot has been added and improved from prior versions. With a full install of Visual Studio and Team Foundation Server, there are many tools available for a Development Team. I will endeavor to list and discuss the relevant ALM tools, but I won't explore the practice of using each. In my opinion, some tools are better left in the toolbox, allowing the team to exercise higher-valued collaborative practices instead.

CHAPTER 1

Scrumdamentals

Scrum is a framework for developing and sustaining complex products. Software is a complex product. Scrum is ideal for managing the development of software. Scrum is not a methodology or a process, although you can employ various processes within it. Software development doesn't generate the same output every time, given a certain input. Scrum embraces this fact and is empirical, which means that it promotes the use of observation and experimentation in order to inspect and adapt. This enables a team to regularly see the effectiveness of its development practices and make changes accordingly.

Even today, more than 60 years into the evolution of software development, the chances are a medium-sized to large software project will fail. Fortunately, the industry has finally noticed, understands, and has started to respond to this problem. Some organizations have turned this around. Things are improving. Evidence shows that Agile practices, such as Scrum, are leading these successes.

> **Tip** Using a software development analogy, you can think of Agile as being an *interface*. Agile defines 4 abstract values and 12 abstract principles (*http://agilemanifesto.org*). While there are many ways to implement these values and principles, Agile does not describe them. Scrum does. You can think of Scrum as a *concrete class* that *implements* Agile.

Agile teams know that they must continuously inspect and adapt—not just their product, but their practices as well. Being book-smart on Scrum, Application Lifecycle Management (ALM), and Microsoft Visual Studio is a good start. Having experience using them together in practice is better. Being able to identify and act on opportunities for improvement as you use them is awesome. That should be your goal. Don't just settle for a non-failed project. Strive for completing the project better, faster, and cheaper than the stakeholders thought possible.

The *Scrum Guide*

Scrum has been around since the early 1990s. During that time, Scrum's definition and related practices have come from books, presentations, and professionals doing their best to explain it. Unfortunately, those messages were not always accurate and almost never consistent. Scrum, as it has emerged today, doesn't look like it did 10 years ago.

In 2010, Scrum.org codified Scrum by creating and publishing the *Scrum Guide* for free. This roughly 15-page guide represents the official rules of Scrum and is maintained by Scrum's creators, Ken Schwaber and Jeff Sutherland. It is available in 30 languages and downloadable at *http://www.scrum.org/scrumguides*. It is a great reference that you can use even as you are reading this book. As you read the guide, you will see that Scrum is lightweight and quite easy to understand. Unfortunately, it is extremely difficult to master. The *Scrum Guide* will continue to be updated and may supersede the guidance you read in this chapter and the rest of the book.

> **Tip** You can think of Scrum as being like the game of chess. Both have rules. For example, Scrum doesn't allow two Product Owners just as chess doesn't allow two kings. When you play chess, it is expected that you play by the rules. If you don't, then you're not playing chess. This is the same with Scrum. Another way to think about it is that both Scrum and chess do not fail or succeed. Only the players fail or succeed. Those who keep playing by the rules will eventually improve, though it may take a long time to master the game.

The Scrum framework consists of the Scrum team and the associated roles, events, and artifacts. Each of these items serves a specific purpose, as you will see in this chapter. The rules of Scrum, as defined in the *Scrum Guide*, bind together the roles, events, and artifacts. Following these rules is essential to the success of a team's ability to use Scrum to develop a high-value, quality software product.

Scrum in action

If you study the *Scrum Guide*, you will understand the components and related rules. You won't necessarily see how they flow together. This requires you to actually experience Scrum while developing software on a team. As a substitute for that experience, Figure 1-1 was created by a fellow professional Scrum developer to illustrate the Scrum framework in action.

In Scrum, the Product Backlog is the single source of requirements for any changes to be made to the software product. This list includes features to be added, as well as bugs to be fixed. It is the Product Owner's responsibility to ensure that the Product Backlog is available, transparent, understood by the Development Team, and ordered (prioritized). The Development Team collaborates with the Product Owner, and others as needed, during Sprint Planning and Product Backlog grooming to understand and estimate the effort required to deliver the items in the Product Backlog.

The Sprint is a time-boxed event that contains the other Scrum events. Sprints should be a month or less in duration. The first event within a Sprint is the Sprint Planning meeting. In this time-boxed event, the Scrum team collaborates to plan the work of the upcoming Sprint. The Product Backlog items (PBIs), ordered at the top of the Product Backlog by the Product Owner, are discussed. The Development Team forecasts those Product Backlog items that it believes it can complete by the end of the Sprint. A Sprint Goal is crafted, and the Sprint Backlog emerges. The Sprint Backlog contains those items selected by the Development Team plus a plan for delivering them. The Sprint Backlog shows the work remaining in the Sprint at all times.

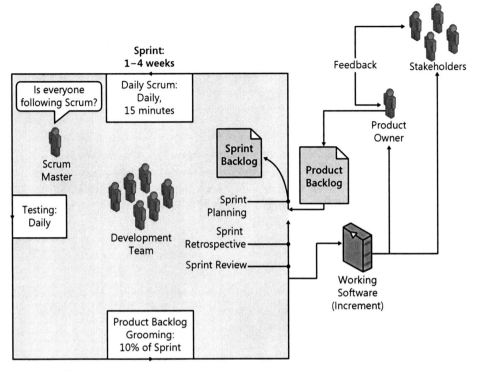

Sprint:
1–4 weeks

Is everyone following Scrum?

Daily Scrum: Daily, 15 minutes

Scrum Master

Testing: Daily

Sprint Backlog

Development Team

Sprint Planning

Sprint Retrospective

Sprint Review

Product Backlog Grooming: 10% of Sprint

Feedback

Stakeholders

Product Owner

Product Backlog

Working Software (Increment)

FIGURE 1-1 The Scrum framework in action.

The bulk of the Sprint's time-box will be spent developing the items in the Sprint Backlog. The rules of Scrum are fairly silent on what occurs each day during development. The Development Team must meet regularly for the Daily Scrum. This short meeting is for the Development Team to synchronize on what work will be executed in the next 24 hours. The Development Team should also meet with the Product Owner to groom the Product Backlog. During grooming, items in the Product Backlog are given additional detail, and estimates are given by the Development Team. This keeps the Product Backlog healthy so that the Product Owner can plan the software product's release and make better decisions on the items to develop next.

During the Sprint, the Development Team completes items in their Sprint Backlog according to each item's acceptance criteria and the team's Definition of "Done". This definition lists the practices and standards that must be met for every item before it can be considered complete. The definition is created by the Development Team but must be understood by the Product Owner. Both parties must understand that if work does not meet the Definition of "Done," it is not done and cannot be released. Ideally, the Development Team collaborates with the Product Owner throughout the Sprint to ensure that all criteria are being met. If the Development Team completes their forecasted work early, they should collaborate with the Product Owner to find another suitable Product Backlog item to work on. Conversely, at the first indication that the Development Team knows that they *won't* be able to complete their forecasted work, they should collaborate with the Product Owner to identify and discuss trade-offs and modify the Sprint Backlog to reflect the reality of the Sprint without sacrificing quality.

Sprint Backlog items done according the Development Team's definition are demonstrated during the Sprint Review meeting. The Product Owner may invite various stakeholders to this meeting for their feedback on the Increment. This Product Owner and stakeholder feedback might be captured and end up as new items in the Product Backlog. Existing items may also need to be updated or removed. The Product Owner may decide to release the Increment as soon as possible or delay it. This should be a business decision. Regardless of when the Increment is released, the Development Team should always develop the Increment as though it were *going to be* released as soon as possible.

The last event in the Sprint is the Sprint Retrospective meeting. This meeting provides an opportunity for the Scrum Team to inspect themselves and identify what went well and what needs improving. If improvements are identified, the team should create an actionable plan for the next Sprint. Nothing is out of scope during this meeting—people, relationships, process, and tools can all be discussed. The Scrum Team may also decide to adjust its Definition of "Done" to increase product quality. After the meeting, the next Sprint begins.

Scrum roles

The group of individuals who are responsible for, and committed to, building the software product is known as the Scrum Team. The Scrum Team is a superset of the Development Team. The Scrum Team consists of the following Scrum roles:

- Development Team

- Product Owner

- Scrum Master

As you will learn, there is an implied equality (that is, lack of rank or seniority) of the developers on the Development Team since Scrum does not recognize titles. That is not the case with the Scrum Team as a whole. The Product Owner is the visionary leader who chooses what is built, when it is ready to release, and when to stop or cancel the project. If you think of the roles in terms of providing service, the Development Team serves the Product Owner, while the Scrum Master serves both the Development Team and the Product Owner. Therefore, the Development Team has strong influence to select (that is, hire or fire) the Scrum Master. Correspondingly, the Product Owner has strong influence to select the Development Team he or she wants to turn the Product Backlog into done Increments. Because of this separation of duties, the roles should be played by separate individuals. This mitigates any chance of a conflict of interest. That said, smaller teams may find it necessary to combine roles.

> **Note** Scrum Team != Development Team. The Scrum Team refers to the Development Team *plus* the Product Owner and Scrum Master. The Development Team refers to the subset of the Scrum Team that contains only the developers who will be developing the Increment. When someone uses the unqualified term "team" during conversation, it could refer to either. You may want to ask the person using the term to provide additional context.

The Development Team

The Development Team consists of between 3-9 professionals who are capable of building and delivering a potentially-releasable Increment of software at the end of a Sprint. The size of 6 +/– 3 developers allows the team to be small and nimble, while being large enough to complete increments of complex development. A team with only 2 developers doesn't need Scrum, as they can simply communicate directly and be productive. Also, there is a greater chance that the 2 developers won't have the skills required to do the work. On the other hand, teams with more than 9 developers require too much coordination. These larger teams tend to generate too much complexity to derive value from Scrum's empiricism.

> **Note** The Product Owner and Scrum Master are not on the Development Team and are not included in the 6 +/– 3 Development Team size count. However, if the Product Owner or Scrum Master is *also* a developer who will be executing development tasks during the Sprint, then you should count them.

In Scrum, Development Team members are called "developers," regardless of their background, job title, or skill set. Development Team members may have experience in software engineering, testing, architecture and design, graphic design, database administration, business analysis, technical writing, or other similar specialties. Regardless of what their resume says, they are now "developers" as far as Scrum is concerned. They should burn their business cards and focus on delivering value in the form of working software. Also, there are no subteams in Scrum, such as testing or QA. The Development Team performs all of the work required to deliver the done increment of the software product.

It's important to note that just because a team member is called a developer, this does not necessarily mean that they will be developing (writing) code. Depending on the task, they may be *developing* architecture, *developing* user interface or design, *developing* test cases, *developing* database objects, *developing* installers, or *developing* documentation, etc. Everyone *develops* something. Table 1-1 lists the high-level activities that a Scrum Development Team will perform.

TABLE 1-1 Development team activities within Scrum.

Activity	When
Collaborate with the Product Owner to forecast the Sprint's work and craft a Sprint Goal.	Sprint Planning.
Collaborate with fellow developers on a plan to implement the forecasted work (including task estimation).	Sprint Planning, Daily Scrum.
Attend the Daily Scrum meeting.	Daily Scrum.
Develop the Increment according the acceptance criteria and the Definition of "Done."	After Sprint Planning and prior to Sprint Review.
Collaborate with the Product Owner to groom the Product Backlog (including PBI estimation).	During the Sprint. Product Backlog grooming makes up to 10% of Development Team's capacity during the Sprint.
Collaboratively identify additional development when forecasted work is completed early.	During the Sprint as needed.

Activity	When
Collaboratively discuss trade-offs and create a contingency plan for when the forecasted work can't be completed.	During the Sprint as needed.
Demonstrate each Increment allowing inspection by stakeholders and Product Backlog adaptation.	Sprint Review.
Reflect upon itself and its practices making delivery improvements.	Sprint Retrospective.
Continuously learn and improve.	Always.

Don't assume that a developer will execute only those types of tasks that he or she is good at or familiar with. For example, just because Dieter has a background in Microsoft SQL Server programming, that doesn't mean he'll be the one executing those types of tasks. If, during the Sprint, the team decides that the next logical task to execute requires SQL Server programming and Dieter is busy or unavailable, another developer should jump in and take on that work if at all possible. During development, the person who is best suited to perform a given task will emerge based on many factors, including expertise and availability. It is for this reason that estimates are made by the Development Team, not individuals—even if those individuals are experts in those domains. It's also why you should have more than one developer with a necessary skill set.

Tip I find very few teams whose members refer to each other as "developers." There is still a reflex to equate "developer" to programmer or coder. Our industry reinforces this. For these teams, and for the time being, using the term "Development Team member" or "team member" is a suitable substitute in my opinion.

Development Teams are cross-functional. This means that there is at least one developer on the team who has the necessary skill set to execute some type of work required for the Increment. Put a different way, it means that the Development Team has all the skills needed to complete its work. Being a cross-functional Development Team doesn't mean that each developer is cross-functional. Ideally, there will be more than one developer who has a required skill set. If not, then the team should strive to improve that by pairing and sharing, or by leveraging some other instructional techniques during development. Having one single developer on a team with a key skill is a recipe for dysfunction.

The composition of the Development Team does not change during the Sprint. If it must change, it may only change "in-between" Sprints. This is typically the result of a decision made collaboratively during the Sprint Retrospective meeting. Changes may include adding a new team member, swapping a member with another team, removing a team member, or changing a team member's capacity. Any change to the team composition is a disruption. Since Velocity is typically computed empirically, by looking back at the Development Team's accomplishments in prior Sprints, any change to the team composition will most likely cause a variance. It will take time for the Velocity to normalize. In other words, productivity will initially decrease for a time and then should (hopefully) increase.

Note Velocity is a measure of Product Backlog items that a Development Team delivers in a single Sprint. Velocity can be measured in the number, size, or business value of those items. Velocity of a single Sprint is not useful, but trending this number of several Sprints shows the general direction of productivity of a Development Team. Once Velocity has normalized, it is useful in planning Sprints and releases. For example, if a Development Team has an average Velocity of 20 points per Sprint and the Product Backlog shows 12 PBIs totaling 96 points yet to be developed in this release, you can expect the release to be available in roughly 5 Sprints, or 2 1/2 months given a 2-week Sprint duration. The term "Velocity" is rooted in the User Story practice, so it is not an official Scrum term. That being said, it can be adapted to other kinds of Product Backlog items, such as use cases, and used in Scrum as a planning tool.

Tailspin Toys case study The Tailspin Toys Development Team consists of seven cross-functional developers with varying backgrounds, skill sets, and skill levels. The team members are Anna, Art, Dave, Dieter, Raj, Toni, and Wade. Art and Anna have architecture, design, and some C# experience. Dave, Wade, and Raj have solid C# experience. Raj and Dieter have SQL Server and Windows Server experience, including Windows PowerShell. With the exception of Raj and Dieter, the Development Team is co-located and spends the majority of their time on the Tailspin Toys development effort. As a team, they all went through professional Scrum developer training and achieved passing assessment scores.

The Product Owner

The Product Owner represents the voice of the user. This means the Product Owner not only knows the product, its domain, and its vision, but also the users. Good Product Owners are in touch with the needs of the users. Great Product Owners will actually share in user's passion. Either way, the Product Owner should understand users' requirements and expectations. Just knowing how the product works and what to fix is not enough to be a competent Product Owner.

Note Over the years I've heard that the Product Owner is the voice of the *customer*. Lately, however, I've been seeing that the Product Owner is the voice of the *user*. I tend to agree with the latter, but what's the difference? Fellow professional Scrum developer Jeroen van Menen explains the subtle difference: the customer is the one who *buys* the software, where the user is the one who *uses* it.

Therefore, the Product Owner must represent the needs of the user and drive value in his or her direction, rather than just trying to satisfy the person writing the check. There is only one Product Owner on a Scrum Team. This helps avoid confusion. When the developers have a question about the product, their first instinct should be to ask the Product Owner. The Product Owner may need to consult other domain experts and stakeholders for the answer, especially for very large and complex products. The Product Owner should be considered the go-to person for all questions about the product's vision, value, release goals, features, and bugs.

The Product Owner is responsible for maximizing the value of the product through the work of the Development Team. The Product Owner's primary communication tool for doing this is a well-groomed and -ordered Product Backlog. The Product Owner collaborates with the Development Team on what and when to develop. A common misconception is that the Development Team develops the product. In fact, it's done through the collaboration and cooperation of the Development Team and the Product Owner. Table 1-2 lists the Development Team's interactions with the Product Owner.

> **Tip** The ideal Product Owner should know the product, know the product's domain, know the product's customer, know the product's users, know Scrum, have authority to make decisions related to the direction of the product, be highly available to the rest of the Scrum Team, and have good people skills. Unfortunately, I've never met a Product Owner who had all of these attributes, but I have met many Product Owners who desired to improve in all these areas and worked toward that goal.

TABLE 1-2 Development team interactions with the Product Owner.

Interaction	When
Collaboratively plan the Sprint and forecast work.	Sprint Planning meeting.
Answer product and product domain questions.	During the Sprint as needed.
Groom the Product Backlog (including estimation).	During the Sprint. Duration should be up to 10% of Sprint length.
Take on additional work.	During the Sprint as needed.
Collaboratively plan contingency work.	During the Sprint as needed.
Demonstrate the Increment and adapt the Product Backlog.	Sprint Review meeting.
Collaborate to inspect the Scrum Team's practices and plan for improvement.	Sprint Retrospective meeting.

High-performance Scrum Teams understand the separation of duties between the Product Owner and Development Team and have come to rely on each team member doing his or her part. Although the *Scrum Guide* doesn't explicitly state that the Product Owner cannot be the Scrum Master or a Development Team member, I think those are good rules to set and follow. Keeping the Product Owner focused on *what* to develop, the Development Team focused on *how* to develop it, and the Scrum Master focused on ensuring that everyone understands and follows the rules of Scrum is a recipe for success.

Since the organization may hold the Product Owner accountable for the profit or loss of the product, he or she should maintain a constant vigil for optimizing the product's value. Passionate Product Owners tend to be engaging Product Owners. They continuously want what is best for their software product and, more importantly, the value provided to its users.

Tailspin Toys case study Paula is the Product Owner of the Tailspin Toys web application. She is the daughter of Buzz, the company's founder, and shares his passion for aviation and model aircraft. She cares deeply about Tailspin Toys' customers and community. This inspires her to constantly improve and evolve the capabilities of the website. She even likes to brag that she's the site's most prolific user. Her vision is to make Tailspin Toys the number one site for aircraft models and hobbyists. Needless to say, Paula is an informed and engaging Product Owner who is available when necessary and has the authority to make the necessary decisions. Paula has been using Scrum for about three years. She has been through the Professional Scrum Foundations and Professional Product Owner training.

The Scrum Master

The Scrum Master enacts the Scrum values, practices, and rules throughout the Scrum Team and even the organization. He or she ensures that the Product Owner and Development Team are functional and productive by providing necessary guidance and support. The Scrum Master is also responsible for ensuring that Scrum is understood by all involved parties and that everyone plays by the rules.

Note The Scrum Master is not a project manager. He or she is considered a manager, but of Scrum itself, not the project, the people, or the product.

The Scrum Master must be resolute in holding fast to the rules of Scrum, giving the organization time to normalize and realize the benefits. This means keeping any old "waterfall" habits at bay. It also means keeping any unenlightened managers at bay, while continually quashing the illusion that command and control and opaqueness equates to better and faster software development. Sometimes the Scrum Master may become the de facto change agent, leading the effort for an organizational adoption of Scrum. If this is the case, then the Scrum Master's steadfastness must be able to scale!

The Scrum Master has a softer side too. He or she can be called upon to act as a coach, ensuring that the team is self-organizing, functional, and productive and shielding them from external conflicts while removing any impediments to their progress. The ability of the Scrum Master to serve the team by removing impediments to their success is a vital piece of Scrum. As a *servant leader*, the Scrum Master achieves results by giving priority attention to the needs of the team. Scrum Masters may also be of service to stakeholders and others in the organization, helping them understand the Scrum framework and expectations from the various players. Servant leaders are often seen as humble stewards of the people and processes in which they are involved. By having a "What can I do for you today?" attitude, it fosters an environment of collaboration and respect, providing fertile soil for a high-performance Scrum Team. Lao Tzu, the ancient Chinese philosopher, said it best:

When the master governs, the people are hardly aware that he exists. Next best is a leader who is loved. Next, one who is feared. The worst is one who is despised. If you don't trust people, you make them untrustworthy. The master doesn't talk, he acts. When his work is done, the people say, "Amazing: we did it, all by ourselves!"

The Scrum Master is not a technical role. Having a strong background in software development is not necessary, though it can be helpful at times. Scrum Masters must really know Scrum. That's not negotiable. A good Scrum Master will also have good communication and interpersonal skills. He or she may have to facilitate interactions with other team members or enable cooperation across roles or functions. It's important to have those abilities. Keep this in mind when considering who might make a good Scrum Master. Table 1-3 lists the ways in which the Scrum Master serves the Development Team.

Tip In my opinion, traditional project managers *don't* make good Scrum Masters. Unfortunately, this is a common reflex for an organization adopting Scrum. For example, the decision makers decide to send "Roger," their PMI-certified, *Henry Laurence Gantt* medal recipient (look it up), Microsoft Project MVP to Professional Scrum Master training. The expectation is that Roger will lead the change. What I've seen happen is that either Roger's project management "muscle memory" adversely affects the adoption of Scrum, or his old colleagues and managers do.

TABLE 1-3 Ways the Scrum Master serves the Development Team.

Service	When
Help facilitate Scrum events.	During the Sprint as needed.
Identify, document, and remove impediments.	During the Sprint as needed.
Provide training, coaching, and motivation.	During the Sprint as needed.
Coach the Development Team on self-organization.	During the Sprint as needed
Attend required meetings on the Development Team's behalf.	During the Sprint as needed
Be the Development Team's emissary to the organization.	During the Sprint as needed
Shield the Development Team from interruption and noise.	During the Sprint as needed.
Be relied upon less and less.	Over time as the team improves.

The duties of the Scrum Master may not require a full-time commitment. High-performance teams recognize this and may select a Development Team member to play the part-time role of Scrum Master. This role may rotate between developers over time. Full-time Scrum Masters may get folded back into the Development Team, or part-time Scrum Masters may start getting busier as new Scrum Teams emerge in the organization. The Scrum Master role is more flexible than the other roles in this regard. So long as a Scrum Team understands and follows the rules of Scrum and has access to someone who can perform the duties of a Scrum Master when needed, party on.

Tip The skills of a Scrum Master are unique and important. Being a Scrum Master is a career choice for some. In my experience, they tend to be high-performance and continuously improve their skills as they serve the team. These Scrum Masters should remain just that. If possible, they shouldn't be dismissed or converted to another role. They will bring more value to the team and the organization as a full-time Scrum Master.

Tailspin Toys case study Scott was hired by Tailspin Toys last year to serve as Scrum Master. Initially, he only served the web application team, providing the necessary coaching in order to transform them into a high-performance Scrum Team. Upper management plans on using Scott to help other teams within the organization learn and adopt Scrum. Scott is an expert in Scrum and has years of practical, hands-on experience with various companies and teams. He has been through Professional Scrum Foundations and Professional Scrum Master training and is active in the Scrum.org community.

Stakeholders

Although not an officially defined role in the *Scrum Guide*, stakeholders include everyone else involved or interested in the development of the software product. Stakeholders can consist of managers, executives, analysts, domain experts, members from other teams, customers, and users of the software. Stakeholders are very important. They represent the necessity for the software. They also drive the vision and usability of the product by influencing the Product Backlog. Without stakeholders, who would use the software, pay for its development, or derive benefit from it?

In my experience, developers have a tendency to discount non-technical individuals. This is unfortunate. Stakeholders should not be ignored. That said, some stakeholders can take too much interest in the development effort and its status, becoming a distraction. Scrum has clear delineations of when stakeholders and the Development Team can interact, and it's very limited, as you can see in Table 1-4. Inspecting and providing feedback on the product, such as requesting a feature, should be handled by the Product Owner. Inspecting and providing feedback on the development process, such as inquiring about status, should be handled by the Scrum Master. In other words, stakeholders should almost always be kept *out* of the development process.

Tip Burndown charts posted in a common area or on a web portal are a great way to keep stakeholders informed, which This keeps the interruptions of the Scrum Team to a minimum. If anyone has questions about the charts, the Scrum Master can educate them.

The Scrum Master should strive to keep stakeholders out of the various Scrum events, with the exception of the Sprint Review meeting. Stakeholders should not be involved in any planning or estimation meetings unless their domain expertise is required. Attendance to any event is by invitation of the Scrum Team only. Stakeholders should also not attend the Daily Scrum, as its purpose is to allow the Development Team to synchronize with each other on the upcoming work. Even the Product Owner's presence at this meeting is considered a distraction from its purpose.

TABLE 1-4 Development Team interactions with stakeholders.

Interaction	When
Answer any questions the Development Team might have about items in the Product Backlog (estimation, planning, etc.).	During the Sprint as needed.
Review the product Increment built during the Sprint and provide feedback to be captured in the Product Backlog.	Sprint Review.

Tailspin Toys case study The Tailspin Toys company has a rich history in aviation, both commercial and military. As founder of the company, Buzz brought with him many of his pilot buddies to serve as advisors. While they are not technical when it comes to software, they do have deep expertise in the domain of aviation, aircraft, models, and the community. In addition to these experts, there are a number of other stakeholders who provide feedback on the web application. Some of these are die-hard users of the software—affectionately called the Fans of Tailspin. Having previously been an executive of an airline, Buzz understands the importance of capturing user feedback. To that end, he insisted on setting up *wish@tailspintoys.com email address to receive email feedback*. These emails are routed to a support person who triages the content and works with Paula to add the item to the Product Backlog.

Scrum events

The Scrum framework uses events to structure the various workflows of incremental software development. Each event is time-boxed, which means that there is a fixed period of time to execute the activities within each event. Time-boxing ensures that an appropriate amount of time is spent planning without allowing waste in the planning process. Figure 1-2 illustrates how the events and related artifacts flow together.

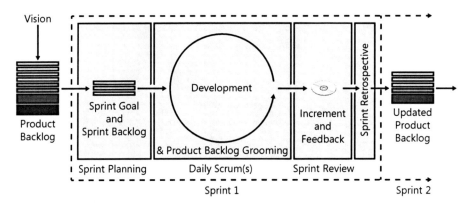

FIGURE 1-2 The sequence of Scrum events and related artifacts.

These Scrum events are meant to establish regularity and a cadence. They are also meant to minimize the need for wasteful or impromptu meetings that are not part of Scrum. All events are a formal opportunity to inspect and adapt something. Inspecting allows the team to assess progress toward a goal, as well as identify any variance in the current plan. If an inspection identifies any unacceptable deviation, an adjustment must be made to the product or process. These adjustments should be made as soon as possible to minimize further deviation. Failure to include or attend any of the Scrum events results in reduced transparency and is a lost opportunity to inspect and adapt. There are five prescribed events in Scrum:

- Sprint

- Sprint Planning meeting

- Daily Scrum

- Sprint Review meeting

- Sprint Retrospective meeting

> **Note** The Sprint is not a meeting. It is a container for all of the other events. This means that the Sprint has begun when the Sprint Planning meeting commences. A notion exists that the Sprint is that time period after the Sprint Planning meeting and before the Sprint Review in which the actual development occurs. This is incorrect. Unfortunately, this "event" doesn't have a name. I refer to it as "development."

The Sprint

A Sprint is the set period of time in which an Increment of the software product is developed. A *Sprint* is Scrum's term for an iteration. Sprints are typically fixed at two to four weeks in length and run end to end, one after another. The frequency of feedback, experience of the team, and Product Owner's need for agility are key factors in determining the length of a Sprint. For example, if the software product is an enterprise desktop application with fairly well defined release goals, longer sprints are fine. If the application is software as a service (SaaS), with demanding customers and several competitors, shorter sprints would be more desirable. Both the customer and the Scrum Team need to collaborate to determine the ideal length of the Sprint.

In Scrum, the Sprint is the outer (container) event for the other four events. In other words, the Sprint Planning, development, Sprint Review, and Sprint Retrospective meetings all take place within the Sprint. This is a change from earlier Scrum guidance, which suggested that the Sprint began once Sprint Planning completed. Once you start using Scrum, you are always in a Sprint—assuming the software still requires development. When this Sprint's Retrospective meeting ends, the next Sprint begins and you repeat the inner events again. There should never be any breaks in between Sprints.

Sprint length   I asked Ken Schwaber once how long a Sprint should be. His answer was, "As short as possible and no shorter." Sprints of longer than four weeks (one month) have a smell—the smell of water falling. When a Sprint's length is longer than a month, the definition of what is being built may change or complexity and risk may increase. By limiting the maximum length of a Sprint, at most one month of development effort would be wasted, rather than several months in a classic waterfall project. Conversely, Sprints with a length of less than one week are possible, but should be executed only by a high-performance Scrum Team. Even with very short Sprints, the overhead of the inner events must be factored in, leaving even less time for actual software development. Teams working in "micro sprints" like these need to be on their A-game every day.

Ideally, the length of the Sprint does not change. If it must, it can only change in between Sprints, as a result of a decision made collaboratively during the prior Sprint's retrospective meeting. Any change to the length of a Sprint will cause disruption to the Development Team's cadence. This will correct over time, as will its Velocity.

Each Sprint is like a mini-project. The Sprint has a definition of *what* is to be developed. It also includes a flexible approach on *how* to develop it. During the Sprint, *all* aspects of the development work are executed. This will typically be more than just designing, coding, and testing. The scope of work may be clarified as more is learned, and the Product Owner may collaborate with the Development Team to renegotiate adding new items or swapping different items in the Sprint Backlog. The Development Team may not decrease any quality goals in order to finish its work. The resulting product Increment is produced and (hopefully) accepted by the Product Owner, who may also decide to release the Increment to production.

The choice of which day of the week to start (and end) a Sprint is entirely up to the Scrum Team. Some practitioners prefer Mondays or Fridays. Most don't. Fellow professional Scrum developer Jose Luis Soria Teruel cautions against teams that try to always start a Sprint on a given day. The team can inadvertently give the day more importance than having a fixed Sprint length. For example, if a holiday falls in the middle of a Sprint, the team might shorten the Sprint so they can stick with it beginning on a Monday. Changing the Sprint length, even by a day, can affect cadence, Velocity, and the ability to achieve the Sprint Goal.

Canceling a Sprint Rarely does a Sprint need to be canceled, but it does happen. If a Sprint's forecasted work becomes irrelevant, then there is no reason to continue developing it. This can occur if the product or organization needs to change direction immediately due to a technology or market reason. Only the Product Owner has the authority to cancel a Sprint. He or she may do so under the advisement of others, including stakeholders, the Development Team, or the Scrum Master. Canceled Sprints require the Scrum Team to collaborate and decide if any done work is acceptable and potentially releasable. The Scrum Team should also re-estimate any undone work, returning it to the Product Backlog. The work done on partially completed PBIs depreciates quickly and may not have any value in the future. Needless to say, canceling a Sprint will generate waste.

Tailspin Toys case study Originally, the Scrum Team tried four-week Sprints. They felt that the longer time-box would be closer to the quarterly delivery schedule they had been accustomed to. Unfortunately, since the team was new to Agile, they continued to take a sequential approach to development. They spent a lot of time on analysis and design at the beginning of the Sprint and deferred QA until the end. The resulting high-intensity crunch in the last few days of the Sprint was not sustainable and was really just a backslide into waterfall habits (a.k.a. "Scrummerfall"). The team did not experience the productivity gains everyone anticipated. When they hired Scott (the Scrum Master), he recommended moving to two-week Sprints. This caused the developers to experience a sense of urgency, change the way they worked, and maintain a comfortable level of intensity throughout the Sprint. Scott also recommended starting the Sprint on a Wednesday. This increased the chances of the whole team being in the office and operating at peak capacity. It also allowed stakeholders to fly in for a Sprint Review and the subsequent Sprint Planning meeting without having to stay over a weekend. The Scrum Team has completed many successful Sprints while on this two-week cadence. Their average Velocity over the last six Sprints is 22.

Sprint Planning meeting

The Sprint Planning meeting is for identifying and planning the development work that will be performed during the Sprint. This is the first event that occurs within the Sprint, and the most important. The entire Scrum Team attends this meeting. The Development Team collaborates with the Product Owner on the scope of work that can be accomplished. A groomed and ordered (prioritized) Product Backlog is required as an input for Sprint Planning. This forecasted work, along with a Sprint Goal and a plan for doing the work (the Sprint Backlog), are the outputs.

The Sprint Planning meeting is time-boxed, so everyone needs to be laser-focused. Distractions, such as non-topical conversations, should be minimized. The length of the Sprint Planning meeting is a function of the length of the Sprint, as you can see in Table 1-5.

TABLE 1-5 Length of the Sprint Planning meeting.

Sprint length	Sprint Planning meeting length
4 weeks	No longer than 8 hours
3 weeks	No longer than 6 hours
2 weeks	No longer than 4 hours
1 week	No longer than 2 hours
Less than a week	In proportion to the above lengths

The forecast During Sprint Planning, the Development Team considers the highest-ordered PBIs from the Product Backlog one at a time. The order is decided by the Product Owner. Each item's requirements and acceptance criteria are discussed. Clarification is provided by the Product Owner as well as other domain experts who might be invited to the meeting. After obtaining a sufficient understanding of the PBI, the Development Team estimates the effort. If the consensus believes that they can deliver the item in this Sprint, the item is added to the forecast. Lack of consensus may require the PBI to be split or deferred until a later Sprint, when more is known. The Development Team moves to the next item in the Product Backlog. This is repeated until the Development Team thinks that they have forecasted a comfortable amount of work for the Sprint, given their capacity and past performance. These forecasted PBIs are moved from the Product Backlog to the Sprint Backlog.

The Development Team may use their Velocity to make the determination of what is an acceptable amount of work. New Development Teams, who don't yet have a normalized Velocity, as well as high-performance teams, may just use their instinct to decide what *feels* like the right amount of work. If the Development Team completes their forecasted work early, they can collaborate with the Product Owner mid-Sprint to identify and develop an additional PBI. Because of this, their Velocity may go up, and a larger forecast might occur at the next Sprint Planning meeting. The Development Team should never forecast more work than they *know* they can complete.

Note In 2011, the *Scrum Guide* introduced a somewhat controversial change to Sprint Planning. The word "commit" was replaced with "forecast". Scrum practitioners had an issue with the word *commit* for some time. The problem was that "commit" implied that the Development Team was obligated to deliver the PBIs at the end of the Sprint. This was especially true when stakeholders, who tend to not understand the complexities of developing software, heard the word. Since software development is very difficult and full of risk, delivering all PBIs every Sprint is unrealistic. The Development Team might have to cut quality in order to make good on their promise and this is essentially forbidden in Scrum. The term "forecast" is more realistic and easier to understand by business stakeholders who have heard terms like "sales forecast." It suggests that, while the Development Team will do their best, given what they know, new information will emerge during the Sprint that might impede their best-laid plans. It will take some time to get used to the new term. It may sound like a weasel word to some, but in the long run, its usage will be deemed more honest and transparent.

The Sprint Goal   After the Development Team forecasts the PBIs that it thinks that it can develop in the Sprint, they should collaborate with the Product Owner to craft a *Sprint Goal*. The Sprint Goal is an objective, in narrative format, that guides the Development Team as they develop the Increment. The Sprint Goal also provides stakeholders the ability to see a synopsis of what the Development Team is working on. While the Development Team only *forecasts* the individual PBIs to be implemented, they actually *commit* to achieving the Sprint Goal.

Note Some teams like to craft the Sprint Goal first, or at least in parallel with the forecasting of work. This way, there is more cohesion with the goal and the PBIs that are developed during the Sprint. This cohesion makes it easier to understand the value of the Increment and how it fits into the goals of the product or release. This approach can be difficult for teams who need to develop disparate features and bug fixes for a given Sprint.

It's important that the Product Owner and Development Team craft the Sprint Goal together and agree on its verbiage and meaning. Everyone on the team should then commit it to memory. Stakeholders should have access to see it as well. Once development has begun (that is, the Sprint Planning meeting is over), the Sprint Goal should not be changed. It is the *theme* that the team has committed to, and the T-shirts have already been printed—so to speak. If the Development Team isn't able to achieve the Sprint Goal, or the goal becomes obsolete, the Product Owner might decide to cancel the Sprint—another indication of the Sprint Goal's importance.

The Sprint Goal gives the Development Team some flexibility and guidance regarding the functionality implemented within the Sprint. Even if the Development Team delivers less PBIs than were forecasted in Sprint Planning, they can still achieve their Sprint Goal. For example, let's assume the Development Team forecasts the following PBIs during Sprint Planning:

1. Add a Twitter feed to the homepage.

2. Create a Facebook page for the company.

3. Create and host a wiki page for product support.

Given this forecast, the Sprint Goal might read, "To increase community awareness of our company and its products." As the developers work, they keep this goal in mind. If the team is unable to finish the third PBI, they didn't fail because they were still able *to increase community awareness of our company and its products* by successfully completing the first two PBIs. If it sounds like Sprint Goals give the Development Team "wiggle room," you are correct. Remember that what developers do is very difficult and full of risk. That's why they should *forecast* the individual items they think they can deliver, but *commit* to the goal that embodies them.

The plan Sprint Planning is not complete until the Development Team has devised a plan for how they will develop the forecasted PBIs. The plan must ensure that all PBI acceptance criteria are satisfied while meeting the team's Definition of "Done." The plan gets added to the Sprint Backlog. On a whiteboard, this might be visualized as a collection of sticky notes in the same row as the associated PBI sticky note. In software, it might be several child records related to a parent record. Regardless of the tool the team uses, the Sprint Backlog contains both the forecasted PBIs and the plan (tasks) to develop them.

> **Tip** Go lightweight during Sprint Planning. Whiteboards are a great medium for sketching ideas and brainstorming tasks. Laptops aren't. Whiteboards can be easily photographed and wiped clean after the meeting. Files on laptops tend to linger and yearn to be updated. They also indicate a finality set in stone that is not necessarily the truth. Using sticky notes to brainstorm tasks in the plan is also good. They can be moved and removed easily from the board. A high-performance Scrum Team will avoid using any software during Sprint Planning unless its value outweighs its distraction. Sticky notes and whiteboard sketches can be translated into digital files later, once the Development Team agrees on the plan.

Because of the meeting's time-box, the Development Team probably won't be able to identify every task required to develop a particular PBI. For expediency, a minimum amount of information should be recorded—perhaps just a title and estimate of effort. Sprint Planning is not the time for detailed design. The Development Team needs to focus on the high-level plan and its tasks.

For example, let's assume that the team will have to create several database tables, stored procedures, and related data access code. Rather than go down the design "rat hole" during the meeting, the team should just identify a couple of high-level tasks: *create database objects* and *create data-access code*. Each of these would include an aggregate estimate of effort to perform all the related activities.

The tasks to be performed first in the Sprint should be decomposed as necessary so that no executable task is larger than can be achieved in one day. Estimates can be in whatever unit of measure the Development Team decides. For tasks, hours are the most common unit. I've seen teams also use days or story points. Personally, I think using story points for estimating tasks can lead to confusion. Rarely would you want to relatively compare the estimations of two tasks that could end up being done by different team members. Regardless of the unit of measure, all of these numeric values will enable a Sprint burndown chart, should the team choose to employ one.

It's important for the Development Team to leave the Sprint Planning meeting with a plan to accomplish the Sprint Goal. This plan should be documented, in the Sprint Backlog, in a way that the Product Owner and Scrum Master can understand the approach. Task ownership is not a required outcome of the Sprint Planning meeting. In fact, it's important to leave "to do" tasks unassigned so that team members who have capacity can pick a relevant task to work on next. That said, it is fine if the team decides to assign one or a few tasks to individuals by the end of the meeting. The Development Team will then self-organize to undertake the work in the Sprint Backlog as needed throughout the Sprint. Table 1-6 lists the activities expected of a Development Team during the Sprint Planning meeting.

TABLE 1-6 Development Team activities during Sprint Planning.

Activity	Where is it captured?
Forecast PBIs to be delivered that Sprint.	PBIs in the Sprint Backlog.
Collaborate with Product Owner to craft a Sprint Goal.	Whiteboard, sticky notes, Microsoft SharePoint, etc.
Develop a plan for delivering the forecasted PBIs.	Tasks in the Sprint Backlog.

Tailspin Toys case study The first Sprint Planning sessions were chaotic. The Development Team were introduced to new PBIs for the first time *at the meeting*. Paula (the Product Owner) wasn't always prepared and the domain experts were sometimes unavailable. Most of the meeting was spent understanding *what* was to be developed, and planning the *how* got deferred until the first few days of the Sprint. This corrected itself over time, as the team members got used to Scrum. Sprint Planning also became much more efficient when the team started meeting regularly to groom the Product Backlog.

The Daily Scrum

The Daily Scrum is a 15-minute, time-boxed meeting for the Development Team to synchronize their activities and create a plan for the next 24 hours. It allows developers to listen to what other developers have done and are about to do. This leads to increased collaboration, as well as accountability. If one developer hears that another developer is about to work in a similar area of the product, they may choose to pair up for the day. On the other hand, if the team hears that a developer is on day 3 of a 4-hour task, it may be time to pair up or inquire about the root cause. Team members need to understand that commitments are being made at this meeting and that these commitments will be tested 24 hours from now.

> **Note** I hear a lot of teams refer to this event as the "daily standup." The event is called the "Daily Scrum." If the team decides to stand during the meeting, they may do so.

The most popular technique that Development Teams use during the Daily Scrum is to stand in a circle facing each other. Each developer, in turn, answers the following three questions:

1. What have I done since the last Scrum?

2. What will I do between now and the next Scrum?

3. What impediments are in my way?

The Development Team can use the dialogue heard during the Scrum to assess their progress. By hearing what is or isn't being accomplished each day, the team can determine if they are on their way to achieving the Sprint Goal. As teams improve in their collaboration, this vibe will become more noticeable—even outside the Daily Scrum. High-performance teams may even outgrow the need for a formal assessment tool, such as a Sprint burndown chart. Stakeholders will only outgrow this need once the Scrum Team has earned their trust, which takes time. The sustained increase of business value being added to the software product should serve as its own assessment.

The meeting should be held in the same place and at the same time every day to reduce complexity and to maximize the likelihood of attendance. Ideally, the meeting is held in the morning so that the Development Team is able to synchronize their work that day. The Daily Scrum is not a status meeting. Problem solving can occur in the meeting, but it is usually deferred to just after the Daily Scrum because the problem solving can often lead to the team violating the 15-minute time-box for the event, as well as conversations that are not relevant to all attendees.

The Daily Scrum is not meant to be attended by anyone other than the members of the Development Team. This includes the Product Owner. In fact, the Scrum Master is not even required to attend. He or she just needs to ensure that the Scrum takes place and that the rules are followed. Any impediments can be identified, tracked, and even mitigated by the Development Team members.

> **Tip** Keep laptops, burndown charts, and other artifacts and props out of the Daily Scrum. These tend to distract from the purpose of the meeting. Each developer should know their own information without having to look anything up. Observations and impediments can be recorded on a whiteboard or using sticky notes. High-performance teams will use a "parking lot" to track anything not relevant to the Scrum, and a follow-up meeting can support those conversations. The Development Team is self-organizing and can decide to meet formally or informally at any time during the day for any reason. The Scrum framework has no guidance on what the Development Team does the other 7 hours and 45 minutes of the day, other than to say that the Development Team should be maximizing their self-organization capability.

Tailspin Toys case study The Development Team has their Daily Scrum at 9 A.M. in the hallway near their team's area. Prior to the meeting, each developer updates their work remaining estimates on their tasks. By doing this, it gives them a fresh perspective on their remaining work and enriches the conversation. A side benefit is that this keeps the burndown reports accurate, which is good if they are consulted at any follow-up meeting. During the Scrum itself, the developers have adopted the practice of tossing a small rugby ball (a "talking stick") to the next developer to speak. Sticky notes are created and placed in a parking lot section of a nearby whiteboard as needed. The Daily Scrum usually takes less than 10 minutes.

Sprint Review meeting

After the Sprint's development time-box has expired, a Sprint Review meeting is held. The entire Scrum Team attends, as well as any stakeholders the Product Owner invites. This informal meeting is for inspecting the increment developed by the team. Stakeholders get to observe an informal demonstration of the working software. Their feedback is elicited and captured. This collaboration can produce new, updated, or removed PBIs.

The Sprint Review meeting is time-boxed. Its length is half that of the Sprint Planning meeting, or 1 hour for every week in the Sprint, as you can see in Table 1-7.

TABLE 1-7 Length of the Sprint Review meeting.

Sprint length	Sprint Review meeting length
4 weeks	No longer than 4 hours
3 weeks	No longer than 3 hours
2 weeks	No longer than 2 hours
1 week	No longer than 1 hour
Less than a week	In proportion to the above lengths

During the Sprint Review, the Sprint Goal and forecasted PBIs should be restated. Keeping their audience in mind, the Development Team may give a short summary about what went well, what didn't, and how they overcame any problems. If applicable, completed PBIs are demonstrated by running the working software, not by showing slides, mockups, or passing tests. Techniques can be employed to provide context and value. For example, the demonstrators might role-play the personas that would be using and benefiting from a particular feature being demonstrated. The Development Team describes what the attendees are seeing and, if necessary, how it works behind the scenes. They will also answer any questions the stakeholders might have.

Tip The Development Team should never surprise their Product Owner at a Sprint Review meeting. This should not be the first time that he or she sees the completed work. High-performance Scrum Teams know the value of continuous collaboration with the Product Owner. At a minimum, the Development Team should ask the Product Owner's opinion on individual PBIs as they approach completion. Product Owner acceptance doesn't have to wait until the Sprint Review meeting. In fact, you don't want Sprint Reviews to become "sign-off" meetings. They are more about improving the product through inspection of the Increment.

The Sprint Review meeting can generate one or more outcomes:

- Unfinished or unstarted PBIs are moved back to the Product Backlog.

- New feature ideas are added to the Product Backlog.

- Unnecessary items are removed from the Product Backlog.

- The Product Backlog is groomed.

- The Increment is released ("Ship it!").

- Product development is canceled.

As previously mentioned, the Sprint Review is an informal meeting. The Development Team should not spend much time preparing for it. Nobody should feel like they are attending a technical presentation at a conference. On the other hand, the team should be organized enough so it doesn't waste the stakeholders' time. If necessary, the Scrum Master can intervene and make corrections to maximize the meeting's value for everyone. Any corrections can be discussed at the Sprint Retrospective meeting and implemented in the next Sprint.

There are many ways to run a Sprint Review. Some Scrum Teams like it to be structured. Others don't. Some like the Scrum Master to kick it off. Others like it to be the Product Owner. Some like to rotate developers so everyone gets a chance to "drive" during the demonstration. Others like their strongest communicator driving. Regardless, the Sprint Review should be down to earth and foster an environment of collaboration and discussion. The Scrum Team should be inquisitive, and all feedback should be welcomed and captured, preferably in the Product Backlog. Later, the Product Owner can provide feedback on any of the captured PBIs regarding business value—or not. Inane ideas will eventually sink to the depths of the Product Backlog.

Being mindful of the time-box, unfinished or unstarted PBIs can also be discussed with the stakeholders. If they have blocked time out of their busy day, don't squander the opportunity to get their feedback on any PBI that might be coming up in an approaching Sprint. These discussions can create valuable input for the next Sprint Planning meeting.

 Tailspin Toys case study Sprint Reviews have always been a big deal for the Scrum Team. They meet every other Tuesday morning in the large conference room and invite all of the stakeholders and even members from other teams. Paula (the Product Owner) kicks off the meeting with a review of the Sprint Goal and forecasted work. Scott (the Scrum Master) then gives a summary of the Sprint, including the team's progress (using the Sprint burndown chart), any obstacles, and how the Development Team overcame them. The bulk of the two-hour meeting is spent by the Development Team demonstrating the completed functionality. They do so in a storytelling way, with the developers playing different personas as they act out the user stories. This fun approach makes everyone in the room feel safe and comfortable in sharing their opinions and ideas. Scott or another team member captures this feedback in real time using Microsoft OneNote. Stakeholders also tend to send feedback in the form of an email after the meeting. This is captured using the product TeamCompanion (*www.teamcompanion.com*). Paula then wraps up the Sprint Review by discussing the forecasted items that didn't get finished or started, as well as her ideas for the next Sprint. Paula may also update everyone present on progress toward a goal via a release burndown chart or other tool.

Sprint Retrospective meeting

The last event in the Sprint is the Sprint Retrospective meeting. In this meeting, the Scrum Team will inspect and adapt its own behaviors and practices, looking for opportunities to improve. The Sprint Retrospective meeting occurs after the Sprint Review meeting and before the next Sprint Planning meeting. The exact time and location are up to the Scrum Team. It's important for the Product Owner, Scrum Master, and the entire Development Team to attend. The Sprint Retrospective meeting is time-boxed, as you can see in Table 1-8.

TABLE 1-8 Length of the Sprint Retrospective meeting.

Sprint length	Sprint Retrospective meeting length
4 weeks	No longer than 3 hours
3 weeks	No longer than 2 1/4 hours
2 weeks	No longer than 1 1/2 hours
1 week	No longer than 3/4 hour
Less than a week	In proportion to the above lengths

The purpose of the Sprint Retrospective meeting is for everyone to share their observations, thoughts, and ideas on what went well and what didn't with regard to people, relationships, process, and tools. These discussions can get heated, especially when you are talking about social interaction problems with other people. The meeting should be constructive and it's the Scrum Master's responsibility to keep it that way.

Note Impediments and struggles with the development process and practices can be inspected and adapted at any time, such as during the Daily Scrum or throughout the day or Sprint. The Sprint Retrospective meeting provides a *formal* opportunity for such inspection, as well as time for planning any adaptations.

The output of a Scrum Retrospective is a plan for implementing improvements. These improvements can target the development process as a whole or individual practices within it.

Improvements might include changing the way the Development Team works, or where, or when. Improvements might also include changing the way the developers use their tools, or what tools they use. Improvements might be more aesthetic, such as ways to make the work more enjoyable by making the work area more or less stimulating. Any potential improvement is really just an experiment, since the Scrum Team constantly inspects and adapts its practices. Table 1-9 lists some other changes that the Scrum Team is allowed to make during the Sprint Retrospective or in between Sprints. Some of these changes can be pretty major, so they should be executed only with the consensus of the full Scrum Team and a complete understanding of the ramifications of making the change. Any change made must still abide by the rules of Scrum.

TABLE 1-9 Changes that can be made at the Sprint Retrospective meeting or in between Sprints.

Change	Examples
Increase product quality by updating the Definition of "Done."	Increase the minimum code coverage percentage.
Change the person playing the Scrum Master role.	Relieve Scott of his duty while attributing the role to Dave.
Change the team composition.	Add another developer or drop Wade's capacity to 50%.
Change the Sprint length.	Change from two weeks to one week to increase agility.

Tip Don't be flaccid. Don't just hold the Sprint Retrospective meeting for the sake of the meeting. If problems are identified, make sure solutions are also identified. If solutions are identified, make sure they are actually implemented in the upcoming Sprints. Inspect *and* adapt!

There are many techniques that a Scrum Team can use during a Sprint Retrospective meeting. The most common is to have each Scrum Team member answer three questions:

- What did we do well this Sprint?

- What could we have done better?

- What will we try to do better next Sprint?

There are other approaches to start the conversation, elicit feedback, and brainstorm solutions. Entire books and websites have been devoted to running successful retrospectives and related techniques. Table 1-10 lists some of the techniques that my fellow professional Scrum developers have employed successfully. You will have to search the web for additional information, such as the instructions for using the technique.

TABLE 1-10 Sprint Retrospective meeting techniques and activities.

Technique	Description
Timeline	A timeline for the Sprint is marked on a wall, and team members add sticky notes to it to indicate good and bad events that occurred at that point in time.
Emotional Seismograph	Similar to the timeline, but team members mark their emotional level as a point on a *Y*-axis throughout the Sprint.

Technique	Description
Mad, Sad, Glad	Team members brainstorm on the events that made them mad, sad, or glad during the Sprint. Sticky notes are clustered together, normalized, discussed, and mitigated as necessary.
The 4 L's	Create four posters or whiteboards, one for Liked, Learned, Lacked, and Long For. Team members add sticky notes to the respective board. They are clustered, discussed, and mitigated as necessary.
The 5 Why's	A question-asking technique used to explore the cause-and-effect relationships underlying a particular problem.
Remember the Future	Used to create a vision of what the team wants to achieve by inquiring about a future point in time that follows another future point in time where the hypothetical change was made.
Car Speeding Toward Abyss	Draw a picture of a speeding car heading towards an abyss and use this analogy to identify the engine, parachute, abyss, and bridge comparisons to the current Sprint's work. The *Speedboat* and *Sailboat* are variations on this technique.
Happiness Metric	Similar to the emotional seismograph, but team members track their happiness levels throughout the Sprint using a scale of 1–5 with comments. A chart is produced for the Sprint Retrospective meeting and the peaks and valleys are discussed.
Perfection Game	A technique used to maximize the value of ideas. Team members rate an idea from 1–10 and provide positive feedback on how to make it a 10. No feedback means they've given it a 10.
Fishbowl	Arranging chairs in an inner and outer circle in order to attract team members to an empty chair in the inner circle (the fishbowl) and participate in the conversation.
Starfish	Using a starfish diagram, team members add sticky notes in these categories: do the same (=), do less of (<), stop doing (-), start doing (+), do more of (>). They are normalized, discussed, and mitigated as necessary.
Problem Tree Diagram, or *Ishikawa (Fishbone) Diagram*	A technique for visualizing the cause-and-effect relationships pertaining to a particular problem.
Team Radar	The team defines the factors (that is, communication, feedback, collaboration, etc.) and then each team member rates their interpretation of that factor on a scale of 0–10, where 0 means not at all and 10 means as much as possible. The chart is discussed and saved for later comparison.
Circles and *Soup*	A technique for helping identify what is and what is not the responsibility of the Scrum Team. This is similar to the *Circle of Concern and Circle of Influence* technique.

It's also important during the Sprint Retrospective to celebrate the team's victories. The good things that occurred should be encouraged to persist. Likewise, challenges in this Sprint should be seen as opportunities for victory in the next. This continuous improvement mentality is foundational in a high-performance Scrum Team. They live it every day. Since not every team member is wired this way, encouragement and team building are important and should be part of the retrospective too, if required. Everyone should see that the Development Team is more productive and happy.

Tailspin Toys case study In the early Sprints, the Retrospective meetings would not generate much return on the time invested. The entire Scrum Team would return to the large conference room after lunch and go through the basic questions. To them, it just felt like a longer version of the Daily Scrum and a waste of time. Retrospective notes were captured and the plan for improving was sometimes executed. When Scott joined the Scrum Team as Scrum Master, this changed. He introduced new techniques to get everyone involved. He focused on what went well and team building. He also ensured that any action items were implemented during the next Sprint. He called it his *Scrum Master backlog*. More important, he convinced Paula and Buzz to hold the Retrospective meeting in the back room at Fourth Coffee.

Product Backlog grooming

Maintaining a well-groomed Product Backlog helps the development of a successful product. Product Backlog grooming is the periodic meeting of the Product Owner and the Development Team to add detail to upcoming PBIs. This is the time when the requirements and acceptance criteria are explored and revised. When the Development Team has sufficient understanding of the PBI, they will estimate the effort required to develop it. This estimate may change over time, as more is learned about the item. In fact, the Development Team may re-groom and re-estimate the same PBI several times before it gets forecasted for development—usually as a result of new information.

Product Backlog grooming is a necessary and important part of Scrum. Although it is not a formal event, the *Scrum Guide* says that it is an ongoing process taking no longer than 10 percent of the capacity of the Development Team. The exact where and when of the Product Backlog grooming sessions are up to the Scrum Team. Some teams try to avoid doing a grooming near the very beginning or very end of the Sprint so that it doesn't collide with the other, more formal Scrum events, and closing out the Sprint. It is important to have the entire Development Team involved in grooming because the analysis and estimation will be more meaningful and accurate. Diligently grooming the Product Backlog minimizes the risk of developing the wrong product.

Tailspin Toys case study With the adoption of two-week Sprints, the Development Team now spends every Friday morning in a conference room with Paula for "story time"—a euphemism for Product Backlog grooming. All developers attend the meeting because each has valuable input and may be called on to collectively estimate the effort of the items being discussed. Because of these regular grooming sessions, Sprint Planning meetings have become more productive. The Scrum Team now spends less time forecasting because the most important PBIs and their estimates are fresh in their minds.

Scrum artifacts

Scrum's artifacts represent the work to be done in the product and Sprint, as well as the work that has been done within the product itself. Each artifact has clear ownership by a specific role. Each artifact is structured in a way that maximizes transparency of key information while providing opportunities for inspection and adaptation. There are three artifacts in Scrum:

- Product Backlog
- Sprint Backlog
- The Increment

Note Burndowns (product, release, and Sprint) were removed from the *Scrum Guide* in 2011. Their inclusion was considered too prescriptive. While it's important for the Scrum Team to monitor progress toward a goal, there are many practices that could support this. Burndowns are certainly a popular option and are still acceptable and used by some high-performance Scrum Teams. No technique will replace the importance of empiricism. In complex environments, such as software development, what will happen is unknown. The Scrum Team can only use what *has happened* to influence its decision making.

Product Backlog

The Product Backlog is an ordered list of everything required of the software product. It is the single source of requirements for any potential changes to be made. Each item in the Product Backlog is called a "*Product Backlog item (PBI).*" A PBI can be a *happy* thing that doesn't yet exist in the software product, like a feature or an enhancement. PBIs can also be *sad* things, like a bug to be fixed. PBIs can range from extremely important and urgent to silly and trivial. Because of this variety, I affectionately refer to the Product Backlog as a list of *desirements*. At some point, somebody, somewhere, for some reason *desired* each item in the Product Backlog.

Note The Product Backlog is a dynamic, living document. It is never complete and will constantly change as requirements change. The Product Backlog will exist so long as the software product exists.

These items are considered valid PBIs:

- Feature

- Enhancement

- Behavior

- User stories

- Use case

- Scenario

- Bug/defect

These items should not be PBIs:

- Task (that is, refactor code, write more tests, meet in the lobby for the Daily Scrum)

- Acceptance criterion (that is, page content in German and English, report exportable as PDF)

- Non-functional requirements (when they are used as acceptance criteria)

- Definition of "Done" (that is, code is peer-reviewed, code coverage > 50 percent, all tests pass)

- Impediment (that is, must reset my password on SQL Server, activate Windows)

Each PBI should be clearly identified by a title. This is the minimum amount of information required to add it to the Product Backlog. If the Product Owner decides it's worth the time to describe it further, then a description should be added. This description should be written in a business language, perhaps as a user story description. The PBI should also be assigned a business value and ordered with the other items in the backlog. The Development Team will need to eventually look at it and provide an estimate. This can be done at a Product Backlog grooming session or during Sprint Planning. Table 1-11 lists the ways in which the Development Team interacts with the Product Backlog.

TABLE 1-11 Development Team interactions with the Product Backlog.

Activity	When
Inspect it.	Any time
Add a new PBI to it.	Any time (if allowed by the Product Owner)
Groom it.	Product Backlog grooming, Sprint Planning, or Sprint Review (with Product Owner)
Forecast work from it.	Sprint Planning (with Product Owner)

I'm often asked if being *responsible* for the Product Backlog means that the Product Owner has to be the person who actually creates the PBIs (that is, write the user stories). The answer is no. The Product Owner can have the Development Team or stakeholders, including business analysts and even the users themselves, create the PBIs. The Product Owner has the right to update any item, such as making it more understandable or changing acceptance criteria, or to remove any item deemed unnecessary. The Product Owner or Scrum Master may have to remind people that PBIs should only define the what, and not the how.

User stories A PBI represents a software requirement. It can take any number of shapes or forms. Of all that I have seen, the user story practice is generally the best choice for teams doing Agile software development. This is primarily because user stories are lightweight and *not* technical. User stories describe the requirement from the customer or user's perspective. It is not a requirements document, nor is it a communiqué between the requirements giver and the Development Team. A user story represents a "what" that the software product should do. A well-written user story description will explain who wants or would benefit from the feature, as well as how and why it will be useful. In a single sentence, the user story provides lots of context, as well as a value proposition.

The most popular format of a user story description looks like this: *As a (role), I want (something), so that (benefit)*. An example would be, "As a returning customer, I want to log in with my ID and password, so that I don't have to enter my shipping and billing information each time I order a product." Another example would be, "As a visitor to the Tailspin Toys website, I want to see a list of recent tweets, so that I know that Tailspin and its products are alive and well." Anyone looking at either PBI instantly knows the context and value to the customer.

Having a title and the initial description in user story format is a good start. To properly complete a user story, communication between the Scrum Team and knowledgeable stakeholders is required. A complete user story includes the *three C's*: Card, Conversation, and Confirmation.

The *card* is already done at this point. You have written a title and the description (in user story format) on a sticky note, an index card, or a software record. This allows somebody to reference the user story during conversation, update it, estimate it, stack rank it, etc.

Next, the *conversation* takes place with the customers, users, or domain experts. This conversation is meant to exchange thoughts and opinions. It can take place at any time with the Product Owner and the stakeholders and the Development Team as needed. If the Development Team is to be involved, it should take place at the Product Backlog grooming session, the Sprint Planning meeting, or the Sprint Review meeting. Conversation that yields examples, especially executable and testable examples, is preferred over formal documents and mockups.

Finally, the *confirmation* occurs. Here the user story's acceptance criteria are agreed upon and recorded. These criteria will help determine when the PBI is done. In other words, when all criteria are met according to the team's Definition of "Done," the PBI is done. If and when the PBI gets forecasted for a Sprint, the Development Team will create the appropriate manual or automated acceptance tests to validate the acceptance criteria.

> **Tip** Don't create tasks, tests, or code for a PBI before the Sprint in which you have forecasted its development. Conditions can change rapidly, forcing a change to the PBI or its acceptance criteria. Time spent creating these kinds of artifacts ahead of time will often be wasted. The plan on how to develop a PBI, as well as any code or tests, just like requirements, should be created at the latest responsible moment. Even though you will always know more tomorrow than today, you should avoid falling into the trap of doing things at the last *possible* moment.

Whoever creates a user story should be sure to INVEST in it. The mnemonic *INVEST* is a reminder of the characteristics of a good user story:

- **I–Independent**   As much as possible, the story should stand alone, without any dependency on another story. Try to write stories such that they don't have long "dependency chains."

- **N–Negotiable**   The story can be changed and rewritten up until it gets forecasted, but significant changes after being forecasted should be avoided and minimized. Minor tweaks are okay so long as they don't greatly affect the original estimate for the story.

- **V–Valuable**   The story must deliver value to the customer or user. This value is often delivered in the graphical user interface (GUI), but not always.

- **E–Estimable**   The Development Team must be able to estimate the effort to develop the story. If too little is known about the story, it will be difficult for the team to come to consensus on a story.

- **S–Small** The story must be small enough that the team can develop it in a single Sprint and preferably within a few days. There are many suitable techniques for decomposing stories.

- **T–Testable** The acceptance criteria is clearly understood and can be tested. This is probably the most important characteristic. It relates to the third "C" in the three "C's": confirmation.

Product Backlog iceberg You can think of the Product Backlog as an iceberg (see Figure 1-3). PBIs on the top, above the surface, are what the Development Team has forecasted for the current Sprint. These items should be crystal clear, estimated, and ready to be worked. Below the surface, the Product Owner knows what other PBIs he or she would like in the release, but it won't be clear which ones surface until the next Sprint Planning meeting. These items are generally understood and estimated so that a release plan can be devised. These are the items that will be in scope during upcoming Product Backlog grooming sessions. At the bottom of the iceberg, you will find all of the other PBIs that may or may not make it into a future release. Some of these may only have a title or a vague description of the desired functionality. Some PBIs will remain in these cold, chilly depths for eternity, which is typical of most Product Backlogs.

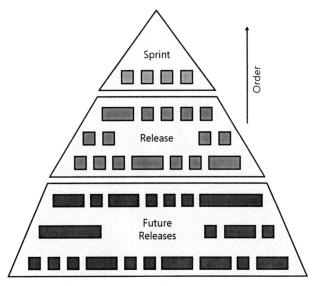

FIGURE 1-3 The Product Backlog iceberg.

Sometimes it's a chicken-and-egg problem when it comes to evolving a PBI. The Product Owner might need an estimate on the level of effort required to develop a PBI before he or she can order (prioritize) it. If it's going to require too much effort, the Product Owner may postpone it for the next release, or beyond. However, the Development Team's time is valuable and they shouldn't waste their time estimating PBIs that may not be developed. A solution I've seen work well is for the Development Team (or a proxy) to provide the Product Owner a rough order of magnitude estimate, such as a T-shirt size (XS, S, M, L, XL). This should give the Product Owner enough insight to be able to order (prioritize) the PBI effectively. A more thorough estimate, provided by the entire Development Team and using a more precise scale, will be performed at a future Product Backlog grooming session.

Note The Scrum Guide uses the term "order" instead of "prioritize". This subtle change has led to some confusion, which is why I've been using both terms together. Fellow professional Scrum developer Jose Luis Soria Teruel explains the difference eloquently. Assume that a Product Owner wants to have some software features as soon as possible, like the ability to sell products and accept payments (priority). However, before those features can be developed, other capabilities must be developed like the shopping cart feature (order).

The Product Owner is responsible for the Product Backlog, including the clarity and precision of its contents. He or she should also ensure that the Product Backlog is visible to all interested parties. The Product Owner will order (prioritize) the PBIs according to his goals for the product or release. The PBIs at the top of the ordered Product Backlog will, more than likely, be what the Development Team works on next. The Product Owner's vision should be discernible by studying the order and content of the PBIs. If necessary, the Scrum Master should help the Product Owner manage the Product Backlog more effectively.

Creating an effective Product Backlog can be very difficult. It can take a long time. It can become political. However, once you've gone through the exercise of creating the Product Backlog, you'll wonder how you ever got along without one.

Tailspin Toys case study Creating the initial Product Backlog *was* difficult. Requirements, feature requests, and bugs were tracked by different people in different formats. Giving up control of those lists started a turf war—but in the end, it was best for the product. When possible, all "happy" PBIs were converted to a user story format. Today, the Scrum Team maintains its Product Backlog in Team Foundation Server. The server administrator gave permissions to anyone on the Scrum Team to manage the Product Backlog. Everyone else can only view it. Paula (the Product Owner) is considering granting access to some additional stakeholders to help her create PBIs.

Sprint Backlog

The Sprint Backlog contains the Product Backlog items forecasted to be developed during the Sprint and the plan (tasks) for developing them. The PBIs were agreed upon and selected through collaboration of the Scrum Team. The plan for developing them was agreed upon and recorded through collaboration of the Development Team. The Sprint Backlog is the output of the Sprint Planning meeting and represents the Development Team's forecast of *what* functionality will be in the next software product Increment, and *how* it will happen. Some teams refer to the tasks as Sprint Backlog tasks (SBTs) or Sprint Backlog items (SBIs). Technically, the forecasted PBIs are also considered SBIs, so additional context will need to be provided when using that term in a conversation.

The Development Team owns the Sprint Backlog. This is to say that the Development Team is wholly responsible for how to implement the PBIs, so long as they do so according to the acceptance criteria and their Definition of "Done." Nobody can tell the Development Team how to develop the

Increment. In other words, nobody except the members of the Development Team can add, edit, or remove tasks from the Sprint Backlog. The Sprint Backlog should be kept up to date and visible to the Scrum Team. It provides a real-time picture of the work that the Development Team plans to accomplish during the Sprint.

> **Tip** Increasing the Sprint Backlog's visibility beyond the Scrum Team is an invitation for the three "M's": meddling, misunderstanding, and micromanaging. Remember that the Sprint Backlog primarily contains the *how* and not the *what*. Allowing stakeholders, or any interested parties, to view the Product Backlog or burndown charts (if utilized) is preferable.

Table 1-12 lists the ways in which the Development Team interacts with the Sprint Backlog.

TABLE 1-12 Development Team interactions with the Sprint Backlog.

Activity	When
Inspect it.	Any time
Move a PBI from the Product Backlog into it.	Sprint Planning or any time afterward (with Product Owner collaboration)
Add, update, split, or remove a task in it.	Sprint Planning or any time afterward until Sprint Review
Take ownership of a new task in it.	Any time (as work demands)
Update status of a PBI or task in it.	Any time (as status changes)
Estimate work remaining for your tasks in it.	Daily

The entire Development Team should collaborate on the plan and create the tasks. Scrum Development Teams must be cross-functional for just this reason. Everyone can and should contribute. This will create a richer and more honest Sprint Backlog than if only one or two code gurus created the plan. A good approach is to start with a conversation in order to understand the PBI and discuss any potential plan. The plan can evolve onto sticky notes or a whiteboard, and then finally to records in a software application like Team Foundation Server. There's zero technical debt in a discussion, and close to zero in a set of sticky notes.

The Development Team must identify *all* tasks in the Sprint Backlog, not just the design, coding, and testing ones. There may be learning, installing, deploying, data entry, design meetings, and documenting tasks. The team's may indirectly require tasks to be created in the Sprint Backlog too. For example, a team's Definition of "Done" might require that every PBI implemented in the Increment has its own installer with notes and instructions in English and German. This self-imposed requirement could drive the creation of several additional tasks for each PBI in the Sprint Backlog.

> **Tip** Have the team's Definition of "Done" nearby during Sprint Planning. It will help the developers as they brainstorm tasks. Also, depending on how the last Sprint went, there may be additional tasks related to improvements identified at the Retrospective meeting.

The developers should estimate their Sprint Backlog items at least daily. This can be done before or after the Daily Scrum, but not during. Most teams I work with prefer to re-estimate their tasks prior to the Daily Scrum, so that any follow-up meetings will have an accurate burndown chart to reference. Some high-performance Scrum Teams won't bother tracking hours or estimating remaining work on tasks. They focus on the Sprint Goal and delivering the PBIs, not the tasks. It is more difficult to assess progress without this information.

Note Scrum does not consider the time spent working on a task. Tracking actual hours is counterproductive to obtaining the Sprint Goal. I would even call it wasteful. If, however, an organization requires its employees to track their time to get paid, that's a separate discussion. The worry is that once such a metric is created, it would be used in a *command and control* way. For example, a manager might see that a set of UX design tasks took 28 hours and then use that as an estimate for future work, or as a stick to beat the designer with if her next set of tasks goes beyond that number—which it could, because software development is very difficult and full of risk.

The Sprint Backlog will be empty at the start of a Sprint. It will begin to emerge during Sprint Planning, and (ideally) be fully populated with tasks by the first few days of the Sprint. For teams new to Scrum or the product's domain, this can be unachievable. These teams may find themselves creating new tasks all the way through the Sprint. This makes it difficult to assess progress, if you don't know what the plan is or when you might achieve it. Even high-performance Scrum Teams need to change their plan sometimes. Each PBI introduces new complexities that can derail an execution plan. New tasks may have to be created mid-Sprint.

Tip In Scrum, work should never be directed or assigned. When creating a new Sprint Backlog task, don't assign it to anyone. For example, you should resist the urge to assign the *testing* tasks to Toni (even though she has a background in testing). Doing so will decrease collaboration and the opportunity for other team members to learn. When the time is right, the team should decide who will take on that task. The team will take many factors into account, including the background, experience, availability, and capacity of the developer.

As the Development Team improves, it will learn to manage risk better, by taking on riskier work early. The team will also become better at identifying the full spectrum of tasks, at least at a high level, during Sprint Planning. It's okay for the more distant tasks to be coarsely defined and overestimated. As the time nears for that piece of work to begin, the eligible developer can decompose and re-estimate it. If Sprint burndown charts are being used, they will be more accurate, earlier in the Sprint. The trend lines, which predict when the Development Team will be done with their work, will also be more accurate. Observers of the burndown charts need to understand that the Development Team will know more tomorrow than they did today—so expect change. The Scrum Master should be able to provide this education.

Tailspin Toys case study During Sprint Planning, the Development Team brainstorms the plan for developing the Increment. When they were just starting out with Scrum, they would only get one or two PBIs planned out and delay the planning of the rest of the PBIs until the Sprint. They've improved in the way they decompose and plan their SBTs. They estimate the tasks in hours, and they've improved the way they've done that. Originally, they would have the "experts" in the various task areas do the estimates. That made estimation go quicker, but during development, they would usually blow their estimates because the expert didn't always do the work. They now estimate the tasks collaboratively and find that they are under as many times as they are over. They can live with that.

The Increment

Scrum is an iterative and *incremental* software development framework. The word "incremental" means "occurring in especially small increments." Each Sprint is an especially small period of time during which the team develops one of these small increments. As we've already discussed, the small period of times (the Sprints) reduce risk by maximizing collaboration and feedback. Incremental delivery of a done software product ensures that a useful version of the working product is always available.

Tip If possible, make the Increment available to the Product Owner and stakeholders throughout the Sprint. Think of it as a hands-on demo or lab environment. As the Development Team finishes a PBI, the demo environment is updated for people to play with the software. This doesn't have to be any kind of a formal testing area, just something that can drive feedback during the Sprint, rather than waiting until the Sprint Review meeting. For example, it would be very convenient to be able to send an email to the stakeholders letting them know there's a "beta" hosted on *http://demoserver1/sprint6/tailspin.*

In Scrum, the Increment is the sum of all the PBIs completed during the Sprint plus all previous Sprints. It's the aggregate of what's currently running in production plus the done PBIs from previous Sprints that haven't yet been released, plus the done PBIs from the current Sprint. Only PBIs done according to their acceptance criteria and the team's Definition of "Done" can be added to the Increment and become potentially releasable.

Note Potentially releasable means that the Increment *could* be released (to the customer or production) if the Product Owner chooses to do so. This is possible because the Increment contains only done PBIs. PBIs aren't done until they meet the level of quality defined by the Product Owner and the Development Team according to the Definition of "Done". The Product Owner may decide to wait until several related PBIs are completed (release by feature), until a certain point in time (release by date), as each PBI is done (continuous deployment).

Definition of "Done"

The Definition of "Done" is not a formal artifact in Scrum, but it should be. Done is the state when a PBI has been developed according to its acceptance criteria and team's Definition of "Done." Scaling that up, done is also the state when the Increment containing all the done PBIs becomes potentially releasable.

The Definition of "Done" is a simple, auditable checklist created by the Development Team. It must be understandable by the Product Owner, the Scrum Master, and any stakeholders. This is why it must be simple and as free of "geek speak" as possible. The definition can be influenced by organizational, product, and release standards and constraints. For example, C# may be a language standard in the organization, but a specific product must be written in C++ for compatibility reasons. Here is a simple Definition of "Done":

- All code compiles without errors or warnings.

- No code analysis errors or warnings exist.

- New code is covered by unit tests.

- An automated build exists.

- An .msi installer exists.

Definitions of "Done" can be quite long and complex. Everything in the definition should be achievable, although some items may not be applicable. For example, if the Development Team is working on a PBI that is mostly graphic-design-centric, there won't be any code to unit-test. For all PBIs that have code, however, the team must create unit tests. It's in the definition. The Development Team should never cut corners by ignoring all or part of the definition in order to finish the forecast. The team has already unanimously decided that quality, as defined by the Definition of "Done", is more important than all-out speed.

> **Note** The Definition of "Done" is a *minimum* standard. There may be times when the Development Team will want to do more than the minimum. This is acceptable so long as the extra effort is justified and not considered "gold plating." Gold plating is when a developer continues to work on a PBI beyond what is fit for purpose. This extra work is typically not worth the value that it adds to the software product.

Undone work

An explicit and concrete Definition of "Done" may seem small, but it can be the most critical checkpoint during a Sprint. Without a consistent meaning of "done," Velocity cannot be estimated. Having a shared Definition of "Done" ensures that the Increment produced at the end of Sprint is of high quality, with minimal defects. High-performance Scrum Teams consider the Definition of "Done" to be sacrosanct. It is the soul of their entire development process. These teams will resist the urge to release undone work, or even demonstrate it at a Sprint Review meeting.

The Development Team should not generate undone work. They should also make sure the "done" means completely done. In the long run, it will be cheaper to hold fast to the Definition of "Done" by improving development practices than to keep sprinting with an unknown amount of work still to be done at the end of the release. If the Product Owner looks at an Increment and doesn't know how much work needs to be done, he or she won't really know when the release will be ready. There may be a need for one or more "stabilization" Sprints at the end of the release just to tackle all of the accumulated undone work.

What's even worse is that the undone work from the Sprints accumulates exponentially, not linearly. Subsequent Sprints will require even more work to reach done: 4 hours of undone work per Sprint for 6 Sprints won't be 24 hours of work, but more like 80 hours. This "undone work" uncertainty has no place in a framework that is supposed to promote transparency and predictability, so every effort should be given to eliminate undone work and "stabilization" Sprints.

As the Development Team improves, it is expected that their Definition of "Done" will improve too. The definition can be changed only in between Sprints. The Sprint Retrospective meeting provides the opportunity to discuss and change it if necessary. The definition should only expand to include more stringent criteria for higher quality. In other words, you should avoid removing items from the definition in order to get more "done" the next Sprint.

The professional Scrum developer

The *Scrum Guide* does not provide guidance on *how* to develop a software product. In fact, during the time between the Sprint Planning meeting and the Sprint Review meeting, the guide is intentionally vague. Other than requiring a Daily Scrum meeting and regular Product Backlog grooming, not much guidance is provided. In fact, the rules state that a Daily Scrum should occur, taking no longer than 15 minutes.

So what about the other 7 hours and 45 minutes of the day? What should the Development Team, and the individual developers, be doing during that time? That's the million dollar question. The short answer is: the developers should be doing the right thing—even when nobody is looking. There are many longer answers. The contents of this book will hopefully reveal several answers to this question.

Remember that developing software is a risky endeavor for both the developer and the customer. The process is a complex undertaking consisting of specifying, designing, coding, and testing. More things can go wrong than right. Any small mistake or fault on either side can lead to wasted effort—if you are lucky. Some mistakes can lead to outright damage. Professional Development Teams understand this, and they make sure their customer understands this. Ideally the customer will share in these risks. This means that the customer and the developers understand that they are both equally responsible for identifying and mitigating these risks, as well as sharing responsibility if a risk evolves into a disaster of some sort.

Let's drop the customer out of the discussion for a minute. Developers on a Scrum Team collectively own their successes and failures, just as they collectively own the code, bugs, technical debt, and other issues. These developers have also learned to rely on their fellow team members and to trust them. They know that they must be resolute, forthright, transparent, and able to compromise in order to reach their goals. These qualities sound similar to those of the chivalrous knights from the Middle Ages —except for the compromising part.

When I'm meeting with a new team, I will often ask what they think the developer's job is. "To write code," is the almost universal flip answer that I hear. Being a career developer myself, I used to agree with that answer. As I've improved my understanding of the profession of software development, this answer now irks me. I believe that a better answer would that a developer's job is *to provide value in the form of working software*. This answer encapsulates the attributes of a professional Scrum developer. Professional Scrum developers understand that:

- They have the right and responsibility to maximize the self-organization capability of the team.

- They should reflect Scrum's values: commitment, focus, openness, respect, and courage.

- They should only do work that provides value to the software product.

- They should plan realistic goals and then commit to achieving them.

- They don't know everything, and they should be always willing to learn.

- They shouldn't be afraid of working outside their comfort zone.

- They should respect the Scrum Guide and its "rules."

- They shouldn't be afraid of asking other team members for help.

- They should be transparent in what they do and how they do it.

- They are part of a team, and their voice is equivalent to others.

- They have a stake in the success (or failure) of the product.

- They look for and minimize waste in their practices.

- They are responsible for the quality of the product.

- They should be honest in their estimates.

- They should say "no" when appropriate.

- They should collaborate when possible.

- They are professionals, not hobbyists.

- They shouldn't release undone work.

- They are more than just a coder.

- They are part of a larger team.

Chapter burndown

Here are the key concepts we covered in this chapter:

- **Scrum Guide**   The *Scrum Guide* codifies the rules of Scrum. You should download it from *http://www.scrum.org/scrumguides* and read it now. Its updates will supersede this chapter.

- **The Development Team**   The Development Team contains a cross-functional group of three to nine professionals who develop the forecasted work during the Sprint.

- **Product Owner**   The Product Owner is the voice of the user and is responsible for maximizing the value of the product and work of the Development Team.

- **Scrum Master**   The Scrum Master is responsible for ensuring Scrum is understood and enacted.

- **Sprint**   A time-boxed event of one month or less that contains the other Scrum events.

- **Sprint Planning**   The meeting where the Scrum Team forecasts the work to be performed during the Sprint, along with a plan for developing it.

- **Daily Scrum**   The daily meeting allowing the Development Team to synchronize activities and create a plan for the next 24 hours.

- **Sprint Review**   The meeting where the Increment is demonstrated and feedback is captured.

- **Sprint Retrospective**   The meeting where the Scrum Team inspects its practices and creates a plan to improve in the next Sprint.

- **Product Backlog**   An ordered list of everything that might be needed in the software product.

- **Sprint Backlog**   The forecasted Product Backlog items plus the plan for developing them.

- **The Increment**   The sum of all done Product Backlog items (PBIs) during this and previous Sprints.

- **Definition of "Done"(DoD)**   A shared understanding of what it means for the Development Team to be done with the development of an individual Product Backlog item or the Increment itself.

CHAPTER 2

Microsoft Visual Studio 2012 ALM

Since Microsoft first introduced what would become Visual Studio Team System (VSTS) back in 2004, .NET development teams have begun improving the way they plan, track, and manage their software development projects. No longer are they tracking code changes in meaningfully-named .zip files or Microsoft Visual SourceSafe, bugs and requirements in Microsoft Excel, and performing automated builds using .bat files. VSTS 2005 (code name *Burton*) integrated those pillars of software development and even tossed in reporting so everyone could stay informed. The game of software development had changed forever. It had gone professional.

In its first iteration, this stack of tools was marketed as only providing support for the systems development life cycle (SDLC). This life cycle included everything to do with developing a software product, such as requirements, architecture, coding, testing, configuration management, and project management. In the subsequent release of VSTS 2008, Microsoft (and the rest of us) refactored its thinking to regard these tools as having much broader capabilities for supporting application lifecycle management (ALM). ALM includes everything that is part of the application lifecycle, not just development. ALM combines business management with software engineering. Scrum, or any other framework, process, or methodology, is encompassed by ALM.

With the 2010 version of Microsoft Visual Studio, Microsoft really doubled down on their support for ALM. They introduced Microsoft Test Manager to allow teams to create and manage their testing effort. Hierarchical work items enabled a richer breakdown of the planned work. PBI work items could now be linked to multiple child Task work items. By using Lab Management, teams could configure environments of virtual machines and automate the build, deploy, test cycle against complex environments. It was during the 2010 product cycle that Microsoft gave us the Visual Studio Scrum 1.0 process template, thus acknowledging and formalizing their support for Scrum. Visual Studio 2012 continues the tradition of providing strong ALM tooling, especially in the area of Agile (Scrum) planning and management capabilities.

ALM is a proven set of tools and processes that help organizations manage the entire lifespan of application development, reduce cycle times, and eliminate waste. It integrates different teams, platforms, and activities with the goal of enabling a continuous flow of business value. ALM includes every aspect of the application's lifecycle, from when it first begins as an idea or need, all the way to its retirement. This lifecycle includes initiating the project, defining and refining requirements, design, coding, testing, releasing, deploying, and even operating, including monitoring.

Note Application *retirement*, otherwise known as *sunsetting* or *decommissioning*, is the practice of ending the life of a software application when it no longer has value to the customer. Just because the software is retired doesn't mean that the need for the software vanishes. Newer, rewritten or commercial, off-the-shelf (OTS) software typically replaces it, along with a migration of the data.

In today's fast-paced, startup, micro independent software vendor (ISV), open source, app store ecosystem, the lifecycle of a software idea can be quite short. Scrum can be used to deliver the vision incrementally, and Agile ALM tools can be used to safeguard that work and the quality of the product. Both can reduce risk and waste. On the other hand, some organizations and products have a very long lifecycle, such as custom line-of-business (LOB) systems. These may need more emphasis on governance and operations and less on Velocity. Regardless, the ALM tools in Visual Studio 2012 support both ends of this spectrum.

In this chapter, we will look at what's new and interesting in Visual Studio 2012 with a focus on the ALM tools that can be used to empower a Scrum Team to deliver value continuously.

Delivering continuous value

For the most part, our industry has emerged from building one-tier, two-tier, and n-tier applications that are internally managed by an organization. On the whole, we now build richer, more immersive applications powered by continuous services. These applications are delivered across a broad spectrum of connected systems—from mobile devices to traditional laptop and desktop computers. In parallel with this trend, software development practices are continuing to emerge that seek to enable continuous delivery of value.

The world is demanding faster and faster cycle times, rapidly realizing the concept released to market. This is putting dramatic pressure on organizations and teams to deliver value rapidly and continuously. If your organization and team are not experiencing this yet, then you will be soon or you will be working for a competitor who is. In order to compete, companies must broaden their focus from merely improving their development practices to improving the entire value stream. This reality has been the impetus behind the main themes for the ALM tools in the latest release of Visual Studio 2012.

Smell It's a smell when management expects that a tool (by itself) will be able to radically reduce cycle times or enable continuous delivery of value. It takes a combination of improving the existing process and practices as well as solid ALM tools. A few years ago, one of my clients asked how Team Foundation Server 2010 would help them reduce their cycle time from 47 days to 7 days. I told them it wouldn't, and that they would have to radically improve their processes, practices, and (most importantly) their culture to achieve that extreme level of improvement.

Here are the main themes for the ALM tools in Visual Studio 2012:

- **Agile software development** Agile techniques and methods, such as Scrum, have helped software development teams improve dramatically in the past two decades. They have fundamentally transformed the industry consensus as to the right way to develop software. Visual Studio continues to add and improve its tooling to support Agile software development.

- **Quality enablement** A shift away from traditional quality control (post-development testing) toward ensuring that quality is defined and delivered as a first-class requirement.

- **DevOps** An integration of development and IT operations to enable faster feedback cycles, reductions in time to fix production bugs, and a focus on pushing smaller packages of features into production more frequently.

- **Continuous delivery (CD)** The rapid flow of incremental business value through the entire end-to-end value chain. CD is made possible through Agile methods, quality enablement, and other practices.

CD of value requires a tuned orchestration of practices and tool usage within ALM. This goes beyond just managing changes to code using version control. As I've always said, the full value of the ALM tools in Visual Studio, especially Team Foundation Server (TFS), cannot be realized unless work items, version control, and automated builds are used correctly. This is certainly the case when a team wants to achieve CD. This orchestration, resulting in a CD of value, can be seen in Figure 2-1.

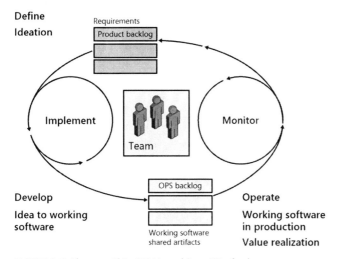

FIGURE 2-1 Phases within ALM to achieve CD of value.

When people view a diagram like Figure 2-1, they don't usually think about subsequent cycles. They tend to step through a diagram like this once, understand each phase, and put it away. In reality, teams rarely begin with a green field environment. Startups tend to be the exception, and even then, that field turns brown very quickly. Once working software is deployed, it affects every part of the cycle. Maintenance work becomes integrated into the Product Backlog alongside new features and ideas. Needless to say, it can be challenging to build a modern application on top of existing technology, manage operations, and try to deliver value while keeping the existing application up and running.

Let's break down software delivery into three phases: define, develop, and deliver. The Scrum framework helps us define by instructing us how to plan and manage work. Smart developers using modern tools and practices have no problem developing the Increment. It's the *delivery* of that value that has been the challenge—mostly because of impediments beyond the control of the Scrum Team. For example, the Development Team delivers a potentially releasable Increment, but operations struggles to get it deployed and running in as timely a fashion. This is just one of many potential impediments. Current Agile and lean concepts have helped to improve the way that teams deliver software. As an industry we're getting better, but improvement is still needed, and the ALM tools in Visual Studio 2012 close the gap.

Delivering the Increment is supported by a variety of different functions that need to be integrated carefully in order to make delivery happen. For example, many organizations still consider quality an afterthought—something tested into a product after the developers are done. This bolting-on of last-minute fixes can produce technical debt that must be repaid (with interest) at some point in time.

The list of impediments keeping a team from achieving CD can go on and on. The only solution is for such a team to start inspecting those impediments and removing them, one at a time. Teams must take every opportunity to improve their development practices in order to improve the entire value stream. This includes impediments that exist beyond the Development Team. Organizations must give these teams the freedom and authority to make these changes, and support the changes to make them persist.

The combination of Scrum and Visual Studio ALM tools is powerful. High-performance Scrum Development Teams know how to apply Agile practices while using tools so that the net result is effective. Through constant inspection and adaptation, waste is identified and eliminated. This may mean starting to use a new feature in the tool or stopping the use of a wasteful feature. Development Teams that blindly use new, shiny tools without thinking are just asking for a drop in Velocity. On the other hand, teams that think that all planning and management tools are wasteful are also missing the boat. For teams that only use whiteboards and sticky notes to manage their work, I hope they never have to "roll back" their task board or recover from a disaster, like a new janitor accidentally cleaning that board. In addition, these teams cannot trace PBIs to source code and even struggle to gather historical data, such as Velocity.

Visual Studio 2012

Visual Studio 2012 is an integrated ALM solution that enables software development teams of all sizes to deliver continuous value with high velocity and high quality. It provides both individual developers and entire Scrum Teams the ability to build business and consumer applications. Visual Studio 2012 includes a feature-rich, comprehensive, integrated environment and new tooling to support a range of Agile practices and methods, such as Scrum.

In June 2012, Gartner's Magic Quadrant report for ALM positioned Microsoft in the Leaders Quadrant. Although this report was based on an evaluation of Visual Studio 2010, I feel that this leadership position will continue to grow when Gartner evaluates Visual Studio 2012. Gartner is one of the world's top IT research and advising companies. You can read more about this report at *http://www.gartner.com/technology/reprints.do?id=1-1ASCXON&ct=120606&st=sb*.

Visual Studio assists everyone on the team in collaborating more effectively while building and sharing institutional knowledge. Project artifacts and data from work item tracking, version control, automated builds, and testing tools are stored in a centralized Microsoft SQL Server data warehouse. Powerful reports and dashboards provide real-time transparency and traceability, as well as historical trending of the progress and quality of both the product and process. Figure 2-2 shows all of the features and major capabilities of these ALM tools.

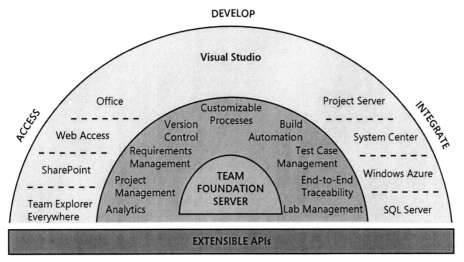

FIGURE 2-2 Visual Studio 2012 ALM features.

Software products are developed by people, not by processes or practices. Processes and practices need to adapt and evolve to accommodate changes in scope and culture. Visual Studio 2012 provides an environment that adapts to a Scrum Team's uniqueness and enhances it with proven Agile practices that can be adopted at any pace. Over time, the team, as well as the organization, will become more productive by using these tools. This assumes that the culture allows this to happen. "Organizational gravity," as fellow Professional Scrum Developer Mike Vincent refers to it, can easily pull the team back into dysfunctional, waterfall behaviors if overt effort is not made to improve.

Professional Scrum development involves more than just coding. It involves the whole range of planning, testing, and management activities. Visual Studio 2012 enables a Scrum Team to incrementally adopt best practices with out-of-the-box support for lightweight requirements, backlog management, task boards, code reviews, continuous integration and deployment, continuous feedback, and more.

These tools also help connect the Scrum Team and stakeholders while optimizing the development process and reducing risk. Integrated feedback tools allow the team to connect remote stakeholder's ideas to every member of the team in real time. This integration helps keep the Scrum Team and stakeholders cooperating efficiently in order to keep development projects on track, and that assists in ensuring that the delivered software is timely, functional, and cost-effective.

Note Visual Studio 2012 provides for full round-tripping project support with Visual Studio 2010 SP1. This means that Visual Studio 2012 can be adopted gradually by a Scrum Development Team that already uses Visual Studio 2010, with no friction and no need to migrate any project.

Editions

There are many different audiences that use Visual Studio. They differ depending on the maturity of the Development Team, the software products they are building, and the speed at which they deliver and maintain the software product. To support various audiences, Visual Studio 2012 is available in different editions. The editions range in price from free (Express editions) to thousands of dollars. You can think of editions as being matryoshka-like in nature, where the next higher (more expensive) edition contains all of the features in the editions below it plus other, exclusive features. Visual Studio 2012 Ultimate edition contains all possible features. You can see this in Figure 2-3.

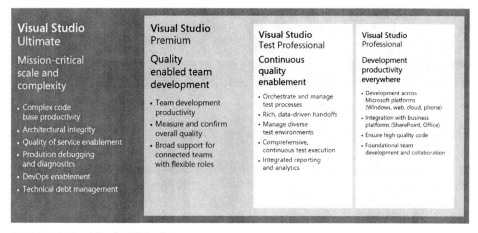

FIGURE 2-3 Visual Studio 2012 editions.

Note Don't confuse *edition* with *version*. The version of Visual Studio is 2012. That version is available in many editions. For a more thorough comparison of the Visual Studio editions, visit *http://www.microsoft.com/visualstudio/11/en-us/products/compare*.

In this section, we will briefly discuss each edition of Visual Studio 2012 and its features.

Professional edition

Visual Studio 2012 Professional edition is the baseline edition to be used in professional software development. With it, a developer can develop Windows desktop and phone applications, including Windows 8 themed applications. These applications can target the web or cloud sites and services while using Microsoft Office and Microsoft SharePoint integration.

Here is a list of the more interesting features found in the Professional edition:

- **Unit testing** Performance of unit testing execution has been improved. Extensibility allows third-party unit testing frameworks, such as nUnit, xUnit.net, MbUnit, QUnit, and Jasmine (a popular behavior-driven development framework for testing JavaScript code) to be used within Visual Studio.

- **Task board** Team Web Access enables visualization and management of the Sprint Backlog. Task work items can be created and moved quickly (via dragging) across the board to a different state.

- **Static code analysis** Analyze and report information about the code, such as violations of programming design rules. C++ code is also supported.

- **Advanced profiling** Analyze performance issues in applications by using one of four approaches: CPU sampling, instrumentation, memory allocation, and thread contention. GPU activity and SharePoint application execution can now be profiled.

Test Professional edition

The Visual Studio 2012 Test Professional edition is not an edition of the Visual Studio integrated development environment (IDE). Instead, it contains Microsoft Test Manager (MTM) and its related capability. It is intended for users who are more involved with test case management, such as creating and running manual user interface (UI) tests. It is ideal for Product Owners as well as stakeholders, such as business analysts and product managers who want to collaborate more on the quality aspects of the Increment and less on the actual coding.

Here is a list of the more interesting features found in the Test Professional edition:

- **Microsoft Test Manager** Manage test plans, test cases, and requirements while streamlining the testing process through manual and exploratory tests. MTM allows test steps to be recorded and played back automatically or fast-forwarded to a specific test step.

- **Exploratory testing** Provides a lightweight mechanism to test applications where developers can explore the application to identify bugs or create test cases. All background information is captured so that work items can be created at any point along the way.

- **Backlog management** Team Web Access supports easy management of the Product Backlog and Sprint Backlog.

- **Sprint Planning** Team Web Access includes tooling for planning Sprints, such as dragging, forecasting, and real-time Velocity and burndown reporting.

- **Microsoft Lab Management** Manage virtual or standard environments of computers to enable developers to spin up complex environments easily in order to run acceptance tests.

- **PowerPoint storyboarding** Use Microsoft PowerPoint to propose ideas and capture feedback and requirements from distributed stakeholders.

- **Request and manage feedback** Use the feedback manager tool to loop distributed stakeholders continuously into the development process by capturing their comments, audio notes, and desktop video.

Tailspin Toys case study Because Paula (Product Owner) and Scott (Scrum Master) aren't involved in the actual software development, they don't need a proper edition of Visual Studio. They do, however, want to be involved with managing the backlogs and planning the Sprints. For this reason, they opted for the Test Professional edition, as it includes this capability. A few other stakeholders have this edition as well.

Premium edition

Visual Studio 2012 Premium edition is a more comprehensive team collaboration suite than Professional edition. It threads quality through all tasks and activities performed by a Development Team while providing multiple engineering tools to help with the development, testing, automation, and diagnostics of the software being developed. Premium edition contains all of the features and capabilities of Professional and Test Professional editions, plus more. This means that MTM and Lab Management functionality is available to users of the Premium edition.

Tip I believe that the Premium edition should be the baseline edition for all members of a high-performance Scrum Development Team.

Here is a list of the more interesting features found in the Premium edition:

- **Code metrics** Code metric data can be generated in order to measure the complexity and maintainability of the code. This can pinpoint where refactoring or increased testing is needed.

- **Code coverage** This determines what proportion of code is actually being tested by tests, such as unit tests. This data can help point out what code hasn't been tested adequately.

- **Coded UI testing** Automated tests that drive the application through its UI can verify that the whole application, including its UI, is functioning correctly.

- **Code clone analysis** This detects similar fragments of code in a solution. This makes it possible to identify wasteful copy and paste problems and where refactoring may be necessary. This is especially useful when working on a legacy code base.

- **Architectural validation** Architectural integrity can be enforced automatically through layer diagram validation. Layer diagrams must be created in Ultimate edition.

- **My Work** This feature lists each developer's pending tasks, displays the status of each task, and provides information on each task in the context of the entire project.

- **Code review** A set of tools and workflows that facilitate collaboration among distributed developers to review the code and propose changes.

- **Task suspend and Resume** This feature sllows developers to visualize their current task. If the developer is interrupted and needs to switch context, Visual Studio can suspend the task, saving all related context. Later, the suspended task can be resumed and the context restored.

- **Continuous testing** Run unit tests automatically after every local build.

Tailspin Toys case study Most developers own a copy of Premium edition. It contains the serious development and testing tools required by the software that they are developing. The fact that Premium edition now includes the Test Professional edition, which includes Microsoft Test Manager, is an absolute bonus. All developers can now be involved directly with creating and managing tests cases and manual tests and executing tests. This is important as they practice acceptance test-driven development (ATDD).

Ultimate edition

The Visual Studio 2012 Ultimate edition is the top-tier toolset that accommodates sophisticated teams executing architectural design and performance testing activities. Ultimate edition contains all of the features and capabilities of the other Visual Studio editions, plus more.

Here is a list of the more interesting features found in the Ultimate edition:

- **IntelliTrace** This feature captures debug data in development and production servers. This data provides developers with the information that they need to fix defects more rapidly.

- **Web performance and load testing** This feature ensures a high quality of service while detecting any scalability problems. Unlimited load testing is now available directly in Ultimate, so there is no longer a need to obtain Virtual User packs.

- **Architecture Explorer** You can understand the structure of an application with architectural discovery tools. Architecture Explorer has been improved to work with big projects, as well as C++ code.

- **Dependency graphs** You can create dependency graphs in order to understand how your code is organized and view its dependencies.

- **Layer diagram and dependency validation** You can enforce architectural integrity and provide automated application validation. Layer diagrams are read-only in Premium edition.

- **UML diagrams** This feature allows you to generate code from Unified Modeling Language (UML) diagrams to create scaffolding. Also, you can reverse-engineer code to UML to understand the big picture faster and with greater comprehension. UML diagrams are read-only in Premium edition.

- **Microsoft fakes** This feature is a unit test isolation framework used to create substitute classes and methods for production and system code that create dependencies in the code under test. This enables the automated testing of hard-to-test code.

> **Tailspin Toys case study** A couple of the developers have a copy of Ultimate edition. They needed some of its specialized features. If, in the future, the team is impeded by not having more Ultimate editions, the impediment will be discussed during a Sprint Retrospective meeting. Ultimate edition is also installed on the build and test agent machines so any developer can run web and load tests as part of the automated Team Foundation Build process.

Express editions

Microsoft has also made several Express editions of Visual Studio 2012 available. These editions are platform-specific and include multiple language support. Each edition provides specialized capabilities and tools required to develop on its platform. Express editions are downloadable for free from *www.microsoft.com/downloads*. Microsoft will also continue to make their Visual Studio 2010 Express edition available for download as well.

Here is a list of the Visual Studio 2012 Express editions:

- **Visual Studio Express 2012 for Windows 8** Developers can build and test applications and then publish them to Windows Store to reach millions of customers.

- **Visual Studio Express 2012 for Web** Developers can build and test HTML5, CSS3, ASP.NET, and JavaScript applications, and deploy them on web servers or to the cloud using Windows Azure.

- **Visual Studio Express 2012 for Windows Desktop** Developers can build and test desktop applications targeted to run on all versions of Windows supported by Visual Studio 2012.

- **Visual Studio 2012 Express for Windows Phone** Developers can build and test applications for the next Windows Phone release.

- **Team Foundation Server 2012 Express** Provides small teams of up to five developers with source code control, work item tracking, and build automation. The sixth and subsequent users each require a TFS CAL. The same CAL exclusions apply as with the full edition of TFS.

While the various Express editions are a frictionless way to get started writing simple applications, they are not intended for *professional* software development. This type of development demands tools that are able to enhance current applications, as well as be able to drive innovation for future applications. By using a more powerful edition, a developer is able to perform all development tasks in one integrated tool: modeling, designing, coding, testing, debugging, and deploying. An organization's return on investing in an edition above Express will be realized when their developers are able to stay focused on their work within a single tool.

Smell It's a smell when I see members of a professional software development team using any Express edition. These editions do not have professional-level code quality and testing tools. More important, while the price may be tempting to management, it tends to reflect their inability to value what the team does or how they do it. It could be that an Express edition was temporarily installed for a team member or stakeholder to perform a spike or another type of experiment.

Team Foundation Server

TFS is the collaboration platform at the core of Microsoft's Visual Studio ALM solution. TFS automates the software delivery process by providing the Scrum Team, as well as the stakeholders, with the applicable tools they need to manage their software development projects effectively throughout the entire lifecycle.

TFS provides services for source control, work item tracking, and automated builds. The respective data is stored in a SQL Server data warehouse and is used as the basis for many reports that provide timely information about the quality of the product and process. TFS can be installed on-premises using an organization's infrastructure. It is also available as a software as a service (SaaS) offering from Microsoft, hosted on their infrastructure and managed by them. The hosted offering is referred to as *Team Foundation Service*, which I will discuss shortly.

Here is a list of the high-level features and capabilities found in TFS:

- **Project management** Create and manage team projects.

- **Work item tracking** Create and manage PBI, Bug, Task, and other types of work items.

- **Version control** Manage changes to the source code and other files in the application.

- **Team Foundation Build** Automate the building, deploying, and testing of the application.

- **Project portal** Use the Windows SharePoint portal as a place for additional collaboration, such as sharing documents. This feature is not available for the Express edition or for the hosted Team Foundation Service.

- **Reporting** Run management and quality reports derived from data in the data warehouse. This feature is not available for the Express edition or for the hosted Team Foundation Service.

These are important features to teams of every size, especially Scrum Teams, and serve to unify the entire team in various ways. Without TFS, each team member would be designing, developing, and testing within his or her own silo. This is a problem that should be avoided by all teams, especially high-performance Scrum Teams.

Team Foundation Service

The Team Foundation Service is a cloud-based, hosted ALM solution. Much like the on-premises version of TFS, the hosted service can be accessed by members of the Scrum Team as well as stakeholders, using the same client applications and tools. Software projects can be planned and developed collaboratively from anywhere.

Work items, source code, build definitions, and other artifacts are stored on Microsoft's Azure-based servers. These assets can be accessed and managed online via a web browser, Visual Studio, Eclipse, or other familiar client applications. This management can be seen in Figure 2-4.

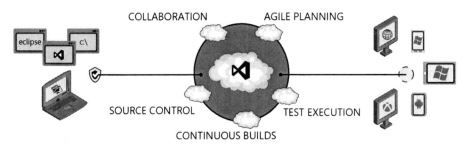

FIGURE 2-4 The hosted Team Foundation Service is a cloud-powered ALM solution.

Using the hosted Team Foundation Service is very much like using an on-premises TFS server. It looks and feels the same from Visual Studio, Office, the command-line utilities, or Team Explorer Everywhere in Eclipse. The only major difference is how a user authenticates. Rather than using a Windows logon, a Microsoft Live ID is used. This means that users will need a Live ID, if they don't already have one.

The main benefit of Team Foundation Service is that an organization or team can get started quickly. There is no infrastructure to provision or manage. In fact, developers can go from zero to their first team project in minutes, including the sign-up process. In addition, Microsoft has a three-week cadence to release new capabilities to the service. This means that, internally, Microsoft has adopted a CD approach of their own, releasing new capabilities to the service about every three weeks.

Note At the time of this writing, the hosted Team Foundation Service is still in preview, and pricing has yet to be finalized. However, full-featured accounts are free during this time period, and there will continue to be a free level of the service as Microsoft transitions out of preview. There will also be paid levels of the service for users who need more than what the free level provides. Benefits for MSDN subscribers, as well as other program membership, have yet to be announced. Microsoft will share more information about purchase options and integration with other programs at a later date.

Microsoft hopes that those users who preview the hosted Team Foundation Service today will remain once the service goes live and transitions over to the new licensing model. If a developer, or team of developers, wishes to leave, however, Microsoft has promised that their code and project data will be able to be exported prior to closing the account. For more information, take a look at the service FAQ here: *http://tfspreview.com/en-us/support/faq*.

You can find a comparison of the benefits of the on-premises Team Foundation Server with the hosted Team Foundation Service in Chapter 4.

Hosted builds

Since all of the new Agile (Scrum) planning and management tools are web-based, users of the hosted Team Foundation Service get to enjoy them as well. Even continuous integration (CI) builds, hosted on Microsoft's build servers, are available.

The hosted builds are provided by a pool of Windows Azure virtual machine (VM) roles that can expand and shrink as needed. This is why some refer to it as an *elastic* build service. When a Development Team starts a build, a VM is allocated from the pool to run the build. The build executes, the output is copied off the build machine, and then the VM is restored and returned back to the pool for someone else to use.

Once configured, a developer can create a new build definition, queue the build, monitor its progress, and view its results in the same manner as an on-premises build. The one difference is that, when creating the build definition, the developer must pick the "Hosted Build Controller" rather than a local build controller.

The hosted build service allows a team to skip the complexities of installing, managing, and patching their build servers. However, there are limitations in what can be installed and configured with the hosted build service, so if the team prefers, they can configure and use their own dedicated build servers to build, test, and deploy their apps locally.

Agents for Visual Studio 2012

Agents for Visual Studio 2012 include test controllers and test agents that can be used to scale out load generation, support distributed data collection, and distribute test execution. A team can also use agents to manage testing, workflow, and network isolation for VMs that are used with Lab Management. Lab agents and test agents, from previous versions of Lab Management, are now combined into one type of agent—the test agent.

Agents for Visual Studio 2012 enable these types of activities:

- Run automated tests remotely using Visual Studio

- Distribute automated tests to multiple machines using Visual Studio

- Run tests and collect test data remotely using Microsoft Test Manager

- Use a lab environment

- Deploy an application in a lab environment using a build-deploy-test workflow

- Run tests in lab environment

The agents are available to MSDN subscribers with Visual Studio 2012 Test Professional, Premium, or Ultimate editions. Keep in mind that while the agents can run load tests, that feature remains exclusive to licensees of the Ultimate edition. Load tests can now execute with an unlimited number of virtual users.

> **Note** Visual Studio Agents 2012 are no longer restricted from use in a production environment. This means that they may now be deployed and enabled for production load testing.

Visual Studio Team Explorer Everywhere 2012

Although Visual Studio 2012 is the ideal client for TFS, it is not the only development environment being used in the world. Many organizations don't use Visual Studio. They may not even run Windows. Eclipse is a popular, cross-platform IDE that is prevalent in the industry. It runs on Windows as well as several non-Windows platforms, such as Linux and Mac OS X.

An important feature of TFS is its ability to integrate with other operating systems and tools, enabling developers to continue to use a familiar environment while still being able to collaborate as a team. Visual Studio Team Explorer Everywhere 2012 enables a Scrum Development Team to collaborate while using Eclipse or from the command line on certain non-Windows operating systems.

Team Explorer Everywhere includes both the TFS plug-in for Eclipse and the Cross-platform Command-Line Client for TFS. Team Explorer Everywhere provides similar capabilities as those that are available in Visual Studio 2012. For example, you can view and edit your work items, employ version control over your application code, track bugs, generate reports, and get an up-to-date view of the entire project. The Team Explorer pane integrates directly into the Eclipse IDE.

> **Note** Team Explorer Everywhere enables popular Eclipse-based IDEs, such as IBM's Rational Application Developer, Adobe Flex Builder, and Aptana Studio, to connect to TFS.

MSDN subscriptions

The preferred way to obtain Visual Studio 2012 is through a Microsoft Developer Network (MSDN) subscription. MSDN subscriptions enhance an organization or team's investments by providing comprehensive access to resources that help software development teams build high-quality applications for web, mobile, cloud, and Windows. Subscriptions also provide a cost-effective way for organizations to obtain software, services, training, and other resources for their development needs. With a simple, per-user licensing model, MSDN subscriptions help enhance developer productivity via access to past and prerelease software, professional and community support, e-learning, magazines and online concierge, in addition to the software tools and services.

Visual Studio 2012 Ultimate, Premium, Professional, and Test Professional editions may be purchased through an MSDN subscription. In fact, only Visual Studio 2012 Professional edition, as well as the Express editions, can be obtained *without* an MSDN subscription. When purchasing Visual Studio through an MSDN subscription, you are licensed to install and connect to an on-premises TFS. For more information, visit *http://msdn.microsoft.com/subscriptions*.

> **Note** Understanding the licensing of Visual Studio 2012, especially when it comes to accessing the shared resources of TFS, can be difficult. The nuances of when a user needs a license, and what kind, are very complex when you consider using features such as Team Explorer, Team Foundation Build, Team Web Access, SharePoint project portal, and SQL Server Reporting Services. Thankfully, Microsoft has published the *Visual Studio 2012 and MSDN Licensing White Paper,* which provides an overview of the Visual Studio 2012 product line, including MSDN subscriptions, and the licensing requirements for those products in common deployment scenarios. For more information, visit *http://www.microsoft.com/visualstudio/licensing*.

Chapter burndown

Here are the key concepts we covered in this chapter:

- **ALM** Application lifecycle management (ALM) is the fusion of business and engineering activities pertaining to the development of a software product.

- **Scrum and ALM** Scrum is a process framework and fits within the boundaries of ALM. ALM is process agnostic. High-performance Scrum Teams know that a balance of Scrum and ALM practices are required to develop complex software products efficiently.

- **CD** Continuous delivery (CD) is possible through the adoption of Agile practices and the effective use of tooling. Scrum works well within an organization practicing CD.

- **Visual Studio 2012** Many editions are available to meet the varying needs of different types of teams.

- **Professional edition** This is the baseline edition for anyone developing professional applications.

- **Test Professional edition** Includes Microsoft Test Manager for managing the testing effort. This edition also allows the user to manage the Product Backlog and Sprint Backlog. visually Product Owners and other stakeholders who are not directly helping with development should obtain this edition.

- **Premium edition** This is the baseline edition for Professional Scrum Developers. The 2012 version now includes Test Professional edition, which includes Microsoft Test Manager.

- **Ultimate edition** This edition contains advanced architecture and testing tools required to build mission-critical applications. Developers with specific requirements should obtain this edition.

- **Team Foundation Server** Enables team collaboration through the management of work items, version control, and automated builds. A number of client applications can be used to communicate with TFS, including Visual Studio, Office, Windows Explorer, Eclipse, and a web browser.

- **Team Foundation Service** Microsoft also offers a hosted TFS SaaS. Users connect to it using a Live ID credential, and users can also manage work items, version control, and automated builds. These builds can even be hosted in Windows Azure.

- **MSDN** An MSDN subscription is the preferred way of licensing Visual Studio 2012. In fact, Test Professional, Premium, and Ultimate editions can be obtained *only* through an MSDN subscription.

CHAPTER 3

Microsoft Visual Studio Scrum 2.0

Shortly after Microsoft released Microsoft Visual Studio Team Foundation Server 2010, they made the Microsoft Visual Studio Scrum version 1.0 process template available for download. This process template was different from the other, out-of-the-box MSF process templates. This new template was designed from the ground up to embrace the rules of Scrum. While the two MSF process templates were very mature and robust in terms of features, neither supported Scrum very well. That said, teams were able to successfully implement Scrum using the MSF Agile Software Development process template, but only after a fair amount of customization and guidance.

The Visual Studio Scrum process template came into existence as a result of the collaboration between Microsoft, Scrum.org, and the Professional Scrum Developer community. We all knew that Scrum had become the dominant Agile framework in software development. Microsoft recognized this as well. They also knew that teams using Team Foundation Server and Scrum together wanted a more tightly coupled experience resulting in a lower *drag coefficient*. What resulted was a very minimalistic process template that followed the rules of Scrum.

It's important to note that Visual Studio Scrum is a *Scrum* process template. Because of this, many of the workbooks and reports that are found in the other templates are missing. I have heard some teams complain about this missing functionality when migrating to the Scrum template, but overall, not many teams saw this as an adoption blocker. One thing is certain: this Scrum process template is very popular. There have been nearly 100,000 downloads in the first two years.

Team Foundation Server 2012 ships with version 2.0 of the process template. It includes a few bug fixes but also many improvements. Some of the changes relate directly to improvements in Team Foundation Server 2012, such as being able to store start and end dates on the iteration path nodes themselves. The introduction of the new web-based Agile planning tools drove a lot of changes to the template as well. In this chapter, we will go over the basics, as well as highlight what's new In Visual Studio Scrum 2.0.

Dissecting the process template

Prior to Team Foundation Server 2012, Visual Studio Scrum was available as a separate download and required manual installation and configuration. Visual Studio Scrum 2.0 is now one of the built-in process templates. There's nothing to install. What's even better is that Microsoft made it the *default* process template when creating a new team project, as you can see in Figure 3-1. This will further drive awareness, if not the outright adoption, of Scrum among software development teams using Team Foundation Server 2012.

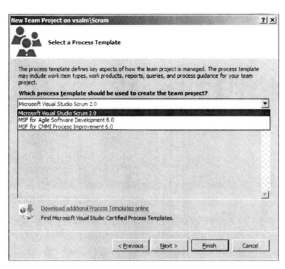

FIGURE 3-1 Selecting the process template when creating a new team project.

Before we analyze the Visual Studio Scrum process template, we need to set a baseline understanding of what a process template is and what it's not. *Logically*, you can think of a process template as what gets "copied and pasted" into a new team project. All of the project's initial settings and behaviors come from the template. *Physically*, a process template is a collection of XML and other types of files arranged in specific folders that define the various elements of a team project during creation. These elements, in turn, define the behavior of the project and how the team can interact with it. Here is an overview of the types of elements found in a process template:

- Process template name, description, version, and plug-ins to execute
- Work item type definitions
- Work item type categories
- Work item link types
- Work items to create
- Work item queries, folders, and permissions
- Agile and planning tools configuration
- Areas and iterations
- Microsoft Project field mapping
- Default groups, teams, and permissions
- Source control behavior, notes, and permissions
- Build settings, templates, and permissions
- Test management, configuration, and other settings
- Lab Management settings and templates
- Microsoft SharePoint portal folders, documents, and dashboards

- Process guidance
- Reports, folders, and data sources

> **Note** Process templates are somewhat analogous to Microsoft Word templates. When creating a new Word document, you can choose from several different templates. There are Microsoft-provided templates, as well as those from third parties. The template only affects the new document's *initial* look and feel. As soon as you change something in the document, like a style or margin setting, it deviates from the original template. It doesn't affect the original template either. This is the same behavior that you'll find in a process template–team project relationship. You can customize a team project by adding a new check-in policy, hiding a field in a work item type, or renaming a query. Changing the team project after creation does not alter the template. The inverse is also true—changing the template after creation does not alter the object created from it.

MSF process templates

You may be wondering about those other two process templates found in Team Foundation Server. They both have *MSF* in their names. *MSF* used to stand for "Microsoft Solutions Framework." It is Microsoft's home-grown approach to planning and managing software projects based on the experiences and documentation of Microsoft Consulting Services (MCS). MSF version 1.0 was introduced in 1993 and was regularly updated through the 1990s and into the 2000s. The software development framework was simply guidance, books, presentations, and training materials. At one point, individuals could become certified MSF practitioners and trainers.

MSF saw a major refresh in 2005 when version 4.0 was released. This corresponded with the release of Team Foundation Server 2005 and the concept of the process template. Through the use of MSF process templates, Team Foundation Server was able to enact the MSF software development process.

Very few people refer to the MSF acronym when discussing the process templates. They refer to them as the "Agile" or "CMMI" templates. CMMI stands for Capability Maturity Model Integration, which is a software engineering process improvement approach created by Carnegie Mellon University. Even fewer people reference the full Microsoft Solutions Framework name. There is a desire inside and outside of Microsoft to drop the MSF acronym from the product alltogether. This may become reality down the road.

Exploring a process template

To explore a process template, you will first need to download it from Team Foundation Server. You can do this from Team Explorer inside Visual Studio. Once you have established a connection to a team project collection, regardless of whether you are connected to a team project, you can click the Settings hyperlink and open the Process Template Manager, as shown in Figure 3-2. From this dialog box, you can see all of the process templates uploaded to your team project collection. You can upload new templates, download existing ones, make a template the default template, or delete a process template. There is even a hyperlink that takes you to a site on MSDN where you can find and download new process templates.

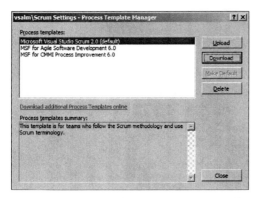

FIGURE 3-2 Viewing and managing process templates from the Process Template Manager.

Once downloaded, you can explore the template using traditional tools such as Windows Explorer, Microsoft Internet Explorer, and Notepad to open and examine the XML and other files. Any changes you make to the process template won't have an impact until you upload the process template back to Team Foundation Server. Any team projects already created using the process template won't be affected by those changes. As an alternative, you can use the Process Editor, installed by the Team Foundation Server Power Tools and found on the Tools menu inside Visual Studio.

The Process Editor

The Process Editor is part of the Team Foundation Server Power Tools. It is installed when you install the power tools and becomes available when you restart Visual Studio. The Process Editor provides a graphical user interface (GUI) for editing Team Foundation Server process templates, work item types, and global lists inside the Visual Studio integrated development environment (IDE), as you can see in Figure 3-3. The Process Editor maintains its own connection to the Team Foundation Server, separate from Team Explorer, and can also be used while disconnected. For example, you can download the process template as mentioned previously, and then use the Process Editor while disconnected from Team Foundation Server.

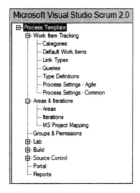

FIGURE 3-3 The Visual Studio Scrum 2.0 process template as viewed in the Process Editor.

You can also use the Process Editor to customize a process template, work item type, or global list. For example, you might want to reduce the number of default *Release* and *Sprint* iteration nodes created when you create a new team, as you can see in Figure 3-4. You would do this by editing the process template and removing the *Release* and *Sprint* nodes that you don't want. You would then save your changes and upload the template back to Team Foundation Server. You might want to rename the template and change its description to indicate the change you made.

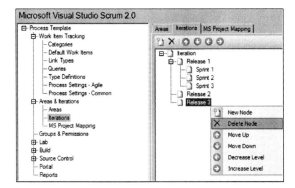

FIGURE 3-4 Using the Process Editor to remove the number of initial *Iteration* nodes.

 Tip If you plan on making any changes to the Scrum or other process templates down the road, consider creating a separate team project in Team Foundation Server, uploading the original template(s), and then managing all changes to the templates as you would any other coding project under source control. This way, you have a history of changes with explanations, allowing you to roll back if you want.

Visual Studio Scrum 2.0

After 100,000 downloads of Visual Studio Scrum 1.0, Microsoft has learned a thing or two about it and the community using it. Primarily, they have learned that teams like it! These teams appreciate its uncomplicated design and its straightforward support of Scrum. As you can see in Table 3-1, there are not a lot of extraneous fields, queries, or reports beyond what is needed to plan and track a project using Scrum. Many teams evaluating Visual Studio Scrum are currently using whiteboards and sticky notes to track their work. Since you can't get any lighter weight than that, any prospective software tool would need to be as lightweight as possible.

 Note My company has seen and helped many teams migrate off of EMC's Scrum for Team System process template. This is the template that was originally created by Conchango and, after EMC acquired Conchango, innovation and support for the template dropped off until it was eventually released to the open-source community. For these reasons, many corporate teams that we talk to want to move off of it and onto Microsoft's template—often simply for the perceived lack of support with an open-source project.

TABLE 3-1 Visual Studio Scrum work item types, queries, and reports.

Work item types	Queries	Reports
Bug	Product Backlog	Backlog Overview
Code Review Request	Feedback	Build Success Over Time
Code Review Response	Current Sprint\Blocked Tasks	Build Summary
Feedback Request	Current Sprint\Open Impediments	Release Burndown
Feedback Response	Current Sprint\Sprint Backlog	Sprint Burndown
Impediment	Current Sprint\Test Cases	Test Case Readiness
Product Backlog Item	Current Sprint\Unfinished Work	Test Plan Progress
Shared Step	Current Sprint\Work in Progress	Velocity
Task		
Test Case		

Microsoft started defining work item *categories* in Team Foundation Server 2010. This enabled different process templates to identify what their "Bug" work item type was, as well as their requirement, Test Case, and Shared Steps work item types. This mapping enabled Microsoft to create tools (like Microsoft Test Manager) that can work with any vendor's process template, so long as it supports the requirement work item categories. Team Foundation Server 2012 adds more categories to support their new code review, feedback, and task-board tools. Table 3-2 shows the work item types and their corresponding categories in the Visual Studio Scrum process template.

TABLE 3-2 Visual Studio Scrum work item types mapped to categories.

Work item type	Associated categories	Hidden category?
Bug	Bug, Requirement	
Code Review Request	Code Review Request	✓
Code Review Response	Code Review Response	✓
Feedback Request	Feedback Request	✓
Feedback Response	Feedback Response	✓
Impediment		
Product Backlog Item	Requirement	
Shared Steps	Shared Step	✓
Task	Task	
Test Case	Test Case	

What's new and different

There really hasn't been much improvement to the core functionality of the Scrum process template itself. The majority of the changes are to support the many new features and capabilities in Team Foundation Server 2012, such as the Agile planning tools. There were some architectural changes in Team Foundation Server as well, such as adding the ability to track start and end dates on the iteration path nodes directly. Some changes to the process template were made to support these as well. The next few pages will list what's been added, changed, and removed between the 1.0 and 2.0 versions of the Scrum process template.

If you are an alpha geek like me, you might want to see all of the differences between the 1.0 and 2.0 process templates, even the small ones. First, you'll need to download the 1.0 and 2.0 templates onto your hard drive into separate folders (that is, C:\VSScrum1 and C:\VSScrum2). Next, run the Tf.exe command-line utility, passing in the two folders as parameters, to show the folder differences. Here's the command: *Tf.exe folderdiff C:\VSScrum1 C:\VSScrum2*. You will then see a side-by-side comparison of the two templates, as shown in Figure 3-5.

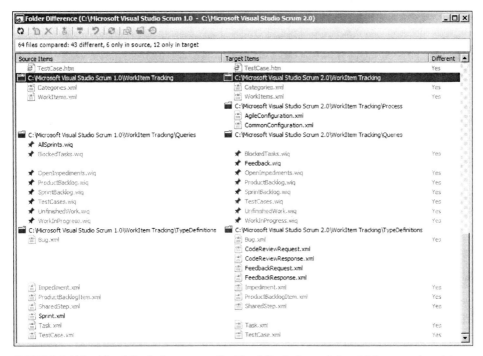

FIGURE 3-5 Using Visual Studio to compare the Visual Studio Scrum 1.0 and 2.0 process templates.

What's new

Here are the artifacts and features that have been added to the Visual Studio Scrum 2.0 process template:

- **Added new Code Review Request and Code Review Response work item types**   These new work item types work together to enable Development Team members to review and comment on each other's code from within Visual Studio.

- **Added new Feedback Request and Feedback Response work item types**   These new work item types enable team members to request and receive feedback on their Increment from stakeholders using the new feedback client.

- **Added new work item categories** Microsoft has added five new work item categories: Code Review Request, Code Review Response, Feedback Request, Feedback Response, and Task. They have also introduced a hidden types category, to hide certain work items from the general-use user interfaces.

- **Added *closed date* field to Product Backlog Item, Bug, and Task work item types** This is a read-only field that is controlled by Team Foundation Server. Setting a work item's state to New, Approved, or Committed will clear the closed date. Setting the state to Done will assign the current date and time.

- **Can now link Product Backlog items to storyboards** You can now associate a Product Backlog item to one or more storyboards. These storyboards can be created using Microsoft PowerPoint and saved to a shared location.

- **New Product Backlog Item and Bug state transitions** You can now transition from New directly to Committed or Done.

- **New Bug state transition reasons** You can now choose between New Defect Reported or Build Failure when creating a bug. You can now select Not a Bug or Duplicate as a reason when removing a bug.

- **New state transition actions for Tasks** There are now StartWork, StopWork, and CheckIn actions that can be called to set a task to a specific state. The StartWork action sets the task to In Progress. The StopWork action sets the task back to the To Do state. A CheckIn action can be called to set a task to the Done state from either To Do or In Progress states. These actions enable tools, such as the task board, to be able to programmatically set a task's state.

- **Added new Feedback query** This query enables a team member to see if anyone else has asked him or her to provide feedback.

- **New Backlog Overview report** Some teams that had previously used the MSF for Agile Software Development process template discovered that they missed the User Stories Overview report. Microsoft ported the report over to work on the Visual Studio Scrum 2.0 template and named it the Backlog Overview report.

- **Added process template version to ProcessTemplate.xml** A type identifier as well as a major and minor version identify the version of the process template.

- **Added process template property to Classification.xml** The process template name gets uploaded to Team Foundation Server and is persisted to the collection (operational) database during team project creation.

- **More fields are reported in the data warehouse** *Work item title, area path, iteration path, state,* and *reason* fields are reported as *dimension*. The *backlog priority* field is reported as *detail* for Product Backlog Item, Bug, and Task work item types. This means that you will be able to more easily query, filter, and pivot on these values when analyzing and reporting.

- **Added the *HideReadOnlyEmptyFields* attribute to a work item type definition's *Layout* element** This attribute establishes the behavior of whether an empty read-only field is visible on the form, such as the *Remaining Work* field when a Task is in the Done state. The default value is *true*, which means that these fields are hidden.

What's changed

Here are the artifacts and features that have been changed in the Visual Studio Scrum 2.0 process template:

- **Changed queries to evaluate work item type categories** In Visual Studio Scrum 1.0, queries would evaluate the work item types directly. For example, the Product Backlog query would only include Product Backlog Item and Bug work item types. In Visual Studio Scrum 2.0, the same query evaluates the work item type category to see if it's a Microsoft.RequirementCategory. This is a better approach offering more flexibility.

- **Changed Product Backlog query to include all Sprints** The Product Backlog query in Visual Studio Scrum 1.0 only returned Product Backlog items and bugs that hadn't yet been placed into a Sprint. In other words, it only returned items that were set to the root iteration path. The 2.0 template now users the *under* keyword, so it'll include more work items than previously. If this sounds like a potential for a lot of noise, just remember that the query excludes Done and Removed work items.

- **Renamed *Description HTML* field to *Description*** This is a fairly invisible change that applies to Product Backlog Items, Tasks, Impediments, Test Cases, and Shared Steps. It may affect custom queries, reports, or solutions you have built using the old field. In addition, the refname has changed from *Microsoft.VSTS.Common.DescriptionHtml* to just *System.Description*. The field type is still HTML.

- ***Backlog priority* field is hidden** By default, you cannot see or change a Product Backlog Item or Bug's *backlog priority* value. This value is automatically set by using the drag-and-drop capabilities of the web-based backlog tool. Also, this value no longer defaults to 1,000. A Task's *backlog priority* field hasn't changed.

- **Link types are limited when associating a task to a bug** When linking a bug to a task, the types of link options are limited to child work item links only. Previously, you could link to changesets, hyperlinks, and so on, which was confusing.

- **Renamed *Builders* group to *Build Administrators*** For the last several versions, the Team Foundation Server group within a team project who was responsible for creating and managing build definitions has been the Builders group. This has been renamed to Build Administrators.

- **Default permissions and settings for the default team** A default team gets created automatically when a new team project is created. Its name is the project name followed by "Team" (that is, the Tailspin Team). Settings in the GroupsAndPermissions.xml file define the initial security permissions, members, and area and iteration backlog scope for this team. The default team is a member of the Contributors group by default.

- **Default build template renamed**   DefaultTemplate.xaml is now DefaultTemplate.11.1.xaml, which includes a major and minor version in the file name. The major version is that of Team Foundation Server. Microsoft may release new build templates, incrementing the minor version, to take advantage of new features down the road.

- **Default Lab template renamed**   LabDefaultTemplate.xaml is now LabDefaultTemplate.11 .xaml, which includes a major version in the file name. The major version is that of Team Foundation Server.

- **Test Management files**   The Testconfiguration.xml and Testvariables.xml files have been updated to include entries for Microsoft Windows 8.

- **You can mark a task resolved (done) when checking in**   Previously, you could only associate your changes with a task when checking in. Now a developer can mark the task resolved (*Done*) while checking in, saving an extra step. You will still need to edit the task work item and set the *Remaining Hours* to zero.

- **Done and removed tasks can now be reactivated**   Previously, you could not transition a task from Done to To Do or from Removed to To Do. These transitions are allowed now, even using the default reasons of "Additional Work Found" and "Reconsidering the Task," respectively.

- **Changed reports that depended on the Sprint work item**   Since the Sprint work item was removed, some reports had to be updated to retrieve the start and end dates from the release and *Sprint* iteration path nodes directly. Also, there were other, minor changes made to the look and feel of reports, such as changing titles, default text, and the width of some fields.

- **Microsoft Project FileMapping.xml renamed to FieldMapping.xml**   The purpose of the file remains the same—only the name has changed.

What's removed

Here are the artifacts and features that have been removed from the Visual Studio Scrum 2.0 process template:

- **Removed the Sprint work item type**   Microsoft dropped the Sprint work item type because iterations now have start and end date fields. While this is a welcome improvement, it brings up the question of where to store the Sprint Goal and Retrospective notes. A document or wiki entry on the SharePoint project portal would work. The All Sprints work item query and corresponding work item guidance on the portal are also gone.

- **Default check-in notes have been removed**   In Visual Studio Scrum 1.0, there were three check-in notes defined in the template: code reviewer, security reviewer, and performance reviewer. These have been removed.

- **Removed the "As a <type of user> …" text from a Product Backlog Item description**   Since not everyone uses the user story description format, Microsoft removed this to make the Product Backlog Item work item type even more generic.

- **Releases 2, 3, and 4 don't have Sprint nodes**   Microsoft simplified the initial set of iteration nodes when a team project is created. Four release nodes are still created, but only the first one contains lower-level Sprints.

- ***Stack rank* field removed from Shared Steps work item type**   This field was never used.

Work item types

Work items are the core elements of planning and tracking within Team Foundation Server. They identify and describe requirements, tasks, bugs, and other concepts in the application development lifecycle. Work items track what a team and team members have to do, as well as what they have done. Work items, and the metrics derived from them, can be visible within various queries, reports, and dashboards. A team project's number and type of work items are defined by the process template that was used to create it.

As previously mentioned, the Visual Studio Scrum 2.0 process template defines 10 work item types. In this section, we will go through the details of each one and discuss how, when, and why to use it.

Product Backlog Item

In Scrum, the Product Backlog is an ordered (prioritized) list of the outstanding work necessary to realize the vision of the product. This list can contain new things that don't exist yet (features), as well as broken things that the Product Owner would like fixed (bugs). In Team Foundation Server, the Product Backlog Item (PBI) work item type enables the Scrum Team to capture all of these various requirements with as little documentation as possible. In fact, only the *title* field is required. Later, as more detail emerges, the PBI can be updated to include business value, acceptance criteria, and the Development Team's latest estimation of effort. Figure 3-6 shows you an example of a PBI work item.

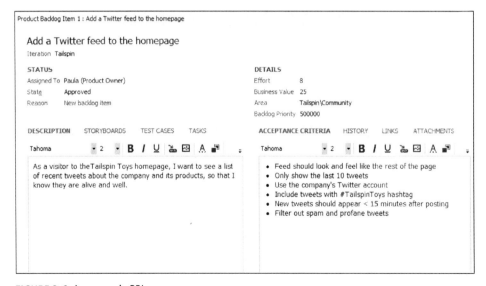

FIGURE 3-6 An example PBI.

As you create or edit PBI work items, consider the following notes and guidance when entering data into the fields:

- **Title (required)**   Enter a short description that identifies the PBI.

- **Iteration**   Select the Sprint in which your team forecasts that it will develop the PBI. If you have yet to forecast the work, leave it set to the default (root) value.

- **Assigned To**   Select the Product Owner.

- **State**   Select the state of the PBI. States are covered in the paragraph after this list.

- **Reason**   Select the reason that the PBI is in this state. This field may be read-only for some states.

- **Effort**   Enter a number that indicates a relative rating for the amount of work that will be required to develop this PBI. Larger numbers indicate more effort than smaller numbers. Story points work well here. T-shirt sizes don't, because this is a numeric field.

- **Business Value**   Enter a number that indicates a fixed or relative business value of the PBI. Business value can represent revenue to be realized from this feature or bug fix. Some Product Owners will establish a subjective range of integers (that is, 1–5) to indicate a specific type of business value (for example, strategic alignment, reduction in costs, competitive advantage, generates revenue, generates awareness, technical value, and learning value). The larger the integer, the more business value.

- **Area**   Select the best area path for this PBI. Areas must be set up ahead of time and can represent functional, logical, or physical areas or features of a software product. If the PBI applies to all areas your team covers or you aren't sure of the specific subarea, then leave it set to its default value. Remember that each team within a team project can have its own corresponding areas as well as a default area. This comes into play when creating a PBI.

- **Backlog Priority**   Enter a number that indicates the relative priority of this item. A larger number indicates a lower priority.

- **Description**   Provide as much detail as necessary so that another team member can understand the purpose of the PBI. The *user story* format (As a *<type of user>* I want *<some goal>* so that *<some reason>*) works well here to ensure that a business value proposition (the "why") is captured. You should avoid using this field as a repository for detailed requirements or designs, especially prior to the Sprint that you forecasted developing the Product Backlog item.

> **Note** Microsoft removed the "As a *<type of user>* ... " default text from the Description field. Since not everyone uses the user story description format, Microsoft removed this to make the PBI work item type even more generic.

- **Storyboards** Add a link to one or more storyboards created using PowerPoint, Microsoft Visio, or a third-party tool like Balsamiq. You can enter a Universal Naming Convention (UNC) path or a URL to the storyboard/mockup document. You cannot create a storyboard from this screen. Also, avoid creating storyboards too early. Ideally, you would create them only during the Sprint that you forecasted developing the PBI.

- **Test Cases** Add a link to one or more test case work items. You can link to an existing test case or create a new one on the fly as shown in Figure 3-7. Before you can create a link to a new task, you must have saved your PBI first. The link type from the PBI to the test case will be *tested by*. The reverse will be a *tests* link type. Avoid creating test cases too early. Ideally, you would create them only during the Sprint that you forecasted developing the PBI.

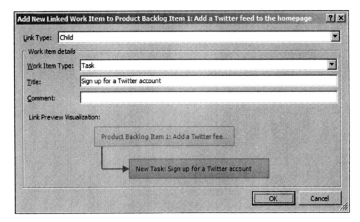

FIGURE 3-7 Creating and linking a child task to a PBI.

- **Tasks** Add a link to one or more task work items. You can link to an existing task or create a new one on the fly—so long as you have saved your PBI first. The link type from the PBI to the task will be *child*. The reverse will be a *parent* link type. Avoid creating tasks too early. Ideally, you would create them only during the Sprint that you forecasted developing the PBI.

- **Acceptance Criteria** Describe the conditions that will be used to verify whether the team has developed the PBI according to the Product Owner's vision. Acceptance criteria should be clear, concise, and testable. You should avoid using this field as a repository for detailed requirements. Bulleted items work well.

- **History** Every time a team member updates the work item, Team Foundation Server tracks the team member who made the change and the fields that were changed. This tab displays a history of all those changes. The contents are read-only, except you can add a comment to add to the historical record. When viewing history, you can switch between *Discussion Only* (shows only team member comments) or *All Changes* (shows all changes made).

- **Links** Add a link to one or more work items or resources (changeset, hyperlink, model link, result attachment, storyboard, test result, or an item in source control). Remember that storyboards, test cases, and tasks are better linked on their respective tabs. This tab can be used to link PBI to other PBI (that is, to represent an epic PBI decomposed into several child PBIs). You may also want to link a Product Backlog item to a Unified Modeling Language (UML) diagram or to an Impediment work item.

- **Attachments** Attach one or more files that provide more details about the PBI. Some teams like to attach notes, whiteboard photos, or even audio/video recordings of the Product Backlog grooming sessions and Sprint Planning meetings here.

A Product Backlog Item work item can be in one of five states: New, Approved, Committed, Done, or Removed. The typical workflow progression would be New > Approved > Committed > Done. When a PBI is created it is in the New state with the default reason, "New backlog item." When the Product Owner decides that the Product Backlog item is valid, its state should be changed from New to Approved with the reason, "Approved by the Product Owner." When the Development Team forecasts to deliver the Product Backlog item in the current Sprint, its state should be changed to Committed with the reason, "Commitment made by the team." Finally, when the PBI is done according to the Development Team's definition, the state should be changed to Done with the reason, "Work finished." The Removed state is used for situations where the Product Owner determines that the PBI is invalid for whatever reason, such as it's already in the Product Backlog, has already been developed, or is an utterly ridiculous idea.

Note Down the road, Microsoft may change the Committed state to Planned. This will better align the Visual Studio Scrum template with the *Scrum Guide*.

Bug

A bug communicates that a problem or potential problem exists. A bug can be found in production, in an Increment done in a previous Sprint, or in the Increment being developed in the current Sprint. By defining and managing Bug work items, the Scrum Team can track these bugs, as well as prioritize and plan the efforts to fix them. A bug could be as small as a typo in a data entry form or as large as credit card data being exposed to the public. Figure 3-8 shows you an example of a Bug work item.

In Scrum, a bug is just a type of PBI; but, the Visual Studio Scrum template defines a separate work item type to track bugs. The reason behind this is that a Bug work item type tracks additional, defect-specific information, such as severity, steps to reproduce, and system information. Otherwise, the Bug and Product Backlog Item work item types are nearly identical. Bug work items don't have a business value field or a tab to explicitly link storyboards. The Product Backlog query includes both PBIs and bugs.

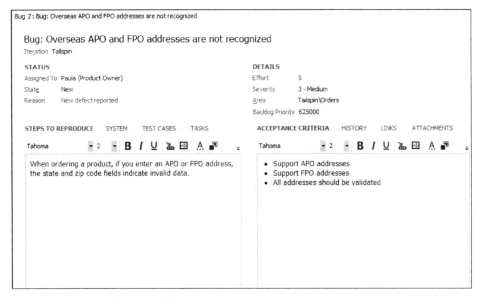

FIGURE 3-8 An example Bug work item.

When you create a Bug work item, you want to accurately report the problem in a way that helps the reader to understand the full impact of the problem. The steps to reproduce the bug should also be listed so that other team members can reproduce the behavior. There may be additional analysis (triage) required to confirm that it is an actual bug rather than a behavior that was by design. By defining and managing Bug work items, your team can track defects in the product in order to estimate and prioritize their resolution. As a general rule, bugs should be removed, not managed.

As you create or edit Bug work items, consider the following notes and guidance when entering data into the fields:

- ***Title* (required)**   Enter a short description that identifies the bug that was found.

- ***Iteration***   Select the Sprint in which your team forecasts that it will fix the bug. If you have yet to forecast the work, leave it set to the default (root) value.

- ***Assigned To***   Select the Product Owner.

- ***State***   Select the state of the bug. States are covered in the paragraph after this list.

- ***Reason***   Select the reason that the bug is in this state. This field may be read-only for some states.

- ***Effort***   Enter a number that indicates a relative rating for the amount of work that will be required to fix this bug. Larger numbers indicate more effort than smaller numbers. Story points work well here. T-shirt sizes don't, because this is a numeric field.

- **Severity**   Select the value that indicates the impact that the bug has on the product. The range is from 1 (critical) to 4 (low). Lower values indicate a higher severity. The default value of this field is 3 (medium).

- **Area**   Select the best area path for this bug. Areas must be set up ahead of time and can represent functional, logical, or physical areas or features of a software product. If the bug affects all areas that your team covers or you aren't sure of the specific subarea, then leave it set to its default value. Remember that each team within a team project can have its own corresponding areas as well as a default area. This comes into play when creating a bug.

- **Backlog Priority**   Enter a number that indicates the relative priority of this bug. A larger number indicates a lower priority.

- **Steps to Reproduce**   Provide as much detail as necessary so that another team member can reproduce the bug and better understand the problem that must be fixed. If you use Test Manager to create a Bug work item, this information is provided automatically from your test case or exploratory test session.

- **Found in Build (System tab)**   Select or type the name of the build in which the defect was found.

- **Integrated in Build (System tab)**   Select or type the name of the build that incorporates the bug fix.

- **System info (System tab)**   Describe the software environment in which the bug was found. If you use Test Manager to create a Bug work item, this information is provided automatically from your test case or exploratory test session.

- **Test Cases**   Add a link to one or more Test Case work items. You can link to an existing test case or create a new one on the fly—so long as you have saved your bug first. The link type from the bug to the test case will be *tested by*. The reverse will be a *tests* link type. Avoid creating test cases too early, unless the bug was created as the result of an existing test case. Ideally, you would only create a test case during the Sprint that you forecasted fixing the bug.

- **Tasks**   Add a link to one or more Task work items. You can link to an existing task or create a new one on the fly—so long as you have saved your bug first. The link type from the bug to the task will be *child*. The reverse will be a *parent* link type. Avoid creating tasks too early. Ideally, you would create them only during the Sprint that you forecasted fixing the bug.

- **Acceptance Criteria**   Describe the conditions that will be used to verify whether the team has fixed the bug according to the Product Owner's vision. Acceptance criteria should be clear, concise, and testable. Consider using this field to document the expected results, as opposed to the actual results.

- **History**   Every time a team member updates the work item, Team Foundation Server tracks the team member who made the change and the fields that were changed. This tab displays a history of all those changes. The contents are read-only, except you can add a comment to add to the historical record. When viewing history, you can switch between *Discussion Only* (shows only team member comments) or *All Changes* (shows all changes made).

- **Links** Add a link to one or more work items or resources (changeset, hyperlink, model link, result attachment, storyboard, test result, or an item in source control). Remember that test cases and tasks are better linked on their respective tabs. This tab can be used to link to this bug to a related bug, link to an article on MSDN or TechNet explaining the root cause, link to the original PBI that failed, or even link to a parent PBI that serves to gather several bugs into one collective "fix" user story. You may also need to link a bug to an Impediment work item.

- **Attachments** Attach one or more files that provide more details about the bug. This could include screenshots, action recordings, and video. If you use Test Manager to create a Bug work item, then this type of information is provided automatically.

A Bug work item can be in one of five states: New, Approved, Committed, Done, or Removed. These are the same states as a PBI. The typical workflow progression would be New > Approved > Committed > Done. When a bug is reported and determined to be genuine (for example, it's not a feature, duplicate, or training issue), a new Bug work item is created in the New state with the default reason, "New defect reported." The reason could also be due to a *Build failure* if it was created automatically from a failed build. When the Product Owner decides that the bug is valid, its state should be changed from New to Approved with the reason, "Approved by the Product Owner." When the Development Team forecasts to deliver the bug fix in the current Sprint, its state should be changed to Committed with the reason, "Commitment made by the team." Finally, when the bug is done according to the Development Team's definition, the state should be changed to Done with the reason, "Work finished." The Removed state is used for situations where the Product Owner determines that the bug is invalid for whatever reason, such as it's already in the Product Backlog, it's actually a feature, it's a training issue, or it had already been fixed in a previous Sprint but not yet released.

Task

A Task work item represents a piece of detailed work that a Development Team member must accomplish when developing a PBI or fixing a bug. Another way to think of it is that all of the tasks form the Development Team's *plan* for achieving their Sprint goal. These tasks, along with their associated Product Backlog items and bugs, form the Sprint Backlog. A task can be design, development, testing, documentation, requirements, or deployment in nature. For example, the team can identify and create Task work items that are development-focused, such as implementing an interface or creating a database table. They can also create testing-focused tasks, such as creating and running test cases. Figure 3-9 shows you an example of a Task work item.

Note Tasks are typically created during Sprint Planning. These tasks are decomposed and additional tasks are added throughout the Sprint as work emerges.

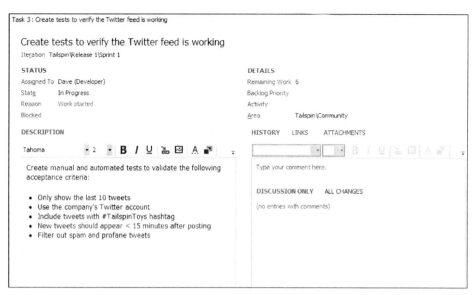

FIGURE 3-9 An example Task work item.

As you create or edit Task work items, consider the following notes and guidance when entering data into the fields:

- **Title (required)**   Enter a short description that provides a concise overview of the area of work in the task. The title should be descriptive enough to allow the team to understand what area of the product is affected and how it is affected.

- **Iteration**   Select the Sprint in which your team will be working on this task. The Sprint should be the same as the associated PBI or bug.

- **Assigned To**   Select the developer who is responsible for ensuring that this task is completed. Leave it blank until someone starts working on it. A task can be assigned to only one developer. If two developers pair up on a task, one of them must become the *owner*. If multiple developers work on a task individually, consider decomposing it into subtasks and ensure that a developer owns each one.

- **State**   Select the state of the task. States are covered in the paragraph after this list.

- **Reason**   Select the reason that the task is in this state. This field may be read-only for some states.

- **Blocked**   Select *Yes* if this task is blocked from being accomplished. The source of the blockage should be identified, either as a note in history or by adding an *Affected By* link to the related Impediment work item. A blocked task shows up on the Blocked Tasks query (assuming that its state is not set to Removed).

- **Remaining Work**   Enter the number of hours that you estimate it will take to complete this task. Ideally, this should be 8 hours or less. If a task is going to take longer than 8 hours, you should consider decomposing it into subtasks. Be sure to update this field as you work on and complete your tasks. In fact, you should update your remaining work estimates daily for all of your tasks. The burndown charts and reports depend on this field.

- **Backlog Priority**   Enter a number that indicates the priority of this task relative to other tasks. Smaller numbers indicate higher priority than larger numbers. The backlog priority reflects the execution order and any technical dependencies.

> **Smell** It's a smell when I see that a team is using the *Backlog Priority* field on tasks. It could be nothing more than a very tricky set of tasks to navigate a complex set of dependencies. My fear, however, is that the priority field is being used instead of collaboration with the other developers. Maybe it's just used to document such collaboration, which is great. A greater fear is that a "lead" developer is setting the priority values as a way to command and control the team. High-performance Development Teams may not need this field, as they continuously synchronize and collaborate with each other.

- **Activity**   Select the type of activity that the task represents. The choices are Deployment, Design, Development, Documentation, Requirements, and Testing. This field allows for queries and capacity planning tools to filter by activity.

> **Smell** It's a smell when I see that a team is usnig the *Activity* field on tasks. Scrum developers know that everything they do is considered a *development* activity, so using this field seems like a waste. My fear is that team members will become conditioned to looking for their favorite type of task. For example, someone with a background in testing may just naturally look for unassigned testing tasks, and that's not necessarily what is best for the team's productivity. A greater fear is that others, not necessarily on the Development Team, will begin using the activity type for resource planning or assigning work!

- **Area**   Select the best area path for this task. Typically, the area will be the same as the associated PBI or bug.

- **Description**   Provide as much detail as necessary so that another team member can understand the nature of work to be performed in this task. This field can also be used to document task-level acceptance criteria. Some teams like to track this for particularly complex tasks.

- **History**   Every time a team member updates the work item, Team Foundation Server tracks the team member who made the change and the fields that were changed. This tab displays a history of all those changes. The contents are read-only, except you can add a comment to add to the historical record. When viewing history, you can switch between *Discussion Only* (shows only team member comments) or *All Changes* (shows all changes made).

- **Links** Add a link to one or more work items or resources (changeset, hyperlink, model link, result attachment, storyboard, test result, or an item in source control). You may want to link larger tasks to smaller, child tasks as you decompose your work. You might also want to link a blocked task to the impediment that describes the blockage using an *Affected By* link type.

- **Attachments** Attach one or more files that provide more details about the task.

A Task work item can be in one of four states: To Do, In Progress, Done, or Removed. The typical workflow progression would be To Do > In Progress > Done. When a task is created, it is in the To Do state with the default reason, "New task." When a developer begins working on a task, the state should be set to In Progress with the reason, "Work started." When the task is finished, the state should be set to Done with the reason, "Work finished." The Removed state is used for situations where the Development Team determines that the task is invalid for whatever reason, such as it doesn't apply anymore or it was a duplicate.

Test Case

The Development Team uses Test Case work items to define manual and automated tests. Test cases allow a team to further define the acceptance criteria of a PBI or bug in the form of executable and verifiable acceptance test steps. Test cases may be defined at a high level initially and will emerge throughout the Sprint as the test steps are added, test runs are executed, and recordings are associated.

Test Case work items can be created within Team Explorer, Team Web Access, and other client applications. Test Manager, however, is considered a better tool to use because it gives full access to the test steps and allows you to create and associate Shared Step work items. Figure 3-10 shows you an example of a Test Case work item.

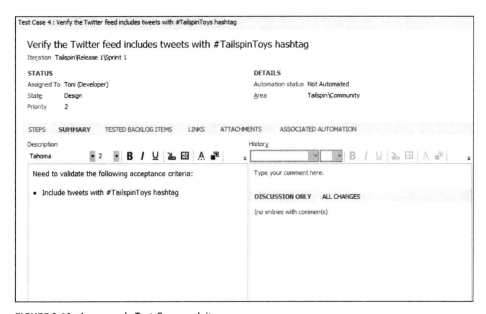

FIGURE 3-10 An example Test Case work item.

As you create or edit Test Case work items, consider the following notes and guidance when entering data into the fields:

- **Title (required)**   Enter a short phrase that describes the criteria to test. A naming convention that you could consider using is *Verify [{criteria/qualification} for] PBI ID and Title*. The *{qualification}* is optional but can be used to distinguish multiple test cases on the same PBI. For example, "Verify the Twitter feed includes #TailspinToys hashtag for 1: Add a Twitter feed to the homepage." Another example might be, "Verify Permissions for 42: User Obtains Ownership."

- **Iteration**   Select the Sprint in which the test case will be defined and run. The Sprint should be the same as the associated PBI or bug.

- **Assigned To**   Select the developer who is responsible for defining the test and ensuring that it is run. Leave it blank until someone starts working on it.

- **State**   Select the state of the test case. States are covered in the paragraph after this list.

- **Priority**   Select the level of importance for the test case on a scale of 1 (most important) to 4 (least important). The default value is 2.

- **Automation Status**   Leave the default value (*Not Automated*) if this test case is a manual test, or select *Planned* if you plan to automate this test case in the future. Later, when you add an automated test to your test case, this field gets set to *Automated*.

- **Area**   Select the best area path for this test case. Typically, the area will be the same as the associated PBI or bug.

- **Steps**   Use Test Manager to define the individual test step actions and expected results. You can add test steps by copying and pasting from Microsoft Excel, Word, or from a plain text file that has a tab-delimited list of actions and expected results. Each step can include an attached file that provides more details, such as a screenshot. You can also use a Shared Steps work item to simplify the creation and management of test cases.

- **Description (Summary tab)**   Provide as much detail as necessary so that another team member can understand the purpose of the test case.

- **History (Summary tab)**   Every time a team member updates the work item, Team Foundation Server tracks the team member who made the change and the fields that were changed. This tab displays a history of all those changes. The contents are read-only, except you can add a comment to add to the historical record. When viewing history, you can switch between *Discussion Only* (shows only team member comments) or *All Changes* (shows all changes made).

- **Tested Backlog Items**   Add a link to one or more PBIs or bugs that this test case tests. You can link to an existing work item or create a new one on the fly, as shown in Figure 3-11. Before you can create a link to a new work item, you must save your test case first. The link type from the test case to the PBI or bug will be *tests*. The reverse will be a *tested by* link type. If you use Test Manager to create a test case from a requirements-based test suite, the new test case will automatically be linked to the requirement.

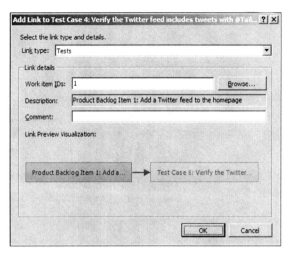

FIGURE 3-11 Linking a test case to an existing Product Backlog item PBI.

- **Links**   Add a link to one or more work items or resources (changeset, hyperlink, result attachment, storyboard, test result, or an item in source control). Remember that Product Backlog Item and Bug work items are better linked on the Tested Backlog Items tab. For example, you may want to link the test case to a bug *discovered* while running the test.

- **Attachments**   Attach one or more files that provide more information about the test case.

- **Associated Automation**   Add an automated test that you wish to associate with this test case. To find the automated test name, click the ellipsis (...) button. All the tests in the currently loaded test project or solution are shown in the list. If a test case already has an automated test associated with it, you must remove this association before you can add a different test. You must be running Visual Studio (not Test Manager) to associate an automated test. Also, when a test case is automated, you can't edit the steps. This is because the automated test method will run instead.

A Test Case work item can be in one of three states: Design, Ready, or Closed. The typical workflow progression would be Design > Ready > Closed. When a Test Case work item is created, it is in the Design state with a default reason, "New." After the test case details have emerged, steps have been added, and the test case is ready to be run, its state should be changed to Ready with the reason of "Completed." When a test case is no longer required, its state should be changed to Closed with an applicable reason, such as testing has been deferred, the test case is duplicated, or the test case is obsolete.

Impediment

The Impediment work item is a report of any situation that blocks the team or a team member from completing work efficiently. By defining and managing Impediment work items, a Scrum Team can identify and track problems that are blocking it. Impediments are typically identified during the Daily Scrum and recorded by the Developer who raised it or Scrum Master, but they can actually be inspected and recorded at any time, by anyone. The Scrum Master is responsible for facilitating the resolution of impediments, as well as improving team productivity. As a general rule, impediments should be removed, not managed. Figure 3-12 shows you an example of an Impediment work item.

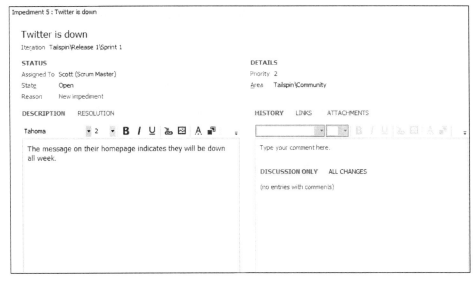

FIGURE 3-12 An example Impediment work item.

As you create or edit Impediment work items, consider the following notes and guidance when entering data into the fields:

- **Title (required)**   Enter a short phrase that accurately and succinctly describes the issue.

- **Iteration**   Select the Sprint in which this impediment occurred.

- **Assigned To**   Select the user who will be responsible for resolving the impediment. If not you, then typically this is the Scrum Master.

- **State**   Select the state of the impediment. States are covered in the paragraph after this list.

- **Reason**   Select the reason that the impediment is in this state. This field may be read-only for some states.

- **Priority**   Select the level of importance for the impediment on a scale of 1 (most important) to 4 (least important). The default value is 2.

- **Area**   Select the best area path for this impediment. Typically, the area will be the same as the associated Product Backlog item or bug. If the impediment applies to all areas your team covers or you aren't sure of the specific subarea, then leave it set to its default value.

- **Description**   Provide as much detail as necessary so that another user can understand the impediment and its impact.

- **Resolution**   Provide as much detail as necessary to describe how the impediment was resolved.

- **History**   Every time a team member updates the work item, Team Foundation Server tracks the team member who made the change and the fields that were changed. This tab displays a history of all those changes. The contents are read-only, except you can add a comment to add to the historical record. When viewing history, you can switch between *Discussion Only* (shows only team member comments) or *All Changes* (shows all changes made).

- **Links**   Add a link to one or more work items or resources (changeset, hyperlink, model link, result attachment, storyboard, test result, or an item in source control). For example, you may want to link this impediment to one or more blocked tasks .

- **Attachments**   Attach one or more files that provide more details about the impediment.

An Impediment work item can be either Open or Closed. When an impediment is created, it is in the Open state with the reason, "New impediment." When the impediment is removed, the state should be set to Closed with the reason, "Impediment removed."

Hidden work item types

Team Foundation Server 2012 introduces the concept of a *hidden* work item type. Work item types that are in this category are not able to be created from the standard user interfaces, such as the New Work Item drop-down list in Team Explorer or in Team Web Access. The reasoning behind this is that there are specialized tools in Visual Studio for creating and managing these types of work items. The hidden work item types are:

- Code Review Request

- Code Review Response

- Feedback Request

- Feedback Response

- Shared Steps

Code Review work item types are created and managed using dedicated pages (hubs) in Team Explorer. Feedback work item types are created and managed using the Feedback client. Shared Steps are created and managed using Test Manager. Microsoft knew that we wouldn't be creating these work item types outside the context of these specialized tools, so they did us a favor and hid them from the various menus where we create work items. You can see this behavior in Figure 3-13.

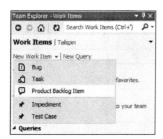

FIGURE 3-13 The Microsoft tools know not to show hidden work item types.

Note These hidden work item types will be discussed in the context of those tools in later Chapter 7, "Acceptance Test Driven Development", and Chapter 8, "Effective Collaboration".

Work item queries

Work item queries allow you to view, understand, and manage your workload. By running the appropriate query, you can identify the Product Backlog Items, Bugs, Tasks, Impediments, and other work items that pertain to you or your team. You can then decide on which of these work items to take action. For example, the Product Owner can view and manage the PBIs and bugs in the Product Backlog by running the Product Backlog query, and the Development Team can inspect the plan for achieving the Sprint Goal by running the Sprint Backlog query.

You can run queries from within Visual Studio or Test Manager, which is convenient when you are working on development tasks. Queries can also be run from Team Web Access, the project portal (SharePoint), Excel, Project, and various other Microsoft and third-party applications.

Team projects based on the Visual Studio Scrum process template contain several default queries. These are available as *shared* queries, meaning that the whole team can access them. You can see these shared queries listed in Team Explorer in Figure 3-14 and explained in Table 3-3. You can also create additional queries, making them shared or private.

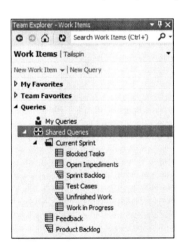

FIGURE 3-14 The default shared queries in a Visual Studio Scrum team project.

You can organize your queries by using folders and subfolders. For shared queries, you can set permissions on those folders and queries to enable or restrict access. You can set permissions for individual users, Windows groups, or Team Foundation Server groups. Only those users with appropriate permissions can view, edit, delete, copy, or manage the query folders and team queries. By default, there is only one folder under Team Queries. It is the Current Sprint folder.

TABLE 3-3 Default shared queries in a Visual Studio Scrum.

Query	Purpose
Product Backlog	Lists PBIs and bugs that are not Done or Removed for any iteration path (not just the root). Work items are sorted by priority and effort.
Feedback	Lists active feedback responses.
Current Sprint\Blocked Tasks	Lists tasks in the current Sprint that are blocked and not in the Removed state.
Current Sprint\Open Impediments	Lists impediments in the current Sprint that are in the Open state.
Current Sprint\Sprint Backlog	Lists PBIs, bugs, and their linked tasks that your team has forecasted for the current Sprint. Tasks in the Removed state are not included.
Current Sprint\Test Cases	Lists test cases for the current Sprint.
Current Sprint\Unfinished Work	Lists PBIs, bugs, and their linked tasks that your team has forecasted for the current Sprint. Tasks in the Removed and Done state are not included. This query is very similar to the Sprint Backlog query, except that it omits tasks that are done.
Current Sprint\Work in Progress	Lists tasks for the current Sprint that are in the In Progress state.

Unfortunately, Current Sprint is just a folder name. The queries inside don't contain any magical automation to know what the current Sprint is. As a result, someone on the team will need to *manually* update each of the queries at the start of each Sprint, changing the Iteration Path value to the next Sprint, as I'm doing in Figure 3-15. If you have created any other custom queries that run for the current Sprint, they will need to be updated as well.

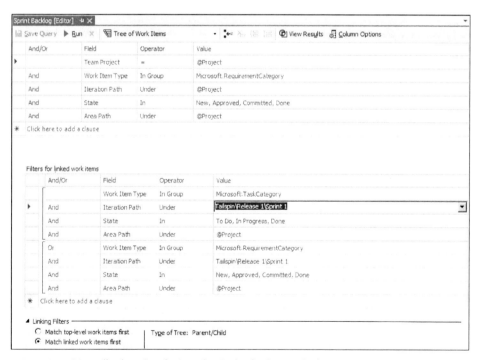

FIGURE 3-15 Manually changing the Iteration Path of a Current Sprint query.

Microsoft knows that this is a pain. They have a feature on their own backlog for something they call "team-based macros." These macros would be similar in functionality to the @*Today* and @*Me* macros available in the Work Item Query Language (WIQL). They are considering a @*Team.CurrentIteration*, which would get substituted during query execution.

> **Tip** Fellow Scrum Developer Mark Michaelis has come up with a good trick to reduce the amount of effort required to fix these queries. Essentially, you would create a fictitious Iteration Path at the release level named "Current." You would then edit each of the current Sprint queries, changing their Iteration Path criteria to be *Under* that *Current* node you just created. This would be the last time you had to edit these queries. At the start of each new Sprint, you would return to the Iterations control panel page and drag the new Sprint up under the *Current* node. You would then drag the old Sprint out. It's a pretty slick trick, although you may have to alter the way you run reports. You can read Mark's full blog post here: *http://intellitechture.com/transitioning-between-sprintsiterations-with-tfs.*

Reports

Reports allow you to quickly assess the progress and quality of your software product being developed. The reports in Team Foundation Server summarize the metrics from work items, source control, test results, and automated builds. Reports can tell you how fast your team is working from Sprint-to-Sprint based on the burndown of actual tasks and PBIs.

Team projects based on the Visual Studio Scrum process template contain four Scrum reports: Backlog Overview, Release Burndown, Sprint Burndown, and Velocity. They also include four engineering reports: Build Success Over Time, Build Summary, Test Case Readiness, and Test Plan Progress.

> **Note** As of this writing, the hosted Team Foundation Service does not support reports. Although the service uses SQL Azure, it does not yet leverage SQL Azure Reporting. Microsoft may add this support in the future.

Backlog Overview report

The Backlog Overview report is a new report added to the Visual Studio Scrum 2.0 template. This report is essentially a Scrum version of the popular User Stories Overview report from the MSF for Agile Software Development process template. It has been tweaked, of course, to work with PBIS rather than user stories. Another difference is that this report doesn't indicate any number or percentage of actual hours completed.

The Backlog Overview report helps you track the progress of each of your PBIs. In addition to listing the PBIs, it shows the number of related task hours in To Do and In Progress states as the number of test points and results (passed, failed, or not run). This report helps a team assess their progress toward completing their Sprint Goal by summarizing how much work remains for each Backlog item, as well as its quality as determined by passing and failing test cases.

Release Burndown report

The Release Burndown report indicates how quickly the Development Team is completing work and delivering PBIs. The primary use of this report is for planning when to schedule a release and to track the team's progress toward delivering on its goals. The graph in this report shows how much work remained at the start of each Sprint in a release. The source of the raw data is your Product Backlog. Each Sprint appears along the horizontal axis, and the vertical axis measures the effort (that is, story points) that remained when each Sprint started.

Sprint Burndown report

The Sprint Burndown report indicates the Development Team's progress against the forecasted work for the Sprint. By reviewing this report, you can track how much work remains in the Sprint Backlog, see how quickly tasks are being completed, and predict when the team should finish its forecasted work. The graph shows how much work remained at the end of specified intervals during a Sprint. The source of the raw data is your Sprint Backlog. The horizontal axis shows days in a Sprint, and the vertical axis measures the amount of work that remains to complete the tasks in the Sprint. The work that remains is shown in hours.

The ideal trend line indicates an ideal situation in which the Development Team burns down all of the tasks that remain at a constant rate by the end of the Sprint. You can think of this line representing the best (steady and sustainable) rate of progress. The bulk of the burndown shows tasks, either in progress (lighter colored) or to do (darker colored). Both types of data are based on the actual progress of your Development Team as it works on tasks in the Sprint Backlog.

Velocity report

The Velocity report shows a graph of the amount of effort that your team has completed in each Sprint. The data comes from the PBIs and bugs completed in prior Sprints. The horizontal axis represents Sprints, and the vertical axis measures the effort (that is, story points) for each work item where the state was Done. In addition to showing how much effort the Development Team has completed each Sprint, this report shows the team's minimum, maximum, and average Velocity across Sprints.

Some Development Teams can use this average Velocity number (or a derivative of it) when forecasting the amount of work they can complete in the next Sprint. Release planning can also make use of this value to more accurately know when the release will be, or what will be in it by a specific date. Empirical data such as this provides the most accurate approach to estimation.

Build Success Over Time report

The Build Success Over Time report provides a graphical variation of the Build Summary report. The Build Success Over Time report displays the status of the last build for each build category run for each day. You can use this report to help track the quality of the code that the team is checking in. In addition, for any day on which a build ran, you can drill down and view the Build Summary report.

The report data is derived from the build information in the data warehouse. The report summarizes build and test results for each combination of build definition (build name), platform (x86, Any CPU, and so on), and configuration (debug, release, and so on). At a glance, you can see which configurations:

- Had a successful build

- Had a successful build with passing tests

- Had a successful build with failing tests

- Had a successful build without any tests

- Had low test coverage

- Had a failed build

- Had no build

Build Summary report

The Build Summary report lists builds and provides information about test results, test coverage, code churn, and quality notes for each build. The report data is derived from the build information in the data warehouse and presents a visual display of the percentage of tests that are passing, code that is being tested, and code that is changing across several builds. The report lists the most recent builds first and contains build results that were captured during the provided date range for all builds that were run. At a glance, you can determine the success or failure of several build definitions for the time period provided.

You can use this report to see the status of all builds over time, including which build succeeded, failed, and partially succeeded. You can also see which builds indicated a significant number of changes to the code (code churn). If the build was configured to track code coverage, the report will show how much of the code was exercised by the tests. All of this information can help make the decision of whether the build is ready to be promoted to another environment, such as production.

Test Case Readiness report

The Test Case Readiness report can be used to determine how many test cases have been defined and are ready to run. This report is useful to run during the Sprint, after the Development Team starts creating test cases. The report helps you track how many test cases are ready to be run, showing the number of test cases in the Design or Ready state.

When someone creates a test case, it is automatically set to the Design state. After it is determined that the test case is valid and ready to be run, its state should be changed to Ready. By reviewing this data, you can determine how quickly the team is designing test cases and making them ready for testing.

Test Plan Progress report

The Test Plan Progress report tracks the team's testing progress. This report is useful after the team has created test cases and has started running tests using Test Manager. The report presents an area graph showing the most recent result of running any test in the specified test plan over time. Ideally, this report shows a steady progress in test plans running and passing. The number of test cases may remain fairly static, but hopefully, the number of passing test cases increases and the numbers of test cases in other states (Failed, Inconclusive, Blocked, Never Run, or Pending) should decrease.

This report helps a team understand how much testing they have completed and still have to do. It also shows them how many tests are passing, failing, or blocked. This aggregation of information will help the team know if they are likely to achieve their goals before the end of the Sprint.

Common customizations

The Visual Studio Scrum process template is a *basic* process template. It is intended to support the core rules of Scrum and does not contain many extras. For example, it does not contain as many engineering reports and additional work item fields as the other Microsoft process templates do. This minimalism was by design and has served Scrum Teams well thus far.

With that in mind, there are some instances where teams may want to customize the Visual Studio Scrum process template. Most customizations apply to work item types. Here are some examples collected over the years from various teams and consultants:

- Add a *Team* field to the Product Backlog Item and Bug work item type to indicate which subteam owns it.

- Add an *Epic* field to the Product Backlog Item type to indicate that the item is too large to be developed in one Sprint and needs to be decomposed.

- Change the *Assigned To* label to read *Owned By*.

- Add a new Ready for Estimation state to the Product Backlog Item type.

- Add a new Groomed or Ready For Sprint state to the Product Backlog Item type.

- Add a new state transition for the Impediment work item type to allow Closed impediments to be reopened.

- Add a *Technical Value* or *Learning Value* field to the Product Backlog Item work item type.

- Change the Committed state to Forecasted to more closely match the *Scrum Guide*.

- Add more options to the state change Reason list for various work item types.

- Add a *Business Value* field to the Bug work item type.

- Add a Storyboards tab to the Bug work item type.

- Remove the *Activity* field from the Task work item type.

- Add a customized Definition of "Done" (DoD) control to the Product Backlog Item and Bug work item types.

- Modify the Blocked Tasks query to include linked Impediment work items that describe the blockage.

- Create a Sprint work item type to track the Sprint Goal and Retrospective notes.

- Add a *Remaining Work* field to the Product Backlog Item and Bug work item types to store the manually rolled-up sum of any child task *Remaining Work* values.

- Add default user story Description text ("As a *<type of user>* I want *<some goal>* so that *<some reason>*") to the Product Backlog Item work item type. Microsoft removed this in Visual Studio Scrum 2.0

- Add default text to the Product Backlog Item and Bug work item type *Acceptance Criteria* fields to suggest a "given-when-then" Behavior-Driven Development (BDD) or "given-when-then-fail" format.

- Add default text to the Bug work item type *System* field to serve as a template for what should be entered.

- Add an *Expected Results* field to the Bug work item type to use instead of the *Acceptance Criteria* field.

- Grant the Contributors group additional permissions so that anyone on the Development Team can thoroughly manage the team project.

- Add a custom report such as a Product Backlog Item Sprint Burndown report, Business Value Burn-Up report, or Earned Value report.

- Change the initial *Release* and *Sprint* (iteration path) nodes automatically created.

Tip Use the process template the way that it was designed for a few Sprints before customizing anything. I've seen teams want to immediately make their new team project look and behave like their last team project. For example, the *Original Estimate* and *Completed* (hours) fields in an MSF/Agile team project were removed from the Scrum process template for a reason: tracking original estimates and actual hours are not of value in Scrum development. Just know what you are doing and why you are doing it before making any "improvements." Don't inadvertently change the rules of Scrum by customizing the tool.

Let's focus for a minute on customizing work item types and related artifacts. If you are making a change to a single team project, then go ahead and use the Process Editor tool found in the Team Foundation Server Power Tools or manually edit the XML files. If you plan on applying those changes to multiple team projects, I'd consider using the witadmin.exe command-line utility to script the importing of the customized work item type to the applicable team projects. If you plan on using the customized work item type in all future team projects, you will need to update the process template with the customized type. Remember that any changes you make to a process template *after* you have created a team project won't have an effect on the team project.

Here is a recap of this guidance:

- To modify a single team project, use the Process Editor or witadmin.exe to export, edit, and import the work item type definitions, link types, or categories.

- To modify multiple team projects, first make the respective changes per above, and then use witadmin.exe to script the importing of those changes to the other team projects.

- To modify the Visual Studio Scrum process template, either modify the XML files manually or use the Process Editor, saving the changes back to Team Foundation Server.

Note As of this writing, the hosted Team Foundation Service does not allow process templates to be customized or a team project's work item type definitions to be changed. Microsoft may add this support in the future.

Chapter burndown

Here are the key concepts we covered in this chapter:

- **Visual Studio Scrum 2.0**   Microsoft has updated this very popular process template and made it the default template for both the on-premises Team Foundation Server and hosted Team Foundation Service.

- **What's new in Visual Studio Scrum 2.0**   There is support for the new features in Visual Studio 2012, such as code review, stakeholder feedback, and storyboarding.

- **What's changed in Visual Studio Scrum 2.0**   The Product Backlog query now returns all Sprints. You can resolve a task during check-in. There are more fields reported to the data warehouse. Reports use iteration path dates rather than Sprint work items.

- **What's removed in Visual Studio Scrum 2.0**   The Sprint work item and default check-in notes have been removed.

- **Work item types**   The Product Backlog Item and Bug work item types together make up the Product Backlog. Tasks and Test Cases should be created and linked only during the Sprint in which you are working on their parent PBIs or bugs.

- **Queries**   You will have to update your Current Sprint queries manually each Sprint.

- **Reports**   A new Backlog Overview report has been added. This report was based on the very useful User Stories Overview report from the MSF/Agile process template.

- **Customizations**   There are many possible customizations you can make. Ensure that you are doing so for a good reason and that it does not implement a dysfunction.

Using Scrum

In this part of the book, I will begin demonstrating how to use Scrum and Microsoft Visual Studio 2012 together effectively. The previous part established a baseline understanding of the three areas of knowledge required before proceeding: Scrum, Team Foundation Server, and the Visual Studio Scrum process template. Over the next several chapters, you will see how these three fit together and how a team can optimize their use to deliver maximum business value in the form of working software.

We will begin with the discussion and activities surrounding product planning. This will take us up to the beginning of the first Sprint. I refer to this collection of activities as the *pre-game*. Everything from envisioning the product, provisioning the Team Foundation Server environment, setting up the team project, organizing the team, building and grooming the Product Backlog, and preparing for the first Sprint falls into the pre-game. As you can imagine, there's a lot in the pre-game. We will stay focused on the intersection of Scrum and Visual

Studio 2012. There are other, more suitable books on the market to explain the intricacies of establishing a new software project.

The remaining chapters will follow the rules of Scrum very closely as I establish how a Scrum Team works within a Sprint using the relevant tools found in Visual Studio 2012. At times, I will focus on using Team Foundation Server to plan and track a Sprint and the daily work. Other times, I will focus on the engineering tools found in Visual Studio 2012 to demonstrate how developers can collaborate effectively to maximize the quality of the code and the product. I will continue to use the Tailspin Toys case study to give examples of how a team might use the many options available.

> **Tip** High-performance Scrum Teams take the "let the team decide" mantra seriously, and they don't abuse it. These teams have learned to effectively live within the balance of increasing value in the product with decreasing waste in the process.

CHAPTER 4
The pre-game

I n the game of rugby, or any professional sport for that matter, there are many activities that must be performed prior to kickoff: prior games are analyzed, sponsors are secured, stakeholder input is provided, rules get re-explained, playing fields get selected, calendar dates get negotiated, teams get selected, and player positions get designated. Scrum software development projects also have a pre-game, where many of these same types of activities are performed. The Scrum pre-game is the time period when the vision is established all the way up to the beginning of the first Sprint. The pre-game is not time-boxed, and not all projects make it out of the pre-game.

There are many important activities that can be performed during the pre-game (in no particular order):

- Establish the vision, scope, and business goals of the product.

- Identify product sponsors and stakeholders.

- Establish the Scrum Team (Product Owner, Scrum Master, Development Team).

- Establish the software development environment (that is, install Team Foundation Server).

- Educate individuals on the rules of Scrum.

- Educate individuals on the Application Lifecycle Management (ALM) tools in Microsoft Visual Studio.

- Define the high-level product requirements.

- Create the initial Product Backlog.

I recognize that some of the activities I outline in this chapter are considered to be *execution* in nature as opposed to *preparation*. An example of an execution activity would be installing and configuring Team Foundation Server. Some Scrum Teams prefer to do these kinds of activities during an actual Sprint, where a timebox and an engaged Product Owner help to prioritize and order the work. Since many of the activities I outline in this chapter are executed one time only and must be performed before development using Team Foundation Server can occur, I have lumped them together into the pre-game.

Smell It's a smell when I see a team spending too much time setting up their environment. Developers do not need the most awesome configuration of tools ever conceived prior to their first Sprint. Just as their software product will evolve, so will their ALM tools and environment. If a team has historically procrastinated getting started on a new project, consider executing these activities in Sprint 1. This forces the team to produce an increment of working functionality in the same Sprint that they set up their environment.

Note The concept of the pre-game (or "Sprint 0" as some call it) does not exist in the *Scrum Guide*. Whatever the team wants to calls it, they are not yet using Scrum. Because of this, most of the pre-game activities I listed above will be out of the scope of this chapter. I will only focus on those activities directly related to provisioning the Team Foundation Server development environment.

Setting up the development environment

It goes without saying that before a Scrum Team can begin using Team Foundation Server and the Visual Studio Scrum process template to implement Scrum, someone will have to install and configure it. This section assumes that the organization has a properly installed and configured Team Foundation Server available for the team to use. We'll also assume that the organization makes available a *helpful* Team Foundation Server administrator to serve the team as needed. In my experience, this is a recipe for success. If the administrator understands software development, that's good. If the administrator does not, that can be an impediment. If the administrator understands Scrum, that's a bonus.

Tip Having a Scrum Team member be the part-time Team Foundation Server administrator is not ideal. A Scrum Team should be allowed to devote as much of their time as possible on developing the software product. High-performance Scrum Teams are ones whose team members can avoid being distracted by activities that don't directly result in business value in the form of working software.

Team Foundation Server: Buy vs. build

When it comes to Team Foundation Server, an organization can purchase, install, and configure their own server, or contract with Microsoft to use their hosted Team Foundation Service. This software as a service (SaaS) model is hosted on Microsoft's Azure platform and enjoys all of the same benefits as any hosted app running in the cloud, including availability, scalability, and durability. The most appealing advantage to the hosted Team Foundation Service is that there is minimal administration required to get started or keep it operating. If a Scrum Team doesn't have the necessary infrastructure or administrator, or needs to establish a hosted ALM solution *today*, using the always-on Team Foundation Service is a no-brainer. Table 4-1 shows a feature comparison between the Team Foundation Service and Team Foundation Server.

TABLE 4-1 Comparing the hosted Team Foundation Service with an on-premises Team Foundation Server.

	Hosted Team Foundation Service	On-premises Team Foundation Server
Who purchases hardware?	Microsoft	Your organization
Who deploys and maintains software?	Microsoft	Your organization
Visual Studio Scrum 2.0	Yes	Yes
Work item tracking	Yes	Yes
Web-based Agile management tools	Yes	Yes
Microsoft SharePoint integration (project portal)	No	Yes (optional)
Reports	No (only on-screen charts)	Yes (optional)
Source control	Yes	Yes
Automated builds	Yes	Yes
Virtual Test Lab Management	No	Yes
Connectivity required	Internet	LAN, WAN, or Internet
Authentication method	Windows Live ID	Windows (NTLM or Kerberos)
Customize process templates	No	Yes
Customize work item types	No	Yes
Licensing model	N/A	Server / Client Access License (CAL)
Frequency of updates	Frequently	Less frequent

Organizations with an existing infrastructure investment may not see the value in using the hosted Team Foundation Service. Likewise, organizations that need to have full control over the software, including the ability to customize and extend Team Foundation Server, should consider going with an on-premises installation of Team Foundation Server. I don't think I've ever run across an experienced Team Foundation Server Development Team that didn't want to tweak at least one work item type definition.

> **Tip** Refer to the *Team Foundation Server Planning Guide* on CodePlex for help in understanding the tradeoffs and planning your Team Foundation Server deployment. It was written by the Visual Studio ALM Rangers and is full of good information. The Visual Studio ALM Rangers are technical specialists that come from the Microsoft product group, Microsoft services, the MVP community, as well as other communities around the world. Their mission is to provide solutions for missing features and guidance. Visit *http://vsarplanningguide.codeplex.com* for more information.

Tailspin Toys case study The Tailspin Toys organization has opted for an on-premises installation of Team Foundation Server 2012. Andy, the Team Foundation Server administrator has installed and configured a single-tier Team Foundation Server on a dedicated Windows Server 2008 R2 server running four cores, 16 GB of RAM, and a single 250 GB SSD. The server's name is VSALM.

Create a team project collection

One of the first decisions an administrator will need to make is whether to use multiple team project collections. Team project collections allow you to organize and manage your team projects. You can group similar projects together in a team project collection in order to assign and share common resources. When you create a team project collection, you specify the logical and physical resources that team projects within that collection can use. All team project artifacts (work items, source control, automated builds, and tests) in the same collection are stored in a single Microsoft SQL Server database. Team Foundation Server administrators or database administrators can back up and restore a team project collection database independent of other collections. Table 4-2 discusses other advantages and disadvantages of using multiple team project collections.

TABLE 4-2 Characteristics of multiple team and single team project collections.

	Multiple team project collections	Single team project collection
Complexity	Increased	Decreased
Work items	Increased security through isolation	No security through increased isolation
Copying work items	Not across collections	Yes
Linking work items	Not across collections	Yes
Querying work items	Within a single collection only	Yes
Source control	Increased security through isolation	No security through increased isolation
Branching and merging	Not across collections	Yes
Automated builds	Each collection requires its own controller	Only one controller required
Offline maintenance	Only projects in collection are affected	All projects are affected
Reporting across all projects	No (just those in the collection by default)	Yes
Supports hundreds of projects	Yes	Yes
Supports hundreds of developers	Yes	Yes
Security management	More complex	Less complex
Can scale out a single project	Yes	Yes (if it's the only team project in the collection)
Can isolate a project for legal or regulatory reasons	Yes	No
Can hand off the team project to the customer when finished	Yes	Yes (if it's the only team project in the collection)
Process template customization	Deployed to multiple collections	Deployed to one collection

If an organization will have several team projects in progress at the same time and these projects will have a need or even *might* have a need to copy, link, or query work items or branch/merge code between their repositories, then create those team projects in the same team project collection.

> **Tip** Unless your organization has a compelling need to isolate its projects (that is, legal or regulatory governance), you should use a single team project collection. The default collection created during Team Foundation Server configuration will work fine. You might want to give it a more interesting name, however.

> **Tailspin Toys case study** After discussing the pros and cons, the organization has decided to create a single team project collection. During the configuration of Team Foundation Server, Andy deferred the creation of the *default* team project creation so that he could provide a better name. When the configuration wizard completed, Andy launched the Team Foundation Server Administrative Console and manually created a team project collection named *Scrum*. Andy named the collection "Scrum," simply to illustrate that it will contain team projects created using the Visual Studio Scrum process template.

Configure Team Foundation Build

High-quality software development teams create high-quality software products. While they may make it look easy, that level of quality doesn't just happen on its own. These teams rely on proven practices and tools to achieve it. One of the best ways to ensure that software reaches and remains at a high quality is through verification. This can be manual or automated. Manual tests are just that— tests that a developer performs manually. These tests can be heavily scripted, with specific steps, inputs, and expected results. They can also be more exploratory in nature, with little or no script provided, relying on the tester's cognitive engagement with the software and ability to manage their time.

> **Smell** It's a smell when I see that a team *isn't* using Team Foundation Build. If I find that they are using another automated build and test tool, then the smell dissipates. More times than not, I find that the team is not using any build and test automation. Typically, the reason is ignorance. They may not have a clue what Team Foundation Build does or how to effectively use it. Fortunately, this is solved by education. When a team tells me that they don't see the value in running automated builds or that Team Foundation Build won't "buy them anything," then that smell becomes a stench. Having Team Foundation Build perform builds and run tests is quite valuable—almost like having another (unpaid) team member continuously integrating and validating your work.

High-performance Scrum Teams have also learned how to work smarter, not harder. They do this by continuously integrating their code changes and using automated tests. Automated tests are more interesting than manual tests because, once created and configured, these tests can be relied upon to ensure that the product maintains a certain level of quality while also ensuring new features work *without* human interaction. In Visual Studio, many types of tests can be "automated." The best candidates are tests that exercise code directly (a.k.a. *white box* tests). Unit and integration tests lend themselves well to automation. You can automate other types of tests, such as configuration tests, user interface (UI) tests, scenario tests, and load tests. Since these types of tests touch more layers, such as the UI, they tend to be more brittle and typically require additional maintenance to keep them accurate.

Automated tests can be executed from inside the Visual Studio integrated development environment (IDE), inside the Eclipse IDE, inside Microsoft Test Manager, or from the command line. They can also be executed during an automated build using Team Foundation Build. The advantage of having Team Foundation Build execute tests automatically is that it's asynchronous to the developer. In a continuous integration (CI) environment, upon code check-in, an automated build launches, binaries are compiled, deployments are performed, automated tests are run, and feedback is returned to the team. Since all of this work occurs on another machine, the developer is not blocked and can continue working on his or her next task. Table 4-3 lists the various quality control activities, such as testing, that are supported by Team Foundation Build.

Ultimately, CI is about reducing risk. When a developer defers integration until late in the day, the week, or the Sprint, the risk of failure (that is, features not working, side effects, bugs, etc.) increases. By integrating your code change with others regularly, throughout the day, you will identify these problems early and be able to fix them when the code is fresh in everyone's mind. The practice of CI is a *must* for a high-performance Scrum Team.

TABLE 4-3 The support for quality control activities in Team Foundation Build 2012.

	Natively supports	Additional software required
.NET Unit Tests (MSTEST)	✓	
.NET Unit Tests (NUnit, xUnit, MBUnit, etc.)		The respective testing framework
Code coverage		Visual Studio 2012 Premium
Test impact analysis	✓	
Coded UI tests		Visual Studio 2012 Premium
Web performance tests		Visual Studio 2012 Ultimate
Load tests		Visual Studio 2012 Ultimate
Ordered tests	✓	
Generic tests		Visual Studio 2012 Premium
Architectural validation (layer diagrams)	✓	
Code analysis	✓	
Code metrics		Visual Studio Code Metrics PowerTool
Code clone analysis		N/A

Team Foundation Build features

Team Foundation Build is installed when you install Team Foundation Server. Installation does nothing more than copying the relevant binaries to the target computer. This computer can be running either a desktop or a server operating system. A configuration step is required before Team Foundation Build can be used. During this configuration, the administrator configures the various features:

- **Build machine** The computer on which the Team Foundation Build service has been installed and is being configured. This machine can be physical or virtual. Preferably, this is a stand-alone machine, but it can also be co-located with Team Foundation Server.

- **Build controller** The process that pools and manages the services of one or more build agents. The build controller delegates the actual work to the build agent(s) within its pool. Each controller is dedicated to a single team project collection. By default, only one controller can be hosted on a build machine.

- **Build agent** The process that does the actual building. Agents perform the processor- and I/O-intensive work, such as provisioning a workspace, getting the code, compiling to one or more configurations, performing code analysis, running automated tests, releasing builds to a shared folder, and publishing results. An administrator can identify the capabilities (that is, what software is installed) of an agent by creating and associating one or more *tags*.

 Tip Think of build agents like shared, network printers in a large enterprise. Each printer can be assigned one or more tags, such as *laser, ink, color, duplex, stapler,* etc. When a user wants to print a document, he or she can request *duplex, laser, color,* and the printing software will find an available printer that meets the criteria and send the job there. Likewise, each build agent can be assigned one or more tags, such as *.NET4.0, .NET4.5, SQL2012 BizTalk, JDK, Telerik, VB6,* or *FoxPro.* More than one agent can have the same tag. When it comes time for an application to be built, the build controller will find an available agent that meets the criteria and send the job there. The only difference is that there is no walking up two flights of stairs to retrieve your binaries.

The specifics of planning and configuring Team Foundation Build are beyond the scope of this book. I recommend downloading and reading the *Team Foundation Server Installation Guide* as a starting point. Suffice it to say that there are numerous ways in which to deploy Team Foundation Build. The simplest topology being the build controller and agent collocated on the same hardware as Team Foundation Server. This would adequately serve a small team working on smaller projects.

A more complex topology would include multiple machines running multiple agents. This would shorten the time required to build and test, thus enabling more team members to build more projects. An enterprise-scale build environment would have multiple controllers and agents running on dedicated hardware available to serve any number of requests from any number of teams and projects.

Tip When provisioning a build agent machine, you should opt for the fastest, most dedicated hardware and I/O that you can afford (multi-core CPUs, solid state drives, adequate and fast RAM, etc.). The time required to compile the binaries is a pittance compared to what testing can demand. Testing can take a substantially greater amount of time than building. Even tactically running tests using naming conventions, categories, or test impact analysis can take time. Anything you can do to increase the speed of the build and test process while reducing the feedback loop time will be greatly appreciated by the team. Continuous integration will be more useful and yield more value to the team.

Tailspin Toys case study Andy has installed and configured Team Foundation Build on a dedicated Windows Server 2008 R2 server running four cores, 16 GB RAM, and twin 250 GB Solid State Drives (SSDs). The server name is *TFSBUILD1*. There is a single build controller named Matrix serving the Scrum Team project collection and two build agents (Smith1 and Smith2). Visual Studio 2012 Ultimate edition has been fully installed, as well as various third-party libraries, controls, and tools required by the Tailspin Toys application. Andy will monitor the build server's performance and feedback from the team. If and when an upgrade is needed, he will probably scale out the build rig by adding new hardware.

Configure Lab Management

For more complicated testing environments, a team may want to use Visual Studio Lab Management. Lab Management automates the build–deploy–test workflow in a test lab environment. This automation results in a shorter feedback cycle, which is especially important when working with complex deployments with multiple tiers supporting different operating systems and services, such as Microsoft Internet Information Server (IIS), SharePoint, and SQL Server. Lab Management automates all of the building, deploying, and testing activities across a complex environment such as this.

Traditionally, test labs have used physical hardware. This hardware usually wasn't the fastest gear in the organization—most likely hand-me-down computers from the Development Team. This infrastructure was usually maintained part-time by a developer or, worse, by someone from the organization's central IT department. These departments usually don't *get* software development or have the skills or mandate to directly support the development effort.

Modern, progressive organizations use virtualization across the board. From servers to desktops, they understand that encapsulating their environment into virtual machines (VMs) makes administrative as well as economic sense. It also helps reduce the amount of hardware in the data center. Modern Development Teams also see the value of virtualization, especially for procuring a testing environment using a self-service model. A team can define several different lab configurations to be ready at a moment's notice, ensuring that testing always begins in a clean, known state. This is important when trying to track down a bug or verify that one has been fixed.

> **Note** In my travels, I see more and more developers working in VMs. The organization will virtualize a standardized development environment, including the proper version, edition, and service pack of Visual Studio, as well as any other utilities, controls, and libraries required. These images are snapshotted and distributed as needed. Furthermore, offsite developers (work from home, contractor, or overseas types) will be asked to "remote in" using a virtual private network (VPN) so that there is no footprint on their personal hardware. This also lessens the chance that the organization's intellectual property might wander off.

In Lab Management, you define an environment as a collection of VMs. Each VM plays a role in that environment. For example, the Tailspin Toys application requires an infrastructure including an IIS web server, a SQL Server machine, and a desktop client. Lab Management is aware of this environment and controls all of the individual VMs in order to test an *n*-tier application. In Team Foundation Server 2010, this only worked so long as the organization was using Microsoft's Hyper-V Server or the Hyper-V role on Windows Server 2008 or Windows Server 2008 R2. There were workarounds for teams using physical environments or environments virtualized using the VMware products, but the lack of first-class support from Microsoft was an adoption blocker for organizations looking at Lab Management.

Team Foundation Server 2012 provides support for *standard environments*. A standard environment is any existing environment of servers and machines, regardless of whether they are physical or virtual, and regardless whether they are virtualized using Hyper-V or VMware. You can now map a Lab Management environment to an existing configuration of machines and then continue to automate the build–deploy–test workflow like before. There is no need to setup Hyper-V servers or configure System Center Virtual Machine Manager (SCVMM) anymore.

Here are the high-level steps to follow in order to use a standard environment:

1. Know the environment, including each computer name and administrator credentials.

2. Configure a test controller for your team project collection.

3. From Test Manager, run a wizard to create a new standard environment.

4. Create a test plan with automated tests and settings to run tests on that environment.

5. Create a build definition using the LabDefaultTemplate.11.xaml template, as shown in Figure 4-1.

FIGURE 4-1 A section of the LabDefaultTemplate.11.xaml build process template.

Another nice feature of Team Foundation Server 2012 is that you do not have to worry about manually installing test agents on any of the machines in the environment. That is done for you automatically. SCVMM environments are still supported in Team Foundation Server 2012. They have been enhanced as well to support the auto-installation of these agents. Also, with an SCVMM environment, you get the additional benefit of being able to use snapshots as part of your testing scenarios. Snapshots allow you to capture the state of a VM at a specific point in time. This snapshot can then be applied later to revert that machine to that known state. For example, you could snapshot a database server containing a specific set of data and then apply it later in order to run some specific tests. Work items can reference snapshots too. Another example could be a developer wanting to associate a specific snapshot of a server at the time a bug was recorded.

Note The details of installing, configuring, and using Lab Management are beyond the scope of this book. Please refer to the appropriate articles on MSDN for more information.

Tailspin Toys case study As the deployment environment is not very complex, the team has decided not to use Lab Management for the initial release. If demand drives the need for a more sophisticated environment, they will go back and revisit the need for Lab Management. The fact that the organization has adopted VMware, and not Hyper-V, as a standard is immaterial.

Setting up product development

This section explores those activities related to setting up software product development within Team Foundation Server 2012. Some of these activities are one-time events, while others are ongoing, such as configuring areas and iterations. Before proceeding, it's assumed that the following activities have already been completed:

- Team Foundation Server is installed (or Team Foundation Service is being used).

- Appropriate client software is installed.

- A team project collection exists.

- The Scrum Team has formed.

- Windows user accounts are known.

- Team Foundation Build is configured (optional).

- Lab Management is configured (optional).

Create a team project

The team project is the container for the software product's development lifecycle. All work items, source-controlled artifacts, test cases, test results, build definitions, and build runs are stored in a team project. Technically, they are stored in multiple tables associated with a team project in the project collection's SQL Server database. To look at it from a Scrum perspective, the team project represents the product being developed and is a container for the Product Backlog, the Sprint Backlog, and the source code and tests that form the Increment. The team project contains queries, charts, and reports that allow a team to assess their progress and the quality of their work.

You can create a team project from the File menu or from within Team Explorer. This will launch the New Team Project Wizard, where you will be asked to provide the name and description of the team project, select the process template (Visual Studio Scrum 2.0), and specify additional information such as SharePoint and source control settings. Depending on the environment, it can up to a few minutes to create a team project, after which you can begin configuring and using it.

How many team projects will you need?

The scope of a team project is a function of the product being developed, its components, and the number of developers and whether they are dedicated to that one product. Remember that a *developer* in Scrum is anyone contributing to the development of the Increment. This includes any team member who performs design, coding, testing, or other activities. The ideal combination is a team of 3–9 developers dedicated to working on a single product. This would yield a single team project containing both the Product Backlog and source code of the product being developed. Unfortunately, I don't see this very often. More common are tiny teams, huge teams, or teams having to split their Sprint across multiple products. Team Foundation Server can support these environments as well.

With a micro-team of only one or two developers, they won't necessarily be using Scrum, but they'll still need a team project. I would hope they would take advantage of the Product Backlog, but as far as planning and tracking work within the Sprint, they may not need tooling for that. For medium-large teams with 10 or more developers, they would want to decompose into teams of 3–9 to work more efficiently within the rules of Scrum. They can still all work within the same team project. Table 4-4 shows a summary of this discussion.

I've seen large products with 80+ developers working within the same team project off of a single Product Backlog. This increased complexity demands using work item areas or a custom work item field to designate the responsible team, not to mention having an effective source control branching strategy. Developers in the unfortunate situation of having to develop or support multiple products at the same time may end up having multiple team projects and bouncing between them regularly.

TABLE 4-4 Creating team projects based on teams, sizes, and commitment.

# of developers	Single product?	Team project(s)	Notes
1–2	Yes	Single	Not using Scrum
	No	Multiple	Not using Scrum; may want to use a common Product Backlog
3–9	Yes	Single	This is ideal
	No	Multiple	May want to use a common Product Backlog
10+	Yes	Single (typically)	Decompose into teams of 3–9 developers
	No	Varies	Strive for development teams of 3–9 developers

Creating a !Backlog team project

It is common for an organization to have more products than teams. I've worked with several organizations that fit this pattern. They tend to have a dozen or more small to medium-sized projects being maintained by a technical staff of 10 or more individuals. These developers tend to pull work from a common queue. This centralized "enterprise" backlog approach can be implemented in Team Foundation Server by creating multiple team projects. The first team project only contains work items and the corresponding area and iteration nodes. The other team projects would contain the source code, tests, and automated builds. I recommend pre-fixing this team project's name with an exclamation point so that it appears at the top of sorted lists, as you can see in Figure 4-2.

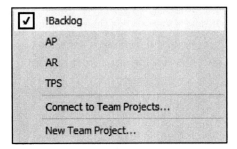

FIGURE 4-2 The enterprise backlog and constituent team projects.

Setting up a single backlog provides these benefits:

- All requirements from all products are visible and manageable in a single backlog.

- Requirements can be prioritized with respect to each other.

- Source control structure, branch, and build complexities are isolated.

This approach requires some additional processes to use effectively:

- The !Backlog project's areas must support all constituent projects, as shown in Figure 4-3.

- All projects must share the same release/iteration schedule.

- Check-ins will be associated with work items found in the !Backlog team project.

FIGURE 4-3 Setting up the area hierarchy in the !Backlog team project.

Tip Once you create the !Backlog project, you should remove access to the source control folders and builds for all but the project administrator. This way, nobody accidentally checks in code or creates a build definition in this project. Also, you may want to do something similar to the constituent team projects to disable the ability to create work items. I've seen teams customize the Visual Studio Scrum process template and create a subset of functionality. Be sure to do your development and testing of such customizations on a test Team Foundation Server. If a separate Team Foundation Server is not available, the next best choice would be to use a separate team project collection. Also, consider creating a separate team project for such work, and check in your changes.

Smell It's a smell when a team is using an enterprise backlog team project. It seems weird that I would suggest an approach, and then turn around and tell you that I consider it a smell if I see it in use. Smells are just that. It may turn out that the underlying reasons for this behavior are sound. My recommendation is that using an enterprise backlog approach like this should be the exception and not the rule. If I find that a team has arranged their team projects this way, or have an environment that would support this, I will attempt to have the hard conversation with the organization about improving their process. We will dive deep into the discussion of waste when work is not being planned or prioritized beyond the current iteration, not to mention when developers have to context-switch. Establishing a single Product Owner usually goes a long way, so long as they focus more on maximizing value in the product and less on making various managers happy.

One organization I worked with claimed to be using Scrum. It had multiple product managers, each vying for the Development Team's time. Needless to say, its queue of work was quite full. One product manager wanted a set of improvements on their system and asked the IT director when she could have them. The IT director performed some high-level analysis and provided a rough estimate, telling the manager that work could be started in about 9 months and, once started, shouldn't take longer than about a month. The manager was displeased. She asked if the developers could start sooner and work on her features in between their other tasks. The IT director replied, "We can do that, but then it will take us 12 months total, put other projects behind, and you probably won't like the quality of the work we did early in the year." The IT director realized that the manager, as well as the organization, had a belief in magic. They thought that developers could work efficiently on multiple things at once, could work at an unsustainable pace when it suited the organization, and could give accurate estimates for unknown, complex problems. Eventually, the IT director became the Product Owner and was able to order the work in a way where the team spent an entire Sprint on project A and then the next Sprint on project B, and so forth. The team was then able to concentrate on one domain at a time and collaborate aggressively to tackle those stories and bug fixes.

Tip If the culture and processes can't be fixed, rest assured that Team Foundation Server can usually implement whatever dysfunctional software development processes an organization can throw at it. For a situation where a small number of developers *must* service a large number of products in a prioritized-just-in-time way, then I suggest they take a look at Kanban. Kanban is a method for developing software with an emphasis on just-in-time delivery. Kanban instructs developers to pull work from a queue using a visual board that shows the work in progress by state.

Supporting the entire lifecycle of the product

A team project can encapsulate the entire lifecycle of the product being developed—from the first release to the last, including all of the Sprints in between. This is done by defining release and Sprint *iterations* and dates as in Figure 4-4. Work items can then be assigned to those iterations. Backlogs, queries, and reports can also be filtered by these iterations. In other words, you do not need to create a new team project whenever you start a new release/version.

Iterations	Start Date	End Date
▲ Tailspin		
▲ Release 1	7/4/2012	9/25/2012
Sprint 1	7/4/2012	7/17/2012
Sprint 2	7/18/2012	7/31/2012
Sprint 3	8/1/2012	8/14/2012
Sprint 4	8/15/2012	8/28/2012
Sprint 5	8/29/2012	9/11/2012
Sprint 6	9/12/2012	9/25/2012
▷ Release 2	9/26/2012	12/18/2012
▷ Release 3	12/19/2012	3/12/2013
▷ Release 4	3/13/2013	6/4/2013

FIGURE 4-4 Managing multiple releases and Sprints.

What should you name your team project?

Let's take a step back. Creating a team project is the easy part; but planning it can be more difficult. It's imperative that you know what product or component of a larger product the team will be developing. If the product has a name, you should consider using that for the name of the team project. If the product doesn't yet have a name, or the name is something like "The ASP.NET web app that consumes the WCF web service from our financial partner," you'll want to give it an actual name first. This is the first step in it becoming a product. It sounds trivial, but having a clear, meaningful name will begin the process of focusing less on *how* the software works and more on *what* it should be doing.

Smell It's a smell if the developers don't know the name of the application they are developing. Maybe it doesn't have a name, or maybe they just don't care to know it. Either way, this demonstrates a lack of product-minded thinking. For a successful adoption of Scrum to occur, this will have to change.

When creating your team project, give special consideration to its name. The name should be short, meaningful, and allow someone to quickly identify the product being developed within. The name does not need to include the version, release, Sprint, subteam, feature crew, feature set, area, or component. All of these items can be tracked within the team project using areas and iterations. For example, if we were creating a team project to plan and track development of the Tailspin application, we should consider naming it *Tailspin* rather than *TailspinV1, TailspinRel1, TailspinSprint1, TailspinDev,* or *TailspinWeb.*

Tip Team projects cannot be renamed. You will need to get it right the first time. This is the most requested Team Foundation Server feature on *http://visualstudio.uservoice.com*. Until Microsoft gives us that functionality, our only recourse is to delete the team project and create it again or use team project descriptions—which can be changed. Team projects can be deleted from within the Team Foundation Server Administrative Console or from the command line using TfsDeleteProject.exe. I prefer the latter. Deleting is a destructive process. If you change your mind, you will have to restore from a team project collection backup. Think twice before you delete a team project.

Tailspin Toys case study Andy created a team project named Tailspin based on the Visual Studio Scrum 2.0 process template within the *Scrum* team project collection.

Source control

Software development activities break down into two broad categories: managing work and software engineering. A Professional Scrum Developer must always attempt to maximize value (and minimize waste) when performing both types of activities. A great way to see the two areas merged successfully is to use Team Foundation Server for change management. Not only does Team Foundation Server track who made what changes to the code and when, but also *why*. Historically, the question of why a developer was making changes was a mystery, at least to everyone but the developer. If asked, they would reply that they were "adding a feature" or "fixing a bug." That may have sufficed in the past, but it's time to become more professional by becoming more traceable. Team Foundation Server lets you prove it by associating your checked-in changes (called a *changeset*) to a work item owned by that developer.

Smell It's a smell when I hear a team member refer to it as *his* or *her* code. High-performance Scrum Teams understand that the *team* owns the code collectively. Individual team members do not own specific components, namespaces, classes, or methods. This alleviates the blame game. An individual should not be blamed for breaking the build, but rather the team should see it as an impediment and work to correct it both in the short term and long term during the Sprint Retrospective. For larger, more complex software projects, the team can use the traceability features in Team Foundation Server, as well as collaboration to track and understand what other team members are doing.

Before we get to the process of checking in and associating work, we should spend some time getting Team Foundation Server configured. The intricacies of setting up the structure and workflows for a particular product are beyond the capabilities of this book. Instead, I will focus on configuring

Team Foundation Server to enable a Scrum Development Team to use its source control capabilities effectively. Here are some of those activities:

- Set up the initial folder structure.

- Create any necessary branches.

- Migrate existing codebase.

- Secure any folders or branches (if required).

- Enable any check-in policies.

- Enable any check-in notes.

- Setup developer workspaces.

- Fix bindings in any migrated solutions or projects.

Set up the folder structure

I differentiate the creating of static folders from that of branches. Both are important, but having an initial folder structure is important regardless of if/when you create branches. For Scrum Development Teams, I recommend keeping it simple. Give your team a consistent folder to work out of (that is, Dev) and a folder to create and manage branches for production hotfixes (that is, Prod). Underneath Dev is whatever folder structure you want. That said, I recommend a top-level set of folders to identify the major components that go into the product. It would be in these folders that the Visual Studio solution (.sln) files would live. Underneath this folder would be the natural Visual Studio project folders managed by the solution. You can see an example of this folder structure in Figure 4-5. This is just one approach out of many that are valid.

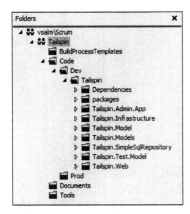

FIGURE 4-5 Sample folder structure for the Tailspin Toys product (initially devoid of any branches).

Your folder structure should be simple to understand and use. Developers should be able to quickly know where they are working each day of the Sprint (that is, under Dev), as well as during emergency hotfix situations (that is, under Prod). They should also be able to quickly find the application (that is, Tailspin) and component. Additional subfolders can be created to group components together further. Visual Studio solutions, projects, and their folders typically constitute the lowest folder levels.

Tip You can create the folder structure manually in Source Control Explorer by using the New Folder command repeatedly until the structure looks the way you want. I prefer to go old school by dropping to the command prompt and quickly creating the folder structure I want. MD and CD commands are my friends. I then return to Source Control Explorer and use the Add Items To Folder command to add the folders (and any files I want) and check in the pending changes.

Tailspin Toys case study The developers discussed the configuration and release management requirements of the product and decided to go with a simple Dev and Prod folder structure, with Dev containing folders for the single Tailspin Toys Visual Studio solution and subprojects.

Choose a branching strategy

Scrum Development Teams work collaboratively on the Product Backlog Items (PBIs) and bugs in the Sprint Backlog until the Sprint's development time-box expires. After this, the Product Owner may decide to release the Increment to production. This pattern continues Sprint after Sprint. In other words, the Development Team is always developing unless something exceptional comes up, such as a production support issue. The team's branching strategy should reflect this process. With respect to source control, when it comes to a work-in-progress, the team should work out of a common (that is, Dev) folder, integrating often.

Many Development Teams have complex to ridiculously-complex branching strategies. Some require a dedicated merge guy to go heads-down for a couple of days at the end of every Sprint or release to merge code manually into an integration branch. In situations like these when I'm asked to help find a solution, I focus on the process, not the tool. Team Foundation Server has some great, shiny features when it comes to working with branches, but it does not have a magic merge button that will do the merge guy's job for him. If integration is delayed, then the team is not practicing continuous integration, and there will be pain—even with Team Foundation Server. Branching is dead-easy. The complexity and cost comes with merging.

Tip I'm passionate about branches. I passionately despise them. Don't get me wrong. If used correctly, they provide a way to solve some specific problems. I list some of these situations in Table 4-5. However, I commonly see branches causing more problems than they solve. By problems, I mean wasted time spent understanding and merging code changes. Before establishing any branching strategy, make sure you fully understand the impact of doing so. Don't branch unless you have a good reason to do so. Don't branch until the latest responsible moment. Perhaps a label will suffice until then. Save your creativity for your product, not your branching strategy.

TABLE 4-5 Situations that *may* require branching.

Situation	Where
Production maintenance/hotfix	Branched from \Dev to a folder under \Prod (that is, \Prod\Bug42)
Large, complex product requiring multiple teams	If necessary, each team works in their own branch under \Dev (that is, \Dev\UX) and integration into the \Dev branch occurs regularly. If each team shares the same release cadence, they should strive to all work in the same branch.
Performing a spike	Branched from \Dev to a folder under \Dev (that is, Spike-HTML5) and if the spike produces useful code, it can be merged back into \Dev at a later date. Consider creating a shelveset instead.
Labels won't work due to compliance	In Team Foundation Server, labels are mutable, meaning that someone (with adequate permissions) can change the files or file revisions within a label without an audit trail.

In Team Foundation Server 2010, Microsoft started differentiating folders from branches. They represented them with different icons in Source Control Explorer. Folders are represented by the traditional manila folder and branches are represented as a small, parent-child link icon, as in Figure 4-6. This differentiation was done so that additional actions, such as branch visualization, could be performed on a branch but wouldn't be supported on a folder. You can explicitly convert a folder to a branch, which will change the icon. You can also implicitly convert the parent (source) folder to a branch when you execute the branch command. This is the default behavior.

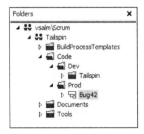

FIGURE 4-6 Branches like Bug42 are represented with different icons than folders.

Working in a private branch throughout the Sprint is easy. It delays the pain of merging your code with others. It also smells like a collaboration dysfunction: Why is this developer working by herself? Table 4-6 lists this and other situations that *may* be hiding a dysfunction.

Regardless of the underlying reason, waiting to merge creates much more work because of the amount of time that has elapsed. The developer will have to reread code, run diffs, and revisit her tasks to understand the context of the change. If another team member merges the changes, this is compounded because he won't know the intent of the code and will have to do even more research. High-performance Development Teams understand that if something hurts, such as integration and merging, then it should be done more often, such as daily or during each check-in.

TABLE 4-6 Situations where branching *may* be hiding a dysfunction.

Situation	Potential dysfunction
Each team member works in his own branch.	The team members can't collaborate effectively or are trying to tackle an entire PBI on their own.
A main, trunk, or other integration branch exists.	Unless the product is being worked on by multiple teams, or the team is using \Main to represent \Dev as in my examples, the mere presence of extra branches can cause confusion and waste.
A QA branch exists.	There is no concept of QA in Scrum. Testing tasks, just like coding tasks, should be done collaboratively under \Dev.
Release branches exist.	Unless the team is supporting multiple versions of the product or they cannot use labels, due to compliance reasons, the presence of release branches can cause confusion and waste.

Labels are cheaper and much more lightweight than branches. When a task or PBI is done, according to the team's definition, a label can be applied to the respective code. When the Increment is finished, another label can be applied, and so forth. These labels serve as checkpoints, allowing the team to return to points in time when the Increment was in a consistent, done state. The team can delete the labels at the end of the Sprint. Ideally, a branch is created only for those exceptional situations, such as a production support issue. Table 4-7 lists a few approaches where a team can use labels instead of branches.

TABLE 4-7 Approaches to using folders, labels, and branches.

Scope of work	Where to find it
Current Sprint development	Located under \Dev (use Get Latest)
Current Sprint PBI is done	Located under \Dev and identified by a label (that is, PBI 42)
Current Sprint Increment is done	Located under \Dev and identified by a label (that is, Sprint 3)
Previous Sprint Increment not yet in production	Located under \Dev and identified by a label (that is, Sprint 2)
Previous Sprint Increment in production	Located under \Dev and identified by a label (that is, Release 1)
Production hotfix	Branched from \Dev to a folder under \Prod (that is, \Prod\Bug42)

Tailspin Toys case study The team has decided to use labels throughout the Sprint and create a branch only when necessary, such as to support a production hotfix. If the team members want to experiment or perform spikes, they will do so locally or use shelvesets to collaborate with other team members.

Local workspaces vs. Git (DVCS)

Distributed version control systems (DVCSs) are very popular today. They are preferred by many Agile software development teams because they enable developers to track changes to files locally, without being connected to a central server like Team Foundation Server. This allows developers to work quickly, while still having revision control and history capabilities. The most popular DVCS implementation is Git, which was initially designed and developed by Linus Torvalds.

Team Foundation Server 2012 introduces local workspaces, which enable you to perform the core version control operations while disconnected. This results in a lightweight experience without the need to be connected to Team Foundation Server all the time. That equals speed. While this is a step in the right direction, there are still a number of advantages of using Git over Team Foundation Server local workspaces:

- Git enables local commits (check-ins).

- Git lets you look at a history of these local commits.

- Git allows local branching.

Local commits are very interesting. Think of them as being a way to establish "checkpoints" as you finish small development tasks, such as during test-driven development (TDD) when you complete a cycle, all of your tests pass, and your method is implemented and refactored. You wouldn't necessarily want to check in to Team Foundation Server because the feature you're working on isn't code-complete. Using a local commit here allows you to create a snapshot of your code in a good working state. Later, you can refer to that history or even roll back if need be.

Tailspin Toys case study A few developers have opted to install and use git-tfs (*https://github.com/git-tfs*) on their local machines to enjoy the benefits of local commits and history while still being able to integrate their code with other developers in Team Foundation Server.

Automated builds

After the Team Foundation Build is installed and configured, the next step is to create one or more build definitions. A build definition contains all of the settings and instructions about what code to compile, which tests (if any) to run, and which additional activities to run. The build definition controls the scope of what is downloaded from Team Foundation Server and compiled. This is done by setting the workspace mappings to include the appropriate folders and files. The build definition can build one or more Visual Studio solutions and projects. This gives the team very granular control over what gets built and tested, from a build that compiles and tests everything in the product down to just compiling a single component of the product. Any MSBuild-based project is fair game, so long as the required binaries (that is, compilers and libraries) are installed on the server(s) that are involved with the building and testing.

There are many types of builds that a Development Team might run during the course of a day, week, and Sprint. These can range from local builds all the way up to nightly builds deploying and running exhaustive end-to-end tests on a complex test environment. With so many types of tests and so many names for those types of tests, I thought it would be useful to standardize the terminology, as you can see in Table 4-8.

TABLE 4-8 Types of builds (in no particular order).

Build Type	Definition
Local or F5	When a developer uses Visual Studio or a script to build (and possibly test) on their local machine
Buddy	When another developer integrates your code with hers and then runs a local build
Integration	A build that verifies the checked-in code compiles and applicable tests pass
Continuous integration	An integration build that triggers automatically during a check-in
Check-in	Another name for a continuous integration build
Partial	An integration build that only compiles and tests a part of the whole product
Full or Complete or System	An integration build that compiles everything and runs all tests
Nightly	A full build that is scheduled to run at night
Private	A buddy build where the *buddy* is Team Foundation Build and it uses a shelveset
Gated check-in	A private build triggered by a check-in, but the check-in gets intercepted and becomes a shelveset; and if it complies with what's currently checked in and tests pass, the original code is checked in
Incremental	A build that doesn't first clean the workspace so that only new/changed files will be compiled
Label	A build that gets its source code based on a label, rather than latest
Branch	A build that gets its source code from a specific branch or folder
Main or Mainline or Trunk	A branch build from a specific branch
Debug	A build that compiles the Visual Studio project using its Debug configuration
Release	A build that compiles the Visual Studio project using its Release configuration, or a full build that also generates installers and other artifacts required to release to production
Queued	A build submitted to Team Foundation Build awaiting a build agent to become available
Partially succeeded	A build that has compiled successfully, but one or more tests have failed

Without knowing the details of your team's product, such as the amount of code and tests, how they are organized within Visual Studio solutions and projects, how long it takes to compile and run tests, and your testing and quality goals, it is impossible to recommend an effective build strategy.

That said, there are some general guidelines that all Scrum Development Teams should follow when setting up their automated builds:

- Have at least one continuous integration build defined for the product.

- If there are multiple teams, each working in a unique area of the product, then each should have its own continuous integration build.

- Continuous integration builds should run only fast, high-value tests, such as unit tests or quick integration tests that apply only to the code being built. Ideally, only the tests that are affected by the code being checked in are run.

- If it takes too long to build and test the entire application using continuous integration builds, then create another build to run on-demand or to be scheduled nightly.

- If you want to run builds that have longer-running integration tests, end-to-end system tests, load/stress tests, or that create installers or rich documentation, you will want to run those on a build agent separate from the one running your continuous integration builds. You could also run those tests and activities as part of the nightly build.

- Inspect your build definitions regularly, and adapt accordingly to ensure that they are fast and provide maximum value to the team.

Continuous integration builds are valuable only if the team actively responds to their outputs. These types of builds are meant to give immediate feedback to the developer who checked in the changeset. Ideally, this feedback is a green light to keep on working on the next task, but red lights should not be ignored. Your code doesn't agree with what's been checked in. Keeping the scope of what is built and tested to a minimum will shorten this feedback loop. Continuous integration without inspection is just continuous compilation, and that's waste!

Tailspin Toys case study The team will create several automated builds. They will create continuous integration builds to compile and run tests for each of the major components (individual Visual Studio projects). They will also create a nightly build of the entire product (the whole Visual Studio solution). The nightly build will output four different flavors: 32- and 64-bit in both debug and release configuration. This gives the team some options each day on which one to deploy and test against. Continuous integration builds were selected over gated check-in builds under the Dev folder, but gated check-in builds will be used under the Prod folder when performing production hotfixes.

Project portal

As previously mentioned, the Visual Studio Scrum 2.0 process template no longer contains a Sprint work item type. Therefore, the Scrum Team will need to find an alternative location for documenting and publishing the Sprint Goal and Sprint Retrospective notes. Sticky notes or whiteboards work fine, but these can make it challenging for stakeholders to find the information. Also, if you want to track changes or control access of who can change these items, an electronic solution is preferred. The obvious solution is to use a team project's project portal, which is hosted on SharePoint by default.

On the project portal, you can easily create a wiki entry or upload a document to track these items. You can also make visible other pieces of documentation on the portal if you wish, such as:

- Product and Sprint Backlogs

- Release and Sprint burndown charts

- Velocity chart

- Calendar showing releases and Sprints

- Development Team's Definition of "Done"

- Development Team's standards and practices

- Stakeholder contact list

- Links to build reports and build drops

- Additional documentation and notes

Having a project portal is optional, but highly recommended. If you decide to configure one, it can be hosted either on SharePoint (WSS3/2007 or 2010) or on another website. The advantage to using SharePoint is that, when properly configured, it enables you to view and manage your documents and document libraries from within Team Explorer. The project portal settings can be managed from Team Explorer, as you can see in Figure 4-7.

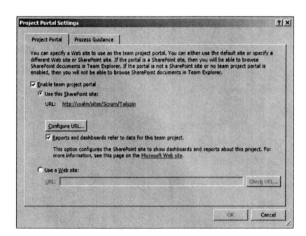

FIGURE 4-7 Configuring project portal settings.

Note The hosted Team Foundation Service, the Basic Team Foundation Server installation, and Team Foundation Server Express don't enable SharePoint integration. These configurations won't show a Documents folder listed in Team Explorer. You can, however, configure an alternative website as a project portal. Referring to Figure 4-7, you would do this by enabling a team project portal, selecting Use A Web Site, and specifying the Uniform Resource Locator (URL).

Definition of "Done"

A team should not hide its Sprint Goal or its Definition of "Done." Make these broadly available so that all stakeholders know what you are working on and what your definition of quality is. In addition, teams may want to increase transparency by publishing their burndown and Velocity reports. I've even seen teams go so far as to publish these in the break room or cafeteria. Now that's confidence!

A great place to store the Definition of "Done" in SharePoint is to use the wiki. You can see an example of this in Figure 4-8. The wiki is a site that enables ideas to be captured, shared, and collectively updated by a community of authors (the team). This community ensures the accuracy and relevance of the content.

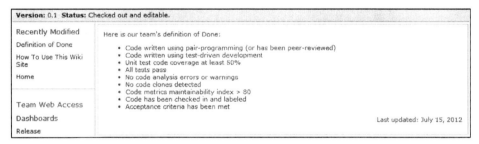

FIGURE 4-8 Use the SharePoint wiki to capture a team's Definition of "Done."

When using SharePoint to host the Definition of "Done," security permissions should be configured for individuals or groups of users. For example, you might want all members of the Scrum Team to be able to change the Definition of "Done," but not the stakeholders. A best practice is to create and manage membership in Windows groups and then assign those groups respective permissions in SharePoint.

Tailspin Toys case study Andy opted to install and configure SharePoint Foundation 2010 at the same time as Team Foundation Server 2012. When Andy created the Tailspin team project, a corresponding Tailspin portal was also created. This project portal will be used for the Scrum Team, stakeholders, and other interested parties to monitor the development progress. The Scrum Team has created a wiki entry to track its Definition of "Done" and plans to create separate wiki entries for Sprint Goals and Sprint Retrospectives as well. Andy has given all of the members of the Scrum Team Full Control permissions and a few stakeholders the Read permission. Andy will tighten the permissions if the team abuses them.

Reports

In the previous chapter, we looked at the reports available in the Visual Studio Scrum process template. These reports break down into two categories: tracking progress and tracking quality. I sometimes refer to the two categories as *process* and *product*. You can see the full list of reports in Figure 4-9.

FIGURE 4-9 Visual Studio Scrum reports listed in Team Explorer.

All of these reports were in the Visual Studio Scrum 1.0 process template, with the exception of the Backlog Overview report. This new report is essentially the popular User Stories Overview report from the MSF for the Agile Software Development process template. It has been tweaked, of course, to work with the Visual Studio Scrum 2.0 template. For example, it reports on PBIs rather than user stories. Table 4-9 lists each report and the reasons why a Scrum Team might want to run it.

TABLE 4-9 Reports in a Visual Studio Scrum team project.

Report	Process	Product	Why run it?
Backlog Overview	✓		Helps you track progress for each of your PBIs. Shows the number of hours remaining and the acceptance test results for each PBI.
Release Burndown	✓		Indicates how quickly the team is completing work and delivering PBIs. Its primary use is for planning when to schedule a release and to track the team's progress toward delivering on its goals.
Sprint Burndown	✓		Indicates the team's progress towards completing its work for a Sprint.
Velocity	✓		Indicates the amount of effort the team is putting in to complete each Sprint.
Build Success Over Time		✓	Helps you track changes in the quality of the code that the team has checked in. Shows test results for the last build of each day.
Build Summary		✓	Helps you determine the status of each build. Shows a list of builds with test results, test coverage, code churn, and quality notes.
Test Case Readiness		✓	Helps you track how many test cases are ready to be run. Shows the number of test cases in each state of preparation.
Test Plan Progress		✓	Helps you track the progress of your test plans. Shows the results of running the tests over time.

With reports, you get out of them what you put into them. I have worked with a number of teams over the years who ask me why their reports are empty. When I ask if they are using work items or automated builds, their answer is "No." I tell them that's why their reports are empty. You can't expect Team Foundation Server to provide rich, meaningful reports if you don't do the work. You need to use all three *pillars* of Team Foundation Server for all of the reports to be populated: source control, work items, and automated builds.

Even if you are using Team Foundation Server properly, you still need to make sure that you put the data in correctly. This includes using the correct states, linking to the correct work item types, and updating the right fields. I've seen several Scrum Teams using Team Foundation Server effectively, but without knowing about a key state or linkage, only to find that their reports don't work and they aren't able to assess progress easily. Here is some guidance on what actions to take to get more meaningful data from your reports:

- **Backlog Overview report** Link PBIs to tasks. If you divide a task into subtasks, specify hours *only* for the subtasks because these hours are rolled up as summary values for the parent task. Update hours remaining on the tasks each day. Link PBIs to test cases using *tested by* links. Run your tests and mark them as pass or fail. Ensure that all work items are in the correct area, iteration, and state.

- **Release Burndown report** Provide an *effort* value for each Product Backlog Item and Bug work item. Set the *iteration* of the Product Backlog Item or Bug work item when it is forecasted to be done in that Sprint. Ensure that all work items are in the correct area, iteration, and state. Done and Removed work items are ignored.

- **Sprint Burndown** Ensure the *Sprint* node has start and end dates defined. Link PBIs to tasks. If you divide a task into subtasks, specify hours *only* for the subtasks because these hours are rolled up as summary values for the parent task. Update hours remaining on the tasks each day. Ensure that all tasks are in the correct area, iteration, and state.

- **Velocity** Provide an *effort* value for each Product Backlog Item and Bug work item. Set the *iteration* of the Product Backlog Item or Bug work item to the Sprint that it was forecasted to be developed. Ensure that all completed Product Backlog Item and Bug work items are in the Done state.

Tip What should you do with tasks that are *not* directly related to the PBIs and bugs that a team has forecasted for the Sprint? I encourage teams to record all significant activities and I let the team decide the definition of significant. If the team wants to create "stand-alone" Task work items for activities such as setting up hardware, installing software, and attending meetings, then they can do this. Realize that any tasks, even those not related to PBIs or bugs, will influence the Sprint Burndown report. Remember that nearly all of the work a Development Team does during the Sprint should originate from the Product Backlog, as this is what has been negotiated between the Product Owner and the business, as well as the Product Owner and the Development Team. If the team decides not to track these kinds of activities as Task work items, they can still rest assured that their efforts will be reflected in the measured Velocity. Transparency and visibility really helps everyone keep their focus on the Sprint Goal. If things get too far off, they should be visible by others and handled by the Scrum Master/coach or in the Retrospective.

 Smell It's a smell when reports are empty. Scrum doesn't officially acknowledge reports or any other artifacts as being required. The rules do say that a Scrum Team should assess progress regularly. Team Foundation Server reports are a great way to do that, but if the team is able to forecast progress using some other method, I'm fine with that. Also, I've worked with high-performance Scrum Teams that choose *not* to create Task work items during a Sprint and instead formulate the plan using sticky notes or through conversation. In this case, the Sprint Burndown report would be empty because no Task work items exist. Without tracking tasks, there would be no long-term transparency into what occurred during the Sprint either.

Reports can be opened from Team Explorer and displayed within Visual Studio. If you know the URL of the SQL Server Reporting Services Report Manager site, you can go there directly to view and manage the reports. Team Explorer makes this shortcut available, as do the SharePoint Project Portal and Web Access sites.

Security permissions should be configured on reports for individuals or groups of users to allow them to or deny them from running reports. Normally, I'm a fan of maximizing permissions for the Scrum Team, but when it comes to reports, there's really not a lot of interesting things you do with them on a daily basis other than to run them. In other words, there's not a lot of value in giving the Scrum Team anything more than the Browser permission. You can see an example of setting permissions in Figure 4-10.

There are times when you may want to edit a report and tweak its caching options or add a subscription. You may even want to upload an entirely new report *.rdl file in its place. The user making these types of changes will need the Team Foundation Content Manager permission. By default, only administrators have this permission.

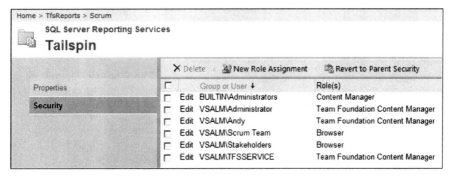

FIGURE 4-10 Setting report security for the Scrum Team and stakeholders.

Tailspin Toys case study Andy configured SQL Server 2012 Reporting Services when he configured Team Foundation Server. As a result, each project created, such as Tailspin, will have all available reports. Since the team will be spending a lot of time in the Agile planning tools, they will use those built-in burndown and Velocity charts, as they are updated more frequently than reports that depend on the data warehouse and cube. The team plans to follow the practices outlined in this book to ensure that the reports contain meaningful data and can be used to measure progress. During their regular Sprint Retrospective meetings, they will review the costs of tracking certain data and compare that against the benefit of producing meaningful queries and reports for them and the stakeholders to determine if there is any waste in their process.

Security groups

By default, team projects contain four project-level groups with a default set of permissions. These are created at the time the team project is created, and they are all empty. The exception is the Project Administrators group, which contains the user who created the team project. This group is populated by the user who created the project, which is typically a Project Collection administrator. The project administrator must decide who else needs access to the team project, and what level of permission they need. Here are some details about the built-in groups:

- **Project Administrators** Members of this group can administer all aspects of the team project, although they cannot create new projects. A Team Foundation Server administrator is required to create the team project.

- **Contributors** Members of this group can contribute to the project in multiple ways, such as adding, modifying, and deleting code and creating and modifying work items.

- **Build Administrators** Members of this group are contributors with additional, build-related permissions, such as being able to create and manage build definitions, delete and destroy builds, and manage the build queue and qualities.

- **Readers** Members of this group can view the project but not modify it.

The obvious choice here is to add all of the members of the Scrum Team (including the Product Owner and Scrum Master) to the Contributors group, and stakeholders to the Readers group. I think this is a valid choice, but it can lead to impediments during the Sprint. For example, if the project administrator is unavailable, the developers might be blocked from adding a new work item Area node or creating a shared query. These sound like minor things, but they can add up during the course of a day or a week. I believe that if a team has a certain level of proficiency in the tool, and the members trust one another, that they should all be project administrators. This epitomizes the self-organization and self-managing qualities of the Development Team. You can easily do this by adding a Windows group, such as Scrum Team, to the Project Administrators security group, as I've done in Figure 4-11.

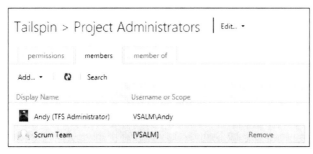

FIGURE 4-11 Adding the Scrum Team (Windows) group to the Project Administrators (TFS) group.

Tailspin Toys case study After Andy created the Tailspin team project, he added the Windows group Scrum Team to the Project Administrators group. During Sprint Retrospectives, the team will discuss and decide if this level of permission should be ratcheted down for any team members.

Teams

Teams are a new concept in Team Foundation Server 2012. They allow the grouping of collaborating team members who will be working on similar areas and iterations of the product. They also enable access to the new Agile planning tools. Behind the scenes, teams are implemented as Team Foundation Server groups and have a similar set of permissions. In fact, a new team has the same permissions as the Contributors group by default. Teams differ from groups in that they enable their members to access and use the Agile planning tools in order to define and manage their Product Backlog, Sprint Backlog, and task board.

When a team project is created, a default team is created with the same name as the project. Developers can be added to this team and start using the Agile planning features right away, without the need for additional configuration. The project administrator can create additional teams as well. Team members can be members of more than one group.

Note When you create a new team, Team Foundation Server will also create a similarly named area path by default. This ensures a strong connection between teams and areas. As you can see in Figure 4-12, you can skip this by clicking the Settings tab of the Create New Team dialog box and clearing the Team area option. Also, keep in mind that if you rename your team, it will not rename the area path. You will have to do that manually.

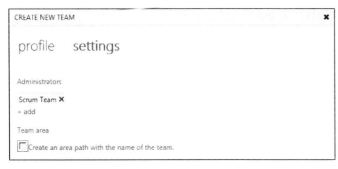

FIGURE 4-12 The option to create a matching area path when creating a new team.

The user who created the team becomes the team's administrator. Team administrators can edit the membership of the team, as well as delete the team. All team members, even non-team administrators, can edit the properties of the team, which include team areas, team iterations (Backlog and Sprints), and team favorites.

After creating a team, its iterations and areas can be specified. Iterations that the team selects will appear in the Backlog as Sprints on the left side. A user can drag Product Backlog Item and Bug work item types to these Sprints for planning. The areas that a team specifies determine what work items show up in the team's Backlog. Teams can also designate one of those areas as its default. This is then suggested when creating work items from the Product Backlog and work items hub within Web Access, as well as within Team Explorer and Team Explorer Everywhere. It does not get offered as a default value in Microsoft Excel, Microsoft Project, Test Manager, or when running reports.

> **Note** If you have only one team then it is considered the *default* team. You can think of this team as the "root" team, which exists at the team project level. You can rename this default team, but you can't delete it. To delete it, you have to create a second team and make it the default first. You might just as well have renamed it. Also, if you want to configure the default team's areas and iterations, you will do it on the team project's control panel page, not the team's.

Team Foundation Server allows a user to belong to more than one team. Before considering this, make sure that it makes sense to do so. Rarely do developers belong to more than one Scrum Team within the same product. If they are a shared resource between a few, but not all teams, then this would make sense. You can see an example of this in Figure 4-13. If the goal is to add the Product Owner or Scrum Master to each team, then they should be added to the default team instead. This will have the same net effect with less overhead.

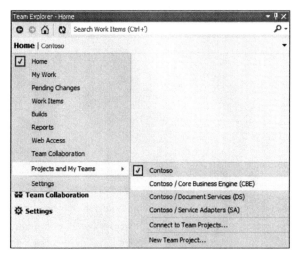

FIGURE 4-13 Selecting a team within Team Explorer.

Tailspin Toys case study Andy renamed the default team to *Scrum*, uploaded a team photo, and added the Scrum Team group in Windows group to it. Knowing that the team members are familiar with the tool and trustworthy, Andy also made them all team administrators. He did this by again adding the Scrum Team Windows group as a Scrum team administrator. During Sprint Retrospectives, the team will discuss and decide if this level of permission should be ratcheted down for any team members.

Chapter burndown

Here are the key concepts we covered in this chapter:

- **Team Foundation Server** You can either pay to play on the Microsoft-hosted Team Foundation Service or license, install, and use an on-premises Team Foundation Server.

- **Team Project Collections** Team projects within the same collection enjoy the ability to copy, link, and query work items, as well as branch and merge code across projects.

- **Team Foundation Build** Use Team Foundation Build to automate the compiling and testing of either your entire application or just components of it. Install build agents on dedicated machines with fast hardware and I/O to shorten the build–test feedback loop.

- **Team Project** The team project is the container for your product's lifecycle management. One team project can support the development of multiple areas, releases, Sprints, and teams.

- **Source Control** Plan and create an initial folder structure to support the development of your product and its components. Establish a branching strategy that reduces complexity and the need to merge. Save your creativity for your product.

- **Project Portal and Reports** Use SharePoint and SQL Server to increase transparency by extending information to your stakeholders. Use the SharePoint wiki or document library to manage your definition of done and Sprint Goals.

- **Security Groups and Teams** Add all Scrum Team members to the Project Administrators group and Team Administrators group to avoid impediments. Ratchet this back as Retrospectives deem it necessary.

CHAPTER 5

The Product Backlog

The Product Backlog is an ordered list of everything that might be required of the software product. It is the single source listing all requirements for any changes to be made to the product. It includes features to be added, changes to be made, and bugs to be fixed. Each item in the Product Backlog is called a Product Backlog item (PBI). PBIs can range from extremely important and urgent to trivial.

While the Product Owner is responsible for the Product Backlog, he or she may have others create and update its items. However, it is the Product Owner's responsibility to ensure that the items in the Product Backlog are clearly defined, understood by the Development Team, assigned a business value, and ordered (prioritized) correctly. The Development Team collaborates with the Product Owner—and other domain experts, as needed—during Product Backlog grooming sessions, Sprint Planning meetings, and the Sprint Review to understand and estimate the items in the Product Backlog.

This chapter will focus on how to use Microsoft Visual Studio Team Web Access to create and groom the Product Backlog. You will also see how a healthy Product Backlog can enable release planning, and how to do that using these tools. If you are more interested in the concept of the Product Backlog, and less on how to use tools to interact with it, you may wish to read Chapter 1, "Scrumdamentals."

Creating the Product Backlog

You create the Product Backlog one work item at a time. Both PBI and Bug work item types appear in the backlog. By default, only a title is needed in order to save a new work item to the Product Backlog. Yet the Product Owner will probably require more information in order to assign the item a business value and order it. The Development Team will definitely need more information than just a title in order to estimate it. Having a title is a good start, though.

> **Note** In Scrum, there is only the PBI. A PBI can be a bug. Microsoft Team Foundation Server, however, differentiates between a PBI and a bug. This is because the Bug work item type tracks different information (reproduction steps, system information, etc.). If you don't care about tracking these additional details, then you can use a PBI work item type for a bug.

According to the *Scrum Guide*, the Product Owner is responsible for the Product Backlog. This doesn't necessarily mean that he or she is the one *doing* the data entry. It just means that the Product Owner is responsible for ensuring that each PBI is clearly defined and understandable. In Team Foundation Server, anybody with the appropriate permission can create work items. A project administrator can control this ability at a high level in the team project security settings, and at a more detailed level at the area and iteration security settings. As stated previously, I feel that everyone on the Scrum Team should be able to contribute to the Product Backlog—at a minimum. The Product Owner may also want other stakeholders, such as business analysts, customers, or the users themselves, to be able to create work items. If someone other than the Product Owner creates the work item, a conversation should take place so that person can explain its context, purpose, and business value.

When someone creates a PBI, he or she should focus on its value (the *what*), and avoid descriptions of *how* the Development Team should develop the item. When it comes time, the Product Owner can order the Product Backlog based on each item's value, risk, priority, or necessity. The Product Backlog can evolve quickly if the business requirements of your product and other conditions constantly change. To minimize waste, detailed requirements should be avoided except for the highest-ordered items. The teams that I have worked with preferred having two to three Sprints' worth of groomed PBIs at the tip of their iceberg.

Team Web Access

In Visual Studio 2012, you use Team Web Access (or Web Access for short) to connect to Team Foundation Server and coordinate your development efforts with other team members. You can use Web Access to manage your work and your team projects. Web Access is a customizable web interface that provides most of the functionality that is available in Team Explorer, as well as additional tools for managing work items. You can use Web Access to find and update work items, view and compare version-controlled files, and queue automated builds. Web Access is automatically installed and configured with Team Foundation Server.

The Scrum Team can manage the Product Backlog and Sprint Backlog by using the backlog page of Web Access. The Development Team can manage its tasks within a Sprint by using the task board page. From these two different pages, team members can perform the following activities:

- Capture the work to be developed in the form of PBI and Bug work items.

- Define epic, theme, or user-story PBIs to capture the vision of the software product and its roadmap.

- Plan a Sprint by dragging work items from the Product Backlog to a Sprint.

- Switch views from the Product Backlog to a Sprint Backlog (past, present, or future).

- Review burndown charts, update tasks, and track progress for the current Sprint.

Note You cannot manage your Product Backlog or Sprint Backlog visually using Visual Studio Team Explorer. If you want to access the Agile management tools, including the "quick add" feature and drag-and-drop functionality, you have to use Team Web Access.

In Web Access, you will use the backlog page to capture the work to be developed in the form of PBI and Bug work items. The PBI work items can be user stories, requirements, or features. The ordered (prioritized) list of work items in the Product Backlog captures the vision and release plan (roadmap) for the software product. Although you can use Team Explorer, Microsoft Excel, or other client applications to manage the Product Backlog, the backlog page in Web Access should be the primary user interface (UI).

Licensing and permissions

At the time of this writing, the Web Access licensing details are still being sorted out. There will be three levels of licensing: limited, standard, and full. These can be viewed and managed on the Web Access tab of the Control Panel root page, as you can see in Figure 5-1.

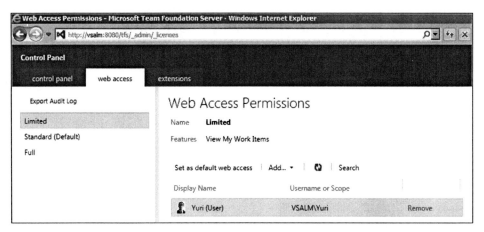

FIGURE 5-1 Assigning Web Access permissions.

Here is a short explanation of the different licensing levels:

- **Limited** Users can create and view only their own work items, such as Bugs. This is similar to the Work Item Only View (WIOV) licensing from prior versions. This licensing level doesn't require a copy of Visual Studio or a Team Foundation Server Client Access License (CAL).

- **Standard (default)** Users can use the standard Web Access features, including the task board. These users *cannot* use the backlog pages to view and manage the Product Backlog or Sprint Backlog. They also cannot solicit stakeholder feedback using those tools. This licensing level is intended for developers using the Visual Studio 2012 Professional edition or any stakeholder with a Team Foundation Server CAL.

- **Full** Users can use all of the Web Access features. This is intended for developers using the Test Professional, Premium, or Ultimate editions of Visual Studio 2012. I recommend that everyone on the Scrum Team is licensed at this level.

The edition of Visual Studio that you have installed has no effect on the access-level license. License compliance is based completely on the honor system. By default, everyone is in the *Standard* group, which is simply a convenience. An administrator will need to ensure that a new user is put into the correct licensing group.

Tailspin Toys case study Paula (the Product Owner) and Scott (the Scrum Master) each own a license of Visual Studio 2012 Test Professional edition. Each of the developers owns a license of Visual Studio 2012 Premium or Ultimate edition. Therefore, everyone on the Scrum Team is licensed to use the full set of Web Access features, including the backlog management features. There is discussion that some stakeholders might purchase a Team Foundation Server CAL or use the limited, CAL-less licensing mode solely to create work items for the team's consideration.

Membership in one of the licensing groups is not enough to interact with a team project; however, an administrator must also add the user to one of the built-in permission groups: readers, contributors, or project administrators. To manage the Product Backlog or a Sprint Backlog, including adding and editing work items, a user must at least be a member of the contributors group or have the Edit Work Items In This Node permission set to Allow for the team project.

Tip My guidance for high-performance Scrum Teams is to make everyone, even the developers, a project administrator. This minimizes impediments caused by the tools, such as not being able to create new areas and iterations, or manage many details around source control and build features. Remember that members of a high-performance Scrum Team trust one another and know how to use the tools too.

Using the "quick add" experience

The easiest way to create a new PBI or Bug is to use the *"quick add"* panel on the backlog page. As you can see in Figure 5-2, you can use this panel to add a PBI or Bug work item quickly. It's fast, because you only have to provide a title. You can enter several items in rapid succession. This can be helpful during the Sprint Review meeting, when ideas are flying about the room.

The "quick add" feature is on by default. If you want some more screen real estate, you can turn it off. You can do this by either clicking the Close button in the upper-right corner of the panel or by clicking the *on* hyperlink next to the "Add Items" label on the right side of the screen. To show the panel again, click the *off* hyperlink in the same area.

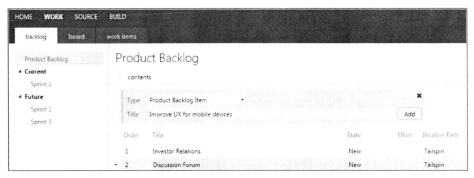

FIGURE 5-2 Using the "quick add" panel to add a PBI.

Work items that you add this way will only have the title specified. The rest of the fields will be assigned their default values, some of which might need to be changed, such as the Assigned To field. Most Scrum Teams I work with like to assign PBI and Bug work items to the Product Owner, since he or she is the owner until the Sprint in which the team forecasts its development. It is blank by default. Over time, as more is known, the work item will get updated. To open the work item, you can just double-click it in the backlog page.

Note In a future version of Visual Studio, I'd like to be able to specify more information about the Scrum Team. I'd like to be able to indicate the team's Product Owner and Scrum Master. By doing this, Team Foundation Server could auto-assign PBI and Bug work items to the Product Owner. I hope this is on Microsoft's backlog.

When you add a work item using the "quick add" feature, it will appear above whatever item you have selected in the backlog. If you have the last item selected, then it will be added below that one. Work items added through other applications, such as Team Explorer or Microsoft Test Manager, will appear at the bottom of the list. This behavior is due to the fact that the Product Backlog is sorted by the Backlog Priority field of a work item. Work items with a null Backlog Priority appear at the bottom of the list. You will, more than likely, want to reorder these items by dragging them elsewhere in the list.

There are many other ways to add work items to the Product Backlog. From the team project's home page, there are shortcuts for adding PBIs and Bugs, as you can see in Figure 5-3. You can also add work items from the work items page. While there is no "quick add" experience on the work items page, it does offer many time-saving features such as Bulk Edit, Clone, Copy, and Link shortcuts.

Tip After adding or editing a work item, you may have to refresh the screen manually. Also, there is no button or link to click to refresh. You'll have to refresh the browser manually by pressing F5.

FIGURE 5-3 Work item shortcuts found on the team project's Home page.

Tailspin Toys case study During Sprint Review meetings, as the Increment is being demonstrated, the stakeholders in the room tend to get excited and start rapidly coming up with new ideas and features. This "feature frenzy," as the Development Team calls it, will generally bear good fruit, while other times, these ideas should be thrown into the fire. Either way, the feedback should be captured, and the "quick add" panel makes this possible.

Removing an item from the Product Backlog

From time to time, you may want to remove a work item from the Product Backlog—or anywhere else in Team Foundation Server, for that matter. The work item may have been entered in error or was a duplicate. You cannot delete work items from Web Access, Team Explorer, Test Manager, or Excel. This is by design. The recommended way of "deleting" a work item is to set its state to Removed, and then add a comment to the discussion on the History tab. By default, PBI and Bug work items in this state are not displayed in the Product Backlog or other views.

If you want to remove a work item permanently, you can use the Witadmin.exe command-line utility. Just pass it the `destroywi` command, along with the team project collection URL and work item ID. These work items are removed from the Team Foundation Server database and cannot be restored or reactivated.

Customizing the "quick add" panel

You can customize the "quick add" panel and add more fields. You might want to do this for important PBI and Bug work item fields that don't have a default value, such as *Description*, *Business Value*, or *Effort*. You can also add additional work items to the drop-down list by adding them to the Requirements work item category, as discussed in Chapter 3, "Microsoft Visual Studio Scrum 2.0." You probably won't be doing this if you are using the Scrum template though, because it already maps perfectly to Scrum.

Here are the high-level steps to follow in order to customize the "quick add" panel:

1. Use Witadmin exportagileprocess.config to export the Agile Process.xml configuration file for the team project.

Note You can also use the Process Editor found in the Team Foundation Server Power Tools.

2. Edit the exported configuration file and locate the *AddPanel* element.

3. Add a *Field* element that specifies the reference name of the field that you want to add to the panel. For example, you could add the *Microsoft.VSTS.Common.BusinessValue* field, as shown here (see bold):

```xml
<?xml version="1.0" encoding="utf-8"?>
<AgileProjectConfiguration>
  <IterationBacklog>
    <Columns>
      <Column width="50" refname="Microsoft.VSTS.Scheduling.Effort" />
      <Column width="400" refname="System.Title" />
      <Column width="100" refname="System.State" />
      <Column width="100" refname="System.AssignedTo" />
      <Column width="50" refname="Microsoft.VSTS.Scheduling.RemainingWork" />
    </Columns>
  </IterationBacklog>
  <ProductBacklog>
    <AddPanel>
      <Fields>
        <Field refname="System.Title" />
        <Field refname="Microsoft.VSTS.Common.BusinessValue" />
      </Fields>
    </AddPanel>
    <Columns>
      <Column width="400" refname="System.Title" />
      <Column width="100" refname="System.State" />
      <Column width="50" refname="Microsoft.VSTS.Scheduling.Effort" />
      <Column width="200" refname="System.IterationPath" />
    </Columns>
  </ProductBacklog>
</AgileProjectConfiguration>
```

4. Save the file.

5. Use Witadmin importagileprocess.config to import the updated configuration file back to the team project.

 Note The "quick add" panel cannot be customized for the hosted Team Foundation Service.

After you have re-imported the configuration file, you must refresh the backlog page. After that, you can start using the new field(s) as you add items to the Product Backlog. Figure 5-4 shows the customized "quick add" panel.

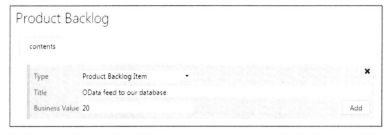

FIGURE 5-4 The customized "quick add" panel showing the additional field.

Handling epic PBIs

An epic PBI is any PBI that is too large to be completed in a single Sprint or by a single team. For example, if the Development Team has a Velocity of 18 points, they should not forecast a PBI that is 21 points. Even if a team is not using Velocity as a forecasting tool, they should never take on more work than they feel they can accomplish. In either case, the PBI must be decomposed. The intricacies of how to split a PBI effectively are beyond the scope of this chapter. Suffice it to say that it's a combination of science, art, magic, and a bit of luck at times.

> **Smell** It's a smell when I see an epic PBI near the top of an ordered Product Backlog. It should be decomposed well in advance of the Sprint in which it is forecast to be developed.

The relevant question then becomes, how do we track the original, as well as the decomposed PBIs in Team Foundation Server? There are three approaches as I see it, and unfortunately, Web Access doesn't provide direct support for any of them.

Let's assume that you have an epic PBI to "Improve UX for mobile devices," as seen in Figure 5-5. (UX stands for *user experience*.) Since this PBI's effort is larger than our Velocity of 18, it must be decomposed.

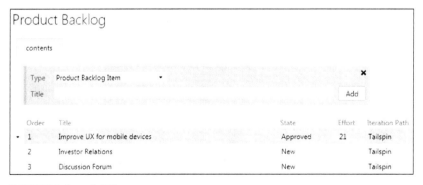

FIGURE 5-5 An epic PBI.

The first approach would be to create additional, child-linked PBIs. Each of these would have smaller efforts, achievable in a single Sprint. The epic parent PBI would become a permanent placeholder. The team would never directly forecast or develop it. When all of the child PBIs were developed, someone would have to set its state manually to Done. The advantage to this approach is that it establishes a visual context.

To create the parent-child hierarchy, simply drag the child work item underneath the parent work item. If the parent already has children, as in Figure 5-6, you can drop it above the first child or in between any of the children. If your intention is to make the work item the *last* child in the hierarchy, then you will need to drop the work item on the parent's *Order* field (which you can see as the darker square on the left side of Figure 5-6). Dropping it on the parent's title, or anywhere else in the row, will just order the work item above the parent. To break an existing parent-child relationship, just drag the child out from under the parent to somewhere else in the Product Backlog.

> **Note** You can also establish the parent-child relationship manually by creating the respective links to the parent from the child (or vice versa). While you are creating the links, you may also want to tweak the Backlog Priority value, as it influences the order that the children are listed under the parent.

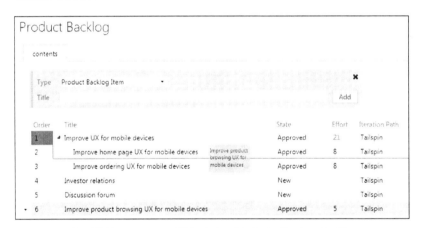

FIGURE 5-6 Establishing a parent-child relationship in the Product Backlog.

A disadvantage to using this parent-child approach is that you cannot order the child PBIs individually. They must stay together as an atomic unit. As soon as you drag the first child PBI above (or below) the parent PBI, the hierarchy is destroyed. Another disadvantage is that you now have something in your backlog which isn't really a PBI. Some of my fellow Professional Scrum Developers would consider this noise, or even waste. Also, if you accidentally (or on purpose) left the parent PBI's effort value, it could mess up any forecasting or release planning. The forecasting tool in the Product Backlog list is smart enough, however, to not double-count the effort of the parent and its children. Other queries, reports, or manual processes may not be that smart. To be safe, you should set the epic parent PBI's Effort to zero after the children are linked. Figure 5-7 shows a completed parent-child relationship of an epic PBI with the parent's Effort removed.

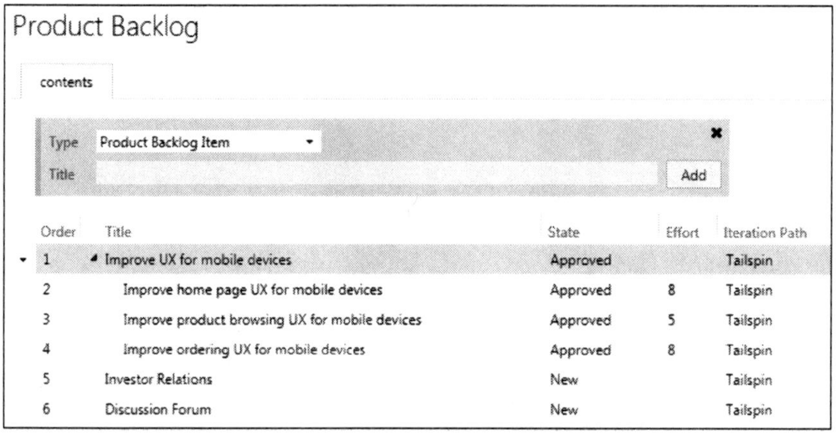

Product Backlog

contents

Type	Product Backlog Item ▾			✖
Title				Add

Order	Title	State	Effort	Iteration Path
▾ 1	◢ Improve UX for mobile devices	Approved		Tailspin
2	Improve home page UX for mobile devices	Approved	8	Tailspin
3	Improve product browsing UX for mobile devices	Approved	5	Tailspin
4	Improve ordering UX for mobile devices	Approved	8	Tailspin
5	Investor Relations	New		Tailspin
6	Discussion Forum	New		Tailspin

FIGURE 5-7 Decomposing an epic PBI into child PBIs.

> **Tip** From the work items page, you can right-click the epic PBI and Select Link Selected Item(s) To A New Work Item. You can then choose a child to link to a PBI. At the time of this writing, this capability is not supported on the backlog page.

The second approach would be to edit and rename the original PBI, making it one of the eventual children. Then you would add two more PBIs as siblings of the first one, as shown in Figure 5-8. You will lose the "big picture" of the epic, as well as the context that they were once related under a common epic PBI, but you won't have any dummy items in your Product Backlog. If you can't live without this information, you can keep them associated by using a title naming convention, description, or history note. You can always review the change history of the first PBI to see that it used to be an epic PBI.

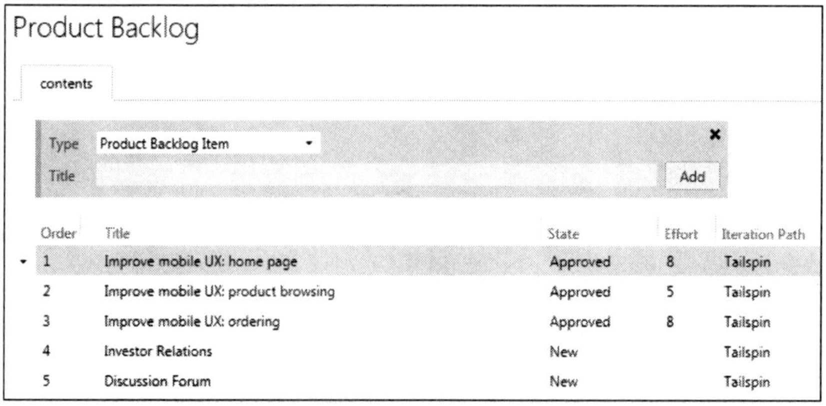

Product Backlog

contents

Type	Product Backlog Item ▾			✖
Title				Add

Order	Title	State	Effort	Iteration Path
▾ 1	Improve mobile UX: home page	Approved	8	Tailspin
2	Improve mobile UX: product browsing	Approved	5	Tailspin
3	Improve mobile UX: ordering	Approved	8	Tailspin
4	Investor Relations	New		Tailspin
5	Discussion Forum	New		Tailspin

FIGURE 5-8 Decomposing an epic PBI into sibling PBIs.

The third approach is really just a variation of the second. Rather than have a naming convention in the title or some common text in the description, you add a custom field to the PBI work item type to register the original epic PBI's title. This can be done manually using Notepad, or by using the Process Editor in the Team Foundation Server Power Tools. Once you have created a new field, you can customize the Product Backlog list in the backlog page to include the new field as a column.

So which approach is best? This is a classic "let the team decide" moment. For teams new to Scrum, I recommend starting with the first approach and creating the child PBIs. This helps everyone visualize and understand the breakdown of work. It also helps the Scrum Team explain to stakeholders that, "We had to do it this way because we couldn't physically build the whole feature in one Sprint." As the organization starts to grow Scrum, they can move to the second or third approach to keep the Product Backlog lean.

Tailspin Toys case study The Scrum Team is currently using the second approach. They ensure that each of the related sibling PBIs have a similar prefix or preamble in their titles. To date, nobody in the organization has requested a list of all epic PBIs. The search tool, or custom queries, have satisfied their ad hoc query needs thus far. If a report was requested, Scott (the Scrum Master) put one together manually.

Importing existing PBIs

Prior to the adoption of Team Foundation Server or Scrum, it's likely that an organization will maintain several lists of work. One might track high-level requirements of the software. Another list tracks the feature requests from the users. Yet another list tracks the bugs. These lists can range from a beautiful arrangement of sticky notes, to an Excel spreadsheet, to a Microsoft SharePoint list, even to a dedicated, third-party application lifecycle management (ALM) tool. Merging all of this data into a common Product Backlog can be difficult, and I'm not just talking about navigating the politics. Meaningful data must be extracted, transformed, and loaded.

Excel to the rescue! Excel is extremely easy to use, and everyone in the office has it. I've personally used it to create dozens of Product Backlogs over the years. Most people don't know that it can be used as an extract, transform, and load (ETL) tool. Okay, maybe it's not advertised as such, but with regards to Team Foundation Server, it's true. Using Excel, you can extract the data from your existing list (using copy/paste, one of the *Get External Data* functions, or some form of automation). The data can be transformed (normalized) and then loaded (published) to Team Foundation Server.

There are a number of ways to import existing backlog items using Excel. Here is a basic step-by-step approach that I recommend:

1. Open Excel.

2. Rename the Sheet1 worksheet to **Source** and Sheet2 to **Target**.

3. In the Source worksheet, load your data using a *Get External Data* function or the Clipboard.

4. Select the Target sheet.

5. From the Team ribbon, select New List and then Input list.

6. From the Team ribbon, select Choose Columns.

7. Select Product Backlog Item, and select the additional columns you'll want. As you can see in Figure 5-9, Description, Acceptance Criteria, Area Path, Business Value, and Effort are good columns to start with.

8. From the Source sheet, copy the respective columns and paste them into the Target sheet. Set the *Work Item Type*, *Product Owner*, and other fields manually.

9. Clean up the data, especially if you are importing *Area Path*, *State*, or any numeric data.

10. From the Team ribbon, select Publish. If an error occurs, read the message, correct the error(s), and then publish again.

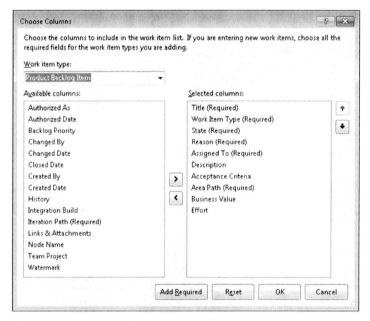

FIGURE 5-9 Selecting additional PBI columns to import.

 Tip Fellow Professional Scrum Developer, Simon Reindl, prefers to start with a custom query that already has the interesting columns selected. These queries are especially useful if he has to run a similar migration again in the future.

The normal state transition workflow of a PBI or Bug work item is New > Approved > Committed > Done. When importing historical items, it can be tedious to change the state several times, saving in between. Microsoft made a nice improvement in the Visual Studio Scrum 2 process template that helps in this situation. When you first create a work item, the state is New. You can now change it directly to Committed or Done. This saves a couple of steps and save operations.

Once you've published the work items, you can continue to use the Excel spreadsheet to make bulk edits to that set of data. You should save the file if you plan on doing this. If this was a one-time import and you are happy with the results, then you can discard the document.

You can also use Web Access to make bulk edits to work items. You will need to be on the work items page. The backlog page doesn't support bulk editing. After running the query you want on the work items page, use the Ctrl and Alt key combinations to select the work items you want to bulk-edit. With the rows selected, click the small drop-down arrow, and then from the pop-up context menu, select Edit Selected Work Item(s). You can also quickly assign the work items to a new team member, move them to a different Sprint, or link them to a work item.

Editing a work item is different than opening it. When opening, it opens the Work Item form, allowing you to see and change all the fields as normal. Editing a work item (or items) allows you to specify a value for one or more fields. As you can see in Figure 5-10, all selected work items will be updated. You can also set a note for the history, which I recommend, to increase traceability.

FIGURE 5-10 Using Web Access to bulk-edit work items.

 Smell It's a smell when I see tasks, impediments, statements, goals, gripes, or guidance in the Product Backlog. What I'm talking about is a PBI titled, "We should back up the database each night" or "Let's stop meeting in the hallway for our Daily Scrum." The Product Backlog should only contain items that represent a potential change in the software product being developed. This is not to say that a valid PBI couldn't have some goals or guidance attached to it—you just don't document them in the Product Backlog.

If you plan on importing items regularly or have a lot of complex data scrubbing to perform, you might consider building a custom import tool. You can use the Microsoft .NET Framework to read the source data and perform any transformations that are required. You can then use the Team Foundation Server object model to connect to the team project and create the work items. The Team Foundation Server Software Development Kit (SDK) contains sample code, as do a number of projects on CodePlex.

> **Tip** The TFS Integration Platform on CodePlex (*http://tfsintegration.codeplex.com*) is a framework that helps other tools integrate with Team Foundation Server. It contains good sample code and approaches to creating work items and dependencies. You can also check out the Test Case Migrator Plus project (*http://tcmimport.codeplex.com*). Although it is more focused on importing test cases, it contains some great sample code that you can repurpose for a custom tool.

Reporting a bug

Bugs are backlog items too. In Scrum, there is no differentiation between a feature and a bug. Both represent something that must be developed in the software product. Team Foundation Server does differentiate. In Team Foundation Server, the Bug work item type tracks additional information over a PBI work item, such as the steps to reproduce the bug, the severity, the system information, and the build number that the bug was found and fixed in. Bugs are treated just like other PBIs, insofar as they are groomed, estimated, forecast, and decomposed into tasks during Sprint Planning.

One field that a Bug work item doesn't have is *Business Value*. PBI work items have a *Business Value*, but Bug work items do not. Instead, the Bug work item has a *Severity* field. It's not quite the same as a business value, but it does let the Product Owner or a domain expert set the criticality of the bug on a scale of 1 (critical) to 4 (low).

> **Note** Having bugs in the Product Backlog is a fundamental difference between the Visual Studio Scrum process template and the other MSF Agile and CMMI templates. Both of the MSF templates dissuade teams from tracking bugs in their Product Backlog. In fact, they treat bugs as completely separate items.

Each team may handle the discovery and classification of bugs in their own way. Before reporting a bug, someone should ensure that it is a valid bug. It could be that the odd behavior that someone experienced was by design, or a training issue, or something that had already been reported. This identifying and sorting process is known as *bug triage*. Triage also includes identifying the severity, frequency, risk, and other related factors. Triaging bugs can sometimes be a collaboration of the Development Team and the Product Owner. Sometimes stakeholders, such as business analysts and experts, should be consulted to elaborate on specific domain issues and risks.

Smell It's a smell when I don't see bugs in a Product Backlog. One concern is that the Development Team isn't testing the product. It could also be that the users aren't reporting bugs. From a planning perspective, I'm more worried that bugs are being reported in another system. Many large organizations have centralized trouble-ticket or issue-tracking systems. Software bugs found in production typically start here. They shouldn't end up here though. Those bugs should be triaged and, if applicable, added to the Product Backlog. Without having bugs in the Product Backlog alongside feature requests, the Product Owner won't be able to order the items effectively to maximize the work of the Development Team and the value of the product.

Anyone should be able to report a bug. Bugs, just like everything else in the Product Backlog, are validated, estimated, ordered, and (hopefully) forecast to be fixed. It's the Product Owner's prerogative to approve the reported bug, leave it in its current state (New), or remove it from the Product Backlog.

Tailspin Toys case study Currently, anybody internal or external to the organization can email Paula or the public alias about an issue or bug in the software. Paula will see that these emails are triaged and, if prudent, that a Bug work item is created.

What makes a bug report good?

A bug report is just that—it's the reporting of a bug or other unwanted behavior in the software product. In order to write a good bug report, and thus create a good Bug work item in Team Foundation Server, it must contain enough information for the Scrum Team to understand it and gauge its impact on the business.

A good, clear title is a must. A developer should be able to grasp the essence of the bug from the title alone. If there are many work items, having a clear title will help the team as they work with the bug through grooming, forecasting, and development. It saves a user from having to read the whole work item to get its context.

Tip At the time of this writing, the backlog page doesn't differentiate between PBI and Bug work items. There are no icon or coloration differences. The work item is not listed either. Needless to say, it will be hard to tell which items are the bugs. You could consider prefixing bug titles with "Bug:" so that they stand out in the Product Backlog, as shown in Figure 5-11. Another option would be to customize the backlog columns and add the *System.WorkItemType* field. You'll learn how to do that later in this chapter.

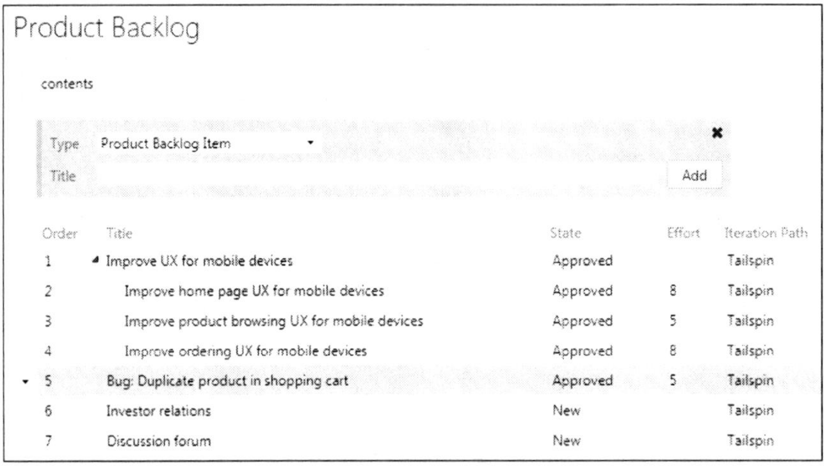

Product Backlog

contents

Type	Product Backlog Item ▾			✖
Title				Add

Order	Title	State	Effort	Iteration Path
1	◢ Improve UX for mobile devices	Approved		Tailspin
2	Improve home page UX for mobile devices	Approved	8	Tailspin
3	Improve product browsing UX for mobile devices	Approved	5	Tailspin
4	Improve ordering UX for mobile devices	Approved	8	Tailspin
▾ 5	Bug: Duplicate product in shopping cart	Approved	5	Tailspin
6	Investor relations	New		Tailspin
7	Discussion forum	New		Tailspin

FIGURE 5-11 Prefixing Bug work items with "Bug:" to distinguish them from PBI work items.

You should report only one bug per work item. If you document more than one bug, some of them may be overlooked. Atomic bug tracking helps in the same way atomic testing does—it provides a very precise understanding of what's working and what isn't.

A picture is worth a thousand words. Sometimes words just can't demonstrate the issue as a screen shot or mockup can. Developers will appreciate these extra efforts because they need to find the problem in the shortest amount of time. Any helpful documentation can be attached to the Bug work item or stored in SharePoint or another website, and then linked to the work item.

It is also a good idea to specify system information, including the build number that produced the failure. This build number can either be the one generated by Team Foundation Build or an assembly or product version number. This number will provide more information and help the developers identify the exact problematic build. Otherwise, if the team uses a more current version, they might search for a problem that was already fixed. If they use an older build, the problem code may not yet have been integrated.

The Bug work item has two fields to track the build number. The *Found in Build* field tracks the build that produced the failure, while *Integrated in Build* tracks the build where the bug was fixed. When adding or editing a Bug work item, the drop-down control for these fields allows you to pick a build number from a list of unique build names that was generated by Team Foundation Build automatically. Fortunately, the drop-down control only suggests these values. You can type whatever you want in these optional fields, such as an assembly or product version.

Bug work items should always contain the observed as well as the expected results. This is a good practice because sometimes developers don't think that the bug is a real bug. The variance between expected and observed should prove the case. Generic descriptions like "This is a bug" are not helpful because the bug in question is not immediately obvious to the other developers.

Note You can use the *Steps to Reproduce* field to track the observed results, but unfortunately, the Bug work item type does not have a field explicitly designated to track the expected results. Rather than customize the work item type and add one, you should consider using *Acceptance Criteria*, as shown in Figure 5-12. Either way, knowing the expected results can help the Development Team create better tests. If there are additional acceptance criteria to list, you can do that below the expected results. Be careful though; you should avoid adding new "features" to a bug fix. If there are other improvements to make, you should create a separate PBI work item. *Gold plating* should be avoided, even when fixing bugs.

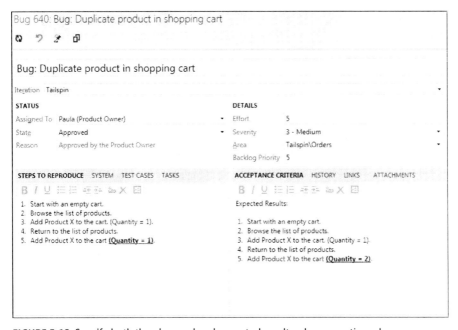

FIGURE 5-12 Specify both the observed and expected results when reporting a bug.

Be professional. Don't write titles like: "Help!"; "It's broken"; "Got an error"; "What happened?"; or "Dude!" These kinds of titles are devoid of content at best and irritating at worst. Titles should be short and concise. Save the explanations for the other fields on the work item. Your fellow developers don't have telepathy. Don't include notes like, "Do you get what I mean?" Try your best to explain yourself. Don't assume the developers will just follow things that are written on the bug report. Also, don't play politics. Using a bug report to score political points is detrimental to the health of the team and the product.

You've probably experienced firsthand that if you don't document the exact steps to reproduce an issue, you'll forget them very quickly. Be specific. Proofread the fields before saving. A proofread work item has a much higher chance of being understood by others and thus of being fixed. Table 5-1 lists a summary of the preferred practices when reporting bugs.

Note If you are creating the bug from Test Manager, you can take advantage of the action recording, system information, IntelliTrace, and video recording features. Test Manager automatically creates and attaches these to the Bug work item.

TABLE 5-1 Preferred practices when reporting bugs.

Practice	Reason
Triage the bug	To determine if it is a valid bug and not a feature, training issue, or by design.
Keep titles concise but descriptive	To save the user from having to read the entire work item to get the context.
One bug per work item	To estimate, order, and forecast each bug independently.
Consider prefixing bug titles with "Bug:"	The Product Backlog list doesn't differentiate between PBI and Bug work items.
Include screenshots	An annotated screenshot is an effective way to report a bug.
Include system information, the build number, and/or the version number	To provide as much context to the Development Team as possible to help them identify and fix the source of the failure. Use the *System Info* field.
List repeatable steps to reproduce the bug	To provide as much context to the Development Team as possible to help them identify and fix the source of the failure. Use the *Steps to Reproduce* field.
Provide expected results, as well as observed results	Knowing how to make it fail is one thing, but also knowing what success looks like when the Development Team fixes the bug is very important. Use the *Acceptance Criteria* field to track expected results.
Proper grammar, spelling, and tone	Don't play politics. Be professional.

Where do bugs come from?

Bugs can be introduced in a software system any number of ways. There is little point in attempting to place blame for any particular bug because there are so many sources. Besides, blame has no place in Scrum. Determining *why* something failed can sometimes take two or three times the amount of effort over just fixing it. Make sure the time spent analyzing the root cause adds value to the product or the process. The Sprint Retrospective meeting is a good place to discuss any findings and correct for the future. Whatever the finding, remember that the Development Team collectively owns the quality (good or bad) of the software product.

Here are a few reasons that bugs occur in software:

- Poorly understood requirements

- Poor coding

- Inadequate tooling

- Poor test coverage

- Inadequate process

- Inexperienced developers

Real bugs, as in the tiny crawly creatures, also have a well-defined lifecycle, according to their species. Their metamorphosis is a good metaphor for software bugs. It often starts with a simple observation of a probable source of customer dissatisfaction (the egg); proceeds to a well-defined report of the observed symptoms, steps to reproduce, and a technical investigation (the larva); to a fix for the problem (the chrysalis); and finally to a working build with the verified fix (the adult). Like real bugs, not all software bugs survive to adulthood. Of course, unlike real bugs, software bugs can retreat back to their larval state when the fixes are unsuccessful. Those are called *reactivations*.

> **Tip** I often meet developers who feel the need to trace a newly discovered bug back to the original PBI. While this linking can be done easily in Team Foundation Server, I always ask, "Why?" If they want to see what the original acceptance criteria were, that's valid. They should consider copying and pasting the applicable criteria into the new work item. If, instead, they are looking for a reason *why* it broke, that can be better answered by looking at the code or tests. If they want to find out how many story points that PBI was worth so they can deduct it from their velocity—that's a dysfunction. Cycles spent dwelling on past mistakes are cycles that can't be used to achieve the Sprint Goal. Discuss your findings during the Sprint Retrospective meeting. Remember, software development is very hard and full of risk. We're not always going to get it right. Focus on improving in the next Sprint.

In-Sprint vs. out-of-Sprint bugs

Not all bugs are equal—so they shouldn't be treated equally. Bugs found in code running in production, or in a done Increment waiting to be released to production, are out of the scope of the team's forecast work for the Sprint. As such, they should be handled the same as any feature request. The bug should be added to the Product Backlog, groomed by the Scrum Team, and forecast for a later Sprint.

If the Product Owner deems the bug as being critical and requiring an immediate fix, then the Development Team should drop what they are doing and fix the bug. The hotfix may or may not require the full Development Team's capacity. Regardless, everyone must realize that the Sprint's forecast may be missed, and that achieving the Sprint Goal might even be in jeopardy. The Product Owner weighs these risks and, after collaborating with the Development Team, makes the decision.

> **Note** Unplanned events are just that. You can't plan them at the start of the Sprint. If the Development Team plans its tasks to the point where they consume 100 percent of the team's available time, they will have no capacity left to handle unplanned work like an emergency bug fix. When the emergency does happen, it will probably cause a drop in Velocity. Since Velocity is an input to Sprint Planning, a decreased Velocity provides *slack time* in the Sprint for handling bugs and other work that might arise. High-performance Scrum Teams watch their capacity while maximizing the value that their work produces.

I refer to bugs found in the code that the Development Team is working on during the Sprint as *in-Sprint* bugs. These may not be bugs according to the classic definition, but rather, the code is just not quite there yet. Most teams' Definition of "Done" includes "code compiles," "no errors," or "no bugs found in new code." In these cases, it's not really a bug—the developers just aren't *done* yet.

The goal for in-Sprint bugs is to *fix* them, not manage them. Ideally, you want to fix all bugs discovered during the Sprint. If you don't, they could affect the Development Team's ability to achieve its forecast or Sprint Goal. Here is the guidance I give the Scrum Team for handling in-Sprint bugs:

- If it's a small bug (< *n* hours to fix) and *won't* affect the burndown, then just fix it. The Development Team decides what *n* equals. A value of 2 feels right to me.

- If it's a larger bug (> *n* hours to fix) and *won't* affect the ability to achieve the Sprint Goal or forecast, then create a Bug work item, associate a Task work item, and have a developer code the fix during the Sprint. The work items will explain the reason behind the hiccup in the burndown.

- If it's a larger bug (> *n* hours to fix) and *will* affect the ability to achieve the Sprint Goal or forecast, then create a Bug work item and discuss the situation with the Product Owner. She may value the bug fix over another PBI in the forecast. If not, then the bug will be left in the code this Sprint and the Bug work item will be groomed and fixed in a future Sprint.

- If another team member finds a small bug and it's not possible to collaborate on an immediate fix, then a Bug work item should be created and assigned to the current Sprint. The Development Team must decide if it can be fixed in the current Sprint or in a later one. If the bug is left in the code, the Product Owner should be consulted. Everyone will need to realize that the Sprint's forecast may be missed and that achieving the Sprint Goal might be in jeopardy. What's worse is that you have now added technical debt to your software product.

I refer to bugs found in production code, or in a done Increment waiting to be released to production, as *out-of-Sprint* bugs. Typically, these bugs don't affect the code associated with the forecast work that the Development Team is working on. If code is affected, then treat them as *in-Sprint* bugs. Otherwise, consider the guidance I give a Scrum Team for handling out-of-Sprint bugs:

- If the Product Owner determines that the bug is critical, the Development Team should do whatever needs to be done to get a fix into production. Everyone must realize that the Sprint's forecast may be missed and achieving the Sprint Goal might be in jeopardy.

- If the bug is not critical, then create a Bug work item. The Product Owner will decide if and when the bug is groomed and forecast in a future Sprint.

- If the number of critical bug occurrences increase, consider adjusting the Development Team's capacity or dedicating a developer to supporting maintenance issues like these. The Scrum Team should also look for the root cause of these critical bugs and a solution during the next Sprint Retrospective.

> **Note** If you suspect a bug exists, write a failing test to verify it. The test could be automated (that is, a unit test) or manual (that is, a Test Case work item). I know that I've said that unplanned items in the Product Backlog should not have any associated tasks or test cases. My reason for this guidance is to reduce waste, like defining the *how* (through tasks and test cases) too early. The exception to my guidance would be a situation where the Test Case work items existed *before* the Bug work item. If this happens, don't discard the Test Case. It may still be of value in a future Sprint when the fix gets forecast.

Bug reactivations

Reactivations occur when bugs have been closed prematurely. Frequent reactivations are a smell of a deeper dysfunction. People sometimes mark bugs as done when the underlying problem has not been fixed. When this happens, it introduces waste into the process. A developer has to write and run a test and reopen the Bug work item. The original code may need to be refactored or scrapped, and then retested. At a minimum, the reactivation doubles the number of context switches and usually more than doubles the total effort required to complete the corresponding work.

Watching the rate at which reactivations occur is important. A tiny amount of waste might be acceptable, but a medium-to-high (or rising) rate of reactivations should be a smell, warning the Development Team to diagnose the root cause and fix it. Although sloppy development practice is an obvious possibility, other potential causes include poor bug reporting, inadequate test lab management, and overly aggressive triage. The Sprint Retrospective is a great venue for such discussion.

> **Tip** Consider creating an All Bugs shared query. Microsoft forgot to create one of these in the Visual Studio Scrum process template. You can add whatever criteria you want (state, iteration, severity, effort, etc.). You can even make the query a team favorite so it'll show as a slick tile on the team project's Web Access home page. You can also add build definitions and version control paths to the team favorites area.

Effective Product Backlog creation

Writing a book about the fusion of Scrum and tools is difficult. I have to constantly balance any guidance I offer with that of the team's ability to self-organize. Most of my recommendations are for teams new to Scrum and the ALM tools in Visual Studio. I understand that these teams will develop their own behaviors over time. My goal is that these behaviors are healthy ones. To that end, Table 5-2 lists some of the preferred practices that I recommend when creating a Product Backlog.

TABLE 5-2 Preferred practices when creating a Product Backlog.

Tip	Reason
Keep titles short and to the point	Sometimes the user will have only the title to go by.
Consider prefixing bug titles with "Bug:"	The backlog page doesn't differentiate between PBI and Bug work items.
Leave items in the root iteration	Don't set the iteration path of a PBI or bug until the Sprint in which they are forecast for development. Things change, and your effort could be wasted. For release planning, consider using the forecasting tool.
Don't create and link tasks or test cases	You should wait until the Sprint in which the PBI or bug is forecast for development. Things change, and your effort could be wasted.
The Assigned To user should be the Product Owner	Since the Product Owner is responsible for the Product Backlog, it makes sense that he or she be the person assigned.
Use the right tool for the job	Use the backlog page for ordering, planning, and grooming. Use the work items page for added tool-support, such as bulk editing or linking. Use Excel for an offline bulk-editing experience or creating ad hoc charts or graphs.
Link to documents rather than attach them	Documents stored on SharePoint can be linked to the work item, as well as discovered independently. Attached documents are harder to find.

As your Product Backlog grows, you could find yourself looking at hundreds of items potentially. At the time of this writing, there is no pagination support or a way to group or organize the Product Backlog other than ordering it. Ordering a large Product Backlog can be very tedious, as you may have to drag up or down several "screens" of items. It might be faster to set the *Backlog Priority* field manually than to drag a PBI up several hundred rows.

When viewing the Product Backlog, only New, Approved, and Committed PBI and Bug work items are displayed. Done and Removed work items are not displayed. You would need to run a standard work item query or use the search feature to find Done and Removed work items. PBI or Bug work items in the Committed state and assigned to a Sprint are also not displayed in the Product Backlog. You would need to go to the respective Sprint Backlog to see those work items.

If your organization has multiple Scrum Teams working on a software product, then you will see only those PBI and Bug work items assigned to the area paths specified as belonging to your team. For example, let's assume there is a Red team that owns areas R1, R2, and R3 and a Blue team that owns areas B1 and B2. If a user on the Red team changes the area of one of their PBIs to B1, it will disappear from their Product Backlog and appear on the Blue team's Product Backlog. The Red team user would need to use the search feature or create a custom query to locate that work item in the future.

Tailspin Toys case study Currently, the Tailspin Toys website is small enough that a single Scrum Team (Paula's team) can handle all of the software development. Because of this, the Scrum Team has complete authority over all areas and iterations (Sprints) of the team project.

Grooming the Product Backlog

Product Backlog grooming is an ongoing, part-time activity where the entire Scrum Team meets to better understand the upcoming items in the Product Backlog. When the time is right, the Development Team will estimate the effort required to develop the item. When and where the Scrum Team meets to groom the backlog is up to them. The *Scrum Guide* only recommends doing it, and that it takes no more than 10 percent of the team's capacity during the Sprint.

> **Tip** Fellow Professional Scrum Developer, Simon Reindl, recommends that a Scrum Team discuss (groom) a PBI three times before considering it ready for forecasting.

Initially, a PBI or Bug work item need only have a title to be added to the Product Backlog. The values for the other fields will begin to emerge and continue until the time that it the item is forecast for development. It may even pivot a bit after that. Prior to forecasting the work item, the Scrum Team should have a solid understanding of the requirement, its value to the customer, what success looks like, and a level of effort required to develop it. This evolution can occur at the Product Backlog grooming session, Sprint Planning meeting, or Sprint Review.

> **Tip** Scrum Teams generally groom their Product Backlog from top to bottom, first making sure that there is understanding and consensus around the highest-ordered items. There are times when you may want to jump to a specific work item or bug that isn't easy to find. To find a work item, I recommend using the search in the upper-right corner of Web Access. Searching will take you to the work items page and display the search results just as though you ran a query. By default, it looks in the work item's title, description, and repro steps (for bugs). You can add filters to the search by prefixing *a:* (for assigned to), *c:* (for created by), *s:* (for state), and *t:* (for work item type). As you can see in Figure 5-13, I am searching for all (shopping) cart bugs assigned to Paula.

FIGURE 5-13 Searching for shopping cart bugs assigned to Paula.

As details emerge, and consensus forms, you should edit the work item and make any updates. This can occur during Product Backlog grooming or any time during the Sprint. Here are some example edits that a team member might make as a result of grooming the Product Backlog:

- **Set state to Removed** The Product Owner determines the PBI or Bug is a duplicate or otherwise unnecessary.

- **Set state to Approved** The Product Owner decides that this is a good requirement.

- **Improve description** A description that explains the who, what, and why is added.

- **Assign business value** The Product Owner assigns a business value.

- **Add acceptance criteria** After collaborating with the customer or experts, criteria is added.

- **Link documents** Any supporting documents are linked or attached.

- **Estimate effort** After reaching a baseline understanding, the Development Team estimates the effort required to develop the item.

When a PBI or Bug work item is initially created, it is in the New state. When the Product Owner decides that the item is valid, its state should be changed to Approved. When the Development Team forecasts to deliver the item in the current Sprint, its state should be changed to Committed. Finally, when the PBI or Bug work item is done according to the Development Team's definition, the state should be changed to Done.

The Removed state is reserved for situations where the Product Owner determines that the item is invalid for whatever reason. It could be that the item is already in the Product Backlog, was already developed, or is not realistic.

Done and Removed PBI and Bug work items don't show up in the Product Backlog. On the backlog page, this will always be the case because the behind-the-scenes query is hard-coded that way. On the work items page, however, you can edit the Product Backlog to include these additional states. I recommend leaving the Product Backlog query untouched and creating another query instead. You could call it *Product Backlog (all states)* or something.

> **Note** At the time of this writing, you cannot type in the *Reason* field. You can only select items from the drop-down list, and the choices are limited. If the reason that you want is not listed, you should add a short comment to the discussion on the History tab. Customizing the work item type might also be an option.

Specifying acceptance criteria

A high-performance Scrum Team won't forecast any work until they know what success looks like. For example, there's not a lot to go on if a PBI is titled "Monthly sales report," with a description that reads, "As a salesman, I want to see a monthly report of my sales activity so that I am better informed." A Development Team would be able to build any of a hundred different reports that are fit for this purpose. Rather than commune this information on the fly, or build the wrong thing, the Development Team needs to take a more measured approach to knowing what to develop and what *done* looks like. This is done by collaborating and identifying acceptance criteria, which is the Product Owner's responsibility.

Using acceptance criteria is a lightweight, agile way of establishing requirements and defining success for a PBI or bug fix. Think of it as the work item's own Definition of "Done," as established by the Product Owner. Acceptance criteria should define the *what*, but not the *how*. The Development

Team should have free rein over what to build (and how to build it) so long as it meets the acceptance criteria and the Definition of "Done." Figure 5-14 shows a PBI with an emerging set of acceptance criteria.

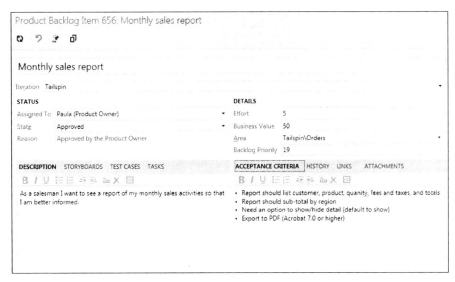

FIGURE 5-14 A PBI's acceptance criteria.

Each individual acceptance criterion should be testable. In other words, you should be able to create and execute a manual or automated test to verify that each bullet is done. Sometimes it might take multiple tests to verify one criterion. Sometimes one test can verify multiple criteria. We will dive deeper into this idea in Chapter 7, "Development."

Scope creep (a.k.a. Feature creep)

So what happens when the Product Owner needs to change the acceptance criteria? If the PBI or Bug work item hasn't been forecast yet, there's no problem. Change the criteria and re-estimate the item at the next grooming opportunity.

If the Development Team *has* already forecast the work for the current Sprint, the reflex is to resist the change. After all, don't the rules of Scrum "unionize" the Development Team to protect against practices like *scope creep*? Some might think so, and they would be wrong. The Product Owner is responsible for maximizing the value of the product, as well as the work of the Development Team. Sometimes these two responsibilities conflict, especially when business or market drivers demand an immediate change.

The correct response is for the entire Scrum Team to collaborate on how to bring value to the product with respect to this new requirement. This is the N (negotiable) in the INVEST acronym we talked about in Chapter 1. Yes, the forecast may slip. Yes, the Sprint Goal may not be achieved. Yes, there will probably be waste. But, in the mind of the Product Owner, the immediate change to the software product is worth the waste to ultimately avoid much greater waste. The Sprint Retrospective meeting should be used to better understand what happened and how to keep it from happening again in the future.

Tailspin Toys case study Because Sprints are only two weeks long, scope creep is not much of a problem. When it does happen, the Development Team is professional and collaborates with Paula to maximize the value of the website. Just as Paula has learned to trust the developers' abilities, so have they learned to trust her judgment.

Estimating items in the Product Backlog

Higher-ordered items in the Product Backlog are clearer and more detailed than lower-ordered ones. More accurate estimates are made based on the increased clarity and detail. The lower in the order, the less detail. This is why you want to estimate the items toward the top of the Product Backlog rather than in the middle or at the bottom. You would be wasting your time, and that of the entire Development Team, if you estimated items too far down. I discussed this, and the concept of the Product Backlog *iceberg*, in Chapter 1.

Each item in the Product Backlog is unique. It's difficult to estimate something unique that is being built for the first time, especially if it is unlike anything built before. Traditional estimation techniques do not work. As weird as it sounds, if you want to be more accurate, you should be less precise. It's okay to be precise on small things, like Sprint tasks (that is, "create a web form," "update a stored procedure," "create a data-driven unit test," etc.). For larger items, such as PBIs and Bugs, you want to use a scale that is less precise, like T-shirt sizes (XS, S, M, L, XL) or a Fibonacci sequence of numbers (1, 2, 3, 5, 8, 13, 21, 34, etc.)

The Development Team is responsible for all estimates. It makes sense that the people who will perform the work (that is, the Development Team) make the final estimate. In smaller teams, where the Product Owner and/or Scrum Master are also Development Team members, then they will have input on the estimations as well. Never underestimate how long good estimation takes, but also realize that too much analysis and estimation can have a diminished return on the time invested.

Tip Scrum offers three formal opportunities to groom the Product Backlog: the Sprint Planning meeting, the Product Backlog grooming session, and the Sprint Review meeting. It's best to do the bulk of your estimation during Product Backlog grooming. This way, the Development Team can spend less time forecasting work at the next Sprint Planning meeting and more time on creating a plan to develop it.

Estimation should be performed as late as possible. Early estimates are less accurate than later ones. You always know more today than you did yesterday. You also don't want to waste the Development Team's time estimating items that are "way down the list." Proper ordering of the Product Backlog can reduce waste when estimating. The Product Owner should know what's coming up next or soon thereafter, and focus on those items. He or she should wait until larger (epic) PBIs are decomposed.

Sometimes it's a chicken-and-egg problem though. The Product Owner needs an idea of the cost (effort) of a PBI before he or she can order it. A solution for adding value to the estimation process is for the Development Team (or a proxy) to provide the Product Owner a rough order of magnitude estimate, such as a T-shirt size (XS, S, M, L, XL). This can give the Product Owner enough insight to be able to order the item effectively. A more thorough estimate, provided by the entire Development Team and using a more precise technique, can be performed at a future grooming session.

The *Scrum Guide* does not prescribe any particular estimation technique or unit of measure. Teams can use whatever practice and values they wish. Planning Poker® is a very popular method. Story points are very popular too—although some teams prefer to call them "complexity points" or something very abstract like "acorns." I once worked for a team building pharmaceutical software which went so far as to use the term "Vicodins." (Vicodin is a prescription pain medication, which is fitting given some of their painful user stories.) Whatever term you decide on, using an abstract measure like a story point is preferred for Agile estimation. Abstract values have an advantage over temporal values (hours, days, ideal-days, weeks) because their usage doesn't imply a plan or a commitment or anything that smells like a schedule. For example, if you were estimating in days, a stakeholder might have a specific expectation.

> **Note** Agile estimation is not a silver bullet. In fact, it's the worst form of estimation except all the others that have been tried. Agile estimation techniques won't remove uncertainty from early estimates, but they also won't waste unnecessary time. Estimates will become more accurate over time. This is due to the empirical nature of agile estimation techniques, where actual work is taken into account.

Planning Poker

Planning Poker is a tool for estimating software development projects. It is a technique where each Development Team member selects an estimate card such that it cannot be seen by the other players. After everyone has selected a card, all cards are exposed at once. The Product Owner and Scrum Master don't participate in the estimation game unless they are also on the Development Team. Ideally, the Scrum Master "chairs" the process. The Product Owner should offer support where needed, such as answering questions. Other stakeholders or domain experts may attend the grooming session to offer support, but not to estimate.

The units represented are typically story points in a limited Fibonacci sequence (0, 1, 2, 3, 5, 8, 13, 21, 34, etc). The cards are numbered in this sequence to account for the fact that the larger an estimate is, the more uncertainty it contains. Thus, if a developer wants to play an 8, he is forced to reconsider that some of the perceived uncertainty does not exist and play a 5, or accept a conservative estimate accounting for the uncertainty and play a 13. Some decks may also contain larger numbers, question marks, infinity symbols, or coffee break cards.

Typically, the most knowledgeable developer or domain expert for a given item provides a short overview. The Development Team is given an opportunity to ask questions and to discuss and clarify assumptions and risks. A summary of the discussion can be recorded if the Scrum Team decides. As the Development Team considers the effort, they should reference a few "golden PBIs" that they've worked on recently. These will be used as a baseline for this relative estimation technique. These referenced items don't have to be similar to the one being estimated, but it helps. When you estimate a new item, you compare the work required relative to this baseline. As the Development Team improves, it can decide to rebase its efforts and select different "golden" PBIs.

Estimation commences and Development Team members with high estimates and low estimates are given an opportunity to justify their estimate as discussion continues. The team should repeat the process until a consensus is reached. If consensus is not reached after a few rounds, estimation should be tabled until the next grooming session. More will be known later.

Avoid anchoring

Anchoring occurs when the Development Team openly discusses their estimates prior to the playing of the cards. A team normally has a mix of conservative and impulsive estimators. Some developers may have an agenda too. Developers are likely to want as much time as they can have to do the job, and the Product Owner is likely to want it as quickly as possible. Compromise through collaboration becomes important at this juncture.

The estimate becomes anchored when the Product Owner, or one of the more experienced developers, says something like, "This should be easy" or "I could do that in a day." Anchoring can also go the other way, when someone says something foreboding like, "Isn't that the component riddled with technical debt?" Whoever starts the conversation with the statement, "That'll take the entire Sprint!" immediately has an impact on the thinking of the other team members. Their estimates have now been anchored. They are now likely to make at least a subconscious reference to that estimate. For example, those who were thinking 5 points are likely to increase their estimate.

This becomes a particular problem if an influential team member makes the original statement. Because the remainder of the team has been anchored, they may consciously or otherwise fail to express their original unity. In fact they may fail to even discover that they were thinking the same thing. This can be dangerous, resulting in estimates that are influenced by agendas, attitudes, alphas, or opinions that are not focused on getting the job done right.

Note A study by K. Molokken-Ostvold and N.C. Haugen (IEEE) found that estimates obtained through the Planning Poker process were less optimistic and more accurate than estimates obtained through mechanical combination of individual estimates for the same tasks. For more information, search for *Combining Estimates with Planning Poker—An Empirical Study,* at *http://ieee.org.*

White Elephant game

There are many methods that an Agile software development team can use to estimate the size or effort of a PBI. While Planning Poker is the most popular, several of my fellow professional Scrum developers use the White Elephant game. It is loosely based on the idea and workflow of a white elephant gift exchange.

You start with the Development Team standing in a half circle, facing a whiteboard with five columns (swim lanes): XS, S, M, L, and XL. On a nearby table is a shuffled deck of PBIs and a timer. The cards can be index cards, sticky notes, or a hybrid. The cards contain the titles of the items that you are about to estimate. The Scrum Master starts the timer, and the first Development Team member performs these steps:

1. Pick the top card off the deck.

2. Read the item out loud.

3. Stick the card to the whiteboard in one of the columns.

4. Provide a reason to the group for the decision.

5. Start the timer for the next player.

Everyone should have laser focus and be listen actively to the estimator's reasons. Everyone else should remain silent. There should be no discussion or judgment. If the developer does not stick the card to the board within one minute, the card is placed in the M (medium) column. The player then restarts the timer for the next player.

After a few rounds, there should be an assortment of cards stuck to the whiteboard. Team members can now, on their turn, choose to move one of the cards to a different column instead of selecting a new card from the deck. The player should read the item out loud, as well as state the reason supporting the decision to change the estimate.

Eventually, all of the cards will be stuck to the whiteboard and estimated. Each player, on their turn, can either move a card between columns or simply *pass*. Passing means that they are satisfied with the current estimates. If a developer does not make a decision within one minute, it will be generally understood to be a pass. The estimation game ends when the pile of cards is now on the whiteboard and every developer signals pass.

Tracking estimates in the Product Backlog

In a PBI or Bug work item, the *Effort* field holds the estimate. Microsoft designed these work items to be generic. Therefore, there is no label or tooltip that suggests or recommends a particular practice or unit of measure. The *Effort* field indicates the relative rating for the amount of work that the PBI or Bug implementation will require. Larger numbers indicate more work than smaller numbers. In contrast, Sprint Task work items should be estimated in hours, since respective queries, charts, and reports expect that.

Tip I'm often asked if *size* is the same as *effort* in Scrum. My answer is yes, so long as we agree that the unit of measure is abstract and not temporal. In other words, effort = size = story points. Some high-performance Scrum Teams use the term *size* to represent the initial T-shirt size estimate and then *effort* to be the more precise estimation after grooming. Other teams consider *effort* to be more generic—just a mix of complexity and the volume of work. Regardless of your practice or vernacular, the data entry field in Team Foundation Server is called *Effort*. You'll need to live with it or customize it. I recommend living with it.

Tailspin Toys case study The Development Team still uses Planning Poker to estimate the effort of the PBIs and bug fixes in the Product Backlog. This occurs primarily at the Product Backlog grooming sessions on Friday mornings. Since they have been working together, on the same domain, using familiar tools and technologies, the Development Team's baseline is well established and consistent. They have many golden PBIs to use when performing relative estimation.

Ordering the Product Backlog

The Product Backlog should be ordered by the Product Owner to maximize the value of the software being developed. He or she will know what features and bug fixes need to be developed before others. Release planning depends on the backlog being correctly ordered. The order can be based on many factors: business value, risk, priority, technical value, learning value, or necessity.

Items at a higher order are clearer and more detailed than lower-ordered ones. Effort estimates are more accurate on these items as well. In fact, the higher the order, the more a PBI or bug has been considered, and the consensus is greater regarding it, its value, and its cost.

Smell It's a smell when I see Development Team members ordering the Product Backlog. This is typically the responsibility of the Product Owner. It could be that the pertinent items need to be arranged according to technical dependencies, and the Product Owner is aware of this. The worry is that the Scrum Team has an *absent* Product Owner who defers the "what" decisions to the Development Team.

In Web Access, you can order the Product Backlog by dragging items. If you click and hold on an item, you can drag it above or below another item and then release it. You can see this in Figure 5-15, as the Monthly sales report PBI is dragged to the top of the Product Backlog. When it is dropped, it will be the highest-ordered item in the Product Backlog.

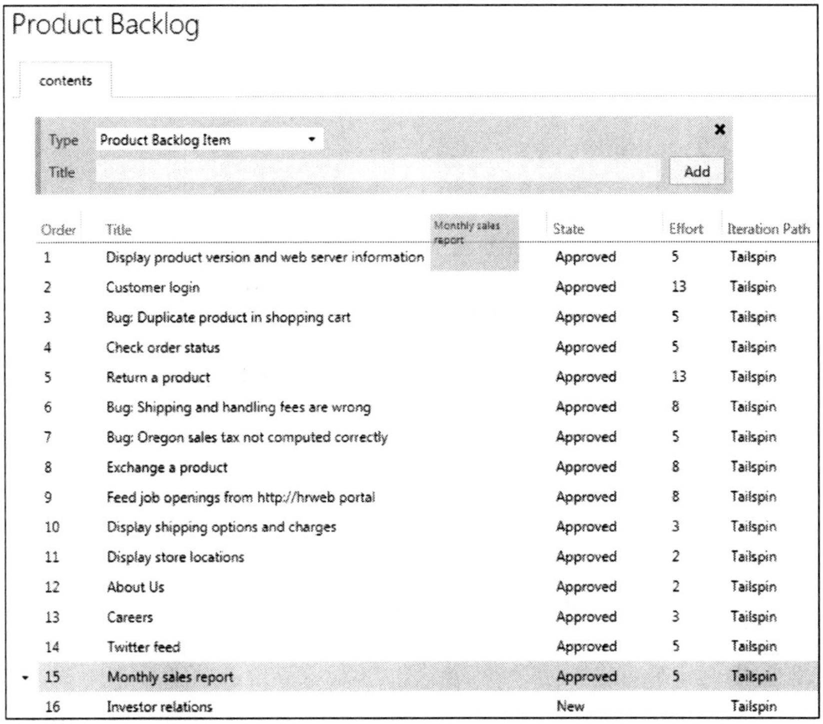

FIGURE 5-15 Ordering the Product Backlog by dragging a PBI.

The work item's position in the Product Backlog is tracked behind the scenes in the *Backlog Priority* field. If you add a new work item using the "quick add" panel, the new work item will be half of the value of the current highest-ordered item. For example, if the current highest-ordered PBI has a *Backlog Priority* value of 6250, the newly added PBI will have a *Backlog Priority* value of 3125.

If you are curious, you can see the *Backlog Priority* field value when you edit the work item. You can also compare the current value with the previous value by reviewing the change history on the work item's History tab (as seen in Figure 5-16). You can change the *Backlog Priority* value manually too, which is important if you are not licensed to use the Web Access backlog page or want to change the execution order of the PBI or bug once the work has been forecast.

Since the order is persisted in the *Backlog Priority* field, other lists and queries can use it. For example, when you assign the forecast PBIs and bugs to a Sprint, the Sprint Backlog will display those PBI or Bug work items in the same order. This is good, because if the Product Owner has signaled that the *Monthly sales report* is the most important item, then the Development Team should see it at the top of the Sprint Backlog and consider executing its work first.

FIGURE 5-16 Viewing previous and current *Backlog Priority* values in the work item History tab.

Note Each time you drag in the backlog page, history is generated. Microsoft is considering ways to limit this in the future. Until then, be mindful of your drag-and-drop activity.

Tailspin Toys case study Paula uses the drag-and-drop features on the backlog page to set the order of the Product Backlog. Once she has it set for the release plan, the order doesn't change that often. Rarely does she have to drag something up from the bottom of the list, or vice versa. This is good because her Product Backlog contains over 100 work items.

Customizing the backlog columns

By default, the backlog page only shows the title, state, effort, and iteration path of the work items. It also shows an order number, but this is auto-generated by Web Access and is not persisted. While ordering the Product Backlog, it might be helpful to see additional columns of data, such as area path, business value, and the work item type.

You can customize the columns and column sequence for the backlog page. You can add or remove columns, change the sequence of the columns, or change the column width for the pages that display the Product Backlog or Sprint Backlog. Here are the high-level steps to follow in order to customize the backlog columns:

1. Use Witadmin to export the Agile process configuration file for the team project.

Note You can also use the Process Editor found in the Team Foundation Server Power Tools.

2. Edit the exported configuration file and locate the *Columns* element within the *ProductBacklog* section. If you want to customize the Sprint Backlog page, you'll need to make edits within the *IterationBacklog* section.

3. Add a *Column* element that specifies the reference name of the field that you want listed and the width in pixels. You can also remove any columns or change their widths. For example, you could add the *System.AreaPath* and *Microsoft.VSTS.Common.BusinessValue* fields as I did here (see bold):

```xml
<?xml version="1.0" encoding="utf-8"?>
<AgileProjectConfiguration>
  <IterationBacklog>
    <Columns>
      <Column width="50" refname="Microsoft.VSTS.Scheduling.Effort" />
      <Column width="400" refname="System.Title" />
      <Column width="100" refname="System.State" />
      <Column width="100" refname="System.AssignedTo" />
      <Column width="50" refname="Microsoft.VSTS.Scheduling.RemainingWork" />
    </Columns>
  </IterationBacklog>
  <ProductBacklog>
    <AddPanel>
      <Fields>
        <Field refname="System.Title" />
        <Field refname="Microsoft.VSTS.Common.BusinessValue" />
      </Fields>
    </AddPanel>
    <Columns>
      <Column width="350" refname="System.Title" />
      <Column width="80" refname="System.State" />
      <Column width="150" refname="System.AreaPath" />
      <Column width="100" refname="Microsoft.VSTS.Common.BusinessValue" />
      <Column width="50" refname="Microsoft.VSTS.Scheduling.Effort" />
      <Column width="100" refname="System.IterationPath" />
    </Columns>
  </ProductBacklog>
</AgileProjectConfiguration>
```

4. Save the file.

5. Use Witadmin to import the updated configuration file back to the team project.

Note At the time of this writing, the backlog columns cannot be customized for the hosted Team Foundation Service.

After you have imported the configuration file, you will need to refresh the backlog page. You will then see the new columns displayed, as shown in Figure 5-17.

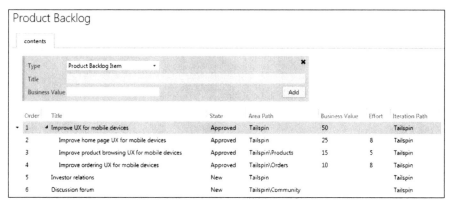

FIGURE 5-17 The Product Backlog displaying additional columns.

Tailspin Toys case study Andy has customized the backlog page to include the *Area Path* and *Business Value* fields. This has helped Paula order the Product Backlog, as well as locate individual PBIs. Originally, Andy also added the work item type column, but later he removed it in lieu of just prefixing Bug work items with "Bug:" and reclaiming some screen real estate.

Planning a release

After the Product Backlog has been groomed, a release plan can be created. This plan can be formal or informal. A formal plan can be documented to include expectations and dates, then made visible to the stakeholders. An informal plan is just an understanding between the Product Owner and the Development Team that by a certain date, they will ship what's done, or they will ship a specific set of functionality when it's done. Either way, you will need the Product Backlog to be in good shape.

Note Release planning is no longer an official event in Scrum. It's assumed that every organization will do some level of release planning. As far as Scrum is concerned, keeping the Product Backlog healthy and estimated is the best input for accurate release planning.

A release plan establishes the goal of the release and includes the highest-ordered PBIs, the major risks, and the overall features and functionality that the release will contain. It also establishes a probable delivery date and/or feature set, and a cost that should hold if nothing changes. The organization can then inspect progress and make changes to this release plan on a Sprint-by-Sprint basis.

The release plan will probably start with a large margin of error unless the Development Team is already established with a known Velocity. The plan will become more and more refined (and accurate) as development progresses and empirical data is gathered. The key to release planning is to have the Product Backlog in good shape. This is a result of an engaged Product Owner and constant grooming by an engaged Scrum Team.

Most organizations already have a release planning process. In these processes, most of the planning is done at the beginning of the release and left unchanged as time passes. In an organization practicing Scrum, the Product Owner defines the overall goal with stakeholders and works with the Development Team to define probable outcomes. This style of release planning requires substantially less time than to build a traditional release plan.

Traditional release efforts are up-front "guesstimates" that seldom prove true. Scrum's just-in-time planning is ongoing during all of its events. In Scrum, release efforts probably consume slightly more effort than in traditional release planning efforts. Empirical methods usually do take longer than guessing. Scrum's approach, however, adds more value and probability of success.

Time-driven vs. feature-driven releases

If the project is time-driven (a.k.a. "release by date"), then the Development Team's Velocity can help predict the total effort that can be expended by the deadline. Starting at the highest-ordered Product Backlog item, the team will work down the list until the cumulative effort reaches the total available. This will show the set of features that can be delivered by the deadline, given the current Velocity and capacity of the Development Team.

If the project is feature-driven (a.k.a. "release by feature"), then the Development Team can calculate the cumulative effort required to build the desired feature set. This can be divided by the team's Velocity to estimate the amount of time (number of Sprints) required for delivery, given the current capacity of the Development Team.

Release planning provides a view of *what* functionality can be developed by a given date. Conversely, it can provide a view of *when* a fixed set of functionality can be developed. Release planning is something that occurs all the way through a software product's lifecycle, not just at the beginning. Release planning typically corresponds to the version increment of the software product.

As the Development Team progresses through the Sprints, their actual Velocity can be applied to the Product Backlog to assess how the release plan compares to reality. If a release burndown chart is being maintained, it will include data from past Sprints and can provide a view of the progress. This information is an important input into release planning, as well as inspection and adaptation.

Tailspin Toys case study Originally, the Tailspin Toys website released quarterly. As the team and tools got better, this changed to monthly. Management hopes that the new tools will help their high-performance Scrum Team move to a continuous deployment (CD) release model.

Controlling and prioritizing scope

It is a fact of life that developing the desired functionality will require more than the available time and budget. Based on project progress, you can make changes to the variables available (time, team capacity, and scope) but never compromise quality. The most effective variation to make is to the scope. Scope control, at its simplest, is the deferral of developing PBIs until a later release, thus reducing the scope for the current release.

It's not enough for the Development Team to sit back and quote the *Scrum Guide* to the Product Owner. Yes, there are rules in place to keep scope creep from occurring during the Sprint. Unfortunately, the Scrum values, as well as the Agile Manifesto values, outweigh them. It is important that PBIs be "negotiable" so that their desired outcome can be achieved by pragmatically adjusting the sophistication of the implementation. In other words, it's more important to deliver business value in the form of working software than to follow a plan.

A high-performance Scrum Team should always ask itself these questions:

- How can we turn the vision into a winning product in the best possible way?

- How can we meet or exceed the desired satisfaction and return on investment (ROI)?

Using Velocity to estimate

If the Development Team has completed multiple Sprints, it can use this empirical data to plan its releases more effectively. The Development Team can review how many PBIs it has completed, according to its Definition of "Done," over the past few Sprints. This data can be used to compute the team's Velocity.

Velocity is how much effort a team can develop in a single Sprint. Once established, a team's Velocity can be used to plan Sprints and releases. Velocity is most accurate when the team composition, Sprint duration, Definition of "Done," and estimation techniques remain constant.

> **Note** I'm often asked how a team's Velocity can be meaningful when PBIs are estimated using such crude precision and in such abstract values as story points. Fortunately, it is. According to the law of large numbers (LLN), the average of the results obtained from a large number of trials (Sprints) should be close to the expected value and will tend to become closer as more trials are performed.

A key piece to maintaining a consistent and honest Velocity is having a solid Definition of "Done" and sticking to it. It may seem small, but it can be the most critical checkpoint of a Scrum project. Without a consistent meaning of *done,* Velocity cannot be estimated. Conversely, a common Definition of "Done" ensures that the Increment produced at the end of the Sprint is of high quality, with minimal defects. High-performance Scrum Development Teams will gradually add to (a.k.a. ratchet up) their Definition of "Done" knowing that it may affect their Velocity for a short period of time, but after that, both the quality and Velocity should go up. This is the epitome of continuous improvement.

There are several Agile practices that, if adopted, can increase a team's Velocity. Here is a partial list:

- Create and maintain a clean Product Backlog.

- Use Agile planning to plan releases and Sprints just-in-time.

- Test early and often.

- Build, deploy, and test continuously.

- Avoid accumulating technical debt.

- Branch strategically, and for good reason.

- Use models effectively, and for good reason.

- Learn from your mistakes.

- Inspect and adapt.

After the Scrum Team has completed a few Sprints, the Velocity chart in Web Access will become more valuable. On the backlog page, a thumbnail of the Velocity is visible at all times in the upper-right area of the page, as shown in Figure 5-18. This small representation of the Velocity chart is hard to see, but it does give you a sketch of how the current Sprint (in the rightmost column) compares with the previous ones. When you look at the Velocity chart onscreen, you'll notice that some of the vertical bars are green and some contain blue. The green color represents the effort that is in the Done state. The blue color represents effort that is in the Committed state.

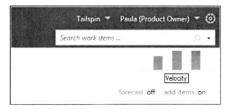

FIGURE 5-18 The Velocity thumbnail visible on the backlog page.

If you click on the Velocity thumbnail, it will open to a larger chart. You can see this in Figure 5-19. This zoomed-in view allows you to actually see the number of story points by Sprint and state. For past Sprints, only work items in the Done state are displayed.

Note At the time of this writing, the Velocity chart does not compute an average Velocity across the Sprints. You also don't have the ability to filter out work item effort in the Committed (blue) state. These would both be nice features to have in a future release of Web Access. Until then, you will have to compute the average Velocity using whatever method the Scrum Team decides on, or run the Velocity report, which provides an average.

Team Foundation Server also provides a Velocity report. This report also includes a graph that shows the amount of effort that the team has reported as done for each Sprint. The source of the raw data is the Product Backlog itself—just like the charts in Web Access. The horizontal axis represents Sprints, and the vertical axis measures the sum of effort from the done PBI and Bug work items. The report includes a horizontal line that represents the average Velocity across all the Sprints on the report. You can see this line in Figure 5-20.

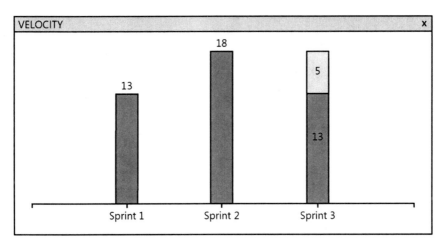

FIGURE 5-19 The full-sized Velocity chart.

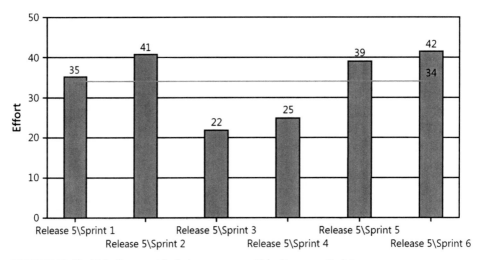

FIGURE 5-20 The Velocity report includes an average Velocity across Sprints.

Another difference between the chart in Web Access and the report is the data on which they are based. The Web Access chart is based on the operational databases, so its data is up to date in real time. The reports data comes from the data warehouse and the SQL Server Analysis Services (SSAS) cube—both of which must be updated by a scheduled event. This difference may cause the graphs to show different information.

Tailspin Toys case study The Development Team's Velocity seems to have normalized around 21. This has been the average of their last few Sprints.

The forecasting tool

By using the forecasting tool in Web Access, you can plan the number of Sprints it will take to complete a set of work. The forecasting tool is available only in the Product Backlog, not any of the Sprint Backlogs. Prior to being able to use the forecasting tool, your Product Backlog must have PBI and Bug work items already created with the effort specified.

You can turn on forecasting by clicking the Off hyperlink next to Forecast on the right side of the backlog page. The first time you do this, Web Access prompts you for the Velocity. Using your Development Team's Velocity, Web Access will add a Forecast column and horizontal lines to the Product Backlog. In the Forecast column, it will display the Sprint that it predicts the PBI or Bug work item will be developed in. As you can see in Figure 5-21, it's a very slick and visual way to see a forecast over several Sprints.

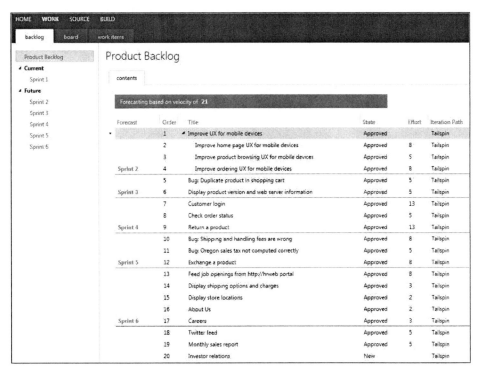

FIGURE 5-21 The forecasting tool uses Effort to predict which items will be forecast and when.

The tool is not based on magic. In fact, its algorithm is quite simple. The forecasting tool walks down the ordered backlog, adding up the points of effort of each item. Once the sum is greater than the Velocity, it increments the Sprint number. When it's out of work items or Sprints defined for the team, it stops.

Note The forecasting tool will sometimes forecast two items in the same Sprint whose combined effort is greater than the team's Velocity. At first glance, this may seem like a bug, but it's actually by design. It's happening because the forecasting logic assumes that PBIs can split across Sprint lines. For example, it might assume that a larger PBI can be started in Sprint Five and be finished in Sprint Six. The Scrum Team may or may not want to adopt this practice. I think the healthy practice to adopt is to have the team split the PBI prior to using the forecasting tool. Microsoft knows this and may change the behavior or make it selectable in a future release.

Using the backlog page, a team can forecast and plan the work in the current Sprint. The team can then review and track its progress against the backlog by using the task board. The task board displays Task work items that are associated with the forecast PBI and Bug work items in the current Sprint. The task board shows the state of each task as it progresses towards completion. We will dive deeper into using these tools to plan and execute a Sprint in the next chapter.

Tailspin Toys case study When the Development Team was first learning Scrum, Velocity meant everything. It was their one true metric. They could endeavor to improve it each Sprint. Everyone in the organization could see it on the reports and dashboards. As the team improved, they learned that business value in the form of working software was the most important metric, and that Velocity was just the trailing indicator. The Development Team still uses Velocity, but only as one of several inputs into Sprint Planning. They now just forecast the number of PBIs that *feels* like the right amount of work, given all of the variables. Paula still uses Velocity, and the forecasting tool in the backlog page, for release planning.

Release Burndown report

The Release Burndown report displays a sum of remaining effort for PBI and Bug work items across Sprints. By reviewing the Release Burndown report, you can understand how quickly the team is delivering items in the Product Backlog.

The report also tracks how much work must still be performed to complete a release. As you can see in Figure 5-22, the graph shows how much work remained at the start of each Sprint in a release. The source of the raw data is the Product Backlog. Each Sprint appears along the horizontal axis, and the vertical axis measures the effort that remained when each Sprint started. The amount of estimated effort on the vertical axis is in whatever unit that the team has decided to use (that is, story points).

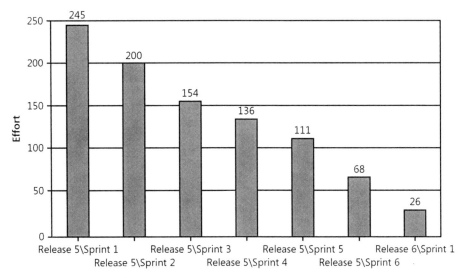

FIGURE 5-22 The Release Burndown report shows the work remaining in the release, by Sprint.

For this report to reflect reality, the Scrum Team needs to be diligent about setting the iteration path and state for each PBI and Bug work item, as they are forecast. As the Development Team completes the work, the state must be changed to Done for the report to acknowledge the end of that effort.

> **Note** There is no release burndown chart in Web Access. You will have to run the Release Burndown report if you want this information.

Chapter burndown

Here are the key concepts we covered in this chapter.

- **Team Web Access** This web-based portal is used to view and manage a team project, including the Product Backlog and Sprint Backlogs.

- **The backlog page** A customizable view within Web Access allowing licensed users to create and manage the Product Backlog and Sprint Backlogs.

- **Quick Add** A customizable panel at the top of the backlog page allowing the user to add a PBI or Bug work item quickly to the Product Backlog.

- **Epics** Any PBI that is too large to be developed in a single Sprint. Epics can be decomposed within the Product Backlog in a couple of different ways.

- **Reporting bugs** Bugs found in-Sprint should just be fixed; otherwise, use the Bug work item to report a bug. Bugs coexist in the Product Backlog alongside other PBI work items.

- **Grooming** The part-time activity where the Product Owner and Development Team understand and estimate the items in the Product Backlog.

- **Agile estimation** Use empiricism and decreased precision to estimate the size or effort of items in the Product Backlog. Only the Development Team estimates.

- **Ordering the backlog** Use a drag-and-drop approach in the backlog page to order the Product Backlog. This can be tedious with large Product Backlogs.

- **Velocity** Use the built-in Velocity chart in Web Access to see (in real time) how many points of effort the team is able to complete per Sprint. The Velocity report also computes an average.

- **Forecasting** Use the forecasting tool and the team's Velocity to view which items in the Product Backlog will potentially be developed in each upcoming Sprint.

- **Release planning** Use a groomed Product Backlog to forecast *what* will be released by a specific date, or *when* a specific set of functionality will be released.

- **Release Burndown** A report that displays a sum of remaining effort for items in the Product Backlog across Sprints.

CHAPTER 6

The Sprint

The Sprint is a fixed-length event (30 days or less) in which the Development Team forecasts items from the Product Backlog and develops the items in the Sprint Backlog according to the acceptance criteria and their Definition of "Done."

At the beginning of the Sprint, the Scrum Team attends the Sprint Planning meeting. The input elements for this meeting are the existing Increment and a groomed Product Backlog. The Development Team's velocity, capacity, and the Definition of "Done" are also helpful inputs because they assist the Development Team in identifying a comfortable amount of work to forecast for the Sprint. The output elements of the Sprint Planning meeting are the Sprint Goal and Sprint Backlog. The Sprint Backlog contains the forecast Product Backlog items (PBIs) and the plan for developing those PBIs.

Each day of the Sprint, the Development Team meets for the Daily Scrum. This is a time-boxed meeting, lasting no longer than 15 minutes. The Development Team uses this opportunity to synchronize with each other and develop a plan for the next 24 hours. The Development Team updates their remaining work daily so that they can assess the progress of their forecast work. Beyond that, what the Development Team does during the course of the day depends on what is required to get the forecast work done. Professional Scrum developers make sure that the work performed is always of value to the organization.

This chapter focuses on how to use tools in Microsoft Visual Studio Team Web Access to plan and manage the work in the Sprint Backlog. If you are more interested in the concept of the Sprint and the Sprint Backlog, and less on how to manage them using Visual Studio, you can read Chapter 1, "Scrumdamentals."

> **Note** In this chapter, I refer to the Product Backlog list on the backlog page as the *(product) backlog page* and the Sprint Backlog list on the backlog page (also known as the "iteration backlog") as the *(Sprint) backlog page*. This will help me set the context when I am talking about the specific behaviors on the backlog page. I will also refer to the board page as the *task board*.

Creating the Sprint Backlog

The Sprint Backlog contains the forecast PBIs. In Microsoft Team Foundation Server, this equates to the PBI and Bug work items that the Development Team will work on during the Sprint. In addition, the Sprint Backlog contains the plan for developing these items. In Team Foundation Server, this plan materializes as Task and/or Test Case work items linked to the respective PBI and Bug work items. The majority of that plan should be created during the Sprint planning, but it will continue to emerge into the Sprint.

Forecasting the PBIs

Assuming that the Development Team has already come to a consensus on what feels like the right amount of work, the act of forecasting the PBIs in Team Foundation Server is trivial. In fact, there are really only two settings to make in order to forecast a PBI or Bug work item:

- Set the *Iteration Path* from the root to the current Sprint.

- Set the state to Committed.

The easiest way to set the *Iteration Path* for a PBI or Bug is to drag the work item in the (product) backlog page to the current Sprint on the left side. You can see this in Figure 6-1. After you drop the item, the *Iteration Path* will be updated immediately. If you don't have access to the backlog page, you can set the *Iteration Path* manually and see the same result.

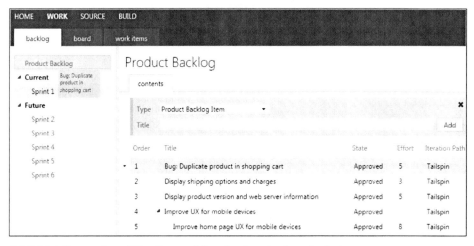

FIGURE 6-1 Forecasting a PBI or Bug work item by dragging it to the Sprint.

Note If a Sprint is not visible on the left side of the backlog page, it's because it hasn't been selected on the Iterations page in the Control Panel. You can get to that page by clicking the Administer Server link (the small gear icon) in the upper-right section of the page. There is also a *Configure schedule and iterations* shortcut on your team project's home page that will take you there. It may seem like extra work to have to select the Sprints, but it's actually a nice feature that keeps the list of Sprints small and more manageable on the backlog page.

Work items that have been assigned to a specific *Iteration Path* will remain visible in the (product) backlog page. They will also be visible in the Sprint Backlog. When the state of the PBI or Bug is changed to Committed, the work item will disappear from the (product) backlog page. The reason is that the query behind the scenes doesn't consider the *Iteration Path*, only the *State*. Ideally, those forecast PBI and Bug work items will never return to the Product Backlog—because the Development Team got the work done.

Tip To "un-forecast" a PBI or Bug, just drag that work item back to the Product Backlog link listed above the Sprints. This will reset the *Iteration Path* back to the root value, indicating that the item is no longer planned for development in any particular Sprint.

Mechanically, the other step in forecasting a PBI or Bug work item is to set its *State* to Committed. Unfortunately, the drag-and-drop operation does not do this for you automatically. You will need to set the state by manually opening each work item one at a time. This isn't so painful if you have only a couple of items forecast in the Sprint.

For a larger number of items, you can use the bulk editing feature on the work items page. First, run the Sprint Backlog query to see the PBI and Bug work items in that Sprint. If the query doesn't return the expected work items, you may have to edit it and change the *Iteration Path* criteria to the current Sprint. In fact, you should probably edit all the *Current Sprint* queries while you are at it.

When the query returns the correct PBI and Bug work items, you need to multiselect and edit them. You can do this by using the standard Windows keyboard combinations of the Ctrl and Shift keys, while clicking the rows. Notice that I mention the Ctrl key. This is because sometimes there will be items in the Sprint Backlog that you don't want to select, such as an epic parent PBI. Microsoft designed the tool to include parent work items in the Sprint Backlog for reference. Work item 905, in Figure 6-2, shows an example of this.

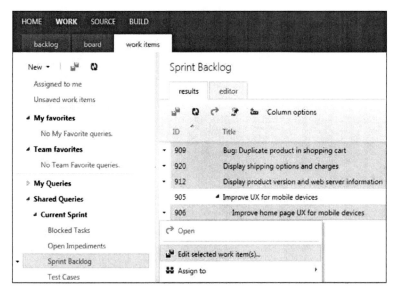

FIGURE 6-2 Selecting multiple work items to edit.

The Edit Work Items screen lets you specify the field(s) that you want to change for the selected items. In addition to setting the *State* to Committed, I recommend adding a quick note for the historical record. You can see an example of this in Figure 6-3.

FIGURE 6-3 Changing the *State* and adding notes for the selected work items.

From the perspective of Team Foundation Server, once the *Iteration Path* and *State* fields are set, those PBI and Bug work items are forecast for that Sprint. They will no longer appear in the (product) backlog page in Team Web Access or in the Product Backlog query results. They *will* appear in the (Sprint) backlog page and on the task board.

Tailspin Toys case study Typically, Paula (the Product Owner) is the user who edits the items in the Product Backlog, setting the *Iteration Path* and *State*. Other Scrum Team members have done this in the past as well. The backlog page is typically used, but Microsoft Excel also provides an easy way to make bulk edits quickly to work items. These changes are done during the Sprint Planning meeting, and the user who is "driving" the keyboard decides which tool to use.

Capturing the Sprint Goal

After the Development Team forecasts the PBIs and Bugs that it believes it can develop in the Sprint, they collaborate with the Product Owner to craft a Sprint Goal. The Sprint Goal is a vision or objective—in narrative form—that guides the Development Team as they develop the Increment. The Sprint Goal also provides stakeholders the ability to see a synopsis of what the Development Team is working on.

Note The Sprint Goal doesn't have to be captured electronically. It can simply be written on a whiteboard in the Development Team's area or another public place. The advantage of using an electronic format is that it can be shared with stakeholders outside the office. A list of past Sprint Goals can be maintained as well, for reference.

Unfortunately, there is not "first-class" support for capturing a Sprint Goal in Team Foundation Server 2012. In the prior version, the Visual Studio Scrum 1.0 process template had a Sprint work item type. This type had *Sprint Goal* and *Sprint Retrospective* fields for the Scrum Team to use. Because version 2.0 no longer supports this work item type, the team will need to be more creative in where and how it records these elements of the Sprint.

Smell It's a smell when a Scrum Team doesn't have a Sprint Goal. Yes, it's difficult to craft a good goal, especially when the forecast work spans many areas and features. Having a goal, however, gives the Development Team something to focus on and commit to. It's good for people to have goals. High-performance Scrum teams understand the psychological value in having a Sprint Goal, working toward it, and achieving it.

One option for capturing the Sprint Goal electronically is to use Microsoft SharePoint. I recommend that Team Foundation Server be installed and configured with SharePoint, and that each team project be configured with its own project portal. For teams using the hosted Team Foundation Service or who don't have SharePoint installed, they will have to find another method of recording the Sprint Goal. Having a SharePoint portal gives the Scrum Team a great place to create lists, documents, and Wiki pages to capture details like the Sprint Goal, Sprint Retrospective notes, and their Definition of "Done." Figure 6-4 shows a Sprint Goal being recorded in a SharePoint Wiki.

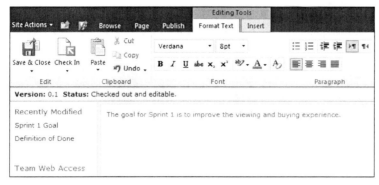

FIGURE 6-4 Capturing the Sprint Goal in a SharePoint Wiki.

Tailspin Toys case study Paula and the Development Team craft the Sprint Goal together. Typically, this is done after the work is selected; but some Sprints in the past have had the goal in mind before the work is selected. Either way, the Sprint Goal is recorded in SharePoint as a Wiki entry. Past goals are combined and saved in a separate Wiki entry.

Creating the plan

Forecasting the work items and crafting the Sprint Goal are only two of the outputs of the Sprint Planning meeting. The Development Team must also identify the plan for implementing those items. This plan emerges after the Development Team has collaborated on a design. In Team Foundation Server, the plan is represented by a collection of Task work items associated with their parent PBI or Bug work item. This emerging hierarchy of work items can be seen and managed in the (Sprint) backlog page and task board.

Tip Team Web Access knows what the current Sprint is. It shows the high-level details on the project's home page, including the Sprint number, start and end dates, remaining work, and a Sprint burndown. Clicking the summary information, as shown in Figure 6-5, will take you directly to the (Sprint) backlog page. Clicking the burndown thumbnail will simply expand it.

FIGURE 6-5 Clicking the Sprint summary on the home page takes you to the (Sprint) backlog page.

Prior to the Sprint, there shouldn't be any Task work items in the Sprint Backlog. Ideally, the Development Team creates its tasks during the Sprint Planning meeting and not before. It is possible that during some previous Product Backlog grooming sessions, an idea for the plan emerged. These ideas should be captured as notes, however, rather than Task work items. Plans change. The latest responsible moment for creating an actionable plan is during the Sprint Planning meeting. Not only does this allow the developers to create a plan with the latest information available, but it also reduces waste.

From the (Sprint) backlog page, you can create an associated Task work item by clicking the large plus sign (+) icon next to the PBI or Bug work item. The new task will default its *Iteration Path* and *Area Path* to that of its parent. The Development Team should give the task a *Title* and *Remaining Work* (in hours) at a minimum. Additional details can be entered into the *Description* field.

> **Tip** Remember, the Development Team should estimate the number of hours for each task as a team. It should not be assumed that any particular developer will be doing any particular piece of work. In other words, don't let the developer with the *best* skills in a functional area provide the estimate. In reality, it might be someone else that ends up doing the work, and in that case those estimates will be off. Once a developer owns the task, he or she will be responsible for re-estimating it regularly until it is done. The overall variance should be a wash because since some team estimates will be lower and others higher than that of the actual developer's.

As the Development Team brainstorms its tasks, it's best to leave the *Assigned To* field blank. Since all the work will be done *after* the Sprint Planning meeting, it's difficult to know who will be performing each task. That said, I know some teams prefer to leave the meeting with each developer having at least one task to get started on. This is one of the many behaviors that the team can decide to adopt.

> **Tip** Fellow Professional Scrum Developer Simon Reindl recommends not having Visual Studio running at all while the plan is being formulated. Keystrokes and mouse clicks can interrupt a productive conversation. Sticky or whiteboard notes can be converted to work items after the meeting.

> **Tailspin Toys case study** The Development Team likes to work on sticky notes or a whiteboard during the Sprint Planning meeting. When consensus is reached and estimates are made, they will convert these into Task work items in Team Foundation Server. Sometimes they use Team Web Access, but Excel is still a favorite tool for being able to blast in a large batch of tasks quickly.

Usually, only 50 to 80 percent of the total plan will be identified during the Sprint Planning meeting. The rest should be "stubbed out" for later detailing, or given rougher estimates that will be decomposed later in the Sprint. The act of decomposing work implies that the Development Team has a consensus about how the work will be accomplished. High-performance Scrum Teams are good at reaching consensus.

> **Note** I get pushback from some teams who think that creating Task work items, or any type of work item for that matter, is waste. Before I argue or agree with them, I like to find out more about their team. If they are a high-performance Scrum Development Team, then perhaps they don't need to track individual Task work items. They can maintain a burndown manually at the PBI level and let the team decide how to decompose and track its work. I explain that if you create and track Task work items in Team Foundation Server, even to the point of associating them with code check-ins, you will gain traceability and transparency. This is important to the Product Owner and stakeholders, as well as your fellow developers, who want to trace which forecast work was developed by which check-ins, and vice versa. Development Teams new to Scrum can also use this information to learn what they are actually capable of and to improve their confidence for the next Sprint.

When decomposing PBI and Bug work items into tasks, do what works for your team. Consider decomposing along design seams. The goal is to achieve independence from other tasks, or at least to achieve sequential dependence. In other words, you should try to avoid interdependence and initial blocking tasks. Initial blocking tasks are those that have to be done first, usually by a single developer (or a pair), and prevent a majority of work from moving forward until they're complete. Ideally, each developer (or a pair) can work on one task at a time and have made meaningful progress when it's done.

Here are some questions to consider as the Development Team creates its plan:

- Does this task provide a meaningful step towards the completion of the item?
- Does this task have criteria for being done (either explicit or implicit)?
- Can this task be worked on by a pair of developers effectively?
- Can this task be worked on by multiple pairs effectively?
- Does this task depend on any other tasks being done first?
- Do other tasks depend on this task being done first?
- Can the task be completed in one day or less?
- Has anyone else created this task already?
- Is this task already done?

Remember, Sprint tasks are what you actually must do during the Sprint. They include work across all disciplines: analysis, design, coding, database, testing, documentation, deployment, security, etc. The tasks must bring together everything required from the perspective of the PBI or Bug fix, as well as the software product's quality needs and the nature of the people doing the work. Completion of all Sprint tasks for a PBI or Bug fix should result in the Definition of "Done" being met for that item. You can see an example of just such a plan in Figure 6-6.

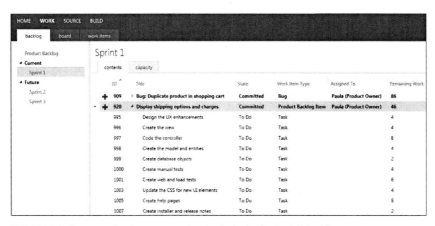

FIGURE 6-6 An example plan represented by tasks in the Sprint Backlog.

Tailspin Toys case study The Development Team has become quite good at envisioning the plan during the Sprint Planning meeting and then creating a representation of it using Task work items. They don't always get the Task work items created during the meeting, but they are keyed in shortly thereafter. If new tasks emerge during the Sprint, they are usually identified during the Daily Scrum and are created later by the developer who brought them up.

Capacity planning

The (Sprint) backlog page in Team Web Access provides the ability to enter and track the Development Team's capacity for the Sprint. Daily capacity (in hours) can be specified by team member. This capacity can even be scoped to a specific activity type (deployment, design, development, documentation, requirements, or testing). In addition, you can enter the number of days off by Development Team member, as well as for the entire team.

The purpose for entering these capacity details is to enable the (Sprint) backlog page to help the Development Team plan its work for the Sprint. By turning *work details* on, additional graphs are displayed on the right side of the screen. These graphs show the total hours of planned work compared to the capacity of the Development Team and the individual team members.

> **Smell** It's a smell if I see a Development Team using capacity planning tools of any kind. While it might be helpful for teams new to Scrum to avoid forecasting too much work, high-performance Scrum Teams recognize capacity planning as a potential dysfunction and a source of waste. They are aware of their capacity and upcoming days off, and they will use that as an input when forecasting a comfortable amount of work for the Sprint. Planning capacity by individual or activity type is counter to the self-organizing and self-managing attributes of the Development Team. Let the team decide what seems like the right amount of work, what to work on next, and who should do what type of work.

Customizing the (Sprint) backlog page

By default, the (Sprint) backlog page shows the *Work Item ID, Title, State, Work Item Type, Assigned To, Remaining Work, Activity Type,* and *Effort.* Just like the (product) backlog page, this page can be customized. For example, the Development Team might want to remove the *Activity* field and related behaviors.

Here are the high-level steps to follow in order to remove the activity column and features:

1.   Use *witadmin exportcommonprocessconfig* to export the common process configuration file for the team project.

> **Note** You can also use the Process Editor found in the Team Foundation Server Power Tools.

2.   Edit the exported configuration file, and then locate and remove the element that identifies the *Activity Type* field. You can see this element in the following boldfaced line:

```
<?xml version="1.0" encoding="utf-8"?>
<CommonProjectConfiguration>
  .
  .
  .
```

```
<TypeFields>
  <TypeField refname="Microsoft.VSTS.Common.Activity" type="Activity" />
  <TypeField refname="Microsoft.VSTS.Common.BacklogPriority" type="Order" />
      .
      .
      .
</TypeFields>
    .
    .
    .
</CommonProjectConfiguration>
```

3. Save the file.

4. Use *witadmin importcommonprocessconfig* to import the updated configuration file back to the team project.

After you have imported the configuration file, you will need to refresh the (Sprint) backlog page. You will then see that the *Activity* column has been removed. In addition, activity is no longer an option in the capacity planning tools and charts. This simplifies the view and removes a tool that could enable a dysfunctional behavior. The customization affects only the targeted team project, not all team projects in the collection. Also, all teams and team members will experience the change. It affects all teams on the team project.

> **Note** Microsoft always intended the Activity feature to be optional. Removing it by customizing the configuration file won't have any negative side effects. If a team wants to completely remove all references to Activity, they would need to customize the Task work item type and remove the *Microsoft.VSTS.Common.Activity* field. This behavior cannot be customized for the hosted Team Foundation Service.

> **Tailspin Toys case study** Andy has customized the (Sprint) backlog page and removed the *Activity* field and related behavior.

Daily Scrum activities

What the Development Team should be doing in between the Sprint Planning and Sprint Review meetings is rather vague in the *Scrum Guide*. This is by design. Besides meeting for the Daily Scrum and ensuring that progress is tracked and monitored, the developers are on their own to self-organize and manage their own work. This is how it should be.

Once the Sprint has been planned, the Development Team must execute the work. It is important to make progress on a daily basis so that at the end of the Sprint, the Development Team accomplished what it set out to do. Team Foundation Server includes a number of tools that can help run the iteration and track the progress of the team.

Developers can use the task board to help visualize the work in progress, what work has been done, and what work remains. The Development Team can use this task board collectively or individually, as each developer keeps track of his or her work and the overall work for the team. The Development Team can also use the burndown chart that is calculated automatically to review the rate of progress. As the Sprint progresses, these calculations and tools can be used to decide whether to adjust plans, add more work, or make changes to help deliver a done Increment of the software product.

The rest of this chapter includes those Scrum-related activities that the Development Team needs to perform throughout the development portion of the Sprint. Software engineering-specific topics won't be covered in this section, but many will be covered in the chapters ahead.

The Daily Scrum

As we learned in Chapter 1, the Daily Scrum is a 15-minute, time-boxed meeting for the Development Team to synchronize their activities and create a plan for the next 24 hours. It allows developers to listen to what other developers have done and are about to do. This leads to increased collaboration, as well as accountability. Team members need to understand that commitments are being made at this meeting and that these commitments will be tested 24 hours from now.

The Development Team can use the dialogue heard during the Scrum to assess their progress. By hearing what is or isn't being accomplished each day, the team can determine if they are on their way to achieving the Sprint Goal. As teams improve in their collaboration, this vibe will become more noticeable—even outside the Daily Scrum. High-performance teams may even outgrow the need for a formal assessment tool, such as a Sprint burndown chart. Whatever method they choose to use must be transparent, however.

Handling impediments

During the Daily Scrum, it is likely that someone will raise an impediment. An *impediment* is anything that blocks or slows down the progress of the Development Team. In my experience, most impediments are small and can be resolved quickly. It usually just takes some collaboration with someone else in the organization, such as a colleague, stakeholder, or IT support person. Larger impediments usually require more steps in order to be removed, such as adding a skillset to the team or co-locating distributed team members.

> **Note** Some teams refer to smaller impediments that can be quickly resolved as *issues*. They reserve the word *impediment* for larger, more organizational issues. In these cases, a strong Scrum Master might be required to resolve them.

Impediments must be cleared in order for the Development Team to be productive. In Scrum, there are two formal opportunities to identify impediments—at the Daily Scrum and at the Sprint Retrospective meeting. Impediments can occur at any time, however, and the Development Team should be ready to handle them.

> **Tip** Remove impediments—don't manage them! Successful Scrum adoption hinges on the ability to inspect and *adapt*. If impediments are identified but are not being removed, the Scrum Master needs to become more actively involved.

Impediments that surface during the Daily Scrum should be briefly discussed. If the developer experiencing the blockage cannot remove the impediment themselves, another Development Team member should offer to help. The Scrum Master, or the Development Team member playing the role of Scrum Master, should ensure that this happens. As a last resort, the Scrum Master should take ownership of removing the impediment.

Impediments should be removed as early as possible, but just not during the Daily Scrum. Problem-solving discussions detract from the real purpose of the Daily Scrum. If it is necessary, time to discuss the impediment and its resolution can be scheduled after the meeting.

> **Smell** It's a smell when I hear members of a Development Team repeatedly telling each other that they have no impediments. Occasionally this can be true; however, developing software is a complex process. It is fraught with risks and the potential for problems every day. In my opinion, developers tend to be optimistic, problem-solving individuals and, in their opinion, nothing ever blocks them. They have lots of (other) work they can be doing. This attitude is more common on teams new to Scrum where team members might be hesitant to share their problems openly. High-performance Scrum Teams know that it's about the team, and not the individual. They know the importance of raising impediments early, being transparent about progress, and feeling confident enough to ask others for help.

If the impediment cannot be resolved immediately, an Impediment work item can be created in Team Foundation Server. You can see an example in Figure 6-7. It is not required that impediments be tracked this way, especially if the Development Team expects the impediment to be resolved quickly.

Open impediments can be tracked by running the *Open Impediments* shared query found in the Current Sprint folder. This query returns all impediments in the Sprint that have a *State* of Open. Once an impediment is resolved, its *State* should be changed to Closed. For impediments that are scoped to a release or the entire product development, an additional query will need to be created.

FIGURE 6-7 Creating an Impediment work item.

Tip Fellow Professional Scrum Developer Simon Reindl has found it helpful to have managers and other executives regularly query the list of impediments. By returning the impediments by date, they can see the organizational changes taking place, including the level of inspection and adaption that is occurring. Seeing indicators that the team is improving can be as powerful as seeing the software product improving.

Note If the Development Team wants, the new Impediment work item can be linked back to the related Task work item(s) affected by the impediment. In addition, those tasks can be marked as Blocked, which will surface them on the Blocked Tasks shared query. While these extra steps provide context, they should be used only if the Development Team decides that there is value in tracking the additional detail.

Tailspin Toys case study The Scrum Team has very few open impediments. The team members have become quite good at removing them quickly. Because of this, they don't bother marking tasks as Blocked or linking impediments. Regular team communication keeps everyone aware of the current issues and what they might be blocking.

Taking on work

As needed during the Sprint, the Development Team works on the tasks required to develop the forecast work and achieve the Sprint Goal. Ideally, all tasks were identified during the Sprint Planning meeting, but this rarely happens. High-performance Scrum Teams will broadly identify all tasks at a high level, to be broken down later. Teams just getting started with Scrum might find themselves still working out the plan (that is, identifying tasks) well into the Sprint. All teams will do this to some degree. Being able to envision and capture the plan before starting the actual work is a skill that comes with the experience of working together as a team, on the same domain, using the same tools and practices.

Task ownership is not a required outcome of the Sprint Planning meeting. In fact, it's important to leave "to do" tasks unassigned so that Development Team members who have capacity can pick a relevant task to work on next. In Scrum, work should never be directed or assigned. When creating or updating a task, don't assign it to anyone who doesn't request the work. Resist the urge to assign tasks to the *ideal* person for the task. Doing so will decrease collaboration and the opportunity for other team members to learn. When the time is right, the team decides who will take on that task. This decision takes many factors into account, including the background, experience, availability, and capacity of the candidate developer.

Ironically, in Team Foundation Server, ownership is tracked using the *Assigned To* field. When the time is right, the developer who will be performing the work should change the task's *Assigned To* field to his or her name. He or she can ask another team member to do it as well. Task ownership can be set from the (Sprint) backlog page, the task board, or from the work items page.

> **Note** In Team Foundation Server, a work item can be assigned only to a single user. If two developers are going to pair up on a task, one of them will need to be the *Assigned To* user. High-performance Scrum Development Teams may not even care about who the task is assigned to, so long as it gets completed and progress against it can be assessed.

Decomposing tasks

The *Scrum Guide* tells us that work planned by the Development Team is decomposed to units of one day or less. This aligns with the guidance that I have always given developers. If the Development Team is using tasks, then a task should be small enough to be completed in a single day—whether by a single developer or a pair. This constraint forces developers to create more specific, granular, atomic tasks that elevate efficiency by reducing bottlenecks and risks. By pursuing smaller units of work, complex problems can be decomposed more easily to a level of detail that can be understood and achieved. Smaller tasks also lead to improved transparency and more accurate predictions of when the remaining work will be completed.

Note Traditional project management thinking might be opposed to this level of granularity. Not only would it cause their Gantt charts to explode, it would be way too hard and risky to identify all those tiny tasks ahead of time. Fortunately, there is no "ahead of time" in Scrum. The Sprint Backlog is created just-in-time by the developers who will be doing the work and is discarded at the end of the Sprint.

Assuming the one-day (eight-hour) task size limit, you might find "epic" tasks in the Sprint Backlog. Similar in concept to epic PBIs, these are tasks that are too large to be completed in a single day. More than likely, the task should be decomposed. The relevant question then becomes if and how to track the original task as well as the decomposed tasks in Team Foundation Server. Just as with epic PBIs, there are a couple of options for how to do this.

Tip Fellow Professional Scrum Developer Jose Luis Soria Teruel even recommends decomposing tasks that are in the six- to eight-hour range. Developers new to Scrum may try to plan their entire (eight-hour) day's capacity. This is not realistic. People take breaks, check email, have impromptu meetings, and perform other activities that distract from development. Keep these factors in mind as you decompose tasks.

The first approach would be to create additional, child-linked tasks. Each of these would have smaller remaining work values, achievable in a single day. The parent task would become a permanent placeholder. A team member would never directly work on that task. When all its child tasks are done, someone would have to set its *State* to Done. The advantage to this approach is that it establishes a visual breakdown of the work. This can be helpful for teams new to Scrum.

A disadvantage to this approach is that you now have something in your Sprint Backlog that isn't really a task. If you accidentally (or on purpose) left the parent task's remaining work value, it could mess up a burndown chart or other assessment. To be safe, you should set the parent task's *Remaining Work* field to zero after the child tasks are linked.

Note Unfortunately, the (Sprint) backlog page does not support task hierarchies. It doesn't have drag-and-drop linking capability or the ability to display multiple levels of tasks. It will display only the lowest (leaf) level of tasks. If you want to visualize the task hierarchy, you should run the *Sprint Backlog* query found in the Current Sprint folder, as shown in Figure 6-8.

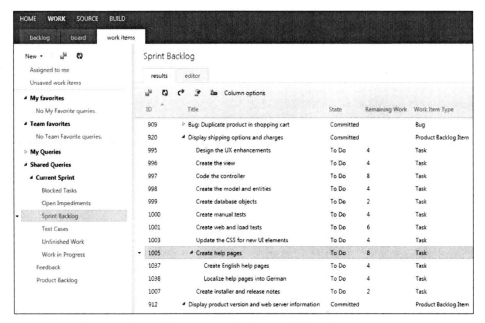

FIGURE 6-8 Using the *Sprint Backlog* query to visualize a task hierarchy.

The second approach would be to edit and rename the original task, making it one of the eventual children. Then you would add additional tasks as siblings of the first one. You will lose the "big picture" that the tasks were once related under a common "epic," but you also won't have dummy items in your Sprint Backlog generating noise and waste. You can always keep them associated using a title naming convention, description, or history notes. By reviewing the change history of the first task, you can see that it used to be the parent task.

I tend toward the second approach because tasks have such a short lifespan anyway. Because they only serve the Development Team, it is doubtful that somebody else would want to see how work breaks down during the Sprint. This approach keeps the Sprint Backlog lean and reduces the chances that a burndown or other assessment tool might provide misleading information.

Smell It's a smell when I see several "epic" tasks in the Sprint Backlog by the middle or later part of the Sprint. Either the Development Team isn't breaking down their work, or they aren't using tasks to plan and track their work. It's also a smell when I see one task per PBI with a generic title like "Develop it."

The task board

A task board is a collaborative tool used by the Development Team to communicate its plan for developing the forecast PBIs. It also provides visibility into the team's progress by displaying the relevant tasks by state. Observers can quickly see what work is done, currently being worked on, and not yet started.

The task board is not a reporting tool. It's not meant to be used by management to hold the team accountable for their progress. In other words, it should not be used as a "blame board." Once these behaviors start to surface in the organization, the developers will be less inclined to be honest and transparent about the tasks they are working on. The fear is that they will revert to their old ways and focus on making the burndown look good, even if that means stretching the truth.

> **Note** You can think of the task board as an information "radiator." It's always on, constantly updated, and relays useful, visual information to anyone who happens by and cares to take a look. You can learn more about information radiators here: *http://guide.agilealliance.org/guide/radiator.html.*

In Team Foundation Server, the task board can be found on the *board* page of Team Web Access. Unlike the backlog page, this one is two-dimensional. In the default *backlog items* view, the forecast PBI and Bug work items are listed down the left side. Across the board are the associated Task work items in one of three states: To Do, In Progress, and Done. You can see an example of this in Figure 6-9.

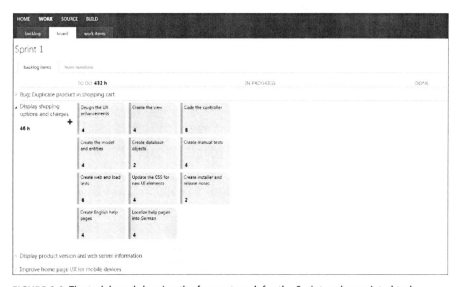

FIGURE 6-9 The task board showing the forecast work for the Sprint and associated tasks.

The task board displays PBI and Bug work items that are assigned to the current Sprint. These backlog items can be in any workflow state (other than Removed). The items don't have to have any associated tasks to be displayed either. If a PBI or Bug work item is assigned to another Sprint but has linked tasks in the current Sprint, you will see them listed here as well. Tasks not associated with a requirement (a.k.a. "free-floating" tasks) are not displayed on the board. Some see this as an impediment in that the board does not show the "big picture" of all the work the Development Team must do during the Sprint. I feel that this is okay, because work performed outside that required to develop the forecast work and achieve the Sprint Goal, while important, is not required to be tracked as part of Scrum.

Smell It's a smell if any of the PBI or Bug work items listed on the task board isn't set to the current Sprint or isn't in the Committed state. It's also a smell if any of the associated Task work items are in a different Sprint. It could be that it is an older task from a prior Sprint and that the parent PBI or Bug work item wasn't completed.

The *tasks* that are displayed on the board don't have to be "Task" work items. The board is flexible enough to display whatever work item type is designated as the Task work item category. For example, if a team were using a custom process template containing an *SBT* (Sprint Backlog task) work item type, the administrator would need to ensure the SBT type was marked as the Task work item category. Once that customization was performed, the developers could drag SBT work items across the task board. Process templates and work item categories were discussed in Chapter 3, "Microsoft Visual Studio Scrum 2.0." It just so happens that in the Visual Studio Scrum 2.0 process template, this equates to the Task work item.

Each task on the board displays four pieces of information:

1. The task's title

2. The task's owner (which will be blank if unassigned)

3. The task's remaining work value to complete the task

4. The task's state (represented by the column that the task is in)

The Development Team can view and update the task board to reflect the status in work items visually via dragging. Anybody viewing the board can see the progress that the Development Team is making against each PBI or Bug. Developers can quickly focus on the remaining pieces of work. The board leads to increased transparency, honesty, and accountability.

 Note You can only manage Task work items (or whatever work item is of the *Task* category) on the task board. In other words, you cannot drag the PBI and Bug work items themselves across the various states. For high-performance Scrum teams that choose *not* to use Task work items, this renders the task board useless. Also, you cannot view past Sprints on the task board. You can only do that from the (Sprint) backlog page, or by running an appropriate work item query. Requests for these features are quite popular on the *http://visualstudio.uservoice.com* website.

An integrated, real-time Sprint burndown chart is also embedded in the task board. The burndown shows the remaining work (in hours) in the Sprint. The task board is available to users in the standard license. In other words, a user only needs to own the Team Foundation Server Client Access License (CAL) to use the board. Team Web Access licensing was discussed in Chapter 5, "The Product Backlog."

There are a number of activities a developer can perform in the task board:

- View the plan (tasks) for developing the forecast work.

- View the progress of development.

- Add tasks to a PBI or Bug work item.

- Make edits to a specific task.

- Change the state by dragging between columns.

- Change the remaining work value.

Smell It's a smell whenever I see someone outside the Development Team changing the Sprint Backlog. According to the rules of Scrum, only the Development Team is allowed to add, delete, or change the contents of the Sprint Backlog. The task board is fun to use, and sometimes Scrum Masters, Product Owners, or other users want to "play" with it. This is fine, so long as they are making changes according to the Development Team's wishes.

Tailspin Toys case study The entire Scrum Team, and even a few stakeholders, use the task board to some degree each Sprint. Developers refer to it throughout the day as they see what work remains to be done, what their colleagues are working on, and to take on new work themselves. Scott (the Scrum Master) uses the task board to keep an eye on the big picture. He watches the amount of work in progress while looking for bottlenecks. Scott's goal is to help the Development Team deliver Paula's (the Product Owner) PBIs in the order she wants them. Paula and the stakeholders also monitor the task board, but they know that they should not touch anything.

Viewing tasks by team member

The default view in the task board is by backlog item. This provides a visual of the work in progress for each of the forecast items in the Sprint Backlog. By default, all tasks are displayed in light blue. You might think that this is just the color the task board uses for tasks. In reality, the blue is the *highlighted* color. By default, tasks for all team members are highlighted.

If you want to see the tasks owned by a particular team member or those tasks that are unassigned easily, you can click the hyperlink next to the person label on the right side of the screen and select the team member, as shown in Figure 6-10.

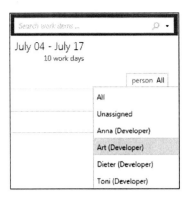

FIGURE 6-10 Highlighting tasks by Development Team member.

Using this feature causes the Task work item(s) owned by that team member to be highlighted, and all other tasks to be displayed in a lighter, gray color, as shown for Anna in Figure 6-11. The contrasting colors makes it easy for you to see the tasks undertaken by a given team member. Unfortunately, these colors cannot be customized. There also is no support for coloring tasks differently when they are blocked, done, larger than one day, etc.

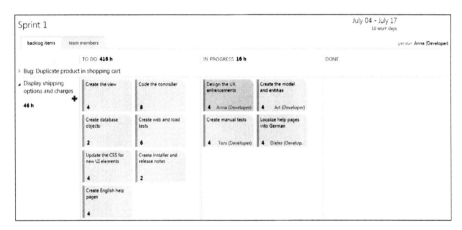

FIGURE 6-11 Highlighting Anna's task.

The highlighting feature is also helpful when a developer is looking to take on a new piece of work. By selecting *Unassigned*, those tasks that are not assigned to anyone will be highlighted in blue. Ideally, they will all be found in the To Do column.

Tip The highlight by person feature has another subtle benefit: any tasks created on this screen (by clicking the large plus sign icons) will default to the filtered user. This can be useful when one person is driving the tool during a planning meeting. Personally, I'd rather the tool just default tasks to the currently logged in user, or no user at all. That would better support the self-organization and self-managing qualities of Scrum.

Smell It's a smell if I see unassigned tasks in the In Progress or Done columns. If a Developer has started working on a task, then that person should claim ownership of it all the way through to Done. If a Developer stops working on a task to the point where he or she has essentially abandoned it, then he or she should move it back to the To Do column and remove himself or herself from the Assigned To field. It's also a smell if I see tasks in the To Do column that are owned by somebody. How can the team know if that Developer will be available when the need for that task arises? Task ownership should be declared as late as is responsible, ideally as that Developer starts working on the task. Seeing "preowned" tasks makes me wonder if there aren't some capacity planning or command and control dysfunctions at play on the team.

There is another way to view tasks on the board. It's the *team members* view, and you can select it by clicking that tab in the upper-left corner of the screen. You can use this view to pivot the task board to display tasks by team member. This view shows the developers down the left side of the screen rather than the backlog items. You can see this in Figure 6-12. The first row lists those tasks that are unassigned. The "highlight by person" feature works on this screen as well.

FIGURE 6-12 Viewing tasks by team member rather than by requirement.

 Note You cannot drag tasks vertically in this view. In other words, you cannot hand off a task to another developer by dragging it up or down to that person's row.

 Tailspin Toys case study The Development Team rarely uses this view, and when they do, it's to get a feel for all of the unassigned tasks, regardless of the backlog item they are linked to. By expanding the Unassigned group, they can see all those tasks.

Adding new tasks

As the Development Team identifies new work or wants to decompose larger pieces of work, new Task work items will be created. Ideally, this is done at the beginning of the Sprint, perhaps even as a result of the Sprint Planning meeting. The reality is that there will be new tasks or re-tasking occurring all throughout the Sprint because developers always know more today than they did yesterday.

Over time, the Development Team will improve in its ability to identify and create the plan—in the form of Task work items—earlier in the Sprint. The important thing to remember about the task board is that it should accurately reflect the remaining work in the Sprint, to the best of everyone's knowledge.

There are several places in Visual Studio and Team Web Access to create a new Task work item. We'll focus on creating one from the task board. Next to each PBI or Bug work item is a large plus sign (+) icon, as you can see in Figure 6-13. When you click it, a new Task work item form will open that allows you to create the task. The *Area, Iteration*, and *Link To The Parent Work Item* are all defaulted for you. Also, if the view is currently being filtered by team member, then that person will be the default *Assigned To* user.

> **Note** You can only add tasks to the backlog page of the board. You cannot add tasks when viewing the board by team members. Also, there is no "quick add" experience when adding tasks like there is when adding PBI and Bug work items on the (product) backlog page.

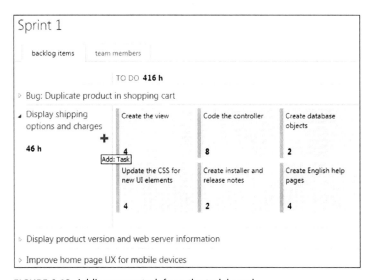

FIGURE 6-13 Adding a new task from the task board.

If you are adding a task of substantial complexity, you should have another developer (or two) review it. They should also assist in estimating the effort required to complete the task. Don't spend too much time estimating the task. Record a quick consensus value. You can adjust it later when you know more information. Be sure to let the Development Team know about the task by adding a good description and maybe discussing it at the next applicable Daily Scrum meeting.

Setting task ownership

It's quite normal to have tasks that are not assigned to anyone. In fact, I believe that it reveals a healthy team behavior. As Development Team members have availability, they should take ownership of the next most important task in the Sprint Backlog. This is decided by the Development Team, possibly during the Daily Scrum but at any point throughout the day. Professional Scrum developers know that selecting and taking ownership of a task should not be based on what task they *want* to do next, or what task they feel they are *best suited* to do. If possible, they should take ownership of the next most important task, as determined by the Development Team, required to complete the current PBI or Bug before moving on to the next one.

The purpose of the Daily Scrum is to identify the plan for the next 24 hours. This means the developers synchronize what Task work items each will be working on or pairing up to work on. The developers can then go back to their desks and take ownership of those tasks in question. Taking ownership, as well as changing ownership, can happen at any time during the day.

In the task board, you can take ownership of a task quickly by clicking in the area just to the right of the remaining work value. You can see this in Figure 6-14. This will cause a drop-down list to appear that will allow you to select a user or reset the task back to Unassigned. You'll notice that the drop-down list only displays those users already assigned to other work items. It won't contain the entire list, as you'd see when editing a work item in the work item window. While this abbreviated list is cleaner and easier to work with, it requires additional effort when a user is not found in the list. You can't type the name in the field. Instead, you'll have to double-click the work item and edit it normally in order to select the correct developer. Once saved, the user will appear in the quick drop-down list.

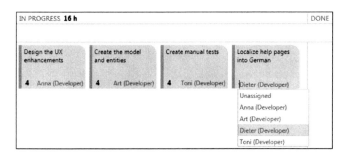

FIGURE 6-14 Using the task board to take ownership of a task quickly.

> **Note** I'm often asked by teams new to Scrum and Team Foundation Server if the developer should be the one who physically changes the *Assigned To* field. My answer is to let the team decide. This might be a useful practice for a new Scrum Development Team to adopt in order to shed any of its old command and control style behavior. If no such behavior exists, then I suggest letting any Development Team member change the *Assigned To* field. The Scrum Master can do this as well. If there's ever a problem or disagreement, remember that Team Foundation Server tracks who changes a work item, what was changed, and when.

Tailspin Toys case study For the most part, each individual developer manages his or her own task ownership. Occasionally, during a Daily Scrum or other planning meeting, the task board will be displayed on a projector and one of the developers will be driving. He or she creates and manages the tasks as the team decides. Dave shows off sometimes by bringing his Windows 8 tablet and manipulates the task board using touch.

Changing a task's state

A Task work item can be in the To Do, In Progress, Done, or Removed state. The natural progression is from To Do > In Progress > Done. These three states map to the three columns on the task board. A Task work item can be dragged to one of these state columns. When dropped, the task's *State* field will change to that value and be saved automatically. When dropping a task in the Done column, the *Remaining Work* field is set to 0 (blank).

These rules, including the rules defining which state transitions are allowed, are defined by the process template used to create the team project. Team projects created using the Visual Studio Scrum 2.0 process are allowed to drag task work items from:

- To Do > In Progress

- To Do > Done

- In Progress > To Do

- In Progress > Done

- Done > In Progress

- Done > To Do

Note When dragging a task from Done to In Progress, an error will be displayed, as shown in Figure 6-15. You will need to provide a *Remaining Work* value to dismiss the error.

FIGURE 6-15 Error message displayed when dragging a Done task back to In Progress.

Smell It's a smell when I see a developer regularly having more than one task at a time in a state of In Progress. There are situations where this can occur, but developers should strive to limit their work in progress in order to maximize their productivity.

Tip Be careful when dragging another person's task to a different state. If you are currently filtering on another team member, that team member will be assigned automatically to that task. For example, if I am filtered on Anna's tasks so I can see them highlighted in blue, and then I decide to move one of *my* tasks to the Done column, the tool will automatically set Anna as the owner of my task when I drop it.

The task board is very flexible in that it supports any number of different process templates—even ones that haven't been invented yet. The support includes what column headings appear on the task board and how they correspond to the workflow states assigned to the default task type assigned to the Task Category. In the Visual Studio Scrum 2.0 process template, the column sequence corresponds to the natural progression of the workflow transitions, moving from left to right. The Task work item's workflow states (To Do, In Progress, and Done) each match a valid *metastate* (Proposed, In Progress, and Complete). This flexibility is provided by mapping definitions found in the *CommonConfiguration.xml* file, as you can see in the bolded text here:

```xml
<?xml version="1.0" encoding="UTF-8"?>
<CommonProjectConfiguration>
  .
  .
  .
  <TaskWorkItems category="Microsoft.TaskCategory">
    <States>
      <State value="To Do" type="Proposed"/>
      <State value="In Progress" type="InProgress"/>
      <State value="Done" type="Complete"/>
    </States>
  </TaskWorkItems>
  .
  .
  .
</CommonProjectConfiguration>
```

Note No column is mapped to the Removed state. If you want to remove a task from the Sprint Backlog, you will have to double-click it and manually change its state to Removed.

Updating remaining work estimates

A high-performance Scrum Development Team may update their remaining work estimates daily. This enables the tool to assess the progress made against the forecast work. You can update the *Remaining Work* field quickly by clicking the number on the task and selecting a new one from the drop-down control that appears. The drop-down list displays the next five numbers lower than the current number, as well as a "zero" option. If the current number is less than five, the drop-down list will start showing fractional numbers. If the number is already zero, the drop-down list shows the first six numbers in the Fibonacci sequence (1, 2, 3, 5, 8, and 13). Any change to *Remaining Work* takes place immediately. There is no need to save your changes.

Tip If the number you want is not in the drop-down list, you can just type it into the tiny field. It can be difficult to do this for a "zero" hour value because nothing is displayed. You will have to guess where the number would be displayed. If all else fails, you can just double-click the task and edit it in the regular work item window.

Microsoft chose this drop-down list population scheme based on the findings of studies that it performed internally. The Development Team analyzed the deltas when hours were reduced. Whenever a developer updated their remaining work, they tracked the average change from the original number to the new number. After studying six months of data, they found approximately 80 percent of all deltas were within five of the current number. Interestingly, they also found that about 2 percent of the numbers were over 20 hours to begin with. Regardless of these findings, or how the drop-down control behaves, your Development Team can choose to record whatever numbers are accurate for them.

Smell It's a smell when I see a Development Team tracking actual hours worked. Remember that Scrum is a *team* effort. Tracking actual hours turns it into a collection of individual efforts. If management is really after the knowledge of whether you are ahead of schedule or behind it, a Sprint burndown chart should suffice. It *is* acceptable for the Development Team to discuss how long a specific task or PBI took to complete during the Sprint Retrospective meeting. An output of that discussion might be a way to improve estimation for the next Sprint.

Tailspin Toys case study Each developer updates his or her remaining work estimates at least daily, and sometimes several times throughout the day as new determinations are made. In addition, each developer takes a look at the upcoming, unassigned tasks to see if the remaining work estimates still feel right. If changes are recommended, they discuss them at the Daily Scrum or at a follow-up meeting and, collectively, decide what the new estimate should be.

Chapter burndown

Here are the key concepts that we covered in this chapter:

- **Forecasting the PBIs**   Set the Iteration Path to the current Sprint and the state to Committed for the forecast work items.

- **Capturing the Sprint Goal**   There is no first-class support for Sprint Goals in Team Foundation Server. Consider using the SharePoint Wiki to record the Sprint Goal.

- **Creating Sprint tasks**   Ideally, tasks are created early in the Sprint. It's to be expected that additional tasks will be identified and created later in the Sprint.

- **Handling impediments**   Impediments should be removed rather than managed. Create an Impediment work item as a last result.

- **Taking on work**   Developers take ownership of Task work items by setting the *Assigned To* field to their user name. In Scrum, work is never assigned.

- **Decomposing tasks**   Tasks should be small enough to be accomplished in a day. Create larger tasks as you brainstorm the plan, but decompose them later in the Sprint.

- **The task board**   The task board is a great way to visualize the work in progress, as well as the work yet to be done in the Sprint. Only the Development Team should make changes to the Sprint Backlog.

- **Changing a task's state**   A developer can change the state of task by dragging it to the respective column in the task board. The board should accurately reflect the work the Development Team is doing.

- **Updating remaining work**   Each developer should re-estimate the remaining work for their tasks each day. Use the task board to update these values quickly.

CHAPTER 7

Acceptance test-driven development

Traditional software development directed us to hand off a code-complete application to testers at the end of a lengthy development cycle. As our craft improved, we sought shorter development cycles, but we still handed off to testers. As we embraced Scrum, we removed the handoff by building a cross-functional Development Team able to perform all of the required activities. We're getting better, but I contend that there is still room for improvement.

The physics of software development tells us that testers must have a stable, finished piece of software to click and poke. On the surface, this sounds like an honest appraisal. I mean, why bother wasting time testing software that isn't code complete, right? Isn't Scrum about identifying and removing waste? Yes it is, and I contend that there is waste to be removed when testing efforts are *delayed*.

Acceptance test-driven development (ATDD) is a relatively new practice that moves testing activities to an earlier place in the Sprint. ATDD encourages the Development Team to discuss collaboratively the acceptance criteria with the right people. These conversations yield practical examples that give way to understanding the features and scenarios that become the basis for acceptance tests, and even coding specifications. All of this can be accomplished prior to any application coding. A benefit of ATDD is that it provides the Development Team with a shared understanding of what it's developing and what *done* looks like at each step of the process.

This chapter introduces ATDD and shows how to implement it using Microsoft Visual Studio 2012.

Note In this chapter, when I mention a *PBI*, I'm referring to the Scrum concept of a Product Backlog Item, not the Team Foundation Server work item type. Remember that in Scrum, a PBI can be any number of possible types of requirements, such as a feature request or a bug fix. Because bugs have acceptance criteria that can be verified through acceptance tests, ATDD can also be used as a practice to determine when a bug has been fixed.

Keep the conversation going

I can't stress enough the importance of conversation. It's one of the tenets of Scrum, and Agile software development in general. I'm not talking about developers talking to other developers about tools and technologies. I'm talking about the Development Team talking with the Product Owner, domain experts, and other stakeholders in order to better understand what they are developing and if they are on the right track.

A common misconception about Scrum is that, after Sprint Planning is over and development begins, the Development Team becomes sequestered. This is true in terms of non-developers being allowed to interrupt the team. But the opposite is not true. If the Development Team has questions or concerns about the work that it's performing, the developers should reach out to whoever can help. Even if there's a chance that development may have to change direction abruptly, the discussion needs to happen. In other words, the conversation should not stop just because work has been forecast, a plan has been devised, and development has started. None of these are immutable if there is no value in what's being developed.

> **Tip** Sometimes it's hard to have an honest and open conversation with people outside your immediate circle. This is especially true when you have to break some bad news, such as sharing the reality of a missed forecast. Professional Scrum developers should always practice *HARD* communication with others. *HARD* is a mnemonic for Honest, Appropriate, Respectful, and Direct.

When talking with the Product Owner, domain experts, and stakeholders, the Development Team also has to be careful about the language they use. They speak *tech*, while the other side speaks *business*. It's plausible that enough words might sound similar enough so that a conversation can actually take place and a consensus can be reached by both sides. For critical decisions, like defining what is acceptable behavior for a feature, a more precise language should be used—language that is mutually understood and devoid of ambiguity.

A good approach for coming up with this common language is to collaborate on identifying the behaviors for features, by creating real-world tests using real-world examples. Discussing and capturing test ideas like passing cases, failing cases, boundary conditions, configurations, and user interactions leads to an understanding shared by both sides.

> **Smell** It's a smell when I see a PBI in the Sprint Backlog without any definition of success, such as acceptance criteria. It could be that the item is so simple that it doesn't require any further explanation or have need for validation. More likely, the item made it into the Sprint with the expectation that additional details would emerge. While it's true that some additional details will emerge during the Sprint, I will question the Development Team's ability to forecast work when it doesn't know all the key acceptance criteria. Knowing the adequate level of requirements in order to be comfortable forecasting a PBI is a skill that will improve over time.

Collaborative specifications

When the Development Team begins developing a PBI, they should already have an idea what success looks like. In fact, I would hope that they have more than just an idea. Success is defined by the PBI's acceptance criteria. When each criterion in that list is satisfied, according to the Definition of "Done," the Development Team is finished with the PBI. Unfortunately, there can be a lot of distance between what was built and what should have been built. Conversations are the best way to bridge that gap, and those conversations should be recorded in a testable format.

In Chapter 1, "Scrumdamentals," we learned that the most popular format of describing a user story looks like this: *As a (role), I want (something), so that (benefit).* Figure 7-1 shows an example of this.

FIGURE 7-1 Describing a PBI with a user story description.

This description only defines, at a high level, the purpose and value proposition of the PBI. Acceptance criteria can be used to describe the PBI further. This can be expressed as a simple bulleted list in the *Acceptance Criteria* field of a PBI work item, as shown in Figure 7-2.

FIGURE 7-2 Acceptance criteria expressed as a simple bulleted list.

The reality is that acceptance criteria may morph during the Sprint to some degree. A competent Development Team understands and even expects this to happen. For example, the Development Team might realize that their server doesn't support the level of encryption required or the Product Owner may become concerned after reading that a popular social networking site was hacked due to an inadequate encryption technique. Both of these are valid, business reasons for a change in the scope of work.

> **Tip** Major deviations from the plan in the Sprint Backlog should be discussed with the Product Owner so that risks can be assessed, tradeoffs discussed, and a new plan formulated.

During conversation, you may find that a PBI will break down into multiple features. A *feature* is a discrete unit of functionality that delivers value to the user or business. A PBI may be large enough to have several features. For example, a "Customer logon" PBI will have features for creating the logon, logging on, changing the password, resetting a forgotten password, and so on. A PBI may also be small enough that the PBI *is* the feature. It's important that the Scrum Team identify these features prior to the forecast. But, just as with acceptance criteria, a feature may be discovered during the Sprint that is of high enough value to the Product Owner that a tradeoff is considered.

A feature may break down into multiple scenarios. A *scenario* is a narrative that describes a workflow or sequence of steps through the feature that exercises one path toward achieving an expected result. These steps could be taken by a user or the software. Scenarios provide more depth to features by expanding on the context and actions that take place within the feature. For example, the Reset a Forgotten Password feature will have scenarios for validating the email address, sending the email, approving the password reset, resetting the password, etc.

Even a small PBI, consisting of only a single feature, could still have multiple scenarios. There will be at least one scenario that includes the normal sequence of steps where everything goes as expected, with no exceptions or error conditions. These are known as *happy path* scenarios. Professional Scrum developers will also include at least one scenario that tests for the occurrence of exceptions or error conditions. These are known as *sad path* scenarios.

Note Some more security-minded Development Teams will identify *evil path* scenarios. These scenarios are similar to those of the sad path, but identify the steps that a malicious user, such as a hacker, would take when using the feature.

Some Scrum Teams will record these features and scenarios in the PBI work item from the very beginning of the PBI's life cycle. This requires a certain level of understanding and commitment by everyone involved with the creation, grooming, and understanding of the items in the Product Backlog. I applaud teams that are doing this, as it signals a shift from thinking about PBIs as "desirements" to thinking about them as "specifications." In addition, these forward-thinking teams can easily convert "yes-but's" that are overheard during review meetings into a sad path scenario that everyone will understand.

Tip When grooming the Product Backlog, the Scrum Team should try to identify all the PBI's features, but not necessarily all the possible scenarios. The full set of happy and sad path scenarios will emerge during the Sprint as the PBI is being developed. Ultimately, it's the Scrum Team's decision as to what is recorded and when, but I would only suggest spending a minimum amount of time on analysis in order to reach a consensus on the estimate of effort. This will minimize waste in the event that the PBI isn't forecast any time soon.

Neither the Visual Studio Scrum process template nor Team Foundation Server, in general, provides first-class support for recording a PBI's features and scenarios. Teams are free to use the *Description* field, as I've done in Figure 7-3, or the *Acceptance Criteria* field. Customizing the PBI and Bug work item types is another possibility.

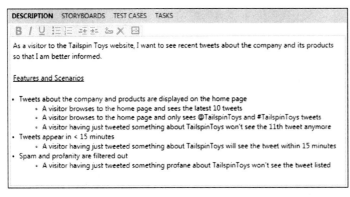

FIGURE 7-3 Recording a PBI's features and scenarios using the *Description* field.

 Note Fellow Professional Scrum Developer Jose Luis Soria Teruel likes using the *Acceptance Criteria* field to track features and scenarios. He considers them to be inseparable from the acceptance criteria and therefore should be located in the same field.

Executable specifications

When the Development Team begins developing a PBI, they should have an idea of the required features and the essential scenarios. These scenarios can begin as simple statements, as shown in Figure 7-3. This syntax is adequate for the Development Team to collaborate with the Product Owner, domain experts, and other stakeholders in order to estimate the level of effort and even forecast the PBI for development. Once development is underway, however, these scenarios should be refactored into a more testable format. This will make it easier to create acceptance tests, especially automated ones.

 Note Acceptance tests verify that a PBI meets the expectations set forth by the Product Owner. This occurs by comparing the observed behavior against the expected results. This behavior can be as large as a test that exercises the entire PBI, or just a feature, or just a specific scenario within a feature.

Scenarios, and their associated acceptance tests, are typically expressed in a natural language that enables the developer, Product Owner, and stakeholders to have a shared understanding of what the expected behavior should be and how to verify it. Having a readable set of tests that can be understood by a variety of people is a recipe for success and transparency. A popular format is the *Given-When-Then* (GWT) format:

Given [context], When [event occurs], Then [expected result]

The *Given* part of the scenario is used to put the context of the scenario into a known state before actions are taken. The *When* part describes the action(s) taken by the user. The *Then* part describes the behavior that is expected. Each of these parts should be written in non-technical terms, using the language, benefits, and values understood by the Product Owner and stakeholders.

Here are some examples:

- Given the existence of millions of new tweets every minute, when a visitor browses to the Tailspin Toys home page, then only @TailspinToys or #TailspinToys tweets are displayed.

- Given the existence of more than 10 @TailspinToys and #TailspinToys tweets, when a visitor browses to the Tailspin Toys home page, then only the last ten tweets are displayed.

- Given a new @TailspinToys or #TailspinToys tweet is sent, when a visitor browses to the Tailspin Toys home page, then the tweet displays in 15 minutes or less.

> **Tip** If you have several *givens, whens,* or *thens,* you can include *and* or *but* to the steps to make them more readable (fluent). For example, rather than saying, "Given 10 tweets are listed, Given all tweets mention Tailspin Toys ..." you can use *and* to make it more readable: "Given 10 tweets are listed *and* all tweets mention Tailspin Toys ...."

Acceptance test-driven development

During the Sprint, the Development Team, the Product Owner, and any stakeholders required should identify all scenarios, including happy and sad paths. These should be recorded or reworded in a natural language format like GWT. This can be captured in the PBI work item, as shown in Figure 7-4. From that, one or more failing acceptance tests should be created. All of this should be done prior to any coding of the PBI. As coding progresses and the Increment emerges, more and more of these failing tests will pass until finally the Development Team is done with that PBI. Keep in mind that acceptance criteria and related tests will be adjusted and fine-tuned as the coding progresses and the feature emerges.

FIGURE 7-4 Rewording scenarios using the GWT format.

During the Sprint, the Development Team iterates through each feature, developing each scenario. Depending on the complexity of the scenario, the Development Team might need to create multiple acceptance tests. A good practice is to have at least one happy path and one sad path test per scenario. This means that with a moderately complex PBI, there could be a dozen acceptance tests, and with a very complex PBI, there could be dozens.

Smell It's a smell if a Development Team does not have any sad path acceptance tests or if all of their tests are manual. I would suggest they consider this at their next Sprint Retrospective meeting and ratchet up their acceptance-testing practices in the next Sprint.

These acceptance tests should be created before any coding begins and they should be *automated* tests. This can be achieved by pairing a team member who has strong coding skills with another team member with a background in testing. In my experience, this kind of duet can produce automated acceptance tests of high value. Remember, all of these will be failing tests until the scenario is properly coded. For example, if a PBI in the Sprint Backlog has 3 features, each containing 4 scenarios, with 1 happy path and 1 sad path acceptance test, then there should exist 24 failing, automated acceptance tests before any coding on the PBI commences.

As development progresses, more and more acceptance tests will start passing. When the last test passes, the Development Team is effectively finished with the PBI. Assuming that the Development Team kept to their Definition of "Done," and no additional work is required, the PBI should be accepted by the Product Owner and demonstrated at the Sprint Review meeting. The Product Owner can then decide to release the PBI to production. This simplified ATDD workflow can be seen in Figure 7-5.

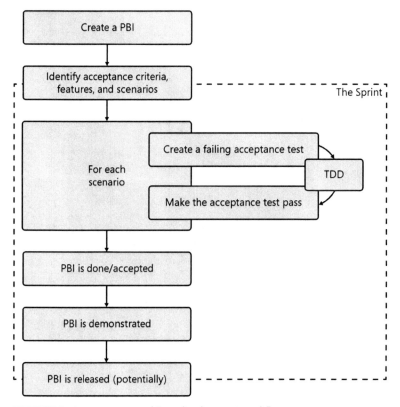

FIGURE 7-5 Acceptance test-driven development workflow.

I'm sometimes asked how ATDD is different from behavior-driven development (BDD), test-driven requirements (TDRs), functional test-driven development (FTDD), or story test-driven development (STDD). I tell people that each of these practices have the same goal: to express an abstract business requirement in a more understandable and testable format.

ATDD can provide added value for distributed teams. Team members collocated with the Product Owner can identify the acceptance criteria, features, and scenarios. They can also create the failing acceptance tests. These tests, written in a natural language, help the distributed team avoid misunderstanding. They provide the requirements and a level of documentation required by the distributed team. Compared to traditional requirements, these executable specifications provide an order of magnitude with more value and reduced waste. Furthermore, having a simple yet concrete goal of "make these tests pass" helps teams who struggle to self-organize.

Tailspin Toys case study The Development Team has started practicing ATDD only recently. Relocating the testing activities earlier in the Sprint was difficult at first, but the developers quickly realized the benefit of not having to delay testing or refactoring their tests. As for breaking down a PBI into features, scenarios, and acceptance tests—they were already doing that, but just didn't use those terms or know that it was ATDD.

Test-driven development

Within the "outer loop" of acceptance test-driven development, the Development Team can employ any development practices that they choose to. Any practice should strive to minimize waste while allowing the developers to develop something fit for the desired purpose. Beyond those basic rules, the Development Team is encouraged to try new approaches to designing, coding, and testing. The usefulness of these experiments can be discussed at the Sprint Retrospective meeting and abandoned, embraced, or enhanced in the next Sprint.

The most popular ATDD "inner loop" practice is test-driven development (TDD). TDD suggests coding in short, repeatable cycles where the developer (or pair of developers) first writes a failing unit test. The failing test specifies a piece of desired functionality in the PBI. Next, the test is made to pass by adding the minimum amount of code required. Finally, the code is refactored to be effective and to meet any standards, such as the Development Team's Definition of "Done." Afterward, the cycle repeats for the next unit of functionality.

> **Tip** ATDD can sometimes be confused with TDD, and I'm not talking about the letters in the acronym. One way to keep them sorted in your mind is that unit tests (TDD) ensure that the team builds the feature right, while acceptance tests (ATDD) ensure that the team builds the right feature.

One of the tenets of TDD is that you do not write a single line of application code until you have written a test that fails in the absence of that code. Advocates of TDD explain that the practice will force requirements to become clearer and mistakes to be caught by developers. Developers will also gravitate towards architectures and design patterns that are more testable and easier to refactor. Another nice side effect of adopting TDD is that the Development Team will end up with unit tests (and acceptance tests), where they may not have had any before.

The strongest argument in favor of TDD is that it uses tests as technical product requirements. Because the developer must write a test before writing the code under the test, he or she is forced to understand the requirements and filter out any ambiguity in order to define the test. This process, in turn, directs developers to think in small increments and in terms of reuse. As a result, unnecessary code is identified and removed as a clear and atomic design emerges. This becomes easier to grow and maintain.

TDD enables continual refactoring in order to keep the code lean. For example, assume a Development Team has high-quality unit tests that cover a high percentage of its code. When refactoring or experimenting, the developer can immediately see failing test results caused by any side effects. A nice safety net like this provides confidence, as well as the ability to code faster, by reducing the number of bugs and side effects that can be introduced accidentally.

> **Note** Having a project with many high-quality unit tests is like having a car with big, high-performance brakes. Both allow their users to operate safely at a high velocity.

Tailspin Toys case study The Development Team members know TDD, understand its value, and are comfortable practicing it. However, they decided as a team during a prior Sprint Retrospective that they don't see value in using it every day. However, if a specific scenario involves a lot of design work or involves working on a highly complex area of the application, the developers will pair up and use TDD to design their way through it.

Automated acceptance testing

All professional Scrum developers agree that automated testing is awesome and is a must-have for software development. The same can be said for automated acceptance testing. In fact, a growing number of professional Scrum developers believe that *all* acceptance tests can be automated. Short of the Product Owner verbally (manually) accepting the work, any scenario that requires human verification can be covered through an automated test. It may not be easy, but by adopting an automated acceptance-testing practice, the Development Team will be able to use these tests throughout the Sprint for ATDD, as well as later, for regression testing.

Note Some professional Scrum developers feel that, while possible, there would be a diminishing return on investment for automating all acceptance tests. An example would be the situation where the Development Team wants to automate the acceptance of user interface (UI) controls being lined up, font types and sizes being consistent, and so on. Manual acceptance user interface (UI) tests would probably make more sense here. My guidance is that if you don't have an automated test and have opted for a manual acceptance test it had better be for a very good reason. It is also something to consider improving in a future Sprint.

Visual Studio 2012 does not include an end-to-end ATDD solution, or any structured acceptance-testing framework for that matter. It does, however, have all the features necessary to wire one together. By using Test Case work items, Microsoft Test Manager (MTM), and various automated tests, such as unit tests, Visual Studio developers can practice ATDD. This section will show you how that is done, by taking the following approach:

1. Create one or more Test Case work items and associate them with the PBI work item.

2. Associate the Test Case work item with an automated test.

3. Make each test pass by coding its feature or scenario according to the specification.

Creating a test case

One way to associate acceptance tests with a PBI is by using one or more Test Case work items. A test case is just another work item type in the Visual Studio Scrum process template. Test cases can be very lightweight, such as only having a title and a description. These work items would merely serve as extra points of documentation. Some Test Case work items might morph to become manual tests, including the actual test steps and expectations. Other Test Case work items can get associated with an automated test, such as a unit test or coded UI test. These are the ones that ATDD practitioners should be using.

Even though the acceptance tests (Test Case work items) are physically linked to the PBI as a whole, you should *logically* link them to a single acceptance criterion, feature, or scenario. As previously mentioned, the scenarios are the tests, so linking them logically to the Test Case work items is preferred. This can be done through naming conventions or comments on the work item link. You can see a diagram of a PBI with features and scenarios defined being linked to multiple test cases which, in turn, are linked to automated tests in Figure 7-6.

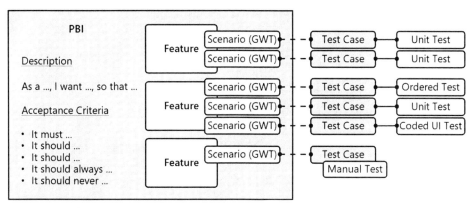

FIGURE 7-6 Linking scenarios to acceptance tests in Team Foundation Server.

Test Case work items can be created separately, and then linked to the PBI in two distinct steps. However, I prefer to create and link at the same time. When brainstorming a PBI's features, scenarios, and specifications, the Development Team will want to capture this information quickly. At first, this can be recorded on the PBI work item. A developer can then click the *New linked work item* icon on the test cases tab when editing a PBI work item. This allows a Test Case work item to be created, specifying a title and comment, and linking it to the PBI all in one step, as shown in Figure 7-7. Notice that my comment provides a logical link to the scenario within the PBI. For those looking at this who are not used to the GWT format, it is readable by humans.

> **Smell** It's a smell when I see only one Test Case work item per PBI. It's a stench when I don't see any. It could be that the Development Team has self-organized around another method to test the acceptability of the items in the Sprint Backlog; if so, that's fine. Professional Scrum Development Teams can use whatever tools and practices that they determine brings them value and reduces waste.

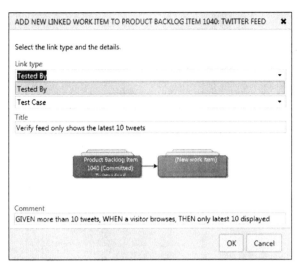

FIGURE 7-7 Using the *Tested By* link type when adding a test case to a PBI.

When linking a PBI to a test case, you should use the *Tested By* link type. If you were ever linking in the other direction, from a test case to a PBI, you would use the *Tests* link type. This link type relationship is more self-explanatory than the standard parent/child link type. After clicking OK, the Test Case work item opens, allowing information to be tweaked, like the owner or description. The test case picks up the Assigned To user, as well as the Area and Iteration paths from the parent PBI.

Smell It's a smell when I see Task or Test Case work items assigned to the Product Owner. These types of work items exist in the Sprint Backlog and, as such, are owned by the Development Team. If the Product Owner wants to change acceptance criteria or suggest new features, he or she would need to discuss this with the Development Team and, after collaborating on the impact and tradeoffs, the Development Team would change the respective work items. If the Product Owner is also on the Development Team, then this smell goes away, but another one shows up that I've mentioned earlier. Having a Product Owner also be a developer can be problematic in its own right, although it would explain why he or she owns these work items.

When associating a Test Case work item, you should reference the scenario or feature that you are testing. You can either use a naming convention when specifying the test case's title, or the link's *Comment* field to do this, as shown in Figure 7-7. You can describe the scenario further in the description of the test case, as shown in Figure 7-8. Logically linking a Test Case work item to a scenario or feature this way is not ideal, but it's the closest integration you can achieve with the current set of tools. Hopefully, in the future Microsoft will add some better support for mapping an acceptance test directly to a feature or scenario within a PBI.

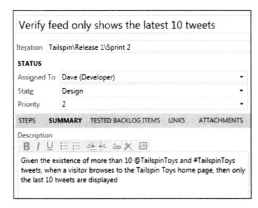

FIGURE 7-8 Using the test case's *Description* field to track the scenario.

Tip There is no "quick add" or other shortcut for adding a Test Case work item to a PBI from the (Sprint) backlog page or the task board. Opening the PBI and adding a link to a new or existing test case is a quick alternative. Fellow Professional Scrum Developer Ryan Cromwell still appreciates the fast, bulk editing approach of Microsoft Excel to creating and linking work items.

If the Development Team is following ATDD closely, then all acceptance tests (Test Case work items) should be created *before* any development begins. The associated automated or manual tests should be completed as much as possible. The goal is to have failing acceptance tests rather than (unit) tests that fail to build. Figure 7-9 shows a PBI with its linked acceptance tests, in the form of Test Case work items. These will be used to verify the behavior of each scenario and feature.

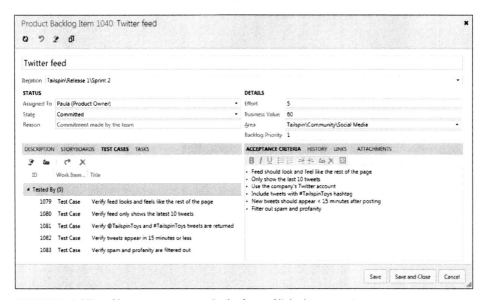

FIGURE 7-9 A PBI and its acceptance tests (in the form of linked test cases).

Once the Test Case work item is created, you can associate an automated test to it or turn it into a manual test. Later, when the test case is run, the associated test will be executed in turn.

Note Manual tests, including how to create and run them, are not covered in this chapter. Until that time when the Development Team is able to have 10 percent of their acceptance tests automated, manual tests still will be required. Visit *http://msdn.microsoft.com/en-us/ library/dd286715(v=vs.110)* for more information on creating a manual test case.

Associating an automated test

You associate an automated test with a Test Case work item using Visual Studio. You cannot use MTM to do this, as it only offers read-only support. Before associating, there are several prerequisites to satisfy. Visual Studio must have the applicable test project open, and it must build successfully. After creating the automated test, the test project must be checked in to Team Foundation Server. This test project must also be part of an automated build using Team Foundation Build. Later, in MTM, this build will be associated with the test run.

I'll begin with the assumption that the Development Team already has a test project or the knowledge of how to create one. That project should contain an automated test that executes a scenario specification and verifies the resulting behavior. This can be a Visual Studio unit test, an ordered list of units, a coded UI test, or another Visual Studio test type. As code is completed, the test should compile and execute without error, but it should also fail because the application code has not been implemented yet.

Tip When practicing ATDD, use the same discipline as when practicing TDD. Never stub out your tests. Spend the time to create each test as completely and thoroughly as possible. It won't be easy. Much of the target code may not exist yet and you may have to use some form of double, such as a mocking framework. The Microsoft Fakes isolation framework helps developers create, maintain, and inject dummy implementations in to their unit tests in order to make testing more robust and scalable. Learn more about the Fakes framework that is built into Visual Studio 2012 here: *http://msdn.microsoft.com/ en-us/library/hh549175(v=vs.110).aspx*.

Note When talking to people about unit tests, I have to be mindful of the context. There's the *theoretical* unit test which is a fast, in-memory, consistent, automated, and repeatable test of a functional unit of work in the software. There's also the *Visual Studio* unit test, which is used to implement a test of a functional unit of work; but it can also be used to implement tests larger in scope than a unit test, such as an integration test. For example, when I say the Development Team can use a unit test as the automation behind an acceptance test, I'm talking about the Visual Studio test type that will call into many functional units to test the entire scenario.

To associate the automated test with the test case, you will have to be connected to the Team Foundation Server and team project. Open up the corresponding Test Case work item and, on the Associated Automation tab, click the ellipsis button next to the *Automated test name* field, as shown in Figure 7-10.

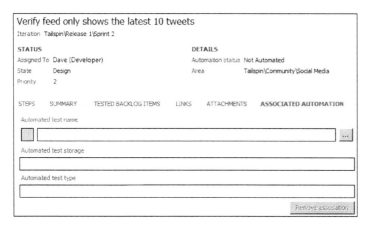

FIGURE 7-10 Associating an automated test with a test case.

You will be presented with a list of automated tests. This dialog box only shows the list of tests that are part of the currently loaded test project or solution. Select the corresponding acceptance test method, as shown in Figure 7-11, and click OK.

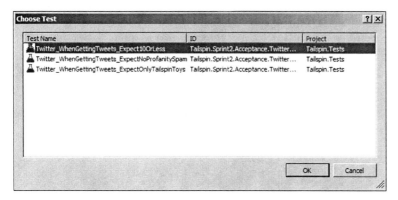

FIGURE 7-11 Selecting the corresponding automated test.

Tip When it comes to a naming convention for your automated tests, such as unit tests, my recommendation is to have one! There are a number of ways to name your test projects, assemblies, namespaces, test classes, and test methods. Some follow a strict BDD format, while others are fine just using clear names that describe the context and expected behaviors. For help getting started, consider visiting *www.stackoverflow.com* to view the latest conversations on the subject.

Only one automated test may be associated with each test case. Once a test has been selected, the Test Case work item's Automation status is changed to Automated. The associated automated test name, storage (assembly file name), and type are displayed on the Associated Automation tab seen in Figure 7-12. If you want to change the associated automated test, you'll need to click Remove Association and start over, selecting a different automated test.

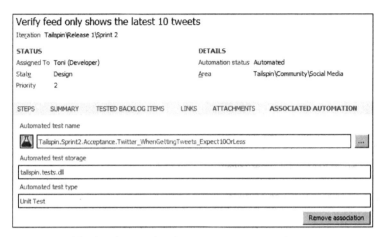

FIGURE 7-12 Viewing the associated test name, storage, and type.

Tip It can be tedious to associate automated tests in this way. If you have several tests, you may want to consider using the Tcm.exe command-line utility to create the test cases and/or associate the automation for you. Each automated test that you select, based on the parameters provided, will have a test case created for it, and the automated test will also get associated. It's not quite the same flow we've been discussing in this chapter, but it can save a lot of time when you need to create many such automated acceptance tests. By using the /syncsuite switch the utility will update existing test cases with automation. See *http://msdn.microsoft.com/en-us/library/ff942471.aspx* for more information.

CodedUI CodeFirst

Code First API Library, Scaffolding & Guidance for Coded UI Tests, or just *CodedUI CodeFirst* for short, is a set of features designed to help you write more maintainable coded UI tests for web applications. It is developed and maintained on CodePlex and installable from the official NuGet feed. You can think of CodedUI CodeFirst as a way to do test-driven webpage development by writing Page Objects that interact with the elements on the page—even before they exist.

CodedUI CodeFirst contains extension methods for UITestControl (to simplify the finding of and interacting with HtmlControls) and Page Object pattern guidance and bases classes. This is helpful for coding, but what's really nice is the support for Test Case work item *scaffolding*. This enables the Development Team to write acceptance tests for web applications using coded UI tests while making them less fragile.

Test case scaffolding reads the steps and parameters from a Test Case work item and creates a test class based on that. By typing in **Scaffold TestCase {test-case-id}** in the Package Manager Console, the scaffolder will create a test class with method names based on the test case. The test method will contain the test steps as comments so that the developer will just have to implement Page Objects and make assertions according to the steps.

There are two types of templates: one for plain test cases and one for test cases with parameters. The class is named the same as the title of the test case followed by its ID. The test method is attributed with metadata such as work item ID and description. The body of the test method contains all the steps from the test case as comments. A parameterized test case will get one test method for each iteration scaffolded. The parameters and their associated values are accessible at run time.

> **Note** The test case scaffolding is implemented as a T4Scaffolding custom scaffolder. A T4Scaffolding provides a fast and customizable way to generate code and build parts of a .NET application via templates. T4Scaffolding is available separately in the NuGet Gallery.

Here is the high-level workflow to practice ATDD using CodedUI CodeFirst:

1. Acceptance test case(s) are created and associated with the PBI.

2. The test case is scaffolded.

3. The pages that are needed to run the test case are identified.

4. A *Page* object is created for each page in the test case.

5. The scaffolded test class is updated to derive from *PageTest*.

6. Developers will implement just enough of the *Page* object and webpage to drive the test case scenario, naming the respective methods according to the actions in the test case.

7. The acceptance tests are executed and they should fail.

8. Using TDD, implement the underlying features in the web application.

9. The acceptance tests are executed and they should pass.

10. An automated build, deploy, and test environment is established to automate the execution of the acceptance tests.

11. Seek feedback and acceptance by the Product Owner.

For more information on CodedUI CodeFirst, visit *http://codeduicodefirst.codeplex.com*. Be sure to check the Wiki for the latest guidance documentation. To download the NuGet package, visit *http://nuget.org/packages/CodedUI.CodeFirst* or execute Install-Package CodedUI.CodeFirst from within the Package Manager Console in Visual Studio to install it.

Executing automated acceptance tests

When implementing automated acceptance tests using Test Case work items, you will use MTM to run them. In order to be able to run these tests and, in turn, execute the associated automated test, you will need to meet some prerequisites.

First, you must have a test controller, connected to a team project collection, and one or more test agents installed. The test controller runs as a service and manages tests on one or more machines by communicating with test agents that are installed on each machine. Each agent can perform tasks such as installing software, running tests, and collecting test data. By using a test controller, a developer can run tests on any machine that has a test agent installed on it.

Depending on the complexity of the software application, you may have to install additional agents and define additional roles. A role represents an individual computer involved in the execution of the software application. You can also think of a role as a location to run tests or collect data. For example, if you have an application that consists of a web server, a database server, and a desktop client, you would define three roles. The desktop client would run the tests and collect data locally, and the other roles would collect any data required on the machine assigned to that role. Multiple machines can be assigned to the same role. Environments and roles are managed using MTM.

Next, you will want to create a test plan and test suite in MTM. Here are the high-level steps for such a setup:

1. Start MTM.

2. Connect to your Team Foundation Server and team project.

3. Select or add a test plan like the one in Figure 7-13.

FIGURE 7-13 Keeping it simple by naming the plan the same as the Sprint.

4. Make sure that the PBIs are added to the test plan as *requirement* test suites like in Figure 7-14.

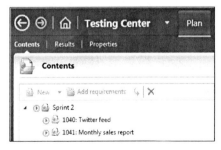

FIGURE 7-14 Adding the PBIs to the Sprint 2 test plan as requirement test suites.

To be thorough, you should also set a few properties on your test plan. You can set these properties by clicking on the Properties link on the Testing Center's Plan menu. The important properties to set are:

- **Name**   The name should refer to the current Sprint.

- **Iteration**   The iteration should be set to the current Sprint.

- **State**   The state should be *Active*.

- **Start Date/End Date**   These dates should match the Sprint's start and end dates.

- **Test Settings**   If you want the ability to collect additional data, such as IntelliTrace, Test Impact, or desktop video, then create custom test settings for manual and/or automated test runs.

- **Test Environment**   Select the standard or virtual test environment that you have set up for testing. This is a requirement to run automated acceptance tests using test cases.

- **Builds**   Select the build definition and/or quality to use as a filter. By default, when a new test case is run, it will select the latest build that meets the filter criteria.

- **Configurations**   Select the default test configurations (operating system type, browser type, and so on) to be used when test cases are run in this test plan.

As previously mentioned, you must be using automated builds in order to run a test case with associated automation. This is a good practice anyway, but in this context, it becomes a requirement because MTM needs to access the relevant test binaries. Also, before you can run a test case, you must associate it with a build number. This can be done just-in-time, as you run the test—which is helpful if you are running acceptance tests on continuous integration (CI) builds. If, however, you are running acceptance tests on a nightly build, you can specify the build number at the test plan level, as shown in Figure 7-15, and it will become the default when running tests.

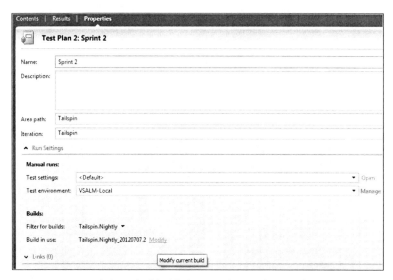

FIGURE 7-15 Associating a build with the test plan on the test plan's Properties page.

Tip Another reason to specify a build when running tests is so that the test results are published and correlated in the data warehouse. The Scrum Team and other stakeholders can view various reports and see how quality is trending higher and higher throughout the Sprint and release.

To run the automated tests, you must be in the Testing Center. You must also make sure that the latest code (for both the PBI and the tests) is checked in and built successfully using Team Foundation Build. The automated build can be triggered to run after a check in of code or at a specific time during the night. When and how often the build runs is a product of how many acceptance tests are to be run, how long it takes to run them, and if there is any value in running them often.

You can easily select and run a single test case, multiple test cases, or all test cases for a specific PBI. It just depends on how many tests you select in the user interface. Figure 7-16 shows the test run results of running all the test cases for a single PBI. As you can see, the Development Team has made half the acceptance tests pass. Because they are practicing ATDD, they can use this as the type of milepost on the road to done.

FIGURE 7-16 Viewing the results of an automated test run.

Tip You can also view the progress of your automated acceptance tests from within Visual Studio. Using the Test Explorer, you can view the results of an automated test run. Depending on your naming convention, you can also use the search box in Test Explorer to find and run only those tests that contain the specified string.

Once an acceptance test is run, its results are associated with the Test Case work item. This allows other developers on the team to see the results. Unfortunately, these results cannot be seen when viewing the test case or its PBI work item from inside Visual Studio or Team Web Access. A developer would need to either return to MTM or run one of the reports, such as the Backlog Overview report to see the test-driven progress of PBI development. You can see an example of the Backlog Overview report in Figure 7-17.

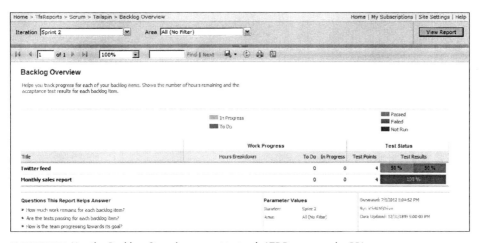

FIGURE 7-17 Use the Backlog Overview report to track ATDD progress by PBI.

When the PBI has been developed, its behavior should be verifiable by one or more passing acceptance tests. When all test cases pass, the PBI should be complete according to the specification. If it's not, then the Development Team probably didn't identify all scenarios or acceptance tests up front. This will improve after practicing ATDD for a while. If, however, all work was done according to the Definition of "Done," then all that's left is for the Product Owner to accept the work.

Reusing test cases

As we've already discussed, when the Development Team sets up their testing for a Sprint, they need to create a test plan and then add the appropriate test suites and test cases. Each PBI forecast for that Sprint should have at least one to two test cases. In addition, test cases from previous Sprints may need to be added to support regression testing. To accomplish this, I recommend creating a standard test suite (which is essentially just a simple folder) in the test plan to hold any regression tests from prior Sprints. You can see an example of this in Figure 7-18.

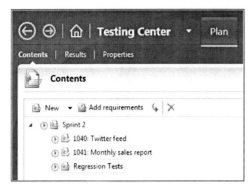

FIGURE 7-18 Creating a Regression Tests test suite.

Tip Check out the Test Release Management guidance by the ALM Rangers. It covers test release management, which includes preferred test case management practices for Agile software development teams. Visit *http://vsartestreleaseguide.codeplex.com* for more information.

By design, a single Test Case work item can be associated with multiple PBIs. For example, you might create a generic test case that verifies that a page request returns a response in 5 seconds or less. Since that is such a common request, you would probably want to reuse this test case for other PBIs in later Sprints. Microsoft recognized this need and, from the very beginning, has included the ability to copy a test suite in order to bring forward references to older test cases into newer test plans.

There *is* a problem with this approach. If you tweak the test case to better support the current Sprint's PBI, such as make it 10 seconds instead of 5, those changes will affect other Sprints' test cases used to verify other PBIs. This could be bad for various regression and regulatory reasons. There is a better way, and we will get to that shortly.

If you right-click the new Regression Tests folder, you can choose the Copy suite from another test plan option. This will let you select a test suite to copy to the current test plan, as shown in Figure 7-19. You can copy a specific test suite, such as a PBI, or all the suites in the source test plan.

Unfortunately, copying test suites like this produces a *shallow copy*. This is to say that the original (Sprint 1) test cases are not copied, but only referenced from the Sprint 2 test plan. You can verify this by looking at the work item numbers of the test cases and seeing that they are the same in both plans. As previously mentioned, any tweaks made to test cases in Sprint 2, for whatever reason, will retroactively affect the Sprint 1 test cases as well. This may be fine for some teams who consider old test cases to be history, like those who release to production every Sprint. But for teams that want to protect their test cases from prior Sprints, like those who don't release for several Sprints, they should make a *deep copy* of the Test Case work items.

FIGURE 7-19 Copying a test suite from another test plan.

> **Tip** You can work around this limitation by first creating a copy of each test case you want in the new plan. This can be done by right-clicking each work item in a query result window and selecting Create Copy. This generates a copy of the selected test cases with new work item IDs. You can then add these work items to the new test plan. The TFS Tester Power Tool, available in the Visual Studio Gallery at *http://visualstudiogallery.msdn .microsoft.com/72576517-821b-46c2-aa1a-fab940752292* helps automate these steps.

Microsoft Test Manager 2012 includes the ability to *clone* a test suite properly by performing a deep copy. Cloning creates new test cases in the destination test plan that are true copies of the test cases in the source test plan. You can change, add, or remove test cases from either the source test suite or the destination test plan as needed, without affecting other test plans. The newly copied test cases won't have any of the historical data like test runs, results, associated bugs, and so on. This feature is available only through the command-line utility Tcm.exe.

During the clone operation, each test case is copied (by value) from the source test plan to the destination plan. They appear as new test cases in the destination test plan. As part of the clone operation, the new test cases can be assigned to a new iteration path.

Here's a list of the objects that are copied during the clone operation:

- **Test case**   Each work item gets a new ID and retains its shared steps and test suite association.

- **Shared steps**   When the test case includes shared steps, that work item is deep copied as well.

- **Test suite**   Names and hierarchical structure are copied and preserved, including the order of the test cases, assigned developers, and test configurations.

- **Action recording**   When the test case includes an action recording, it is copied as well.

- **Attachments**   Any work item attachments are copied.

- **Test configuration**   The test configuration is reapplied in the destination test plan.

Here's a list of the objects that are *not* copied during the clone operation:

- **Test settings**   The test setting for the destination test plan is used instead.

- **Test results**   Any previous test results are not copied.

- **Test runs**   Because links to test runs are applicable only to the source test plan, they are not retained. This also applies to links to exploratory test sessions.

- **Requirements**   Because requirements are specific to a Sprint, when the requirements are cloned, they are created as static test suites in the destination test plan. Cloned test cases will be added as tests under this static test suite. Additionally, cloned test cases will not include links to their original requirements.

- **Bugs**   Any previously linked Bug work items are not copied.

> **Tip** To avoid duplicate clone operations, check the Links tab and see if any links have a comment mentioning TF237027, as shown in Figure 7-20. This is the Team Foundation Server message that indicates that a clone operation has been executed previously.

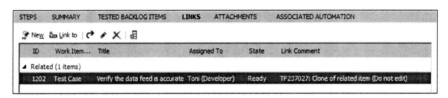

FIGURE 7-20 The link comment indicates that this test case was cloned from another.

You perform the clone operation from the Visual Studio command prompt using Tcm.exe. You must specify the collection, the source and destination suites, and a value for the new destination test plan. You can use the *overridefieldname* and *overridefieldvalue* parameters to specify a new area path, iteration path, or other test case fields. For example, here's the command line to clone a test suite from Sprint 1 (suite ID #6) to a new suite in Sprint 2 (underneath suite ID #26). You can see the results of the cloning operation in Figure 7-21.

```
C:\Projects>tcm.exe suites /clone /collection:http://vsalm:8080/tfs/Scrum
/teamproject:tailspin /suiteid:6 /destinationsuiteid:26
/overridefieldname:"Iteration Path" /overridefieldvalue:"Tailspin\Release 1\Sprint 2"
```

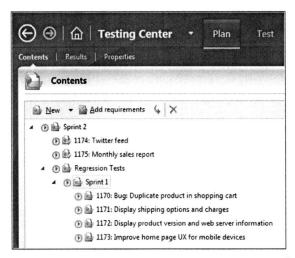

FIGURE 7-21 All acceptance tests from Sprint 1, cloned into Sprint 2's test plan.

Note If you clone a test case with an associated automated test, you must specify a build in the destination test plan. Visit *http://msdn.microsoft.com/en-us/library/ hh543843(v=vs.110).aspx* for more information about cloning test cases.

Tailspin Toys case study Paula (the Product Owner) wants to move to a continuous delivery (CD) model in the near future. She wants each PBI to be released to the production servers as she accepts the work. Once CD is implemented, saving and protecting prior Sprint test cases won't be so important. If and when a production bug comes up, the Development Team will execute a deep copy using the command line of any relevant test cases from the original PBI to be tweaked and used to verify and fix the bug. Until CD is in place, however, several Sprints, worth of finished work can get stacked up prior to release. It's important for the Development Team to ensure that they don't break this backlog of done work. Reference copies of test cases, using the copy feature inside MTM, will work fine for their needs.

Other acceptance-testing frameworks

By now, you should understand why having executable specifications is important. Having specifications that are merely testable by manual acceptance tests is a start, but executable specifications robotically verified by automated tests are ideal. They should be the goal for all professional Scrum Development Teams.

The approach I have outlined so far in this chapter is really just a *partial* ATDD implementation. If the Development Team wants a *true* executable specification, which is one where the framework actually passes the specification data to the test runner to execute, they will need to implement an open-source .NET acceptance-testing framework. With these frameworks, if the specification is changed, then it will automatically affect the test. In the approach using Test Case work items, the link is only a *logical* one. If the specification is changed the test will not be changed automatically.

Even with the latest Visual Studio 2012 tools, a professional Scrum Development Team that wants a full-fidelity, automated acceptance-testing process needs to use one of the open-source frameworks. Visual Studio can integrate with any of these frameworks. By using Visual Studio Generic test, an external test runner can be invoked and the test results imported into Team Foundation Server for reporting. I have listed the most popular frameworks for .NET developers in Table 7-1. There are others available, and new ones seem to appear each day. This is good news because it shows that there is excitement in the developer community.

When evaluating these frameworks, keep in mind that some are *behavior* frameworks, while others are *spec* frameworks. Some frameworks, such as RSpec, support both. Here is the distinction:

- **Behavior frameworks**   Use a shared language and structure to focus more on the PBI and acceptance criteria at the application level. These criteria can then be wired up to code, providing an automated way to run the acceptance tests.

- **Spec frameworks**   Focus at the unit level, using unit tests rather than acceptance tests. These frameworks allow the developer to replace or augment the existing unit test syntax with one that's focused more on behavior.

TABLE 7-1 .NET acceptance-testing frameworks.

Framework	Type	Description
Framework for Integrated Test (Fit)	N/A	An open-source tool first released in 2002. Fit creates a feedback loop between the user and the developers by using Microsoft Office to enter examples that are displayed in HTML and connected to the software using test fixtures. Fit originally only supported Java, but has since been ported to C#. You can learn more about Fit here: *http://fit.c2.com*.
FitNesse	N/A	FitNesse is an integrated development environment (IDE) for Fit that uses a wiki as its client. FitNesse enables the creating, running, organizing, annotating, and sharing of Fit tests throughout the team. You can learn more about FitNesse here: *http://fitnesse.org*.
StoryQ	XSpec	StoryQ is a portable (single DLL), embedded BDD framework for Microsoft .NET Framework 3.5. It runs within your existing test runner and helps produce human-friendly test output (HTML or text). StoryQ's fluent interface adds strong typing, IntelliSense, and documentation to your BDD grammar. You can learn more about StoryQ here: *http://storyq.codeplex.com*.
NBehave	XBehave	NBehave enables defining and executing application requirement goals. You can learn more about NBehave here: *http://nbehave.codeplex.com*.

Framework	Type	Description
MSpec	XSpec	Machine.Specifications (MSpec for short) is an XSpec framework geared toward removing language noise and simplifying tests. MSpec uses named delegates and anonymous functions to increase readability. You can learn more about MSpec here: *https://github.com/machine/machine.specifications*.
NSpec	XSpec	NSpec drives development by specifying behavior within a declared context. It is heavily inspired by RSpec and builds upon the NUnit assertion library. You can learn more about NSpec here: *http://nspec.org*.
SpecFlow	XBehave	SpecFlow is a very popular framework for facilitating acceptance tests as acceptance criteria. It is quite similar to Cucumber from the Ruby world. You can learn more about SpecFlow here: *http://www.specflow.org*.

These frameworks all operate by calling public methods on .NET assemblies and evaluating the results. This is similar to how Visual Studio unit tests execute, but the similarities stop there. With simple unit tests, there's no built-in support for specifying expectations for specific conditions. There is only the developer's word that he or she will name the test method, class, and namespace responsibly in order for others to be able to understand its intent and purpose. Third-party acceptance-testing frameworks, on the other hand, take a more explicit approach by enabling the developer to define the scenario, scenario steps, givens, whens, thens, and bindings/hooks into the application code.

Note Some of my fellow professional Scrum developer colleagues don't see the value in distinguishing frameworks by behavior versus spec. They feel that both types serve the purpose of driving and verifying the intent of the code. While I agree with them, I think it's also important to call out those that are better suited for acceptance testing (XBehave) versus those that are better suited for creating unit tests and domain-driven design (XSpec).

Regardless of which framework you choose, the tests become the executable specification. Investing in a framework is worth it in the long run. Not only will you have a way of knowing your progress during the Sprint, but you'll also have automated tests to use for regression testing down the road.

Tip It can be difficult to find a Product Owner, domain expert, or other stakeholder who is interested in learning and using an acceptance-testing framework. I've found that it's more common that the Product Owner just *tells* the Development Team what he or she wants and leaves the decision of selecting the testing framework up to the developers. If this were a straight "how" decision, I would agree, but acceptance testing is about understanding the criteria, features, and scenarios—it's a "what," and that must involve the Product Owner. The Scrum Team should try out a framework for a couple of Sprints and then abandon, embrace, or enhance it after discussing its value during a Sprint Retrospective meeting.

Tailspin Toys case study The Development Team is evaluating SpecFlow to use as their acceptance-testing framework. Compared to the other frameworks, it is far easier to integrate testing with the entire Scrum Team. The SpecFlow stories are written in plain business English rather than in Gherkin-speak. Paula and the domain experts appreciate this. The fact that SpecFlow integrates into Visual Studio 2012 is also a plus.

Acceptance

As I visit with software development teams, I realize that there is a lot of confusion around the concept of acceptance. For example, a common misconception I hear is that having passing acceptance tests means that the PBI has been accepted. This is not necessarily true. Having passing acceptance tests only proves that the acceptance criteria have been satisfied. It does not necessarily mean that the Product Owner will accept the work. Acceptance testing and Product Owner acceptance are two distinct activities. Table 7-2 lists some other common misconceptions around acceptance.

TABLE 7-2 Common misconceptions about acceptance.

Misconception	Why it's a misconception
Passing acceptance tests is equivalent to being done with the PBI.	The Development Team is done when the acceptance criteria have been validated, the Definition of "Done" has been met, and the Product Owner accepts the work.
Passing acceptance tests is equivalent to the PBI being accepted.	Only the Product Owner can accept a PBI. An engaged Product Owner will want to see/use the PBI firsthand before accepting it.
Acceptance tests must be manual tests.	Almost all scenarios can be verified using automated tests.
Acceptance can occur only at the Sprint Review meeting.	The Product Owner can accept the work at any time during the Sprint. In fact, it can even be released to production mid-Sprint.
Stakeholders can accept the work.	Only the Product Owner may accept the work.

In reality, there's no guarantee that the Product Owner will like what you have built, let alone accept it. High-performance Scrum Development Teams know this and will relentlessly pursue the Product Owner to get his or her opinion about and eventual acceptance of the feature they are developing. This is because it is very difficult to capture, in an executable specification, what somebody "likes." Product Owner acceptance is, and always will be, a carbon-based test, meaning that the Product Owner themselves will need to put eyes and hands on it.

Tip Product Owners are just people. People have a hard time itemizing their wants, desires, and tastes. This is especially true with something as abstract as software. You can count on people telling you what they *don't* like after seeing it. Scrum embraces this fact, and so should you. For example, if you and your colleagues are working on a PBI and have just finished designing the user interface, have the Product Owner look at it and give a nod before any additional work is spent wiring it up.

Tailspin Toys case study The Development Team is fortunate that Paula (the Product Owner) works in the same building and makes herself regularly available for questions and feedback. As the developers get close to finishing a PBI, they make sure Paula likes what they are doing. The same is true when the Development Team is brainstorming complex plumbing or User Experience designs. Paula wants the software to be the best for her users, and she knows that her regular involvement will produce better results. When it comes time to "accept" the work, the odds are Paula has already accepted it, just not in so many words. It's because of this work ethic and mindset that the Scrum Team believes that a continuous delivery model is within their reach.

Chapter burndown

Here are the key concepts we covered in this chapter:

- **Desirements**   Requirements without acceptance criteria expressed as executable specifications are nothing more than just wishful thinking.

- **Acceptance criteria**   The Product Owner's definition of success for a given PBI.

- **Feature**   A discrete unit of functionality that delivers value to the user or business. A PBI may break down into multiple features, or it may be the feature.

- **Scenario**   A narrative that describes a workflow or sequence of steps through a feature. A feature may break down into multiple scenarios.

- **Executable specification**   An initial failing automated acceptance test that verifies a specific scenario.

- **Acceptance test-driven development (ATDD)**   The practice of defining executable specifications in the form of failing automated tests prior to writing any application code. Development is done when all acceptance tests pass.

- **Test case**   A type of work item that can be used as an acceptance test. Test cases can be manual or automated. Professional Scrum developers prefer automated acceptance tests.

- **Associated automation**   Test Case work items can be associated with an automated unit test, ordered test, coded UI tests, and so on. The association is performed within Visual Studio and the test is executed from within MTM or during an automated Team Foundation Build.

- **Regression testing**   Test cases from prior Sprints can be copied or cloned to the current Sprint and used for regression testing.

- **SpecFlow**   The most popular third-party acceptance-testing framework for .NET.

- **Acceptance**   Acceptance testing and Product Owner acceptance are two separate activities. The Product Owner should never accept work that hasn't passed acceptance tests.

CHAPTER 8

Effective collaboration

There's a buzz—a kind of energy that you can feel—when a high-performance Scrum Development Team works in harmony to solve a problem. Each developer gets totally absorbed in his or her task. Each member of the Development Team does his or her part integrating the design, the coding, and the testing. Scenarios and features are completed and verified. Product Backlog items (PBIs) are moved to the done column. Everyone loses track of time. They are experiencing *flow*. Everyone feels happy and satisfied.

Bruce Tuckman wrote about the stages of group development. He identified four stages in the development model: forming, storming, norming, and performing. In the initial, *forming* stage, the individuals come together to form the team. They may not know each other or everyone's strengths and weaknesses. This leads to the *storming* stage, where each developer competes for their idea's consideration while working together to resolve their differences. This necessary stage can sometimes be completed quickly. Unfortunately, some teams never leave this stage. Once the team members are able to resolve their differences and participate with one another more comfortably, they enter the *norming* phase. Here, the entity of the team begins to emerge. The members converge on a single goal and come up with a mutual plan. Compromise and consensus decision making occurs in this phase. High-performance Scrum Development Teams have reached the fourth and final phase, known as *performing*. These teams not only function as a unit, but they also find ways to get the job done smoothly and efficiently. They are able to self-organize and self-manage effectively. In my opinion, very few teams reach this phase, but every one that does has mastered the art of collaboration.

In this chapter, we will look at some practices and tools that enable more effective collaboration. By learning and adopting these practices, a team will increase its ability to reach the performing phase of Bruce Tuckman's model.

Individuals and interactions over processes and tools

The Agile Manifesto clearly states that while there is value in process and tools, there is *more* value in interacting with individuals. This is to say that Agile software development recognizes the importance of people and the value that they bring when working together. After all, it's people who build software, not the process or the tool. If you put bright, empowered, motivated people in a room with no process and inadequate tools, they will still be able to get something accomplished. Their Velocity may suffer, but they will produce value. They will also inspect and adapt their processes, while looking for methods of improvement. Conversely, if the people don't work well together, no process or tool will fix that. A bad process can screw up a good tool, but bad people can screw up everything.

> **Tip** Fellow Professional Scrum Developer Simon Reindl reminds us that to err is human, but to forgive is vital.

Software development is a team sport. To succeed in this sport, game after game, the team must share the vision, divide the work, and learn from each other. In other words, they must collaborate. Even a team of expert craftsmen (rock stars in their own right) is doomed to fail if they don't collaborate with each other. If the striker on a soccer team has his best game ever—scoring four goals—but the other team scores five goals, it is still a loss. The other team, with even mediocre players, probably collaborated better.

A few years ago, Ken Schwaber did a series of podcasts where he answered frequently asked questions about Scrum. My favorite question that he answered was, "Do I need very good developers for Scrum?" His answer was insightful: "You need very good developers for software development. You can do Scrum with terrible software developers, and you'll get terrible increments of functionality every Sprint."

When I hear about teams that have tried Scrum and given up because it was "too difficult," I know that they are not talking about the complexity of Scrum. These are software developers. They are some of the smartest problem solvers you'll ever meet. Besides, Scrum is easy to understand. Chapter 1 pretty much covered it. No, what these people are talking about is the *discipline* of practicing Scrum correctly within an organization that allowed them to do so, every single day. That's why they gave up.

I agree with the Agile Manifesto. This is evident throughout this book as I point out the value of interacting and collaborating with individuals. I have discussed process and tools as well, but have been most vigilant in pointing out that not all application lifecycle management (ALM) tools and automation frameworks are healthy for a team. Most are. Some, however, can lead to one or more dysfunctional behaviors. For example, social networks, televisions with digital video recorders (DVRs), and video games are appealing and fun, but sometimes the kids (or developers in this case) need to get outside and interact with others.

Years ago, I was once asked to build a web-based work item approval system on top of Team Foundation Server (TFS). The client designed it so that email alerts would be sent when a work item changed to a certain state. These emails contained embedded hyperlinks that would redirect the user to a webpage that allowed managers or leads to authorize the state change. It was a sophisticated system—it even knew which users could cover for others if someone was on vacation or out of the office. My company built it. The client installed it. It did exactly what they wanted, but they ended up not using it. The reason they mothballed it was that it was too mechanical and removed the opportunity for two people to meet face to face and have a discussion. This was a learning opportunity for me and something I keep in mind whenever I see a shiny new feature in Microsoft Visual Studio. I ask myself, "Does this feature encourage collaboration or discourage it?"

When it comes time to meet and collaborate with members of your Scrum Team or stakeholders, here are some tips to consider:

- Establish the scope and the goal of the meeting, and stay focused on these topics.

- Meet face to face, especially if you anticipate a substantive conversation.

- Meet at a whiteboard, especially if you're intent on solving a problem.

- Set a time-box for the meeting. Be prepared to explain the concept.

- Leave the gadgets in the other room, unless they are required.

- Employ active listening techniques.

In this section, I discuss some of the general—but important—collaboration practices that a Scrum Team can adopt.

Listen actively

Software developers tend to have a short attention span and be impatient with anybody who is not as smart as them or who doesn't have the answer that they are looking for. Of course, I could just be talking about myself. But as they say, acknowledging that you have a problem is the first step in curing it. For me, *active listening* was that cure.

Active listening is a communication technique where the listener is required to feed back what is heard to the speaker. This can be as simple as nodding the head, writing a note on a piece of paper, or restating or paraphrasing what was said. This demonstrates your sincerity and respect for what the person is saying. It also helps alleviate assumptions and other things that get taken for granted. Opening a laptop and clicking through emails or otherwise getting distracted by anything else is not active listening and may even be considered disrespectful. Even "lightweight" devices such as tablets, slates, and smartphones can fall into this category.

Another part of active listening is waiting to speak. This is my particular problem. I tend to complete other people's sentences in order to move the conversation along to a more interesting topic. In my mind, I think I'm being helpful, but I know that I'm probably coming across as being rude. This is especially true for people who don't know me and is especially apparent to me when I have a conversation with another ADHD individual. Fortunately, there are techniques that can be used to overcome this particular interpersonal dysfunction. My favorite is to take a stack of sticky notes with me and write down the things that come to mind while the other person is talking. Soon it will be my turn to talk, and I can go back through my notes. See what I did? I solved the feedback and interruption problems with a single solution.

I'll re-mention HARD at this point. HARD is a mnemonic for Honest, Appropriate, Respectful, and Direct. It is a reminder of how you should always communicate with people, especially those that don't know you. Actively listening plus HARD communication is a recipe for successful collaboration.

Tailspin Toys case study During a recent Sprint Retrospective meeting, Scott (the Scrum Master) brought up his observations made during the Sprint. He witnessed a few developers having difficulty conversing respectfully with each other (as well as with stakeholders) during a couple of meetings. As a team, they decided to improve their communication abilities, specifically their active listening skills. Scott did some searching online and found several websites dedicated to the subject. During the next few Sprints, Scott coached the team as they adopted more and more of the techniques that they learned.

Collocate

I think we can all agree that communication and collaboration provides more value when practiced face to face, rather than remotely. At least I would hope that everyone knows this, because we experience it every day of our lives. When two people communicate face to face, they exchange more than just words. There are facial expressions, body language, and other nonverbal gestures. This kind of sideband data can be just as important, if not more important, than the text that is exchanged. For example, the look on a Product Owner's face when you suggest a solution to a problem can short-circuit the need for a detailed explanation. Thank you, collocated Product Owner. You just gave me back 20 minutes of my day.

Remember that Scrum has several formal events (meetings) built into the framework where collaboration can occur. In addition, the Scrum Team, and certainly the Development Team, should be continuously "meeting." These are not traditional meetings, where someone speaks and everyone else listens. These are short, collaborative, time-boxed meetings with the specific purpose of solving a problem. In fact, I wouldn't even call them a meeting, but more of a conversation. It's important that they occur as needed, with no logistical impediments. For example, if two developers need to discuss something with the Product Owner, but all the conference rooms are booked, they should meet anyway, somewhere, anywhere. To some degree, business formalities, and even etiquette, go out the window during the Sprint when the Development Team is in the zone, developing and generating business value.

When forming a new Development Team, collocation should be a requirement. This is not just a nice-to-have feature. It's required if you want a high-quality product and process. By collocation, I'm not talking about being in the same time zone, city, or building. While these options are better than some I've seen, I want the team in the same room or in adjacent rooms. The Product Owner should be nearby too, but not necessarily in the same room. This way, the face-to-face communication can occur on demand.

Tip Fellow Professional Scrum Developer Simon Reindl suggests bringing a geographically dispersed team together periodically. This is especially true at the beginning of a new project, so they know with whom they are working.

Professional Scrum developers know the value of collocation, and they strive for it. That said, there may be cultural, political, or financial reasons for not collocating the Development Team. This is the reality that I see as I visit larger organizations. The most common justification I'm given when I ask why the team is not collocated is that it saves money to have one or more of the functions supported or outsourced remotely, usually overseas. When I hear that, I hope that somebody, somewhere is doing the math on that, taking into account the decreased quality of the product and the process. Even if this decrease is not detectable or measurable, the decision makers should consider what the increase in quality *could be* if they were to bring the entire team together.

Note Do I think that developers working remotely as part of a distributed team *can't* be professional? Of course not. They absolutely can be professional and the team absolutely can collaborate, deliver high-quality software, and create business value. That said, an attribute of a professional Scrum developer is to inspect and adapt constantly, such as looking for ways to improve the process. Collocating a dislocated team is one of the biggest improvements that can be made, usually resulting in an increase of quality and Velocity. That team's Product Owner should wake up in the morning and go to bed at night, thinking of ways to maximize the product's value through the work of the Development Team, such as through collocation.

Most organizations consider their custom software as a strategic advantage over their competitors. I will sometimes ask executives where they would be without their line-of-business (LOB) application or public-facing website. They all agree that it would be a complete disaster. Not only has their staff forgotten how to run the business manually using paper and pencil, but they don't even know where to find the paper and pencils. Next, I ask them why they try to save money by limiting the capabilities and productivity of the team developing that custom software. At this point, I'm either asked to tell them more, or I'm escorted out of the building.

Note I recently had a conversation with an IT director of a very large organization. He explained to me that the Product Owner worked out of the main office, as did the programmers. The testers were overseas—nearly 10 time zones away. He shared with me a problem that they'd been having for the past few months. He said the programmers would code a feature and then go home for the night. The testers would come in, download the binaries, begin testing, and run into a bug. This blocked them from doing any further testing until the developers could fix it. The programmers would come in the next day, see the lack of progress, fix the bug, and have to wait until the end of the day for the testers to do their thing. Sometimes this dance would take three to four days before testing could proceed. He asked me how TFS could help him. I answered by asking why the testers weren't collocated with the rest of the team. He told me it was because they save money by sending the work offshore. I'm glad we were having this conversation in person because he was able to see the awesome facial expression I made at that point.

Set up a team room

Having the entire Development Team work in a shared, common room can be a good thing. Whiteboards containing plans and design notes are visible to everyone. Artifacts such as the Sprint Backlog and burndown chart can be updated easily and seen by everyone. During critical design points, the team room can become a war room of sorts as the developers move from strategic planning to tactical planning. Communication becomes more open and happens in real time. Developers tend to focus their productivity toward solving problems, while minimizing time spent on wasteful activities. Team rooms allow everyone, including stakeholders, to feel that buzz that I mentioned in the beginning of the chapter.

However, not every developer wants to work in a war room every day. There needs to be the opportunity to have private conversations, take phone calls, or just take a timeout from the rest of the team. Developers are smart and can self-organize to come up with solutions for these requirements. I've seen developers put on headphones, adjourn themselves to quiet rooms, or work away from the office for a short time as needed. Ideally, the managers and the organization trust their developers to the point where they can accommodate their needs. If they don't, then that is a big impediment to self-organization. Generating business value in the form of working software is a way for the Development Team to earn that trust.

Some personalities and cultures see collocation as an impediment. These developers may actually be counterproductive in such an environment. Remember that Scrum is about people, and people are just human. Their idiosyncrasies map directly to their ability to collaborate and work effectively as a team. The Velocity at which the Development Team is able to create business value is a function of the Development Team's productivity. Perhaps for these people, being in close proximity to, but not in the same shared room with, the rest of the team is good enough at first. A strong Scrum Master, as well as open and honest Sprint Retrospectives, can be used to improve this.

 Note An open-space team room is not the same thing as an *open-plan* office. Open-plan offices are typically inhabited by employees working on different tasks for different projects. Open-space team rooms are inhabited by developers working on a common software product. Both environments can generate noise, but the type of conversations found in an open-plan office will typically be more contrasting and thus, more distracting.

My recommendation is to set up a team room and just try it out. See if management will let the Development Team take over one of the conference rooms for a Sprint or two. If, during the Sprint Retrospective, the Development Team honestly believes that they were productive, then the Scrum Master can work with management to create a more permanent, open-space room.

 Tailspin Toys case study The Development Team has been collocated since day one, with Paula (the Product Owner) in a nearby office. During the Sprint, they regularly meet and collaborate whenever and wherever it is required. Day to day, the developers sit near each other in a large, open-space room with a half-dozen whiteboards (approximately one for each PBI). Because the developers use laptops with wireless connections, there's a minimum amount of cables in the room, and individuals can be more nomadic as they work. When one of the developers needs to concentrate or requires some personal space, he or she will put on headphones or go to a quieter room down the hall. When a developer has to travel or otherwise work remotely, the team will set up a dedicated computer with an always-on Skype connection, including video. Scott (the Scrum Master) has done a good job of educating the organization. Although the stakeholders know where the team room is located, they know to avoid it during a Sprint—unless of course they're invited by the Development Team. Scott still has to remind them from time to time.

Meet effectively

High-performance Scrum Development Teams know to avoid meetings, if possible. To be clear, I'm not talking about the built-in Scrum events, such as the Sprint Planning meeting, the Daily Scrum meeting, the Sprint Review meeting, or the Sprint Retrospective meeting. I'm also not talking about the regular Product Backlog grooming sessions, nor those impromptu but important meetings requested by the Development Team in order to clarify requirements, gather feedback, or seek the Product Owner's acceptance. I hope, in fact, that I've made it clear that these meetings are important and they should be attended by all of the involved parties face to face, if possible. I am talking about all the other meetings that an organization might require its technical staff to attend. You know the ones that I'm talking about They are mandatory, read-only (they don't ask for your feedback), and provide zero business value to the software product being developed or the development process itself. Unfortunately, some of these meetings cannot be avoided. They are a fact of life and a requirement to keep your job and get paid.

When you are invited to such a meeting, try to identify its purpose and expected outcome. This may be stated in the invitation, but if it's not, you may have to query the meeting organizer or sponsor. I know many developers who will not accept a meeting invitation if no clear agenda or objective is given. From this information, hopefully you can determine who the intended audience should be. Will the meeting be technical? Will decisions be made? If you don't fit the audience profile, try to skip the meeting, or send the Scrum Master instead. Being a proxy for the Development Team at meetings like this is one of his or her duties and allows the Development Team to what they do best.

If the tables are ever turned, and you find yourself organizing a meeting, you can follow the same advice:

- Only schedule meetings that are absolutely necessary and that can't be satisfied by one of the other built-in meetings.

- Keep the meeting as short as possible.

- Establish a time-box to enforce it.

- Outline the agenda and expected outcome in the invitation.

- Send invitations only to those people who need to attend.

- At the beginning of the meeting, explain the time-box and its concept.

When someone who is versed in Scrum sets up and runs a meeting, he or she will end up sharing good behaviors and practices, such as transparency, active listening, and time-boxing. This is a good way to get others in the organization more educated on Scrum and some of its attributes and practices. If appropriate, email any retrospective notes to the attendees, including action items. These behaviors may even infect the organization as other business units and teams will want "to get some of that Scrum."

> **Tip** One way to keep meetings constructive is to say "yes, and" instead of "yes, but." If the current topic or solution being discussed is one that there is partial agreement on, saying "yes, and …" comes across as being more constructive. If someone hears "yes, but," then they might think their idea is being discounted, or they may feel limited in what can be accomplished. If, however, they hear "yes, and," they will think that their idea was accepted, or at least understood, and be more prone to ideas. More importantly, the person will be more open to collaborating on a shared solution, which should always be the goal to avoid discussions becoming polarized.

> **Tailspin Toys case study** Paula (the Product Owner) and Scott (the Scrum Master) are good at running interference for the development team. For meetings that are not related to the development of the software product, Scott will try to attend as a proxy for the Development Team. Some meetings, such as the "all hands" meetings, cannot be avoided, and the developers do attend them.

Collaborate productively

Collaboration means working with people. This typically means dividing the work between two or more individuals and working together. Both the process of dividing the work and the actual working together with others can require intense concentration. Getting into this productive state, otherwise known as the *flow* or the *zone,* can take time. Getting out of that state prematurely, as caused by any kind of interruption, can be considered waste. The irony is that collaboration *requires* interruption, and you will need to get used to it and master it.

We are taught at a young age that it is disrespectful to interrupt others. If your team is working in an open-space team room, it's easy to see when a fellow developer is deep in thought or in the zone. Your instinct should be not to interrupt them. When you're working by yourself, however, it may be harder to know when *you* are in the zone. Stopping to take a mental assessment may actually kick you out of the zone. High-performance Scrum developers know how to minimize interruptions in order to maximize productivity. There have been numerous books, blog posts, and white papers written about being more productive.

Here are some of my favorite tips:

- **Cell phone** Turn it to vibrate, turn it off, or leave it at home.

- **Exit Microsoft Outlook** Email can be a great productivity tool, but it can waste a lot of your time as well. If you can't or don't want to turn it off, then be sure to disable all notifications. Having an icon appear in the system tray, seeing the mouse pointer change, or hearing an audible alert when a new email arrives, can have the same conditioning effect as one of Pavlov's dogs hearing a bell ring. Try to check email only three times a day: at the start of your day, after lunch, and before leaving.

- **Exit IM/chat client** Close the program, or at least set your status to busy. The exception to this is if the tool is used by the Development Team to share code or quick questions and feedback.

- **Limit Internet searches** Developers can spend their whole day on the Internet if they are not careful. Time-box the search and keep the scope to just researching the problem at hand.

- **Just get started** Some planning is required before starting a task, but overplanning becomes the antithesis of productivity.

- **Avoid formal meetings** One reason that Scrum is so successful is that it defines the important meetings to minimize the need for unimportant ones. A developer's productivity drops when he or she is away from the keyboard. Feel free to attend the valuable ad hoc meetings over coffee or at another's desk, but send the Scrum Master to the formal meetings in the Development Team's stead.

- **Use active listening** When your colleague is talking, you should listen to what he or she is saying, and expect the same courtesy when you are talking.

- **Stop fiddling** Developers can have complex software environments. These can include multiple versions of software, one or more integrated development environments (IDEs), virtual desktops and servers, databases, frameworks , software development kits (SDKS), testing tools, installers, etc. Do yourself a favor. Get it working, script it, snapshot it, and forget about it. Endless tweaking tends to have a diminished return on value. Solve today's problem today and tomorrow's problem tomorrow.

- **Life happens** We're all human and have a life outside of software development. When issues emerge, be open and honest about it, and take the necessary time to get your head right. Be appropriately transparent with the rest of your team.

Tailspin Toys case study The Scrum Team is always looking to do better. This is evident during their Sprint Retrospective meetings where collaboration practices are almost always discussed as improvement is sought. Everyone knows that the best way to increase Velocity is to improve the individuals and interactions.

Achieve continuous feedback

Developers love feedback loops—the faster the better. As soon as we type a few lines of substantive code, we hit F5 to see what the compiler thinks. As soon as we've got the method refactored, we run our unit tests to see them pass. As soon as we have a tangible user interface (UI), we have a colleague or the Product Owner look at it to tell us how he or she likes it. As soon as we are done with a task, we check in so that the continuous integration build or another developer can evaluate our work. Continuous feedback like this is healthy for the product, as well as the developer.

Automated feedback provided by builds, unit tests, code coverage, code analysis, and acceptance tests are awesome. Developers can call upon Visual Studio or TFS to provide this feedback at any time, day or night. The results tell the Development Team that they are building the feature correctly. High-performance Scrum Development Teams will take advantage of all of these features to ensure that they are well informed about the progress and quality of their work.

Smell It's a smell if the Development Team doesn't ask for feedback from the Product Owner during the Sprint. Passing unit and acceptance tests only ensure that the quality of the feature or scenario has been met. The Development Team will want to make sure that the person requesting the feature (the Product Owner) is happy with its design, function, and usability. The Sprint Review meeting should not be the first time that the Product Owner sees a feature being demonstrated.

Product Owner feedback is just as important as other types of feedback. An engaged Product Owner who knows the product and the desires of its users can quickly give the Development Team positive or negative feedback on a feature being developed. Getting in-person guidance on the usability of a feature early in its development is very valuable. If the Development Team builds the wrong feature, it's essentially the same as if they introduced a bug into the software product. The same advice goes for features as for bugs—it's easier and cheaper to "fix" them earlier in their lifecycle.

Note The Product Owner feedback loop should be as short (fast) as possible as well. This is another argument for collocating him or her near the Development Team.

I'm often asked if the Development Team can reach out directly to the stakeholder (user or customer) who requested the feature in order to gather feedback. Technically, the answer is no. The Product Owner is the one source of feedback to the Development Team. If she wants to establish her own feedback loop to the stakeholders, that's her prerogative. That said, I feel that there are times and conditions where the Development Team can solicit feedback directly from a stakeholder if they decide that bypassing the Product Owner will provide them more value. The Product Owner should be informed and agree to this. During the next Sprint Retrospective meeting, this can be discussed to determine if it was a one-time thing or if there's a deeper dysfunction to address (like an untrained or absent Product Owner).

I see Product Owner feedback as falling into three broad categories in Scrum, with practices and tools that can support each. These are listed in Table 8-1.

TABLE 8-1 Types of Product Owner feedback with the associated practice and tools.

Type of feedback	When is it given?	Practice	Visual Studio tool
Can you give us more details about this PBI?	Product Backlog grooming, Sprint Planning meeting during development	Collaborate with the Product Owner or stakeholder at a whiteboard	PBI work item, PowerPoint storyboarding
Do you like this? Is this the behavior you were expecting?	During development	Sit down with the Product Owner or stakeholder and go through the feature	Microsoft Feedback client
What else do you want, not want, or want developed differently?	Sprint Review meeting	Collaborate with the Product Owner and stakeholders to update the Product Backlog	Team Web Access, Microsoft Excel

The rest of this chapter will discuss some of the more effective collaboration practices and tools.

Collaborative development practices

Even the simplest software product requires a team with many talents. Beyond having the standard capabilities of design, code, and test, there can be many types and levels of talent within each discipline. Every developer has a unique background, set of skills, expertise, and personality. Each brings something different to the team. For example, you may have two C# programmers with similar resumes and experience. The way in which they analyze and solve problems will vary radically. Both approaches can be fit for purpose according to the requirements, but they can be very different.

A high-performance Scrum Development Team understands this reality, and even uses it. These types of teams recognize everyone has a different way of solving problems, and so long as those solutions fit within the parameters of the product and the Development Team's practices, they should be embraced. Long, drawn-out discussions and arguments over approaches and coding styles tend to generate little value, and typically only lower Velocity and morale.

In this section, we will explore several contemporary practices that boost the Development Team's effectiveness during collaboration.

Note A self-organizing Scrum Development Team should pick and choose from these as well as other development practices and try them for a Sprint or two. Later, during a Sprint Retrospective, the team can decide whether to continue to embrace the practice, to amplify it, or to abandon it.

Collective code ownership

Extreme Programming (XP) gave us the notion of *collective code ownership*. With this approach to ownership, individual developers do not own modules, files, classes, or methods. All of those things are owned collectively, by the entire Development Team. Any developer can make changes anywhere in the code base.

Consider the alternative to collective code ownership, where each developer owns an assembly, a namespace, or a class. On the surface, that may seem like a good idea. The developer is the expert on this component , as well as the gatekeeper for all changes. Strong code ownership like this has a tendency to block productivity. Consider the situation where two developers (Art and Dave) are working on separate tasks that both need to touch a common component owned by a third developer (Toni). Dave will have to wait while Art's functionality is coded and tested. A collective code ownership model would allow Dave to code the feature himself. The source control tools in TFS would track who made what changes to which files and enable a merge (or a rollback) to occur if there were any problems. Another potential problem with strong code ownership pops up when refactoring. Modern refactoring tools, like those in Visual Studio, can do this safely, but if the file or files are locked, then productivity is blocked again.

Adopting a collective code ownership mentality can take time. This is especially true if the Development Team used to have strong code ownership. Pairing and shared learning is a way to break up the turf and politics. Just as it takes time for the Product Owner and organization to trust the Development Team's ability to self-organize and self-manage, it also takes time for the individual developers to trust each other.

Tracking ownership in TFS

The biggest advantage with collective code ownership is the boost in the social dynamics of the Development Team. Because each developer has full control over all source code, there are less boundaries and more opportunities to find solutions. Remember that in Scrum, the Development Team owns all the problems and all the solutions collectively. This includes the artifacts of those solutions, namely the source code.

Should you ever have a need to determine who made a specific change to a file, TFS can help you. By right-clicking a file or a folder and selecting View History (as shown in Figure 8-1), you can see a history of changes, including who made them, the type of change, the date and time, and a (hopefully meaningful) comment. If you want to see what was changed between two versions, you can select them both and right-click, choosing Compare as shown in Figure 8-2. The UI will show removed text in red and new text in green. If you want to see who wrote which line of code in a specific version of a file, you can use the Annotate tool as shown in Figure 8-3.

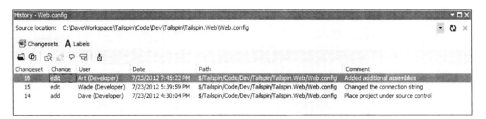

FIGURE 8-1 Viewing a history of changes to a specific file in Team Foundation Server.

FIGURE 8-2 Comparing two versions of a file to see the differences.

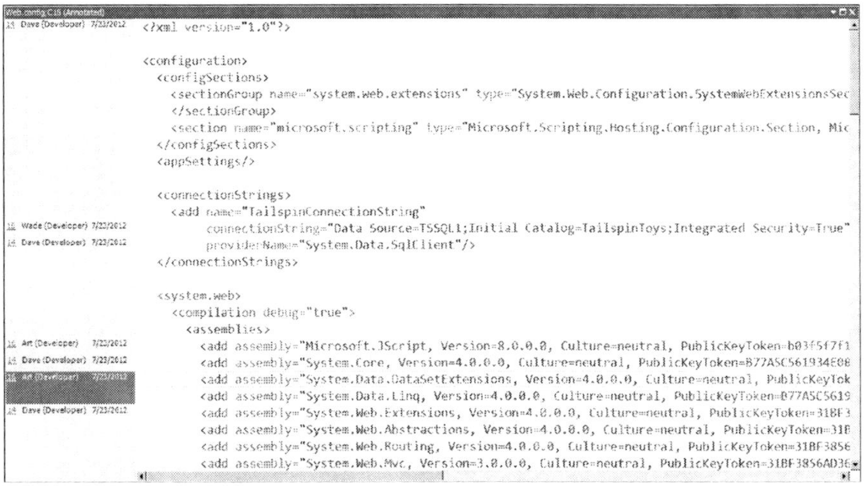

FIGURE 8-3 Using Annotate to see which developer made which changes in a specific file.

Tailspin Toys case study Because each member of the Scrum Team is a team project administrator, everyone has full control over every aspect of the team project. This includes the ability to view, edit, and even delete files from source control. Should the need arise to see who made a change, the developers are all trained in TFS and can view history, compare, and annotate as needed. Sometimes they will use the Annotate feature to praise another developer for good work.

Commenting in code

With collective code ownership comes a certain amount of responsibility. Other developers on the team will need to understand the code. If a developer or pair of developers is working on a rather complex part of the code, they should consider adding some comments. This can be a block of comments that give another developer enough information to understand this code. The comments can also be regularly sprinkled throughout longer algorithms. You can think of comments as being messages to the future, and it might be *you* reading those comments a year from now.

Tip Comments shouldn't tell the reader how the code works. The code should tell them that. If the code isn't clear, then you should refactor the code rather than add descriptive comments.

When commenting in code, only comment about what the code can't say for itself. If the code is well formed and follows popular patterns and principles, it probably doesn't need comments. When someone looks at the source code, its logic and purpose should be apparent. Keep this in mind while you are coding. Constantly ask yourself how clearly your code is telling you, or another developer, what it is doing.

Tip Fellow Professional Scrum Developer Jose Luis Soria Teruel suggests that commenting in perfectly readable code can sometimes be useful too. For example, in Microsoft Visual C#, you can create documentation for your code by including XML tags in special comment fields in the source code directly before the code block they refer to. If you are developing an application programming interface (API) for third parties, you may want to at least use the *summary* tag to describe a type or a type member.

Remember that comments live inside your source code files, and as such, they become inventory just like the code itself. Comments can even be a form of technical debt if they are wrong or misleading. Be diligent about updating your comments or removing them as you refactor and improve your code. Adding more comments isn't necessarily a good thing unless they add value. Perhaps it's time to refactor the code into simpler units rather than adding more comments. You should prefer unit tests over comments. The best comment is a set of working unit tests with high coverage.

Smell It's a smell when I see a file with the author's name at the top. I understand a developer wanting to get credit for his or her work, but this kind of comment tells everyone else to go away. It could be that the code file is really old and hasn't been touched since the team started practicing collective code ownership. If that's the case, someone should remove it. TFS tracks this through changesets, so it is redundant anyway. It could also be an organizational requirement to have predefined headers and require authors to add their names. If that's the case, meet with the decision makers and ensure that the value delivered by the practice outweighs the waste that it seems to generate.

Tailspin Toys case study The Development Team uses popular frameworks, principles, and practices as they design and code. As a result, there's not a lot of opportunity for meaningful comments. Only when they are coding some complex LOB methods do they add comments. The Development Team also knows that when checking in to TFS, they will associate a Task work item (which links back to a PBI or Bug work item) and a meaningful comment. Together, these two items provide more than enough context to explain later *why* the changes were made. Additional comments in code are not required.

Code reviews

A code review is a simple way to assure code quality by having another developer look at the code. This assurance can cover multiple levels of quality. It can assure that the code works, is fit for purpose, is absent of bugs, is absent of avoidable technical debt, is readable, and meet's the team's agreed-upon coding standards, as well as the Definition of "Done." Additionally, the developer whose code is being reviewed can use the conversation as an opportunity to learn about the way that he or she writes code.

Professional Scrum developers recognize that the candid feedback (otherwise known as criticism) given during a code review is targeted at the code and not themselves. For new developers, or developers new to code reviews, there can be a tendency to take these criticisms as an insult, even becoming defensive. Over time, these developers will see that even experienced developers make mistakes. Everyone is human. Everyone screws up now and then. Everyone can improve. Code reviews are just another type of shared learning activity, where any developer can learn from another.

Tip Code reviews can also catch and enforce coding style and standard issues. Be careful spending too much time with these kinds of topics during a code review, as they can become a rathole. A *rathole* is any discussion that detours the original purpose of the conversation. Don't get me wrong—discussions around coding styles and standards are very important, but any debate or decisions around changing existing standards, or establishing new ones, should be deferred until the Sprint Retrospective meeting. High-performance

Scrum Development Teams know that matters of style are not absolute. Developers should be allowed to self-organize and use whatever style is fit for purpose. Once a Development Team has been working together for a while, their coding standards will begin to emerge. These standards may even become part of the Definition of "Done."

When reviewing someone else's code, you should avoid appearing as a "senior" developer. The truth is that you may be the senior developer, but because everyone is equal within a Scrum Development Team, it's all about the sharing and learning. Choose your tone and your words carefully as you identify problems and improvements in someone else's code. Developers new to Scrum may be put on the defensive. Don't aggravate the situation by also going on the offensive.

Code reviews don't have to be a formal process. They can happen spontaneously. They also shouldn't be despised or avoided. High-performance Scrum Development Teams actually look forward to code reviews. This is because those teams know that the code is owned collectively. Problems and criticisms aren't directed at a single developer; rather, they are learning opportunities for the entire team. Every code writer and code reviewer will have different perspectives and approaches to solving problems.

Tip Typically, most developers know the code that needs to be reviewed. This can change, depending on the frequency of the code reviews. Developers can forget the changes that they made and the context if too much time elapses. Fortunately, TFS knows what files a developer has worked on for any given date range. From inside Source Control Explorer, the developer can right-click a parent-level folder and view the history. Unfortunately, this will show activity from every developer. There's no way to filter out other developers' changes. If you drop the command line, however, this filtering can be accomplished using the Tf.exe command-line utility.

Here's an example where Dave is asking TFS to list all of his changesets for a given date range:

```
tf.exe history $/Tailspin/Code/Dev /version:D"07/04/2012"~D"07/17/2012" /user:"Dave
(Developer)" /recursive
```

Professional Scrum developers should build solutions that are fit for purpose while avoiding gold plating. *Gold plating* is any design or coding that is above and beyond what is absolutely necessary for the task at hand. For example, if a PBI requires a method that calculates the sales tax for the state of Washington, and the developer adds additional logic to handle the nearby states, that's gold plating. The developer may try to justify the extra coding as being required down the road for a future Sprint. In order to maximize value and minimize waste, Development Teams should solve today's problem today and tomorrow's problem tomorrow (in the next Sprint, as it is in Scrum). Code reviews can be a good way to unearth gold plating.

Pair programming

You can think of pair programming as a form of code review—one that happens in real time. The practice of pair programming has two developers sit together at one computer. One developer types at the keyboard (drives), while the other observes, navigates, spellchecks, and otherwise reviews the code being typed. The two developers will switch roles frequently.

A benefit of this two-person approach is that the driver can focus on the tactical (coding) activities, while the observer is thinking about the broader, strategic solution to the problem. This collaboration leads to better and simpler designs and fewer bugs, in shorter periods of time. Pairs of developers working in close proximity like this are also less prone to get sidetracked from the task at hand.

During pair programming, knowledge is passed back and forth. The two developers can learn new practices and techniques from each other. Pairing a newly hired developer, or a developer with a different or weaker skill set, with a developer who is stronger will help improve the overall effectiveness and Velocity of the Development Team. Some teams scale this idea using an approach called "promiscuous pairing." Each developer cycles through all the other developers on the team, rather than pairing with only one partner. This behavior causes knowledge of the software product and its inner workings to spread throughout the whole Development Team. This reduces risk if a key developer leaves the team. Figure 8-4 demonstrates the possible outcomes of pairing weaker and strong developers together.

		Developer B	
		Weak	Strong
Developer A	Strong	Mentoring	Flow
	Weak	Danger	Mentoring

FIGURE 8-4 Possible outcomes when pairing developers together.

Tailspin Toys case study The organization has no policies around code reviews. They leave it up to the Development Team to decide. Sometimes the developers perform ad hoc code reviews. These are done whenever a developer hits the wall or needs a better solution for a complex problem. These kinds of code reviews are almost like an impromptu pair programming session. In addition, the entire Development Team likes to sit down in the conference room and use a projector. Each developer in turn shows off code. With a full room, this approach encourages discussion on design and style. As the team has improved, each review begins by showing the automated tests.

Collaborative development tools

Over the years, I have met with hundreds of software development teams. In my opinion, the most productive, collaborative tools for software developers to facilitate a discussion are a whiteboard and a dry erase marker or a laptop running Visual Studio and a projector. Using tools like these implies several things: the collaborators are collocated, they each see the same thing, and they are having a discussion in real time. There are no environmental impediments blocking the flow.

In a perfect world, all discussions and brainstorming meetings would occur like this. Unfortunately, some of us work in a world that is not collocated. Our team members don't work in the same office, or even live in the same city, state, or country. When we are in bed, our colleagues are at work, and vice versa. For environments like this, high-bandwidth collaboration tools like a whiteboard don't have the same impact. Alternatively, electronic tools must be substituted. Fortunately, Visual Studio 2012 includes several good ones.

> **Tip** There are countless more collaborative development tools available as open source or for commercial license. A popular example is *join.me*. It is a free (and ridiculously simple) screen-sharing tool for meetings on the fly. You can learn more at *http://join.me*.

In this section, I will discuss some of the Visual Studio 2012 features that enable collaboration.

Team Foundation Server

Team Foundation Server is the team's hub for coordinating development efforts on a shared code base using shared work items and shared, automated builds. TFS directly supports the first two, and Team Foundation Build (Team Build), a feature of TFS, enables automated builds. The team can use Team Build to automate the compilation, deployment, and testing of its software products. Having at least one automated build for the product should be a goal. High-performance Scrum Development Teams will have several.

TFS should be at the center of the development team at all times, especially when coding. There are challenges, however, when supporting a busy team of developers working on a shared code base. Parallel development such as this can lead to concurrency issues. In the time between a developer getting the latest version of code, making changes, and then checking it back in, one or more developers may have checked in their changes to the same folder. This means that when the original developer checks in his or her code, the probability that a conflict will occur increases with the length of time that the code is not checked in. Because these conflicts usually require a merge operation, you should check in frequently.

Merging occurs when two variants of the same file are combined in a logical way to create a new version of the file. Manually integrating files like this is a time-consuming process and should be avoided. TFS can often auto-merge for you, but not always. One way to avoid having to merge is to enable locking so that each developer locks the file(s) that he or she is working on. While this will prevent anyone else for making changes to the file until the first developer is done, it will block other developers from working on the file and being productive. There is a better way—to integrate, or merge, continuously.

 Smell It's a smell when I see a team project that does not have *multiple check-out* enabled. Either the team has been burned in the past by an inferior revision control system and wants to play it safe, or they haven't learned how to collaborate together effectively. Either way, wholesale locking like this is a recipe for an impediment. To overcome this, I usually start with a bit of education, letting the developers know that even with multiple check-out enabled, they are still able to lock individual files as needed, such as when performing a tricky refactoring operation. I've yet to see a team project that truly required locking of this nature that didn't have a deeper dysfunction driving the need.

Continuous integration

High-performance Scrum Development Teams have learned how to work smarter, not harder. One way that they do this is by continuously integrating their code changes with others on the team and running automated tests to verify the integration didn't break anything. While these same automated tests can be run inside Visual Studio, Team Build can probably run them faster and they will be asynchronous, enabling the developer to work on something else. Another benefit is that the tests can be run in a controlled environment that will show any configuration management problems quickly.

A better way to avoid painful, manual merge operations is to do smaller, less painful merges throughout the day. This is the basis for continuous integration (CI). Automated CI takes this a step further. Upon a check-in, an automated build gets launched, having been triggered by a check-in event. Source code is compiled, binaries are deployed, automated tests are run, and feedback is returned to the team *quickly*.

 Tip Another way to minimize the pain of manually merging code is to *listen* to the other developers during the Daily Scrum. Remember that the purpose of the Daily Scrum is to synchronize and create a plan for the next 24 hours. This means that each developer verbally shares their planned tasks with the other developers. If a developer hears another mention a task that will be in the same file or files that he or she was planning on working on, they should consider pairing up and working on their overlapping tasks together. This should alleviate any need to merge the code manually, as well as increase knowledge and productivity in general.

CI is about reducing risk. When a developer defers integration until late in the day, the week, or the Sprint, the risk of failure (i.e., features not working, side effects, bugs) increases. By integrating code changes with others regularly throughout the day, the Development Team will identify these problems early and be able to fix them sooner because the offending code is fresh in everyone's mind. The practice of CI is a must for any high-performance Scrum Development Team.

A Development Team shouldn't be afraid to break the build and work together to fix it. Refactoring, restructuring classes and methods, and changing internal interfaces can be messy work. There may be times that you want to check in your not-yet-finished code so that another developer can begin working with a part of it. You may also want to see how many errors and warnings and failed tests occur when your changes are integrated with others. This is fine. You are in the middle of the Sprint. This is not production code. Just as a surgeon may need to make some cuts in order to fix a critical problem, so might you have to break some code in the development process. These cuts are temporary, and the CI build and failing tests will illuminate them until they are all healed.

Tailspin Toys case study The Development Team has invested in a very powerful, very fast build server. They keep it quite busy, integrating code changes, building, and testing on every check-in. The developers aren't afraid to break the build, but they are disciplined to check the results of every build to ensure that they don't miss a broken one. Some have installed the build notification tool and others use email notifications to stay connected to the build status.

Builds check-in policy

Scrum Development Teams stay busy. They will work on a design task and when it's done, switch to a coding or testing task, and repeat, and repeat. As they finish a task, they usually check in their work. When CI builds are enabled, the check-in triggers an automated build. The developer then starts working on another task and, hopefully, remembers to go back and check that build's status and quality. Unfortunately, the developer may become focused on the new task or get sidetracked by something else. He or she may forget to evaluate the results of that CI build. Compound several builds on top of each other, and you might have a tangle of build results to work through.

The Builds check-in policy was created as a solution for just such a situation. When you configure a CI build in Team Build, every check-in operation starts a build. When one of these builds breaks, it is important for the Development Team to fix the problem that broke the build before making additional, unrelated changes. You can use the Builds check-in policy as a tool to limit additional check-ins until the broken build is fixed. When this policy is enabled, it literally blocks anyone else from adding new files to any source control folder that is a working folder in/under the build definition. When the policy fails, the developer who is attempting to check in will receive a message like the one shown in Figure 8-5.

When a developer runs into this warning message, the expected behavior is that he or she can query the other team member who "broke" the build. Remember, it could just be that a single test failed, and not some catastrophic system error. Once the Development Team has been consulted, the developer who received the warning can then choose to override it by clicking the Override Warnings hyperlink on the Pending Changes page and providing a comment. All developers will be blocked like this until the CI build completes without errors and all tests pass.

FIGURE 8-5 Builds check-in policy warning when the last CI build failed.

Tailspin Toys case study The Development Team tried the Builds check-in policy for a few Sprints and then, after discussing it during a Sprint Retrospective meeting, decided to disable it. What had happened was, as they improved their CI practice, they got better at proactively watching and analyzing the build results. In addition, some developers have opted to enable the Build Notifications tool.

Build Notifications tool

Rather than having TFS block check-ins when a build fails, some developers would rather just be notified when the build completes and then check the results manually. Fortunately, Microsoft includes a notification tool that does exactly this.

The Build Notifications tool is installed by default, but not configured. The developer will have to start it manually at first. It can be found under the Start menu by pointing to Microsoft Visual Studio 2012 > Team Foundation Server Tools. Each developer can choose the build(s) that they want to monitor. They can also choose to be notified when each build gets queued, starts, or completes. They can also choose to monitor only builds that *they* have started or that anyone on the team has started. You can see an example of the settings in Figure 8-6.

Note The Build Notification tool used to be part of the Team Foundation Server Power tools, but starting with TFS 2010, Microsoft now includes it "in the box," as part of a Visual Studio or Team Explorer installation.

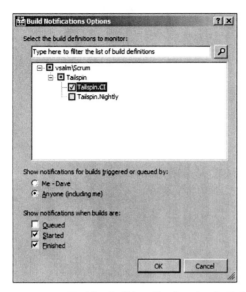

FIGURE 8-6 Enabling build notifications for the Tailspin.CI build.

The notifications will appear in the system notification area (otherwise known as the *system tray*), in the lower-right corner of the Windows desktop. You can see an example of this in Figure 8-7. The notification will appear for a few seconds and then fade away. You can click hyperlinks on the notification to allow you to view the details of the build. If the notification has since disappeared, right-click the Build Notifications icon, in the system notification area, to view a build's status or replay a recent notification.

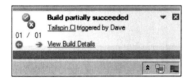

FIGURE 8-7 A notification that a build has finished, but only partially succeeded.

Tailspin Toys case study There is not a team-level practice or requirement to use the Build Notification tool. Some developers on the team, however, have configured it and use it. Others have since disabled it. The most common reason for disabling it is to avoid the "noise" that it generates. As previously mentioned, the Development Team is quite good at watching the CI builds and responding to any problems.

Gated check-in builds

Gated check-in builds are a type of private build, triggered by a check-in, but built using shelvesets in order to ensure that there are no errors prior to checking in. The purpose of a gated check-in build is to verify that the developer's code integrates with the other team members and that tests pass before committing the changes to the main source control repository. This feature was introduced in TFS 2010.

One of the problems plaguing the gated check-in build feature is performance. Even in TFS 2012, the slow performance of the UI notifications become apparent—very fast. Also, each gated check-in definition can have only one running build at a time. Therefore, active teams doing lots of check ins and builds are more likely to develop a large queue of gated check-in builds. Fortunately, there's a new feature in TFS 2012 that helps with performance, which I'll get to in a moment.

Smell It's a smell if I see a team using gated check-in builds on their development codeline. Ideally, the Development Team practices lots of small, frequent check-ins. If one breaks the build, a few minutes later, they should know about it, fix it, and keep going.

Gated check-ins are a solution to a misunderstanding. When the original authors of XP said, "Don't break the build," they didn't mean it literally. They meant that if a developer ever does break the build, it is their responsibility to fix it immediately. Really, the authors should have said, "Don't ever leave the build broken." When I've seen teams use gated check-in builds, they often do so because they are unable to meet the requirement of never leaving it broken. It could be that their build takes too long or they simply don't have the discipline to follow the practice. It also may be because the organization has a low tolerance for broken builds. We need to recognize that these are all dysfunctions of some type.

Tip If your production gated check-in build takes a long time to complete, even without running tests, consider creating a second CI build that builds and runs the tests. The CI build would kick off in parallel with the gated check-in build and provide a measure of quality. It might take a really long time to finish the CI build, but at least the gated check-in build wouldn't get any slower, and you'd still get a sense of the code quality.

For teams running long gated check-in builds, TFS 2012 offers a helpful new feature. Gated check-in builds can now batch together multiple shelvesets into a single build. For example, a team might configure a production build to build up to three submissions simultaneously, as shown in Figure 8-8. These submissions (shelvesets) would get merged and built together on one build agent. If the build succeeds, and all tests pass, each shelveset would be committed (checked in) separately. If the build fails or any tests fail, then each shelveset is built, one at a time, to determine which one caused the failure.

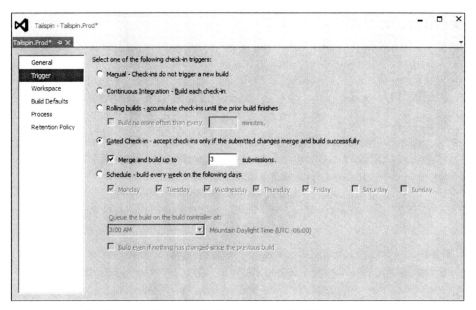

FIGURE 8-8 Configuring a gated check-in build to merge and build up to three submissions.

Tailspin Toys case study The Development Team makes heavy use of CI builds. They were selected over gated check-in builds for development in the DEV folder. Everyone agreed that the practice of CI promotes healthier team behaviors than relying on a tool. The team does use gated check-in builds when fixing bugs in code (in the PROD folder) that has been released.

Email alerts

A developer can also monitor builds by enabling an email alert. He or she can register an email address with TFS to receive an email that alerts them to the fact that a build has completed or a build's quality has changed. In fact, alerts can be established to notify when changes occur to work items, code reviews, and source control files, as well as builds. These are just standard emails (in either plaintext or HTML format) that are sent from TFS to a user's inbox using an intermediary Simple Mail Transfer Protocol (SMTP server). Developers can subscribe to alerts for themselves, for others, or for the entire team.

The body of these email alerts contain hyperlinks that can be clicked to take the reader to the respective information in Team Web Access. Emails pertaining to source control, such as check-ins, will display information about the changeset when clicked. Emails about work items will take the reader to the respective work item when clicked. Emails about builds will direct the user to the build in question.

Before TFS can send any alert email, a TFS administrator must configure the server to use an existing SMTP server. This can be accomplished in the Team Foundation Server Administrative Console in the Application Tier section, as shown in Figure 8-9. At a minimum, the administrator must specify the SMTP Server and the Email From Address. In TFS 2012, Microsoft added the ability to specify optional advanced SMTP settings, including User, Password, Port, and additional security information directly from the console. This was a long-anticipated feature in the product.

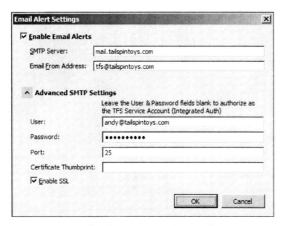

FIGURE 8-9 Configuring SMTP settings so that TFS can send alert emails.

Tip The out-of-the-box emails are very plain. They convey the basic information, and not much else. There are no fancy colors or graphics. If a team wanted to, they could add some style or missing functionality to the content and format of the base email alerts by customizing the associated .xsl transform files. The event service uses these files to transform the XML data for an event into a human-readable email message. Editing the respective .xsl file would provide a different format for the email. You should make a backup copy of the transform files before attempting any customization. Better yet, consider creating a separate team project for such an effort so that you can manage changes to those files. For more information check out *http://msdn.microsoft.com/en-us/library/bb552337.aspx*.

Alert subscriptions are stored on the server and organized by team project. A developer can add different alerts for each team project or team that they are a member of. A developer can also configure a *team alert*, which is new in Visual Studio 2012. Team alerts simplify the administration of setting up the same alert for everyone on the team. For example, if all Scrum Team members, including the Product Owner and Scrum Master, want to be informed when a build has completed or when a PBI is "done," someone can create a team alert such as the one shown in Figure 8-10.

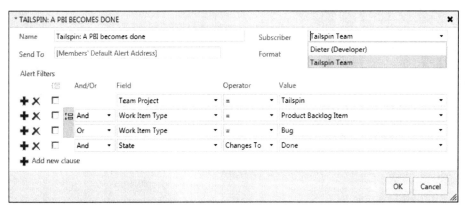

FIGURE 8-10 Creating a team alert so that everyone on the Tailspin Team is notified when a PBI is done.

For build-related alerts, there are two fields that you should be aware of: Requested By and Requested For. The Requested By field is populated by TFS and is always the account that actually queues the build. For manual builds, it contains the user that queues the build, but for CI and scheduled builds, it contains the build service account. If you are interested in knowing who requested the CI build, this won't work. Instead, you should reference the Requested For field. Its behavior is very similar to the Requested By field, except that for CI builds it contains the user who performed the check-in.

Email alerts can also be configured to let a developer, or a whole team, know when a build has completed or failed. This would be an alternative to using the Build Notifications tool previously mentioned. In addition, by using the Requested For field, a single team alert can be created that is smart enough to only email the developer who requested the build, and nobody else. This is done by creating a team alert with the criteria Requested For = [Me], as shown in Figure 8-11. This criteria establishes a behavior which causes an email to be sent to only the person who requested the build. You'll be happy to know that the *[Me]* macro, and its related behavior, is available for all types of alerts.

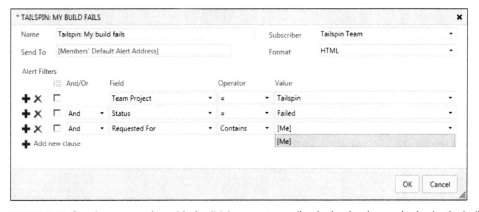

FIGURE 8-11 Creating a team alert with the *[Me]* macro to email only the developer who broke the build.

Shelving

Shelving lets you set aside a batch of pending changes for whatever reason. It could be that you were interrupted by some more important work, or you want to queue a private build, back up your work, or hand something off to another developer. Shelving can also be used when you want to have your code reviewed.

Shelving produces an artifact called a *shelveset*. Shelvesets exist outside of the normal TFS source control repository and are identified by a unique name provided by the developer who created it. Some point in time later, that developer (or another) can unshelve those pending changes into a local workspace and continue working or review the code.

When a developer shelves his or her code, anybody on the team with the appropriate permissions can view and unshelve those pending changes. In other words, to unshelve a pending change, you must have the *Read* and *Check out* permissions set to *Allow*. For a Scrum Development Team practicing my recommended security configuration, this means that any developer can unshelve another developer's pending changes. This is how it should be on a high-performance Scrum Development Team. Any developer can review any other developer's code without being limited by the tool.

If the developer reviewing the code makes any changes, he or she must create a new shelveset or check in the code. This is because the second developer cannot change the first developer's shelveset. What I have seen happen is that the reviewer will create a second shelveset with the proposed changes and comments, and then the first developer will create a third shelveset, and so on. If the two developers are not diligent about cleaning up their shelvesets as they iterate, there will be a big housekeeping task at the end. For this reason, as well as for general efficiency reasons, code reviews should be performed in person, where all developers look at the same screen at the same time.

Smell It's a smell if I see a team using shelvesets as a mechanism for code reviews. If it turns out that they are used sparingly for situations where the coder or reviewer are remote, then that is OK. I will suggest, however, that the developers use a screen-sharing utility such as Microsoft Lync or *http://join.me*. By sharing a screen, you avoid the back-and-forth of shelveset creation or the administrivia of creating them or cleaning them up after the exercise.

Tailspin Toys case study The Development Team primarily uses shelvesets for interruptions and private builds. They also use them indirectly with the new suspend and resume features in Visual Studio 2012.

My Work

Visual Studio 2012 Premium and Ultimate edition users can use *My Work* as a way to see and manage their current, in-progress work. As a developer works through his or her tasks in the Sprint Backlog, they can be started in the My Work page. Work can also be suspended and resumed as needed. Code reviews can be requested and managed. Check-ins can be performed. It's a very powerful page within Team Explorer, and every developer on the team should consider using it.

To begin working on a new task, drag it from the Available Work Items section to the In Progress section, as shown in Figure 8-12. You can also right-click the task and add it to In Progress or click the *Start* link. If the task you want to start isn't visible, you may have to run a different query or refresh the results. It may be that you have to create the Task work item first.

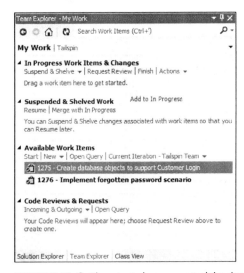

FIGURE 8-12 Getting started on a new task by dragging it to the In Progress section.

 Note Microsoft provides two default queries to get you started in the Available Work Items window: "All Iterations - <project team>" and "Current Iteration - <project team>". The second query is the interesting one. It contains some behind-the-scenes magic to determinate what the current iteration is. If your team has set up the iterations (Sprints) and specified start and end dates, then TFS knows what the current Sprint is. This value is looked up and hard-coded into this query to return Task work items from the current Sprint. This is very convenient, but unfortunately the magic cannot be bottled and reused on other custom queries. Hopefully, Microsoft will give us a *CurrentIteration* macro, or something like it, to use in our queries some day soon.

Dragging the work item to the In Progress section will also change the State to In Progress. More important, it gives you context on what you're doing. For example, even taking 60 seconds to answer a phone call can generate a lengthy "Now where was I?" pause. Being able to see what item you are working on will help return that focus more quickly. If you exit Visual Studio without finishing an In Progress task, it will still be there later when you return.

 Smell It's a smell if I see two or more tasks In Progress. Just because Team Explorer allows it, doesn't mean that it makes sense from a work management perspective. Are you really working on two things at once? Perhaps you didn't create the right tasks in the first place. Maybe you switched context and didn't know how to suspend your existing work before starting something new.

Later, when you are done with your task, you can check in your changes and resolve (rather than associate) the task. You can also just click the Finish link in My Work. Both of these methods will transition the work item to the Done state and set any Remaining Hours to zero. If you click Finish, Visual Studio may prompt you with a warning that you haven't checked anything in. For tasks that don't require a check-in, you can dismiss the warning. The task will be removed from My Work, as will the pending changes when you check them in, allowing you to move to your next task.

Code reviews can also be requested and managed from the My Work page. I will discuss them later in this chapter.

Suspending and resuming work

From time to time throughout the Sprint (or the day on some dysfunctional teams), a developer will experience an interruption. In a perfect world, this never happens, but in the real world, it does. A high-performance Scrum Development Team works to marginalize this reality by either reducing the number of interruptions or making them less painful. When an interruption does occur, switching context to the new problem can be difficult and wasteful.

For example, let's say that you are deep in thought, implementing a complex scenario within a PBI and the Product Owner drops into the team area with an emergency. It's obvious that an urgent bug fix is required and, as this is critical to the business, you *should* drop what you're doing and fix it. Forget your forecast. It's about saving money and customers at this point. What most developers do is to shelve their code, undo pending changes, and close their solution. Others will just start a new instance of Visual Studio, get the specific version of code that's running in production, and go about locating, verifying, and fixing the bug. Visual Studio 2012 now offers a better way.

From the My Work page, the developer can suspend the current work he or she is doing. Behind the scenes, a shelveset is created to save any pending changes to code, tests, and other files. Important elements of Visual Studio are also saved, such as open windows, breakpoints, and other debug states. The developer assigns the suspended work a friendly name in order to find it easily at some point in the future. By default, this name is the title of the In Progress work item, as you can see in Figure 8-13.

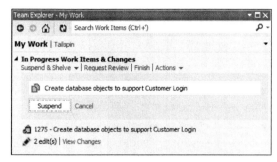

FIGURE 8-13 Suspending in-progress work and giving it a friendly name.

Suspending will shelve any pending changes and then undo the local changes, putting your workspace back into a clean state. It is now ready to handle the new crisis by dragging the new task into the In Progress section. You can see the suspended work listed in the Suspended & Shelved Work section of the My Work page, as shown in Figure 8-14.

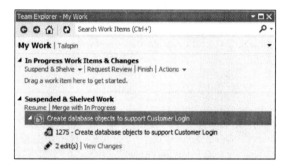

FIGURE 8-14 Suspended work is given a friendly name and persisted as a shelveset.

> **Smell** It's a smell if I see more than one piece of suspended work listed. Maybe you are the kind of developer who spends more time helping, mentoring, and supporting others. This could explain the various pieces of suspended work. Maybe your organization is so chaotic that even the interruptions get interrupted? Maybe you are just the kind of developer who leaves a bunch of half-eaten sandwiches sitting around your house. That's a different kind of smell.

Later, when the crisis has passed and the developer is able to return to the planned work, he or she can select the suspended work and click the Resume link. The original pending changes will be unshelved, and the task will be put back in the In Progress section. Other IDE settings and behaviors will be restored as well.

In the event that your interruption gets interrupted, you may want to suspend it, and return to your original work. If this is the case, then instead of a Resume link, there will be a Switch link. Clicking Switch will suspend the interruption work, and return context to the original task. Alternatively, you can choose to Merge With In Progress and bring all the pending changes from the two tasks together.

PowerPoint Storyboarding

Visualizations allow the Development Team to elicit feedback more easily. This feedback can come from other members of the Scrum Team, as well as stakeholders, especially domain experts. Shapes and lines drawn on a whiteboard to represent components and actions enable ideas to be vetted by the right people. It's faster to sketch out the high-level concepts and their interactions than it is to try to design or code anything in Visual Studio. It's also cheaper to fix a bug in a drawing than later in code.

As previously mentioned, feedback is important when brainstorming how to tackle a problem such as developing a particular feature or scenario. This is especially true when the developers are not familiar with the domain or the workflow is complex. Having the right people involved in the conversation is critical. The more eyes you can put on a problem, the better the chances of finding an optimal solution. Unfortunately, this is not always possible when the required people are geographically distributed.

Smell It's a smell when the Development Team doesn't have access to the people who know the domain. It's the Product Owner's responsibility to either know the domain or collaborate with experts who do. The Scrum Master might have to get involved to make sure the introductions, communication, and collaboration occur effectively. It's also a smell when the opposite occurs, and the Development Team becomes the domain experts. This is natural in an organization that encapsulates its critical business processes into software. The developers know the software, and thus the domain behind it. This is fine so long as the organization doesn't start using their technical staff as the business help desk.

For Development Teams that love their whiteboards, I recommend setting up a laptop with a webcam in the meeting room or team area. By aiming the webcam at the whiteboard, and then strategically standing out of the way after drawing on it, remote attendees can be part of the design session and discussion. This is less ideal than collaborating in person, but still allows for rapid design with a dry erase pen, rather than fumbling with a software design tool.

When the Development Team has a need to present their ideas to (and gather feedback from) remote stakeholders, then the new PowerPoint Storyboarding feature in Visual Studio 2012 can be beneficial. Users of Visual Studio 2012 Premium, Ultimate, or Test Professional editions can install and use PowerPoint Storyboarding, which allows a developer to illustrate a PBI or a specific feature or scenario using Microsoft PowerPoint. The illustration is created by dragging and dropping predefined, inline images and adding formatted text. It can then be linked to a work item, such as the PBI that it describes, and shared with other TFS users.

Smell It's a smell when I see storyboards created *before* the Sprint in which the PBI gets forecast for development. It could be that the Development Team had to iterate on the design of a complex feature or scenario with a remote stakeholder or two before they were able to estimate it. It could also be that the Development Team started working on this

PBI in a previous Sprint and didn't finish it. From my experiences, the more likely reason is that someone on the team got bored, fired up PowerPoint, and started designing something. When a developer has spare time, he or she should help the rest of the Development Team complete their forecast work. If the whole Development Team has spare time, they should meet with the Product Owner to discuss working on an additional PBI.

 Tip Fellow Professional Scrum Developer Jose Luis Soria Teruel has experimented with using storyboards while grooming the Product Backlog. Wary of generating waste, he and the other developers keep them to the right (rough) level of detail. This was a practice that they opted into as a team.

To create a PowerPoint storyboard, there are a few simple steps to follow:

1. Open the PBI work item, choose the Storyboarding tab, and then choose the Start Storyboarding link. You can also start the tool from the Start menu under Microsoft Visual Studio 2012 or by starting PowerPoint directly.

2. Add slides, shapes, and text to the blank presentation to illustrate a PBI, feature, or scenario, as shown with the Customer Login storyboard in Figure 8-15.

FIGURE 8-15 An example PowerPoint storyboard with annotations.

3. Save the storyboard presentation to a network share or Microsoft SharePoint.

4. (Optional) Link the presentation to the PBI work item that it describes, as shown in Figure 8-16.

5. Share the storyboard with others.

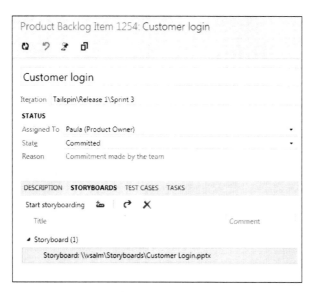

FIGURE 8-16 A PBI work item with a linked PowerPoint storyboard.

6. Others may provide feedback by annotating the PowerPoint document or by using the Feedback client.

As the stakeholders review the storyboard, they can add comments or even make changes to the illustrations using the built-in features of PowerPoint. If the presentation is stored on SharePoint, it can enjoy the dual benefit of broad availability and revision control. Users can check out the presentation and check in any changes. Feedback can also be provided out-of-band, via email, voice, or using the Feedback client, which is covered in the next section.

> **Tip** I'm often asked if a Development Team should use PowerPoint Storyboarding or SketchFlow. On the surface, they appear to be very similar in functionality. SketchFlow is a feature of Expression Studio Ultimate and has a new UI to learn. PowerPoint Storyboarding runs inside PowerPoint, so the learning curve isn't as steep. While SketchFlow is more sophisticated (with a richer set of user controls for designing UIs), it's not as nicely integrated into a development process that uses TFS. Another important difference is that SketchFlow is able to convert (forward-engineer) the prototypes into starter projects. PowerPoint storyboards don't support that. They will always just be illustrations.

Creating a storyboard

To create a storyboard, a developer can select from several layouts that support common user interfaces, such as web and Windows Phone backgrounds. Images can be dragged and dropped from the Storyboard Shapes pane in addition to using all the features available within PowerPoint. These features include clipping and inserting screenshots, hyperlinking from one page to another, animation, inserting images and shapes, and aligning and grouping objects. For example, a developer might create two slides to illustrate the UI for a particular PBI. She might add information about upcoming service appointments to the customer's account page and add buttons that customers can use to schedule, reschedule, and cancel those appointments.

Tip You can save a custom shape to MyShapes and then use it in the same way that you use the predefined storyboard shapes. Also, you can export shapes to share with other developers on the team or import shapes that others have created. Microsoft has also created a Storyboard Shapes Authoring tool to help make storyboard shapes that can be used with PowerPoint Storyboarding. It is available for free at *http://visualstudiogallery .msdn.microsoft.com/75f32d63-8ff2-49f3-b86e-70297d300858.*

Before you can link a storyboard to a work item, you must save it to a shared location. The shared location can be any shared folder on the network or a SharePoint site (such as the team project portal). By linking the storyboard to a work item, you are essentially inviting the rest of your team to access this shared file, so be sure they have the appropriate permissions. They can open the presentation, review it, and add their comments. You can link storyboards only to certain types of work items based on the process template from which your team project was created. In the Visual Studio Scrum process template, you can only link storyboards to Product Backlog Item work items. It is possible to link a storyboard to more than one work item.

Note You cannot create work items from PowerPoint, but you can link to them. This means that if you create the storyboard first, you will have to switch to Visual Studio or Team Web Access to create the PBI so that you may link it. This situation is less likely to occur for a Scrum Team, who should be creating and grooming PBIs a long time before the Sprint.

To create and modify storyboards by using PowerPoint Storyboarding, a developer must have installed either PowerPoint 2007 or later, and one of the following versions: Visual Studio Premium, Visual Studio Ultimate, or Visual Studio Test Professional. Storyboarding is not available in Visual Studio Professional or Express edition. To view storyboards that were created by using the PowerPoint Storyboarding template, users must have PowerPoint 2007 or later installed. They do not need Visual Studio 2012 installed.

Tailspin Toys case study In the past, some developers on the team have used Balsamiq to mock up complex UIs. Over time, the Development Team realized that in-person conversations at a whiteboard provide the most value. They take this approach whenever possible. Occasionally, however, it's not possible because a stakeholder or expert is not available for an in-person discussion. When this happens, they will usually generate and send the storyboard over email or even store them on SkyDrive, allowing the stakeholder to review and comment. Once the feature or scenario is done, the storyboards are deleted.

Feedback client

As you read in the last section, the PowerPoint Storyboarding tool enables a team to create rapidly a UI mockup or illustration of a feature that can be shared with other team members or stakeholders. It's important to close that loop by collecting rich feedback about what those users think of a feature, and whether it is still being brainstormed, under development, or has been released. Feedback should always be welcomed, and even encouraged. If the feature has been released and valid feedback is given, it can be captured in the Product Backlog to be considered for future development.

One of the new features of Visual Studio 2012 is the ability to capture rich stakeholder feedback on features being implemented and bugs being fixed. This is good for distributed organizations who want stakeholders to evaluate the emerging Increment or a design that may still be in flux. The Feedback client is used to gather this type of feedback. It is versatile enough that it can be used to provide feedback on anything the user can see and interact with on the desktop.

> **Note** Users submitting feedback using the Feedback client *do not need* a TFS Client Access License (CAL). A Windows Server CAL may still be required, however. Please refer to the latest version of the Visual Studio 2012 licensing white paper at *http://go.microsoft.com/fwlink/?LinkID=246172*.

This type of feedback can either be formally requested via a work item and email sent from Visual Studio, or it can be provided voluntarily, without solicitation. We will look at both scenarios shortly.

Requesting feedback

The first feedback scenario occurs when a member of the Scrum Team, preferably the Product Owner, solicits feedback from one or more stakeholders. These stakeholders will receive a feedback request through an email that is constructed from the feedback request form. From the email, the stakeholders can install and launch the Feedback client tool, which guides them in providing and capturing their feedback. TFS stores this feedback as a Feedback Response work item.

In order to request feedback, TFS must be configured to use an existing SMTP server in order to send emails. This requirement was mentioned earlier in the chapter in the context of setting up email alerts and, hopefully, it is already configured. To begin, click the Request Feedback link on the Team Web Access home page, as shown in Figure 8-17.

FIGURE 8-17 The Request Feedback link on the Team Web Access home page.

Feedback can be requested on any aspect of the product, from the entire application down to a specific scenario within a feature. Because the feedback request is essentially an email, the requester can be as ambiguous or as specific as he or she wants to be. In addition, one request can be partitioned to ask for feedback on up to five discrete items. For example, if the Development Team is code-complete on three scenarios within a PBI, a request could be created that contains three items—one for each scenario the Product Owner desires feedback on.

> **Note** Regardless of the size and scope of the request, the stakeholders must be able to access physically the application and feature(s) in question, and they must have the time and know-how to do it. This should be considered as the feedback request is created.

When creating the feedback request, one or more stakeholders must be selected. These users must have an email address associated with their user name. Users without email addresses won't be sent a request. The stakeholders should also be told *how* to access the application in question. An address and instructions can be provided for a web application, (rich) client application, or a remote machine. Finally, the item(s) to be evaluated and any related notes are added to the request. Figure 8-18 shows a feedback request ready to be sent to a stakeholder to evaluate the Customer Login feature of a web application.

FIGURE 8-18 Creating a request for feedback on the Customer Login feature.

Tip Consider previewing the request before sending it. It will show what the email that the stakeholder(s) receive will look like and allow you to customize it. It will also show the email addresses rather than the user names, so you can see if there are any discrepancies, such as wrong or missing email addresses associated with the user names. For example, if you add a stakeholder by user name and that user doesn't have an email address associated with his or her account, you will receive an error message like this: *TF400596: Cannot find email addresses for the following recipient(s): 'Chuck'*. If this occurs, you can just add the email address manually and continue with the request. However, you should ask the stakeholder to update his or her profile and provide a valid email address to avoid this error in the future.

As the feedback requester, you will receive a copy of the email submission automatically when you send it. You can also add other email addresses in the To box when previewing the email. Figure 8-19 shows a sample email requesting feedback. If an administrator has not granted permissions to the accounts of those stakeholders that you add, they will not be able to provide feedback through the Feedback client.

FIGURE 8-19 A sample email sent to a stakeholder requesting feedback.

Providing feedback

When the stakeholder receives the request, he or she should first make sure that the Feedback client is installed. If this is the first time providing feedback, it will need to be installed. The email contains a hyperlink to download it, if necessary. Next, the stakeholder starts the feedback session by clicking the large hyperlink in the email, or copying and pasting the supplemental URL into the web browser.

As the stakeholder reviews the new feature, he or she is able to perform the following tasks using the Feedback client:

- Record video of the interaction with the application.

- Record voice comments.

- Capture a screenshot.

- Annotate a screenshot using a program such as Microsoft Paint.

- Type comments.

- Attach a file.

- Rate each item of feedback on a scale of 1–5 stars.

On the Provide page of the Feedback client, one or more items appear for the user to provide feedback. For each item, he or she can get context on what's being asked and then provide free-form feedback through any of the aforementioned methods of input. Figure 8-20 shows the various recording options. If there are multiple items, clicking Next will advance to the next item for which to provide feedback. Recordings appear as images within the Feedback client's text box.

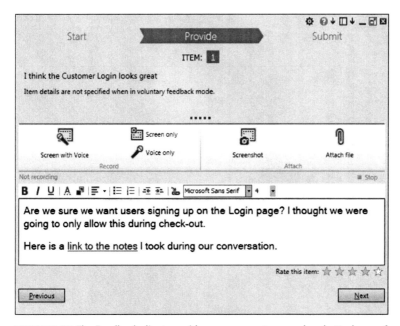

FIGURE 8-20 The Feedback client provides many ways to record and attach your feedback.

By annotating screenshots, the reviewer can indicate corrections or improvements by adding text or images to the screenshot that was captured. By default, Paint opens automatically when the user opens a screenshot image that was captured within the Feedback client. Another annotation tool, such as Paint.NET or Snagit, can be configured instead by clicking on the cog icon at the top of the feedback tool, as shown in Figure 8-21. After feedback has been provided for each item, the user can review, make corrections or additions, and then submit the feedback to the requesting user via TFS.

FIGURE 8-21 Click the cog icon to configure your annotation tool.

Tip Be careful when recording sensitive data, such as user names, passwords, account numbers, etc. If the recording is going, everything will be captured. If you do record sensitive data, you can delete the recording by deleting its representative image in the text box and then record it again.

In order for stakeholders to be able to provide feedback, an administrator must grant them specific permissions in TFS. They can either be added to the Limited license group in Team Web Access or a custom group with specific permissions. The Limited group is provided specifically to support access to TFS for users who do not need a CAL. If the stakeholders have a CAL and you are not going to use the Limited group, then make sure to grant the minimum permissions required, which are project-level permissions to create and view test runs and view project-level information, as well as area path permissions to view and edit work items in the respective nodes.

Regardless of which permissions approach you take, you should try to group the feedback stakeholders together in their own Windows group. Because providing feedback is probably the only way that they will interact with TFS, keeping them grouped together will simplify management and allow the Scrum Team to know exactly who their feedback stakeholders are.

Feedback requests generate a Feedback Request work item assigned to the creator of the request. The Description field contains the body of the email that was sent. Feedback Response work items are created to hold the feedback provided by the stakeholder using the tool. Remember that both Feedback Request and Feedback Response work item types are designated as Hidden types. This means that they cannot be created directly from Visual Studio or Team Web Access. Instead, they are created using the appropriate tool, such as the Request Feedback link and Feedback client respectively.

Smell It's a smell when the Development Team solicits stakeholder feedback directly. Gathering feedback from stakeholders is the responsibility of the Product Owner, not the Development Team. If the developers want to seek feedback from stakeholders or other domain experts, they should do it with the blessing of the Product Owner. If necessary, the Scrum Master can help facilitate this. Visual Studio, however, doesn't know about the rules of Scrum, and it allows anyone to request or provide feedback. If the Feedback client is being used inconsistently with the rules of Scrum, the Scrum Team should discuss it during the next Sprint Retrospective meeting and adapt accordingly.

Tailspin Toys case study The Development Team does not use this feature, but Paula (the Product Owner) does. She will sometimes send a request for feedback to a stakeholder in a remote office, along with a link to the test website. Andy (the TFS administrator) will add any new stakeholders to the Limited license group in Team Web Access so that they have adequate permissions.

Voluntary feedback

Another way to use the Feedback client to provide feedback is for a stakeholder to start it directly. It can be found on the Start menu under Visual Studio 2012. If it's missing, it can be downloaded from Microsoft.

When started, the client will be in *voluntary feedback mode*. There won't be any associated request or instructions, as you can see in Figure 8-22. Hopefully, the stakeholder will already know what application to start, what features or scenarios to evaluate and provide feedback on, and what team project to submit the feedback response to.

FIGURE 8-22 Feedback client running in voluntary feedback mode.

Feedback that has been submitted voluntarily like this can be found in TFS by running the Feedback shared query. This query returns work items that are in the Microsoft.FeedbackResponse Category work item type category. In the Visual Studio Scrum process template, this would only include Feedback Response work items.

When viewing a Feedback Response work item, you will see many of the standard fields, such as *title, created by, state, rating, area*, and *iteration*. The more interesting data will be in the Notes field, as it contains the comments typed by the stakeholder and any references to audio, video, screenshots, or attached files. There won't be any linked stories (PBIs), but the developer can add them as needed. Be aware that any files attached in the Feedback client will appear as Result Attachments links on the All Links tab and not as true work item attachments.

Note Currently, the Feedback client doesn't capture and persist system information. It was available during the beta version of Visual Studio 2012, but it was later removed. Microsoft is considering enabling it in a future update, along with the ability to disable it selectively for organizations that are sensitive to this kind of data being collected.

Tailspin Toys case study During the Sprint, completed features are deployed to a dedicated acceptance testing environment where the Scrum Team (as well as stakeholders) can use the system and provide feedback. Once Paula's remote stakeholders know how to use the Feedback client, they may drop in on the deployed website periodically and provide feedback. The Development Team has created an email alert that watches for new Feedback Response work items being created to let everyone know when an unsolicited, voluntarily provided piece of feedback arrives.

Code reviews

As we discussed earlier in this chapter, code reviews and pair programming are two ways that developers can collaborate to help assure higher code quality. These practices also reduce the risk of creating bugs, technical debt, and gold plating. Visual Studio Premium and Ultimate edition users can use Visual Studio to facilitate code reviews.

Smell It's a smell when I see a *collocated* Development Team using tools to facilitate code reviews. They should be able to practice these reviews in person. Excuses are usually to the effect of "But the developers are busy right now" or "It would be rude to interrupt them." It's obvious that they want to use the asynchronous behavior that the tool provides. I understand that there's a cost to interruptions, and that instant messaging (IM) and Short Message Service (SMS) texts are good for quick questions. Code reviews are not quick interruptions. They require a full stop and context shift in order for the review to have everyone's full attention. As I've mentioned several times in this chapter, conversations that take place face to face are more efficient, reduce ambiguity and misunderstanding, and provide more value than anything facilitated by a tool.

Tip Fellow Professional Scrum Developer Jose Luis Soria Teruel sometimes uses the Code Review tool to ask people *outside* the Development Team to review the code. It's useful to get the opinion of someone not working directly on the code, especially where new technologies are concerned. The Code Review tool provides the opportunity to involve an expert in the matter being reviewed.

From the My Work page, you can request a code review of work that currently has a state of In Progress or that has been suspended. You can also request a code review on a shelveset or changeset. Code reviews can be requested from various other pages and menus as well. Let's focus on the scenario where we want another developer to review some code that is currently In Progress. Assuming that there are pending changes on one or more files, the coder will click the Request Review link from the My Work page. Next, he or she selects one or more reviewers to send the request to. He or she can specify a friendly name for the code review, the area path, and a helpful comment, as shown in Figure 8-23. Unlike sending a request for feedback, this feature just assigns work items to the other TFS users. No email is sent.

FIGURE 8-23 Creating a new code review request for two other developers.

Tip Each code review recipient must have access to the files in TFS. In other words, if some files are off limits to a particular developer, don't ask her to review your changes to those files. She won't get very far. Also, it is possible to add yourself as a reviewer. Microsoft enabled this particular workflow so that you could add comments on your own code to explain the context before the review is sent to others. When those reviewers receive the code review request, they can read your comments first to obtain context and understanding.

When the request is submitted, a Code Review Request work item is created and assigned to the requester. In addition, one or more Code Review Response work items are created and assigned to the individual developers being asked to review the code. All of these work items are in the Requested state. Code Review Request and Code Review Response work item types are designated as Hidden types. This means that they cannot be created directly from Visual Studio or Team Web Access. Instead, they are created and managed using the appropriate tooling in Team Explorer. While you can query and open one of these work item types in Team Explorer or Team Web Access, the data in the form is read only.

The prospective reviewers will see the incoming request in the Code Reviews & Requests section of their My Work window. You can see an example of this in Figure 8-24. A number in parentheses shows, at a glance, how many code reviews are being displayed in the view. This is a quick way to see if any code reviews need your attention. There are several available views that can be selected to show code reviews in different ways. If you are curious, you can click the Open Query link to see the work item query (WIQ) behind any of the views.

Here is a list of the built-in views:

- **Incoming Requests** Shows active code reviews in which you are a reviewer.

- **Outgoing Requests** Shows active code reviews that you have requested.

- **Incoming & Outgoing** Shows both incoming and outgoing code reviews. This is the default view.

- **Recently Finished** Shows code reviews that have been completed in the last seven days.

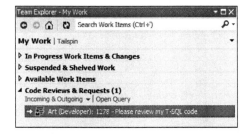

FIGURE 8-24 My Work page showing an incoming code review request.

When a request appears, the prospective code reviewer should open it to learn more. This opens the Code Review page in Team Explorer, as you can see in Figure 8-25. On this page, the reviewer can accept or decline the request by clicking the respective link towards the top. If the developer chooses to decline the request, he or she can provide a reason for declining the request.

FIGURE 8-25 Opening a code review request in Team Explorer.

Reviewing code within Visual Studio consists of performing one or more of the following activities:

- View the associated shelveset or changeset that contains the code.

- Open and review the associated Task work items.

- Add additional reviewers or remove current reviewers.

- Add overall comments.

- Comment on another's overall comment.

- Review the individual files and add inline comments (as shown in Figure 8-26).

- Check the boxes next to each file to ensure everything is reviewed.

- Finish the review.

FIGURE 8-26 Adding two separate comments about the CustomerLogin table.

Once the reviewer is done with the review, he or she can complete and send it with an overall opinion. The opinion choices are Looks Good, With Comments, or Needs Work. At this point, the work item will be closed and the person named in the Assigned-To field will be removed. At any time, the code review requester can expand the outbound request in his or her My Work page and see if the prospective reviewers have accepted, declined, ignored, or finished the request. The requester can also complete the code review as a whole at any time by closing it or abandoning it.

Tailspin Toys case study The Development Team has been performing code reviews and pair programming for some time now. They don't make either practice mandatory, but let the individual developers decide which will serve them best. They rarely use the code review features in Visual Studio, opting for in-person reviews instead. Occasionally, however, they have used this tooling when team members are on the road or otherwise working remotely.

Chapter burndown

Here are the key concepts we covered in this chapter:

- **Collaboration is key** Software development is a team sport. The Scrum Team needs to communicate with each other, as well as stakeholders, effectively.

- **Active listening** Communication techniques that enable better, more effective dialogue.

- **Collocated teams** Development Teams working in close proximity are more productive and generate more business value than teams that are geographically distributed. Large, open-space team rooms can be particularly effective.

- **Meet effectively** Scrum has all the built-in events (meetings) that a Development Team needs. Limit attendance to other meetings, or send the Scrum Master instead.

- **Limit interruptions** Turn off or otherwise neutralize cell phones, email clients, and IM/chat clients. Limit Internet searches and attending non-essential meetings.

- **Collective code ownership** The entire Development Team owns every aspect of the code. Everyone can read, check out, or check in code for any assembly, namespace, or class. TFS will effectively track all changes made.

- **Comments** When commenting code, be sure to explain your actions to others, assuming the code and/or check-in comments can't do it for you.

- **Code reviews** Practice these in person, or consider pair programming as an alternative. Developers should be open to giving and receiving criticism. Use the code review features in Visual Studio only when in-person reviews are not possible.

- **Continuous integration** Merging is painful, so do it more often so it hurts less. Stay in touch with your builds, especially when they fail. Get them healthy again as soon as possible.

- **Builds check-in policy** This check-in policy requires that the last build was successful for each affected CI build definition.

- **Build Notification tool** Configure and use this to receive alerts from TFS in your notification area (system tray) when a build queues, starts, or completes.

- **Gated check-in build** Use this on production code to ensure that the codeline stays healthy. CI is a better practice for the active development codeline.

- **Email alerts** TFS can be configured to send individuals or the entire team an email when something interesting happens, like a build breaking.

- **My Work** A page in Team Explorer that enables a developer to see and manage their current, in-progress work. The page is available to Visual Studio 2012 Ultimate or Premium users. Work can be suspended and resumed as other priorities crop up.

- **PowerPoint storyboards** Mockups and illustrations can be created in a familiar environment and shared with remote stakeholders to obtain their feedback.

- **Feedback client** A freely downloadable, lightweight tool that enables desktop video, audio, screenshots, and notes to be recorded as a stakeholder evaluates a piece of software. This feedback can be requested, or it can be offered voluntarily, without solicitation.

Improving

CHAPTER 9

Continuous improvement

One thing that I hope I have made clear is that high-performance Scrum Development Teams know they can always do better. They can build a better product. They can increase its quality. They can build it faster. They can build with less waste. They can learn new techniques that will help them improve personally and as a team. I use the term *continuous improvement* to categorize all of this.

Knowing where to start is a big part of improving. There are tactical improvements, which help the team successfully deliver the Increment during the Sprint while not generating waste. Mastering some of the common challenges that Scrum Teams run into will help in this regard. There are also strategic improvements, such as learning to become more cross-functional and self-organizing. Teams that improve in these areas will see orders of magnitude increases in capability and performance.

Note The FBI Sentinel Project is just such an example of a Scrum Team realizing this kind of increase in capability. While working in the basement of the Hoover building, the team finished over 80 percent of the work in just 10 percent of the budget—after a large government contracting agency failed to deliver. You can read more about the FBI case study in *Software in 30 Days* by Ken Schwaber and Jeff Sutherland.

In this chapter, we will look at how to handle common challenges, as well as how to identify and overcome various dysfunctions. We'll also look at some healthy behaviors to adopt in order to improve to the point of becoming a high-performance Scrum Team.

Common challenges

There are many challenges facing Scrum Development Teams, as well as any software development teams in general. Software development is a complex effort, and anyone who is not in the middle of it will have difficulty understanding that. Even the smartest developers will run into the dilemma of balancing the values of Scrum against getting something out the door.

For example, when an experienced developer sees the need to refactor one of the larger classes in the application, when should he or she do this? If he puts on a propeller hat, her or his technical side wants to open up the code file and start refactoring right now because it shouldn't take more than a day's time at most. However, when he or she puts on the Scrum robe, he or she wants to spend time wisely and in ways that provide maximum business value to the Product Owner. One developer, two urges. Which one wins? The answer is, of course, "it depends."

And in that, you can find the primary goal of this section—to address some of the more common challenges facing Scrum Development Teams and help them make good decisions.

Bugs

A bug communicates that a potential problem exists in the code that the Development Team is currently developing or has developed. Most teams believe that when a bug is located, it should be reported, perhaps as a Bug work item in Team Foundation Server (TFS). As I've said previously, I think that it should just be fixed. I always prefer that Development Teams fix bugs rather than manage them. There are, of course, exceptions to this rule.

If the bug is associated with work that is being done in the current Sprint, then fix it. I refer to these as *in-Sprint* bugs. The fact is that maybe it isn't a bug at all. It could just be that the developer isn't finished with the work. An extreme example of this would be when a developer forgets to add a semicolon at the end of a line of code and the compiler raises an error. Obviously, the developer should just fix the code rather than create a Bug work item in TFS. This example is silly, but it scales. Consider a larger and more complex issue that is blocking the team from completing its work. Either the bug will need to be fixed or that work will have to be renegotiated with the Product Owner. Bugs that come up during work within a Sprint are just an indicator the complexity of software development.

If, on the other hand, a bug is discovered in code that was previously thought to be done, and the bug's existence doesn't affect the Development Team's ability to deliver its forecast work in the current Sprint, then create a Bug work item in TFS. The bug goes into the Product Backlog like other Product Backlog items (PBIs) and will be groomed by the Scrum Team and ordered by the Product Owner to be fixed in a later Sprint, perhaps even the next one. I refer to these as *out-of-Sprint* bugs.

> **Tip** When you create a Bug work item, you should report the problem accurately in a way that helps your fellow developers understand the full impact of the problem. The steps to reproduce the bug should be listed so that someone else can reproduce the behavior. Also, include the expected behavior that is currently broken. This will serve as acceptance criteria when the team fixes the bug later. This is covered in detail in Chapter 5, "The Product Backlog."

I should be clear: It's always the Development Team's prerogative to create work items in TFS. They may decide that all bugs of a certain size, or larger, should be represented as a work item. On the other hand, the team may decide that if one developer locates a bug, but does not have the skills to fix it, he or she can immediately pair up and collaborate with another developer to fix it rather than creating a work item. While I prefer this type of behavior, it can be a source of interruption for the team. Ultimately, it is the Development Team's decision.

Note Professional Scrum Master Charles Bradley developed a helpful flowchart that encapsulates this type of decision-making process pertaining to the triage and handling of bugs. At the top of the flowchart is the detection of weird behavior in the software product. The possible outcomes, through the rest of the flowchart, are similar to those that I have just mentioned. For more information about the *Bradley Bug Chart*, visit *http://www.scrumcrazy.com/bugs*.

Previously, we have talked about writing and running tests to verify our design, as well as the behavior of new code that we are building. When faced with a potential new bug to fix, tests are also recommended. In fact, writing an automated test to verify the existence of a bug should be one of the first steps performed, possibly even before the bug is put in the Product Backlog.

Note Fellow Professional Scrum Developer Mike Vincent reminds us that writing a failing unit test may not be enough to prove the existence of a bug. A broader integration test or even a user interface (UI) test that exercises the functionality at a higher level may be required.

At a high level, here are the steps that a Development Team should take when handling bugs:

1. Verify the existence of the bug by writing a failing test. These should be automated tests, but not necessarily unit tests.
2. Fix the bug by making the test pass.
3. Verify the bug is fixed, and the fix didn't break anything else, by rerunning all tests.
4. Refactor any relevant code in accordance with your team's Definition of "Done." Avoid "gold plating."
5. Rerun all tests to ensure that the refactoring didn't break anything else.
6. Integrate your code with the latest version from TFS and rerun all tests. A continuous integration (CI) build running on Team Build can automate this.

If the Development Team is using work items to track the bug and the fix:

1. Associate the changeset with the "fix the bug" Task work item.
2. Set the Task and Bug work items to a State of Done.

Impediments

An *impediment* is anything keeping the team from being productive. Impediments can be environmental, interpersonal, technical, or even aesthetic in nature. Regardless of what the impediment is, or its size, if it's blocking the team from being productive, it should be removed. Just as the sweepers in the game of curling keep the path of the stone free from bumps and debris, so should members of the team keep the path of productive software development free of impediments.

Scrum has two formal opportunities to identify impediments: each day during the Daily Scrum, and at the end of the Sprint during the Sprint Retrospective meeting. However, impediments can be identified at any time during the Sprint. More important, they can and should be *removed* at any time. The problem is not finding the opportunity to identify impediments, but rather getting the developers to be honest about their existence.

It's common to hear software developers say that nothing's blocking them. Hearing this repeatedly does not reflect reality and might actually be a smell of an underlying dysfunction. I'm not saying that developers are patently dishonest. On the contrary, they are often just being optimistic. They have a lot of work to do and can easily find something else to work on. They may not realize that "blocking" can also mean that they are experiencing slow or non-optimal progress. Also, nobody wants to bother others with something as depressing as an impediment. What they don't realize is that by sharing their problems with the rest of the team, their honesty and openness will actually invite others to help remove the impediment. The impediment might just disappear sooner than expected.

 Smell It's a smell if I see a Scrum Team relying on their Scrum Master to remove impediments. Servant leadership only goes so far and can be abused by the rest of the team if allowed. While Scrum Masters are typically associated with being impediment removers, a healthier team behavior is for the person who identified the impediment to become the one who removes it, if possible. Don't let any person utter the words "that's not my job."

While the Microsoft Visual Studio Scrum 2.0 process template does contain an Impediment work item type, I prefer the team members not use it. My guidance is the same with impediments as with bugs: Remove them, don't manage them. Only create an Impediment work item if it will be some time before the impediment can be removed. Impediment work items can be in one of two states: Open or Closed. They are created in the Open state with the default reason "New impediment." When the impediment is removed or is no longer blocking productive work, the state should be changed to Closed with the reason "Impediment removed." Additional notes can be added to the work item history.

 Note For products requiring more than one Scrum Team, the recording and sharing of impediments becomes more important. Being able to view impediments across a large project or organization allows management the necessary visibility into any hotspots or trends.

 Tip When an impediment blocks a specific Task work item, be sure to mark the task as *blocked* and create a link to the Impediment work item. This will increase the visibility and understanding of exactly how the impediment affects the team.

Identifying an impediment is just the first step. A more important step is to execute a plan to remove it. Some team members will be able to remove certain types of impediments more easily than others. The Product Owner, or management, may need to get involved as well. Regardless of the level of difficulty or amount of ceremony involved in removing an impediment, it should still be identified. In other words, don't keep an impediment to yourself just because you think it'll be difficult to remove. If you see something, say something. Blow your whistle.

 Smell It's a smell if I see that a team is not dealing with their impediments. Ideally, any impediment that survives to the next Sprint should be resolved during that Sprint. It's the Scrum Master's job to keep a watchful eye on older impediments and appropriately nudge the team to remove them. I think of the impediment list as being the Scrum Master's *backlog*.

Estimation

Estimating the effort required to develop items in the Product Backlog is a team skill that will improve over time. Initially, the team may not have experience working with the domain, the tools, or each other. They may not have a common baseline to use for relative estimation either. All of this will emerge and improve over time.

Regardless of how experienced your team is, when it comes to Agile estimation, always remember and follow the basics:

- **Keep it groomed** A big reason for keeping the items in the Product Backlog groomed is to enable more accurate estimation. The Development Team should have just enough information in order to estimate a PBI, but no more. Specifying additional requirement information beyond what the Development Team needs to estimate, especially when it describes *how* the item should be developed, is wasteful. Once it becomes apparent that a PBI will be forecast in the next Sprint, more refined details, such as acceptance criteria and fresh estimates, are encouraged.

- **Estimate as a team** The entire Development Team should be involved in the estimation. Each PBI will require different types of activities and disciplines. The whole cross-functional team needs to be in the room as each item is discussed and estimated. Estimation by proxy will lead to the wrong estimates.

- **Be less precise** If you want to be more accurate, be less precise. Initially, consider estimating the size of the PBI using T-shirt sizes. This will help with coarse-grain release planning. Later, as it becomes more likely that a PBI will be developed, consider using a more precise unit of measure, such as story points. In the Sprint Planning meeting, as well as during the Sprint, the team can be even more precise as it estimates tasks in hours.

- **Be relative** No two PBIs will ever be the same level of complexity or amount of effort to develop. This is the nature of software development. To mitigate this while estimating, the team should think in terms of how the *size* of one PBI relates to another. This size usually relates to effort, but it can also relate to complexity. It doesn't matter which, so long as the Development Team is consistent. By comparing a new PBI with one of a similar size that was previously developed, the Development Team is able to determine if the new one is more work, less work, or about the same. Over time, working consistently as a team, more baseline PBIs will become available that can be used for comparison.

- **Don't translate** Keep any units of measure abstract. Avoid the temptation by you, or the organization, to translate story points into days, hours, or dollars. Knowing how many days are in a Sprint allows management to reconcile the work the team delivers, or more important, to translate the business value of that work into a monetary value. They already know what it costs to employ the team per Sprint. From this information, they can determine the business value per monetary unit, which should be the ultimate metric for any organization. Similarly, the Product Owner can also use the number of days in a Sprint and the Development Team's Velocity to assist with release planning. Either way, these computations are informative and healthy, and not the type of "translation" I'm referring to here. Trying to figure out how many hours a "typical" story point equates to or how many dollars a "typical" story point costs is pointless, as well as wasteful.

Note Fellow Professional Scrum Developer Jose Luis Soria Teruel stresses that the *process* of estimation is more important than the outcome. The real value is in all the information that is gained and uncertainty that is removed as a result of the conversation that estimation fosters.

When a team new to Scrum estimates features of a new product, in a new domain, using new tools, estimates will be way off. As the team normalizes and becomes familiar with each other as well as the product, this will turn around. Eventually, estimation will occur faster and become more accurate. If this is desirable (and it should be), then keep the team together. They will improve.

Smell It's a smell when I see management break up a high-performance Scrum Development Team. It's actually more than a smell—it's a downright shame. I know what they're thinking. They're thinking that they can distribute these individuals to other teams within the organization as seeds. The seeds will then grow new high-performance Scrum Development Teams. While this may be true, it destroys self-organization and generates waste due to the length of time that it requires to become a high-performance team. I contend that the organization will derive more value by leaving that team intact. Let the Scrum Master plant and water seeds in other teams without dismantling a proven generator of business value. Specific advice and techniques for scaling Scrum are beyond the scope of this book.

Tip Fellow Professional Scrum Developer Chad Albrecht agrees with this guidance. He encourages organizations to keep their high-performance Scrum Development Teams together whenever possible. However, when an organization wants to spin up several new Development Teams in a relatively short amount of time, splitting up a solid team is a good way to go about it, especially when done with professional assistance.

Tracking actual hours spent on tasks and PBIs is not important in Scrum. Although it is easy for TFS to track this information, I recommend teams resist the urges or requests to track or compute actual hours. It can only be used for evil. Once actual hours are tallied by task, or task activity type, somebody somewhere will use it as a measuring stick, or a beating stick, to attempt to improve the team's abilities. As I've previously explained, improving because someone else wants you to improve doesn't work. The desire must come from within, not from a spreadsheet.

Note Tracking hours on a timesheet in order to get paid is a different matter altogether. So is the tracking of hours in order to bill a project or client. If management expects this data, provide it. But do so knowing that the totals you are providing have nothing to do with your efficacy. If tracking hours detracts from the Development Team's ability to develop software efficiently, have the Scrum Master do it.

Tracking original task estimates is also not important. The only estimate that a Development Team should track is the amount of remaining work left to be done. In TFS, this relates to the total number of hours for all Task work items in the To Do and In Progress states in the Sprint Backlog. These estimates can change daily, and therefore should be updated daily. Hopefully, the work remaining estimates go down. Some days, however, they will go up. Some days, new tasks are identified that the Development Team didn't foresee. This is the nature of a complex effort like software development.

Tip When pressed by management for why your original estimates were off, give the honest answer: "What we do is very complex and hard to predict."

For example, let's assume a Development Team estimated that the development of a new mobile-browser-friendly home page would be eight story points and the sum of all the hours of the initial tasks would be 120 hours. Let's also assume that development ended up taking 160 hours to complete the PBI. Should the Development Team be concerned about the gap in their estimates? Sure. They should discuss it during the Sprint Retrospective meeting and determine if they can and how they might make better estimates going forward. Should management be concerned about the deviation from the original estimates? Sure, but they should know that their best people are on the job and they should be given the freedom to make those improvements themselves. Additional "management" won't make estimates more accurate.

Note Some Scrum practitioners are not fond of breaking PBIs down into tasks. They've seen situations where most or all of the tasks were done, but the PBI wasn't. While I would consider this to be a dysfunction that should be repaired, these same practitioners prefer to have smaller PBIs in the first place. This removes the need to break them down into tasks. It also removes the need to estimate because each PBI would be of a small enough size to be completed in one or two days at the most. Unfortunately, the task board found in Visual Studio Team Web Access does not support working with PBIs directly. It expects there to be associated tasks that will move across the board through the different states.

Assessing progress

Assessing progress simply means knowing how much work is left to do before reaching a goal. This is not necessarily the Sprint Goal, but any goal. The goal could be completing a PBI, completing all forecast PBIs for a Sprint, or completing all of the work promised in a release. Progress towards each of these types of goals can be measured in a number of ways. The *Scrum Guide* does not provide guidance on *how* to assess progress other than noting that it should be done by the team daily. Table 9-1 lists some practices that can be used to assess progress.

TABLE 9-1 Practices for assessing progress toward a goal.

Goal	Practice to assess progress	Goal is reached when
Release	Sum story points of undone PBIs in Product Backlog	Sum = 0
	Count undone PBIs in Product Backlog	Count = 0
Sprint	Sum story points of undone PBIs in Sprint Backlog	Sum = 0
	Count undone PBIs in Sprint Backlog	Count = 0
	Count failing tests [assumes acceptance test-driven development (ATDD)]	All tests pass
PBI (and Sprint)	Sum work remaining hours of undone tasks in Sprint Backlog	Sum = 0
	Count undone tasks in Sprint Backlog	Count = 0
	Count failing tests (assumes ATDD)	All tests pass

The most popular way to assess the progress of a release is to maintain a release burndown chart like the one shown in Figure 9-1. This kind of chart shows how much work remained at the start of each Sprint in a given release. The data comes from the Scrum Team's groomed Product Backlog. Each Sprint appears along the horizontal axis. The vertical axis measures the effort that remained when each Sprint started. The unit of measure is whatever your team has decided to use. Story points are the most common.

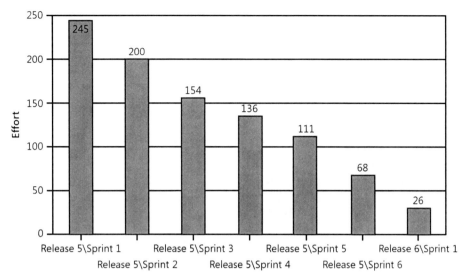

FIGURE 9-1 Example of a release burndown chart.

Note Fellow Professional Scrum Developer Jose Luis Soria Teruel reminds us that for a long-running project, one with multiple releases, the remaining work could actually *increase* over time as the Product Backlog evolves. In cases like this, the release burndown alone won't tell you how quickly the team is completing items in the Product Backlog, especially if the burndown refers to more than one release (as the one in Figure 9-1 does).

The most popular way to assess the progress of a Sprint is to maintain a Sprint burndown chart like the one shown in Figure 9-2. This kind of chart shows how much work remained at the end of specified intervals during a Sprint. The data comes from the Development Team's regularly updated Sprint Backlog. The days of the Sprint appear along the horizontal axis. The vertical axis measures the amount of remaining work to complete the tasks identified in the Sprint. The unit of measure is typically hours.

Sprint burndown charts can show the team how much work remains in the Sprint. These charts will often include an ideal trend line. This line represents the ideal rate at which the Development Team is able to complete all of the remaining effort, at a constant rate, by the end of the Sprint. It is usually manifested as a straight line displayed on the chart. By using the trend line, the team can gauge how it's doing and know if it is on track to finish all forecast work by the end of the Sprint, given the constant rate.

Burndown charts are generated from actual data. Because of this they reflect the reality of the Development Team's activity. For example, if the developers all go away for a three-day training class, the burndown will reflect a flat horizontal line (no movement) for those days. This means that the amount of work completed is the same as the amount of work added, which can happen when new tasks are discovered.

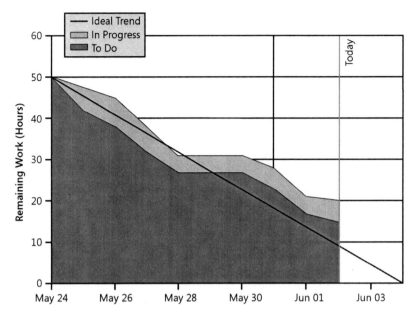

FIGURE 9-2 Example of a Sprint burndown chart.

Burndown charts can also illuminate other facts about how the Development Team works:

- **Actual and ideal trend lines are diverging or are far apart** The Development Team will probably miss their forecast. This will happen from time to time, but more often with new teams. As the Development Team's estimation practices improve and Velocity normalizes, the forecasts should become more accurate. On the other hand, sometimes the actual trend line is *below* the ideal one, meaning the Development Team should complete their forecast work earlier than expected and will be able to collaborate with the Product Owner about adding more work to the Sprint.

- **The total number of hours is increasing** This occurs when additional tasks are added to the Sprint Backlog during the Sprint. Some new tasks are to be expected, but a large number of tasks, or new tasks over several days, indicates poor Sprint planning, a badly groomed Product Backlog, or scope creep. This becomes very evident if the team is using a Sprint burndown chart.

 Smell Fellow Professional Scrum Developer Luis Fraile has seen this as a smell of the Development Team violating the You Ain't Gonna Need It (YAGNI) principle. This principle instructs developers not to add functionality until it is necessary, and not just because they *might* need it in the future.

> **Note** Fellow Professional Scrum Developer Chad Albrecht says that it is normal for an experienced Scrum Development Team to add tasks and actually burn up the first few days of a two-week Sprint. He describes this as a pattern of doing "just enough" planning during the Sprint Planning meeting. Additionally, teams that are practicing single-piece flow (working on a single PBI until it is done before moving to the next one) will witness multiple, small burn-ups during the Sprint. The number of bumps (burn-ups) is typically related to the number of PBIs forecast.

- **Actual performance is significantly above the ideal trend line** The Development Team has really missed the estimates or the amount of work forecast. Attention should be given to both during the next Sprint Retrospective meeting.

- **Tasks move to "Done" prematurely** Reactivating a task by moving it from Done back to In Progress will be reflected on the burndown as a bump. Knowing when a developer is done with a piece of work is a practice that will improve over time.

- **Not creating tasks for large pieces of work** The Development Team should decide when to create a Task work item and when to just do the work. The rule of thumb I use is two hours for a two-week Sprint. This is totally dependent on the Sprint length and other team behaviors. For example, if a developer realizes that a Secure Sockets Layer (SSL) certificate is expired while deploying the application to a staging environment, he or she may want to create a Task for what's about to take a measurable period of time to accomplish.

- **Tasks stay "In Progress" for more than two days** Sprint burndowns don't usually show this level of granularity, but flat spots (or rises) are always a concern. Where this staleness becomes obvious is during the Daily Scrums. Other developers should be concerned, or at least inquisitive, when a fellow developer says they are (still) working on the same task for several days. There may be a lack of transparency or openness in play here. Keep the burndown, and the team, accurate by updating all of the *Remaining Work* fields of your Task work items each day.

- **Burndown actually looks like a "burn-up"** Increasing hours may be due to "scope creep," which occurs when a substantial amount of work is added to a Sprint after it is planned. This is to be expected to some degree. A high-performance Scrum Development Team will strive towards effectively estimating work at the beginning of the Sprint.

When an organization first adopts Scrum, the customers and management will still be expecting to see the old management reports pertaining to software development. The ones they get in Scrum are going to be quite different. There will be a transition period for them to unlearn the old reports and begin understanding the new ones. During this period, the customers and management should also learn what it means for the team to be self-organizing and self-managing. This will also explain why the old reports are not necessary anymore. A good Scrum Master can explain to stakeholders that any report or artifact showing progress is primarily for the team and that they are being allowed access in order to provide transparency.

Note Burndown charts, graphs, and reports used to be artifacts in Scrum. In 2011, they were dropped from the *Scrum Guide* and are no longer a part of Scrum. This is because there are many ways that a team can assess progress. For example, in Chapter 7, "Acceptance test-driven development," we looked at the practice of ATDD. We talked about breaking down PBIs into features and scenarios and specifying the expected behavior in the form of failing acceptance tests. If this practice is adopted by the Development Team, they will have an array of failing tests prior to coding the features. As development proceeds, failing tests become passing tests. At any time, the team can use the remaining number of failing tests as a measure of progress.

Another way to assess progress is to simply ask the Development Team. At the Daily Scrum, simply ask each team member how confident they are in being able to meet the Sprint Goal and complete the forecast work. The numbers can be given a percentage such as 50 percent, 80 percent, 100 percent, and so on, and tracked each day. If the percentages stay the same or go up, that's fine. If they start to drop, that's an indication that something is wrong, and one that can be trusted because it comes directly from the front line. This technique for assessing progress can be just as effective as using a burndown.

Renegotiating scope

In the business world, things can change suddenly. Software being developed to support the business or to sell or support a product or service can quickly become obsolete. Or, thinking about it more optimistically, the software can be modified to take advantage of new opportunities. Regardless of the reason for the change, a Product Owner may determine that one or more forecast PBIs no longer has value once the Sprint has begun. This realization can also be initiated by the Development Team as they determine that a PBI is not able to be developed to any degree that would be fit for purpose.

Note Renegotiating scope can mean that the Development Team has completed all of its forecast work and wants to add more PBIs to its Sprint Backlog (scope increases). In this section, however, I'm talking about the more challenging scenarios where the forecast work was *not* completed or has become irrelevant (scope decreases).

The best case scenario when renegotiating scope is that the Development Team has not yet started on the PBI. Hopefully only an hour or less of the team's time spent planning the work will be wasted. The more complex scenario is where the scope needs to be renegotiated *after* the Development Team has started working on it. Obviously, the further into the development process, the more work will be potentially wasted. The Product Owner should take this into consideration before pressing the "big red button" to stop development. It may be more efficient (less wasteful) to create a new PBI instead. It is the job of the Scrum Master to help the Product Owner understand the costs associated with the potential waste. These costs are probably irrelevant if the work the Development Team is doing is truly without value.

Smell It's a smell if I see a Product Owner regularly renegotiating scope. More often than not, it's a dysfunctional Product Owner at work, trying to continuously introduce new, high-priority work. This dysfunction could also be restated as a lack of proper Product Backlog grooming. It could also be that the Product Owner is new to the role and still getting the hang of effectively ordering the Product Backlog. Either way, the Scrum Master should get involved and make sure that changing scope is truly the exception to the process, and not the rule. Nothing frustrates (and burns out) good developers like an organization that keeps giving priority 1 work, on top of other priority 1 work. If everything is priority 1, then there are no priorities.

Canceling a Sprint

If it is determined that the Sprint Goal becomes obsolete, the Product Owner can cancel the Sprint. In other words, the Sprint could be canceled if the Product Owner determines that there is no chance to realize *any* value in *any* of the forecast work being developed. For example, if a company suddenly decides to abandon support for a particular platform, the Sprint could be canceled if it contained only PBIs targeting that platform.

Note Only the Product Owner has the authority to cancel a Sprint, but he or she can do it under the influence of stakeholders or others on the Scrum Team.

You would cancel a Sprint only if you were unable to proceed and create anything of value during the Sprint. Here are some examples:

- Business conditions change in a way that the PBIs in the Sprint Backlog no longer have value.
- The technology on which you've been building the software proves invalid, and switching to a new technology requires a large amount of new planning.
- The organization might undergo a restructuring where developers get moved off the team.
- Critical production support issues arise and take the team away to the point where it isn't able to deliver any features or value in the Increment for the Sprint.

When a Sprint is canceled, any "done" PBIs should be reviewed to determine if they are potentially releasable. The Product Owner may choose to accept the work. All undone PBIs are moved back to the Product Backlog. They should be re-estimated if required, or left to sink to the dark depths of the backlog if they are not.

When a Sprint is canceled, it means that at least some amount of the work will have to be thrown away. Although Scrum minimizes waste through short iterations and just-in-time requirements, canceling a Sprint should be the last thing considered. Cancellations consume resources, since everyone has to regroup in another Sprint Planning meeting to start another Sprint. They are often traumatic to the Scrum Team and are very uncommon. They are not a good thing.

Tip If your Product Owner is canceling Sprints frequently, consider shortening them instead. I've worked with teams in volatile markets who normalized on three-day Sprints for just such a reason. This is an extremely short Sprint, with a relatively high cost in the overhead of meetings, and should be attempted only by high-performance Scrum Teams.

Undone work

A common problem that Scrum Development Teams face is that of undone work. The Sprint is over, and some things did not get done. Maybe an entire PBI (or two) didn't get touched. More likely, however, is that a PBI is in progress with one or more undone tasks, code half written, tests half passed, the Definition of "Done" not fully adhered to, and so on. I refer to that type of undone work as *unfinished*. Regardless of how much work was accomplished for a PBI, it cannot be released unless it is done. Not only would the feature not work correctly, but the Development Team will have introduced technical debt into the product.

Regardless of the type of undone work, or its level of undoneness, the guidance is the same:

1.   The PBI(s) are not demonstrated in the Sprint Review meeting.

2.   The PBI(s) are moved back to the Product Backlog.

3.   The Product Owner will consider developing the PBI(s) in a future Sprint.

There are other nuances to consider when dealing with undone work:

- **No partial credit** Story points for partially completed PBIs should not be summed into Velocity, even partially. The Development Team is either done with a PBI, or they aren't. The exception to this is when a PBI can be split and partially released during the Sprint (see the next bullet).

- **Decompose and release smaller PBIs** If a PBI can't be delivered in whole, as forecast, and the Development Team determines that it can be decomposed, they should talk with the Product Owner. That discussion could yield a plan to release smaller, logical parts of the PBI as smaller PBIs that are truly done and contain business value.

- **Re-estimate the PBIs** Undone PBIs should be regroomed and re-estimated. This increases transparency because the new estimates reflect the Development Team's latest thinking. Besides, the new estimates will be more accurate, since the team has first-hand experience. They may also be lower than the original.

- **Product Owner owns the order** It is always the Product Owner's prerogative to reorder the Product Backlog at any time, for any reason. This means that an undone PBI from the current Sprint may not necessarily be the top-ordered item, or even in the Sprint Backlog, for the next Sprint.

- **Excluding undone work from the Increment** In the event that a Sprint ends with unfinished work, there may be a lot of manual effort required to exclude the unfinished code and behavior from the rest of the Increment. Single-piece flow (limiting work in progress by swarming on a PBI) is one such approach. The Development Team can just decide that they will not advance to the next PBI in the Sprint Backlog until the prior one is done, documented, and exists with an installer, for example. For some environments, this is not practical, so other, more engineering-centric solutions are required. The two most common approaches are to create a version control branch per PBI or to use *feature toggles* in the application. We will look at feature toggles in the next section.

- **Product Owner cannot override the Definition of "Done"** Under no circumstances can the Product Owner, a stakeholder, or the organization override the Definition of "Done" and say that a PBI or bug fix is done when it isn't. That said, the Product Owner may determine that including an unfinished PBI in the Increment will add more business value to the software product than not including it. This should be done only after carefully considering the tradeoffs, such as the technical debt that will be incurred. Unfinished PBIs should be tracked in the Product Backlog and finished as soon as possible.

Note Fellow Professional Scrum Developer Trainer Chad Albrecht feels that using version control branches to isolate work per PBI is dysfunctional and does not promote good collaboration and CI practices. He has seen many teams do this, and they typically spend a lot of time merging while trying to figure out how everything integrates. Chad prefers using a combination of feature toggles, extensive test automation, and CI behavior to mitigate the chaos generated by unfinished work.

A potentially releasable software product is one that has been designed, developed, tested, and otherwise done according to the Development Team's definition. The only activity left is the actual release of the software. This means that the Development Team must create any build packages, installers, help files, and other artifacts to assist in the actual release before declaring the corresponding PBI, as well as the Increment, "Done." Whether or not the Product Owner chooses to release the feature is irrelevant. The Development Team must complete all work as if the Product Owner *was* going to release it at the end of the Sprint.

Smell It's a smell when a Scrum Team, including the Product Owner, just assumes that undone PBIs will be carried forward to the next Sprint. That may very well be the case, but assumptions like this can lead to unhealthy behaviors, such as compromising on quality, pushing off undone work until the next Sprint, and so on. It's always the Product Owner's decision what work will be considered for the next Sprint. He or she should listen to the Development Team, but it is only one source of input to consider. In other words, it's a dysfunction to assume that the Development Team will just continue working on any current, unfinished PBIs in the next Sprint.

Velocity simply indicates how many PBIs (or the sum of story points) a team usually completes per Sprint. It is not a commitment or a target and should only be used as one of several inputs for release and Sprint planning. For example, just because the Development Team was able to deliver 30 points last Sprint, that doesn't mean they will again. The Velocity for next Sprint is always unknown, and someone can only guess what it will be. These guesses will become more accurate over time. Velocity should also increase over time as the team improves. However, making a commitment based on a guess, even a good one, is still risky. It takes courage to stop guessing and trust that the Development Team will be able to self-organize and forecast a comfortable amount of work and then deliver the best Increment possible given all the constraints.

Smell It's a smell when I hear the term *Velocity* and *"credit"* or *"score"* together, or when management tries to compare the Velocities of two Development Teams. This smells like the developers are being gamed in some way, or even artificially rewarded somehow. Remember that Velocity is just a historical record. It should not be the goal. It is a lagging indicator of how well the Development Team is working together. Using Velocity in any other way diminishes its value. Don't put too much scrutiny, positive or negative, on the numbers. The Development Team should focus on delivering business value in the form of working software, and not on increasing its Velocity. That will occur as the team improves.

Feature toggles

A *feature toggle* is a technique where functionality can be selectively excluded, or disabled, from a release. These types of solutions are not new. I've heard them previously referred to as *feature bits*, *feature flags*, and *feature switches*. Feature toggles are most often used in the context of undone work and in lieu of branching in version control. They allow a Development Team to release an Increment that has unfinished features. These unfinished features are hidden (toggled), so they do not appear in the UI.

Tip Ideally, the Development Team will finish a partially completed feature in an upcoming Sprint, prior to the release. This minimizes waste and also ensures the toggled feature doesn't become long-term technical debt in the product. Even more ideal is that the team gets better about completing its forecast work and doesn't need such solutions in the first place. Be careful releasing a software product with feature toggles, since they can (by design) cause different behavior in different deployments, which can make the process of triaging a bug very complex.

The actual implementation of the feature toggle can vary. Menu items can be disabled. Entries in App.config or Web.config files can be used. Even compiler directives can be used. While these techniques can be implemented easily by most .NET developers, there are some third-party libraries available to simplify the practice further.

Jason Roberts (*www.dontcodetired.com*) has released a simple, yet effective, library called FeatureToggle. It defines a number of different types of toggles and supports many Microsoft run-time platforms. You can download the code at github (*https://github.com/jason-roberts/ FeatureToggle*) or via NuGet.

Here is a short example, taken from the github wiki, that shows how to use a SimpleFeatureToggle. First, create a toggle for the feature that you want to control by inheriting from SimpleFeatureToggle:

```
private class SaveToPdfFeatureToggle : SimpleFeatureToggle { }
```

Next, add an entry to the AppSettings section of the App.config or Web.config file. This will control the value of the SaveToPdfFeatureToggle:

```
<appSettings>
    <add key="FeatureToggle.SaveToPdfFeatureToggle " value="true"/>
</appSettings>
```

In the application, add code to query the state of the toggle in code and behave accordingly:

```
var savePdfFeature = new SaveToPdfFeatureToggle();
if (savePdfFeature.FeatureEnabled)
    ShowSavePdfButton();
else
    HideSavePdfButton();
```

Later, if the Product Owner decides to disable the feature, or it wasn't finished, then return to the .config file and set the toggle to false:

```
<appSettings>
    <add key="FeatureToggle.SaveToPdfFeatureToggle " value="false"/>
</appSettings>
```

Development Teams working in a continuous delivery environment don't necessarily need feature toggles to include or exclude functionality in a release selectively. This is because each PBI is effectively its own release. While the chance of having undone work in a fixed-length Sprint still exists, these teams may use feature toggles a bit differently. They may use the practice to keep a feature disabled until some future date. For example, if an online Software as a Service (SaaS) product wants to begin offering a new paid feature starting November 1, the product team will probably get it installed in the production environment days or weeks earlier, and leave it "switched off" until the release date. Microsoft sometimes takes this approach with their hosted Team Foundation Service.

Handling undone work in Visual Studio

Unfortunately, Visual Studio does not offer any tools for handling undone work. All moving or copying operations will have to be performed manually, and it can be a time-consuming undertaking. Because of this, Product Backlogs and Sprint Backlogs end up in a less-than-desired state of organization due to the amount of work required to organize them properly.

When a PBI is not done at the end of a Sprint, the opportunity to work on it as part of the existing body of work is often lost forever. The reason for this is that when the same PBI or feature is planned in the next Sprint (or a future Sprint), the context for that work may be different. This is why the PBI must be re-estimated and reordered, especially for complex work. Admittedly, this isn't true for simple or even complicated tasks, such as building a CRUD data entry form.

When considering how to handle undone work in the context of Visual Studio, there are basically four approaches:

- **Move to Product Backlog** This is the most common approach and fits with my guidance from earlier in this section. The PBI work item is simply moved back to the Product Backlog by changing its *Iteration path* and *State* fields accordingly. (You can also drag and drop in Team Web Access). Linked work items remain linked. No record, other than notes in the History, shows that the PBI was ever in the original Sprint.

- **Copy to Product Backlog** The PBI work item is shallow-copied and the copy's *Iteration path* and *State* fields are set for it to appear in the Product Backlog. The original PBI work item and all linked work items remain in the original Sprint in the committed State. The new PBI has no linked work items, so a brand new plan (Task and Test Case work items) can be established during Sprint planning.

> **Note** Fellow Professional Scrum Developer David Starr recommends this approach. He prefers to create a new PBI and replan it from scratch during a later Sprint. This is especially helpful when the PBI requires overly complex work to complete such that the new definition of work will be different from the old plan. The old PBI, and any linked work items, should be abandoned and left to the historical record of the last Sprint.

- **Move to (next) Sprint Backlog** If the Product Owner wishes, then the iteration paths of the PBI work item and all linked work items can be changed to the next Sprint. Everything appears just the way it was in the original Sprint. No record, other than notes in the History, shows that the PBI was ever in the original Sprint.

- **Copy to (next) Sprint Backlog** If the Product Owner wishes, then the PBI work item can be shallow-copied and have its iteration path set to the next Sprint. The original PBI work item and all linked work items remain in the original Sprint in the Committed state. The new PBI has no linked work items, so a brand new plan (Task and Test Case work items) can be established during Sprint planning.

There will be times that a Scrum Team may want to use each of these approaches. One cannot be prescribed as the "recommended" one without knowing more about how the team likes to work and other factors. There are also a number of other activities to consider when copying or moving undone work items. I've listed some of these in Table 9-2.

TABLE 9-2 Considerations when copying or moving undone work items.

Consideration
■ Set the PBI's *State* to Approved when moving or copying to the Product Backlog.
■ Set the PBI's *Iteration* to the root when moving or copying to the Product Backlog.
Re-estimate and reorder PBIs after moving or copying them to the Product Backlog.
Clear all *Remaining Work* fields in linked Task work items (re-estimated as needed)
Clear all *Assigned To* fields in linked Task work items (they should not be preowned by anyone).
Set all states and fields appropriately for other linked work items (like Test Cases).
Copy all (or just the undone tasks) to the next Sprint Backlog if the plan still makes sense.
Test Case and other work items could also be copied to the (next) Sprint Backlog if applicable.
Add appropriate notes to the History tab of the various work items.

Spikes

There will be times that the Development Team will be required to develop something that it hasn't done before. Needless to say, they cannot estimate the task with any confidence either. This could include developing a new capability using a new product, component, framework, system, or language. The developers will need to learn and practice in order to develop the feature successfully. They also need this experience sooner, in order to be able to *estimate* the size of the PBI.

Organizations can't expect their developers to gain this knowledge on their own, although some developers will. I know many developers who consider their profession as their hobby. For these geeks, learning new things is just fun. For the rest of the world, this learning will have to come during company time, on the company dime. But how does this fit with Scrum? The answer is to perform a *spike*, which is another word for a technical investigation, proof of concept (POC), or an experiment. The outcome of which is to gain just enough knowledge to be able to give the Development Team some confidence in their estimate. Ultimately, Scrum is about learning from data derived from experiments— so the spike concept fits right in.

> **Note** When fellow Professional Scrum Master Charles Bradley sees the look of sheer panic on the faces of the Development Team when estimating a new PBI, he knows that it's time to perform a spike.

Most spikes are small and executed as needed throughout the Sprint. In fact, I wouldn't even call them a spike. They are just part of development. Some Scrum practitioners call them *spike tasks* (as opposed to the larger *spike stories*). If a developer needs to clarify a technical issue, and another team member cannot help, the developer can create a quick spike instead. Time-boxing should always be used to keep spikes as small as is necessary. The Development Team can decide the criteria for when to track the task in the Sprint Backlog, such as by creating a TFS work item.

Tip A spike is not the same thing as a *tracer bullet*. A tracer bullet is development that cuts vertically through the many layers of architecture. This is sometimes known as the practice of developing thin, vertical slices. *Emergent architecture* is the practice of continually developing in thin slices like this. Tracer bullets can be experimental in nature, like a spike. But, unlike a spike, they are not typically discarded at the end of the experiment.

When a spike takes a large amount of time, or is required to be accomplished *before* the Development Team can estimate a PBI, it should be treated like any other PBI. Spikes are part of the Sprint and should therefore be accounted for in Sprint Planning and be represented in the Sprint Backlog. This means that the spike should be added to the Product Backlog first, and forecast as part of the Sprint. A plan should be created and tracked, just like any other feature or bug fix. There should always be other PBIs forecast for that Sprint, even just a few small ones, so the product (and the Product Owner) will enjoy some increment of business value every Sprint.

Tip Fellow Professional Scrum Master Charles Bradley recommends that a Scrum Team add acceptance criteria to any spike PBI to ensure that the follow-on PBI exists and is properly groomed. This way, the spike is not "done" until another PBI exists containing clear acceptance criteria, and that is estimable (with some level of Development Team confidence).

Smell It's a smell when a spike takes the majority of the team the majority of the Sprint to accomplish. It's a stench when it takes multiple Sprints. I guess it may be possible that the new architecture or technology is so alien that it really does require that much capacity to understand it to the point of being able to use it effectively. In my experience, however, good software developers aren't caught flat-footed like this very often. New tools and technology are pretty similar to the previous ones. Also, don't let the Development Team get into the habit of creating a spike for every PBI that it grooms. Spikes should be few and far between.

Fixed-Price contracts and Scrum

Scrum works well when the Product Owner, customer, and stakeholders trust the Development Team and all are able to work together collaboratively. If the customer has had enough projects fail in the past, this trust won't be there initially. In their minds, it will need to be replaced with a contractual relationship with the development group instead. The customer's hope is that the contract and its clauses and signatures will minimize the customer's risk and provide a legal way of recovering costs if the developers fail to deliver. From their perspective, they only have one shot at getting the software they want, so they want to define everything up front and then manage risk by putting a monetary limit on the cost.

The most common of these contract development agreements are known as *fixed-price* or (*fixed-bid*) contracts. They attempt to predict exactly the cost (and the time) at which the software that's been specified by the customer will be delivered. The common misconception is that it is impossible to use Scrum on a fixed-price contract. The reality is that Scrum handles this in the same way that any other process would. Everything the customer wants is detailed and estimated, generating an idea of a time at which everything can be delivered.

Here are the common challenges with fixed-priced contracts:

- Price is the most important factor and is driven by competition, not quality.

- Requirements are vague, wrong, out of date, or missing.

- Team-based estimation is impossible due to insufficient data.

- No knowledgeable person (such as a Product Owner) exists.

- The Scrum Team doesn't have any incentive to spend time enlightening the (potential) customer about Scrum, or creating and grooming a Product Backlog prior to signing a contract.

- Quality is not defined, only assumed.

- No Definition of "Done," or even a basis for one, exists.

- Deadlines are artificial and impossible.

- Risks are not shared or are ignored.

Tip Beware of fixed-price, *fixed-scope* contracts. Scrum + fixed-price + fixed-scope don't mix. This is the whole idea behind having a Product Backlog and an active Product Owner to order the PBIs. If the customer in a fixed-price contract wants to own both the date and the number of features, the only remaining variable is quality, and sacrificing quality never works out, especially in a contract situation.

Any fixed-price contract should be *variable-scope*. This fits better with Scrum because the team can now apply a consistent Definition of "Done" and establish an uncompromising baseline of quality for all of the work it does. The team then can start using iterative, incremental development to begin delivering increments of working software every month or sooner. This model provides more value and less risk to both parties, but is hard to conceptualize and agree to without knowing more about Scrum and the Development Team.

Perhaps a better name for a fixed-price contract would be simply *fixed-budget contract*. The customer knows how much they want to spend, or at least what the ceiling is. By creating an ordered Product Backlog, the customer will get the most important features before the money runs out. Therefore, the ideal Scrum contract model should be *fixed-budget, variable-scope*.

Here are two rules to consider when using Scrum for a fixed-price project:

- The customer (via the Product Owner) can replace any item in the Product Backlog with another item of similar size, provided the Development Team hasn't started working on it or completed it yet.

- At any point in time, the customer (via the Product Owner) can say that they have enough functionality and effectively end the development effort.

Speaking of risk, it's important for both the customer and the Scrum Team to share the risk. Typically, this means that the customer must become the Product Owner or work closely with a knowledgeable Product Owner to order the Product Backlog and determine the scope. This removes the risk of the Development Team developing the wrong features, or not getting to their "must-have" features before the budget runs out. Some customers, after learning that they will be accountable for this, may decide to walk away and offer the work to a competitor. You should let this happen. In my opinion, this is the right thing to do, rather than running the risk of building the wrong product or a product of questionable quality and value.

Common dysfunctions

Leo Tolstoy told us that "happy families are all alike, but that every unhappy family is unhappy in its own way." This is true of teams that develop software as well. A certain amount of dysfunction is going to exist, even in high-performance Scrum Teams, and it will always be unique. This is because Scrum is about people, and people don't behave like highly predictable machines.

Removing a dysfunctional behavior can be difficult. Identifying it in the first place can be very difficult, especially if you are in the middle of it or the cause of it. Part of becoming good at Scrum is the ability to inspect and detect dysfunctional behavior. At first, this may be the ability to know when your team isn't following the rules of Scrum, according the *Scrum Guide*. But that's not enough.

It may seem like the *Scrum Guide* has an answer for everything, but it doesn't. The complex world of software development will sometimes put you and your team in the middle of two practices that conflict with each other. Your abilities should transcend from just knowing the rules to knowing (and applying) the principles and values of Scrum. Knowing the higher-level reasoning behind Agile software development and why Scrum works allows you to identify and resolve such conflicts.

Teams new to Scrum will fumble with applying the right practice for a given dysfunction. Their heads are down, executing the practice. High-performance Scrum Teams have moved beyond rote practices and think in principles. Their heads are up, looking for dysfunction and ways to generate more value. It's a state of mind, and it comes with experience.

This section serves as a guidebook to the different types of dysfunction that can be found on a Scrum Team, and offers ideas for removing them.

Not getting "done"

You would think that *done* is when a new feature or bug fix has been deployed and is running happily in production. I would agree. If that's the status of your PBI, then you are definitely done with it. From Scrum's point of view, however, this is not always the case. Done doesn't necessarily mean that the PBI is *in* production, but that it easily *could be*. This is the concept of potentially releasable, or potentially shippable, as some of us still say. In Scrum, "done" typically includes everything up to, but excluding being deployed. It's actually up to the Development Team to decide what "done" means, through the Definition of "Done."

What "done" *doesn't* mean is that the PBI has been coded but not yet tested. In Scrum, all software engineering activities, including testing, must be finished before a PBI can be considered done. It's a dysfunction when a Development Team is not able to complete its work according to the Definition of "Done." Perhaps their definition is too stringent. Perhaps the Sprint length is too short. More likely, their Sprint length is too long. Nothing focuses the Development Team like knowing it has a Sprint Review meeting in the same week that the Sprint starts.

> **Smell** It's a smell what I hear a team using the terms *"done done," "proper done,"* or *"really done."* Historically, these terms have meant that both coding *and* testing had been completed, which implies that there was a "done" state where just the coding was finished. In Scrum there is only "done," and the team is either there or they aren't. It is a Boolean state.

In Chapter 1, "Scrumdamentals," I mentioned that the Definition of "Done" is an auditable checklist that each PBI must go through before it is considered done. When each item in that definition is "checked" and the Product Owner accepts the work, the PBI is done. Some Development Teams include an item in the definition verifying the Product Owner's acceptance. Other teams don't, and just understand that it's simply a part of Scrum's workflow for being done. Either approach is fine, so long as it is uniformly applied, understood by the entire Scrum Team, and never undermined.

If a Development Team is not able to complete all of its work—such as performance, regression, stability, security, and integration testing—within a Sprint for each PBI, this work then becomes *undone* work. Sprint after Sprint, this backlog of undone work accumulates and must be addressed at some point prior to releasing the Increment. The work may appear to accumulate linearly, but in fact, the accumulation is more exponential. This is due to the inherently complex nature of software development, as well as the attributes and behaviors of the product and the organization. For example, the organization may not have a proper environment provisioned yet to complete the testing, or a lengthy "route to live." These should be considered impediments. Regardless, additional "release" Sprints must be added to the end of any release to complete this undone work. The number of these Sprints is unpredictable to the degree that the accumulation of undone work is not linear. Needless to say, undone work is a form of technical debt and should be avoided.

Tip There are times that the Development Team will not get done. It is hard to prevent this from happening from time to time. It is important not to make it a habit by forecasting too much work. It is also important to craft a reasonable Sprint Goal during Sprint Planning. Having a Sprint Goal is important because, even if some of the forecast PBIs aren't completed, at least the goal was met and the Sprint was not a failure. Refer to Chapter 1 for more information on Sprint Goals. The Development Team should make good use of the Sprint Retrospective and Sprint Planning meetings by analyzing all of the inputs, checking capacity and recent Velocity, and forecasting a comfortable amount of work each Sprint.

Flaccid Scrum

In January 2009, Martin Fowler wrote a blog post on the topic of flaccid Scrum. Just as the name implies, his observations of many teams doing Scrum was that they were doing poorly. His typical observation would include a team that wanted to use an Agile process, so they picked Scrum. The team adopted the Scrum practices, and maybe even the principles. After a while, progress slowed because the code base became a mess and the team found itself drowning in technical debt. You can read Martin Fowler's article here: *http://martinfowler.com/bliki/FlaccidScrum.html*.

The fact that these teams were using Scrum was orthogonal to the root cause of the problem. It was just another example of teams and organizations considering Scrum a silver bullet. Scrum is simply a framework for planning and managing complex work. It says nothing about specific development and engineering practices exercised within, other than the generic statement: "As Scrum Teams mature, it is expected that their Definition of 'Done' will expand to include more stringent criteria for higher quality."

I surmise that the software products that these teams were developing suffered low quality because the developers were not inspecting, not adapting, or both. Remember that Scrum has built-in opportunities to inspect and adapt, at both the process and the product level. The fact that technical debt was building up to critical levels was because the teams either didn't know (weren't inspecting) or didn't care (weren't adapting).

 Note I've met with many such teams who love to throw around the terms *Sprint, Scrum Master, Product Backlog*, and so on. But when it came to being able to deliver business value within a time-box, they couldn't do it. It seems as though they were using the Scrum nouns, but not doing the Scrum verbs.

To fight flaccid Scrum, the Development Team needs to inspect and adapt its technical practices. This is true especially if there is a lot of technical debt and technical dysfunction present. During the Sprint Retrospective meeting, the team should inspect its current practices and, if improvement is required, agree to adopt, continue using, or abandon any specific practice. They can also take this opportunity to ratchet up their Definition of "Done" and include more stringent criteria for higher quality. Most importantly, in the next Sprint, they can adapt by executing on these improvements.

Tip The Professional Scrum Developer (PSD) program was a direct response to the problem of flaccid Scrum. The program consists of a training course, assessment, certification, and a community developed for the most neglected role in Scrum: the Development Team. The PSD course was developed in cooperation between Microsoft, Scrum.org, and Accentient.

Not inspecting, not adapting

Flaccid Scrum came about because of many reasons. Teams were uneducated. Teams didn't have a Definition of "Done," didn't stick to it, or didn't try to improve it. Teams weren't able to deliver business value in a single Sprint. Teams weren't inspecting. Teams weren't adapting.

Scrum is based on empiricism, which means that the players make decisions based on what *is*. These players must frequently inspect Scrum artifacts and their progress toward a goal (release or Sprint) to detect any undesirable variances. Good decisions can't be made if you don't have the data. Conversely, rich data is useless unless it is acted upon. Not doing either is a dysfunction.

Tip If I want to know how well a Scrum Team is inspecting and adapting, I will ask about their Sprint Retrospectives. In my experience, the Sprint Retrospective is the first to suffer when times get rough. Sure, the team may meet and discuss things, but they may not act on their findings. I contend that "rough times" is code for "we didn't like what we discovered" or "we didn't want to improve." Fellow Professional Scrum Developer Simon Reindl also likes to ask the Development Team to see their automated regression test coverage. This is an indication of how well they are improving technically.

For example, a Scrum Team may be very diligent about scheduling and attending their Sprint Retrospective meetings. They may have rich conversations and discuss the high and low points of the Sprint. They may even identify things to do differently in the next Sprint. Multiple team members capture this information and then do nothing with it. They have inspected, but not adapted.

Tip Fellow Professional Scrum Master Charles Bradley recommends that anything the Scrum Team tries to do differently in the next Sprint remain visible and transparent to the team. There are several strategies for encouraging adaptions. Some teams use a Retrospective Backlog, while others add tasks to the next Sprint's Backlog to represent the work and time needed to adapt their practices. Still others use a small portion of the Sprint Retrospective to inspect whether they made the adaptations suggested from the previous Sprint Retrospective.

Smell It's a smell when I see nobody taking notes at the various Scrum events, such as the Daily Scrum or the Sprint Retrospective. Does the team not have anything interesting to discuss and record? Maybe they have nothing that can be fixed, and thus no action items. For the teams I've worked with, however, this is rarely the case. More likely, nobody wants to be the secretary and do the paperwork. This is a behavior the team should correct. In the meantime, and at the very least, the Scrum Master should be recording any inspections and then ensuring the appropriate adaptations are made. It's also a smell when I hear the *same* item(s) coming up repeatedly. This is a failure to adapt.

On the other hand, formal inspection should not occur so frequently that it gets in the way of the work. In order to minimize this, Scrum prescribes four formal opportunities for inspection and adaptation:

- **Sprint Planning meeting** The Product Backlog is inspected, and the Sprint Backlog is adapted.

- **Daily Scrum** The Development Team's progress is inspected, and their plan for the next 24 hours is adapted.

- **Sprint Review meeting** The Increment is inspected, and the Product Backlog is adapted.

- **Sprint Retrospective meeting** The process and practices, including the Definition of "Done," are inspected and adapted (during the next Sprint).

Development Team challenges

It takes time for a Development Team to be able to self-organize, even with the support of the organization. Development teams that come from a more formal, "waterfall" background are used to the relative safety of the different stages. Hiding behind (the wrong) requirements or in front of (the yet to be run) tests provides a level of safety and cover. Moving to an attitude of understanding that everybody is on the same team, working towards the same goals, and sharing in the same successes and failures will take time.

As I've said before, Scrum is about people. These people work together as a team communicating, listening, complementing each other's skills, sharing objectives, and solving problems together. There must be compassion and respect for each other, as well as trust. These attributes will develop and improve over time. High-performance Scrum Development Teams continually balance the three raw ingredients of a Development Team: people, process, and technology. You can see this in Figure 9-3.

People exhibit different behaviors depending on the context of a situation. There is the normal behavior: how team members usually see each other. There is problem solving behavior: the team members are fully engaged mentally and getting stuff done. There is also stress behavior: quite different from the others and often harder for the rest of the team to deal with. During any given Sprint, each of these behaviors will be observable.

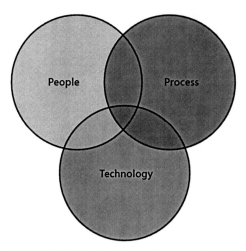

FIGURE 9-3 Achieving high-performance Scrum is a continuous balancing act.

Note There are many frameworks and techniques out there that try to capture and categorize the attributes of people and their interpersonal relationships. In my opinion, these should not be used to "improve" a Development Team unless the current climate is a disaster. FIRO-B is interesting because it focuses on capturing and measuring the interpersonal needs of members of small groups. The theory is based on the belief that when people get together in a group, there are three main interpersonal needs they are looking to obtain: affection/openness, control, and inclusion. The instrument helps teams measure/control feelings when it comes to these needs. For more information on FIRO-B, visit *https://www.cpp.com/products/firo-b/index.aspx*.

Scrum Development Teams need to learn to deal effectively with ambiguity. For most projects, the team won't have all the answers. Effectiveness in the face of ambiguity is a measure of intellectual growth and maturity. Development Teams will find themselves in unusual circumstances that cannot be solved by thinking at the practice level; rather, it can be solved only by abstracting to the principle level. It's up to the individuals to make judgments and not just copy and paste random bits of practice.

In addition to dealing with ambiguity, there are a number of other challenges facing a Development Team. Here is a list of dysfunctions, expressed as "weasel words," that may be found in any given Development Team:

- **I don't have all the requirements and can't get started.** A major theme in Scrum is the ability for the Development Team to self-organize and get the job done. If there are missing requirements, fix that by getting the answers. If you want to add functionality over and above what the Product Owner is asking for, don't. Remember, the Product Owner owns the *what*, and the Development Team owns the *how*.

- **I monopolize the conversation.** Stop doing that. Use active listening skills to improve your ability to communicate and collaborate with others.

- **I tell other people what to do.** The entire Development Team needs to be able to self-organize. This means that nobody, not a Scrum Master, not a Product Owner, not a manager, and certainly not a developer can order another developer to work on a particular task or to do a task in a particular way. Work is never assigned in Scrum. Perhaps you need to excuse yourself from the team for a while so they can learn these skills on their own. The Scrum Master can help you arrange a vacation.

- **I'm quiet and don't like to converse with others.** Effective collaboration requires all parties to communicate. This is more than just actively listening, but also actively talking and sharing ideas.

- **I'm a coder, not a tester *or* I'm a tester, not a coder.** In Scrum, everyone is a developer regardless of what their business card says or what activity they are working on that day. Besides, most tests in Visual Studio are written in code.

- **I'm not to blame, another developer broke it.** In Scrum, the whole team succeeds or fails. If something broke it's because the team broke it. The team will fix it. Focus on being a team player.

- **I'll let the Scrum Master remove the impediment.** If you can remove the impediment yourself, do it. If you cannot, or if you can provide more value by doing something else (such as developing software), consider asking the Scrum Master for help.

- **I write great code by myself.** That's nice to know. Having another developer review your code or pairing with another developer isn't always about you. It can be a learning experience for others, as well as improve the quality of the product. It also helps hedge against the event where you are hit by a bus, or decide to quit your job because you've won the lottery.

- **I'll work evenings and weekends to get this done.** Thank you, but that sounds like an unsustainable pace. Typically, this smell is due to time management or over-forecasting dysfunctions. During the next Sprint Retrospective, the team should discuss this and find an alternative approach to reaching its goals, such as forecasting less work in the next Sprint.

- **I can slack off because others will do my work.** Every day, the entire Development Team meets for the Daily Scrum. During this meeting, each developer clarifies his or her plan for the next 24 hours. If, for example, by the third day, a developer is still working on the same task, the others should notice. The self-managing team can then find an appropriate solution.

- **Nobody on our team has that skill set.** This may be true, especially as a software product delves into new markets and new technologies. The reality is the Development Team needs to acquire the necessary skill set. Attending training, adding a new developer to the team, or learning the technology on their own are all options. Be sure to account for this change in capacity at the next Sprint Planning meeting, and add any large spikes to the Product Backlog.

- **I'll give it to the testers at the end of the Sprint.** There are no testers in Scrum, only developers. Some developers will focus on coding tasks, and others on testing tasks, but this is not written in stone. For a PBI to be done, it needs to be tested as well. Don't wait until the end of the Sprint to do this as it increases the risk of not being able to release the PBI. If you have the capacity, you can do the testing tasks yourself.

- **Nothing is blocking me.** These are commonly heard words during a daily Scrum. But they do not always reflect reality. Developers need to learn that transparency and openness starts within themselves and the team. If there is an impediment or *even the possibility of an impediment* blocking some work, be sure to let others know, regardless of whether you have other things to work on or not. Identifying actual or possible impediments is not whining, and it is not a sign of weakness. In fact, it is quite the opposite. Identifying impediments is about transparency and creating a strong, high-performance Scrum Team.

Measuring performance

A Development Team's performance should be measured by what it is able to develop. In other words, rate the team by its ability to turn requirements into Increments of functionality that are actually deployed to production. This can be measured for a specific Sprint or for the entire release.

Velocity is the measure of how many PBIs (or story points) the team is able to deliver each Sprint. This measure can then be divided by the cost of the team to develop that Increment. You can also use a consistent number such as $100,000 (or 100,000 financial units). Performance can be measured as you see this ratio increasing over time.

> **Tip** From the perspective of the business, Velocity is not a good metric on which to base performance. If the Product Owner tracks business value for each PBI, this provides a better measure than just the number of PBIs or the sum of their story points. Whether the business value is specified in a numeric range, income/profit, or some specific scale, when this number is expressed over a monetary amount, it will tell the business exactly how much value is being returned on investment (ROI). Tracking ROI per PBI or team helps the Product Owner and organization focus on the business value.

The performance of individual team members should never be measured. The team is self-managing and operates as a unit, not as a group of individuals. For a given Sprint or release, some developers may be a lot more heads-down than others. As such, it may appear to stakeholders like these individuals are "working harder" and more worthy of praise. Other developers, those not at the keyboard, may actually be "working harder" while coaching, mentoring, or designing. Invisible metrics like this are hard to measure and can be missed. A better approach is to rate the performance of the team as a whole and by the business value of what they deliver.

Working with a challenging Product Owner

The Product Owner is responsible for maximizing the value of the product and the work of the Development Team. This is a lot of responsibility for a single person, making this the hardest role in Scrum. Needless to say, most Product Owners can find at least one or two dysfunctions to improve upon.

One of the biggest dysfunctions a Product Owner can possess is not knowing their role. They must reflect the real value and priorities of the business, customer, or user with respect to the software product. This is both the biggest responsibility and the biggest potential risk of the role. The Product Owner is one person, not a committee. The desires of the committee, however, may be represented by the Product Owner in the Product Backlog.

> **Note** Organizations struggle to find viable Product Owner candidates among their existing employees. People with technical backgrounds are typically better suited to be on the Development Team, as they like to get involved with *how* things are developed rather than *what* should be developed. Employees with management backgrounds might be inclined to install command-and-control practices. Candidates with strong Scrum knowledge typically gravitate towards being the Scrum Master.
>
> Successful Product Owners tend to have product management and even marketing backgrounds. They understand terms like *"market segment"* and *"sales channel."* When no such candidates exist, I've seen some organizations advertise the position of Product Owner online and in the local papers. Seriously. It sounds weird, but by bringing in someone off the street with the knowledge of what a Product Owner should do, but absent the knowledge of organizational politics and the "old way" of doing things in the organization, is often a recipe for success. They just need to learn the product and the desires of the customer and users to succeed.

Being able to negotiate the politics of an organization, its committees, and the users can be an exhaustive, full-time job. For the Product Owner to succeed, the entire organization must respect his or her decisions. The Product Owner's decisions are visible in the content and ordering of the Product Backlog. No one is allowed to tell the Development Team to work from a different set of requirements, and the Development Team isn't allowed to act on what anyone else says.

Here is a list of other challenges you might encounter when working with Product Owners:

- **Injecting their own version of Scrum** There is only one version of Scrum, and it's documented in the *Scrum Guide*. Anything else risks upsetting the established flow. Any allegiance to old waterfall habits must go. Understand that mental muscle memory takes time to fade.

- **Insufficient acceptance criteria** A good PBI doesn't just stop at a title and description. The Product Owner, with help if necessary, should evolve the requirement and define what success looks like in the form of acceptance criteria. These should be testable, or even written as executable specifications if that's what the Scrum Team is practicing.

Tip When creating a PBI, and specifying its acceptance criteria, remember the *INVEST* mnemonic: Independent, Negotiable, Valuable, Estimable, Small, and Testable. Refer to Chapter 1 for more information.

■ **Absent or doesn't interact with the team** In order to maximize the work of the Development Team, the Product Owner must interact and collaborate. This is especially true during Sprint Planning, Sprint Review, and Sprint Retrospective meetings, and especially the regular Product Backlog grooming. The Product Owner should also be available during the Sprint to clarify requirements, review work, and provide feedback.

Note Fellow Professional Scrum Developer Chad Albrecht reminds us that the Product Owner's primary responsibility is to understand the product. He recommends that a Product Owner spend 75 percent of his or her time understanding the product, its customers and users, the competition, and so on. Only 25 percent of the Product Owner's time should be spent interacting with the Development Team. The Development Team should use their autonomy to make good decisions about development and keep the Product Owner in the loop. This keeps the Product Owner from being an impediment and also engages the Development Team more than if the Product Owner has to make every decision.

■ **Disrupts the team** Whether it's to introduce a new piece of work during the Sprint (scope creep) or just wandering into the team room and asking how things are going, these intrusions can interrupt the flow. The Scrum Master should get involved and help the Product Owner understand this.

■ **Product Owner provides the solutions** The Product Owner must allow the Development Team to self-organize and come up with its own solution. So long as it is fit-for-purpose, meets all the acceptance criteria, and abides by the Definition of "Done," it should be acceptable.

■ **The Development Team elicits PBIs directly** It's good to know that they have that skill, but their time is better spent on deciding *how* to implement the feature, not determining *what* feature to develop. If the Product Owner needs technical assistance expressing a requirement, this should be done collaboratively during grooming.

■ **Indecisiveness** The Product Owner has the authority to make decisions pertaining to the software product. This includes everything from determining the value of a PBI, to ordering the Product Backlog, to changing the scope of a Sprint, and even canceling a Sprint. The Scrum Master can help the Product Owner understand the ramifications of these decisions, but the decisions still have to be made.

■ **Not being prepared** This common dysfunction is especially risky with regard to Product Owners. The plans of multiple people (the Development Team) depend on the decisions made by a single person (the Product Owner). If the Product Owner is not prepared, much waste can be generated. Regularly scheduled Product Backlog grooming sessions can help.

 Tip Fellow Professional Scrum Developer Mike Vincent can't stress enough how important it is for a Product Owner to be prepared. When he or she is not prepared, the Development Team can usually compensate, but at the cost of reduced Velocity. Instead, the Development Team should learn to push back on the Product Owner, saying "no" or demanding more information. A good Scrum Master can help facilitate this, either immediately or at the next Sprint Retrospective meeting.

- **Command-and-control Product Owner** In Scrum, the Product Owner is not the "boss" in the traditional sense. It's acceptable to say no, especially when he or she is asking you to do something that is out of bounds for the Product Owner role or the rules of Scrum in general. The Scrum Master can be called in to referee if necessary.

- **Expects a commitment, not a forecast** An important change was made in the *Scrum Guide* in 2011. The Development Team now *forecasts* the work that it honestly feels that it can deliver during the Sprint, but they don't *commit* to it. If a Product Owner expects a commitment, such as assuming the developers will sleep under their desks until the Sprint Backlog is done, that is an unhealthy, dysfunctional behavior. While this might be possible once every few Sprints, such as during the last Sprint before a release, it is not a sustainable pace. The Product Owner must learn the difference between a forecast and a commitment. A good Scrum Master can help explain this concept.

 Tip Fellow Professional Scrum Developer Jose Luis Soria Teruel wrote a great article explaining the difference between commit and forecast. He also included the reasoning behind the change. You can read his article on Scrum.org at *http://www.scrum.org/About/All-Articles/articleType/ArticleView/articleId/95/ Commitment-vs-Forecast-A-subtle-but-important-change-to-Scrum*.

- **Multiple Product Owners** The Product Owner is one person, not a committee. The Development Team, as well as the stakeholders, should have a "single wringable neck" (or "one throat to choke"). Having multiple Product Owners is confusing to everybody. Pick one, and the others become stakeholders who help the Product Owner create PBIs and order the Product Backlog.

- **Multiple Stakeholders, but no true Product Owner** People often confuse the role of Product Owner with that of a business stakeholder. Just because someone has a large influence on the product, or the business unit that uses the product, doesn't make that person a Product Owner. The Product Owner is a role defined in the *Scrum Guide*. The Product Owner works very collaboratively and closely with the rest of the Scrum team, and fulfills his or her Scrum role dutifully.

- **The Development Team maintains the Product Backlog** Developers typically do not have the proper vision and insight into the needs of the customer and users to maintain the Product Backlog adequately. They are better at solving technical problems. The Product Owner needs to be present and accountable for maximizing ROI in the software product. This is done through the content and order of the items in the Product Backlog. While there may be times that the Development Team gets involved, such as helping the Product Owner understand how technical dependencies affect the delivery order, these should be the exception and not the rule. The Product Owner is responsible for maintaining the content and order of the Product Backlog, and passing that task along to the Development Team smells like a weak or unprepared Product Owner.

- **Acting as a developer** Product Owners sometimes come up through an organization's technical ranks. While developing the product, someone learned everything there is to know about it and ended up becoming its Product Owner. Unfortunately, this increases the chances that person will become involved with *how* it should be developed, when he or she should be focused only on *what* to develop. Having a Product Owner also be a developer is sometimes unavoidable, especially for smaller teams such as startups.

The Product Owner is a full member of the Scrum Team and, as such, should be present at all Scrum events, with the exception of the Daily Scrum. The purpose of the Daily Scrum is for the Development Team to create a plan for the next 24 hours. The Product Owner shouldn't have any input on the plan, nor does he or she need to know about it once it is made. The Product Owner, however, should be available to the Development Team during work time. Being in close proximity and ready to collaborate in person as needed is a recipe for a successful software product. Keep in mind that the Product Owner also needs to work with stakeholders during these same hours, so availability may be limited.

 Smell It's a smell when I meet a Scrum Team who still goes by their old titles. When I'm introduced to the Scrum Master, and he tells me his name is Dave and he's the CIO, I get confused. The rest of his teammates might get confused too. Remember, in Scrum, there are only the Product Owner, Scrum Master, and Development Team roles.

Working with challenging stakeholders

Stakeholders are not an official role in Scrum, but they exist and can be challenging to work with. Remember that a stakeholder is any person who has a direct or indirect interest in the work of the Development Team. He or she may be a customer, a user, a domain expert, a manager, or a company executive. For the most part, the Development Team may not interact with stakeholders too often. The only time the Development Team is guaranteed to interact with stakeholders is during the Sprint Review meeting. They may also interact at any other time, as required during Product Backlog grooming or to help understand a requirement.

Stakeholders may or may not know about Scrum. And what they do know, may not be accurate. Some stakeholders may think Scrum is a "silver bullet" and just by using the nouns during conversations and meetings, the software will develop itself quickly, perfectly, and without bugs.

It's the responsibility of the Scrum Master to squash this illusion and tell the uneducated that Scrum's success depends on empiricism and the commitment of the people practicing it. Stakeholders are welcome, and encouraged, to watch the great experiment take place.

> **Note** Scrum was not designed to keep stakeholders from interacting with the Development Team. On the contrary, Scrum brings the two camps closer together, just in a more structured and productive way. For example, the Sprint Review meeting allows stakeholders to see working software and provide instant feedback, which is captured in the Product Backlog. Most stakeholders are ecstatic that there is a software development process used by the organization that actually allows them to see the working results of the Development Team's effort every few weeks. This is welcome transparency, much like being able to meet the chef at a nice restaurant.

Here is a list of challenges you might encounter when interacting with stakeholders:

- **Doesn't understand the Definition of "Done"** Since stakeholders do not necessarily know Scrum, they may not understand why something "they saw running on your desktop yesterday" isn't done and able to be demonstrated during Sprint Review. You, or the Scrum Master, can explain how the Definition of "Done" ensures an uncompromising level of quality. This should be done using their terms. For example, instead of saying, "Load testing has not been completed," you should say, "We still don't know how the application performs with lots of concurrent users."

- **Doesn't provide feedback** Some stakeholders are just not that interested in the software product. They may be paying for it, or managing the department of employees that will be using it, but they just don't care. If it won't hurt the long-term prospects of the product, consider uninviting them to the next Sprint Review, or at least inviting some other, more interested parties. Whenever possible, invite a few key users. They tend to be passionate about what the team is doing and provide extremely valuable feedback.

- **Injects their own version of Scrum** There is only one version of Scrum, and it's documented in the *Scrum Guide*. Anything else risks upsetting the established flow.

- **Absent or doesn't interact with the team** In order to maximize the work of the Development Team, stakeholders (specifically domain experts) must be available periodically to help answer questions and provide feedback.

- **Disrupts the team** Stakeholders, by definition, have an interest in what the Development Team is doing. They may wander into the team room and ask how things are going. These intrusions can interrupt the flow. The Scrum Master should get involved.

- **Provides the solutions** The stakeholders are free to work with the Product Owner to clarify what is to be developed. The Development Team, however, is self-organizing and comes up with its own solutions.

- **Not able to say "no" to a stakeholder** In Scrum, the stakeholder is not your "boss" in the traditional sense. Unfortunately, he or she may be the owner of the company, and absolutely your boss outside of Scrum. High-performance Scrum Developers are able to balance following the rules of Scrum with remaining employed.

- **Expects a commitment, not a forecast** Stakeholders also must acknowledge the reality of software development and allow the Development Team to forecast the work they can do in a Sprint—not force them to commit to it. The Scrum Master can explain that what the Development Team does is very hard.

- **Acts as a manager** The Development Team is self-organizing and self-managing. Nobody, including stakeholders, can tell the developers how to do their work, or what they should work on next. That said, stakeholders can be very influential as to what should be worked on next. This should be routed to the Development Team through the Product Owner via the Product Backlog, however.

- **Acts as a developer** Some stakeholders may be developers from another team, or have that skillset on their resume. Be cautious of them getting too involved in the development. They can easily become a distraction. If, on the other hand, they have the skills you need and the capacity to help, have them join the Development Team, even if on a part-time basis.

- **Acts as an insurgent** Some stakeholders, for whatever reason, are just anti-Scrum. Maybe they tried it at a previous business unit or organization and were unsuccessful. Maybe they prefer waterfall, or Kanban. Maybe they hate Rugby. Unfortunately, sometimes such a person is necessary to support the successful adoption of Scrum. Hopefully the Scrum Master can help educate him or her.

Working with a challenging Scrum Master

The Scrum Master is responsible for ensuring that Scrum is understood and enacted. Scrum Masters do this by ensuring that the Scrum Team adheres to Scrum theory, practices, and rules. The Scrum Master is a servant-leader for the Scrum Team and a facilitator who supports the team in learning self-organization, and understanding and adopting the rules of Scrum.

A good Scrum Master brings value to the Scrum Team, and the organization, by helping both adopt and progress towards good Scrum in a realistic way. By applying what they know, the Scrum Master can help the team deliver software that is of a higher quality and value faster. This is done by maximizing the benefits produced by Scrum. A great Scrum Master should be putting himself or herself out of a job by teaching the team to identify and solve their own problems.

> **Tip** The key to finding a good Scrum Master is seeing him or her in action. Let the candidate attend a Daily Scrum and tell you what he or she observes. One's knowledge of the rules of Scrum, as well as one's perception of the team's behavior and level of collaboration, should speak volumes about experience and capability.

Beyond supporting the Scrum Team, Scrum Masters can also be responsible for educating the organization and leading the effort to adopt Scrum. This means that they are a help desk of sorts, where the standard questions are asked and answered. It also means that the Scrum Master is a walking Scrum salesperson, always pointing out the benefits of adopting Scrum to new people and potential teams. Your Scrum Master should be able to articulate why Scrum works and is healthy for the organization, even to the loudest critics and detractors.

Here is a list of challenges you might encounter when working with Scrum Masters:

- **Doesn't know Scrum** This is a deal breaker. If there is one person on the Scrum Team, or in the organization, who must know Scrum, it's the Scrum Master. Inform management that the Scrum Master needs more training than just reading the *Scrum Guide* and then send him or her to a Scrum.org training class (*http://www.scrum.org/Courses*). Experience will come with time, but since it's required on day one, hire an experienced Scrum Master, even if only temporarily.

- **Doesn't enforce the rules** A Scrum Master acts as a referee and should be confident in "throwing a flag" or showing a teammate a "yellow card" when the situation calls for it. The rules of Scrum have been fine-tuned over years of use and work only when they are followed. That said, there is room for adaptation once the core principles are embedded in the organization.

> **Tip** It may be challenging for a Scrum Master to *actually enforce* the rules. I tend to stereotype Scrum Masters as being firm and resolved, but in practice, this type of Scrum Master sometimes can create an adversarial environment. As an alternative, a Scrum Master should *coach* their team members to follow the rules of Scrum. If the team wants to step outside the rules of Scrum, the Scrum Master should use powerful questioning and dialogue to probe and discuss. If, after the discussion, the team *still* wants to break the rules, the Scrum Master may want to allow it as a learning experience. Then, during the next Sprint Retrospective, the Scrum Master should talk about the issues that resulted from not following the rules.

- **Focuses too much on rules and practices** A Scrum Master should enforce the rules, but focusing too much on the rules and practices can create a "cargo cult" mentality. In this dysfunction, the team is certainly executing all of the practices, but they are not reaping the intended benefits. A Scrum Master should always make sure that the team is getting the most out the Scrum practices and rules.

- **Doesn't act as a firewall** The Scrum Master should block any wasteful request or interruption of the Development Team's time. This could include going to meetings in place of the rest of the team, tracking and providing actual hours worked to the central Project Management Office (PMO), or educating others in the organization on how to interpret a burndown chart. A Scrum Master should respect the Development Team's flow, and do whatever is possible to protect it.

- **Acts as a manager** The Development Team is self-organizing and self-managing. Nobody, including the Scrum Master, can tell the developers how to do their work. The Scrum Master should avoid even suggesting how a team member does his or her work, or what to work on next. The exception to this is when the Scrum Master is asked for help, or if the Development Team as a whole, or an individual developer, exhibits dysfunctional behavior or otherwise has become an impediment. The Scrum Master has the authority to implement and enact the rules of Scrum, including removing such impediments. I'll leave it at that.

- **Absent Scrum Master** The Scrum Master is a servant–leader and, as such, should be collocated with the team, ready to help. The only time the Scrum Master should be unavailable is when he or she is away educating the organization, removing an impediment, or taking a (much-deserved) vacation.

- **Doesn't manage conflicts** Since Scrum is about people, Scrum Teams will inevitably experience conflicts. Simple conflicts can (and should) be handled by the people involved. More complex and emotional conflicts may require the Scrum Master to become involved. If a Scrum Master is hesitant or doesn't have the social skills required to manage such conflicts, this is a dysfunction.

- **Settles for the status quo** A Scrum Master should be hungry for improvement. Just as a teacher gets excited when students are learning new things and applying what they've learned, so should a Scrum Master thrive on seeing the Scrum Team improving.

- **Poor communication** This is more than just the Scrum Master not being able to communicate clearly, but allowing communication dysfunctions to grow and thrive in the team. A good Scrum Master knows how to teach and foster good communication skills in the Scrum Team. This includes teaching topics such as active listening.

- **Has a day job** Any additional role that a Scrum Master occupies is a conflict that can cause difficulty. Sometimes this is unavoidable, however, especially for smaller teams or startups.

- **Doesn't deal with impediments** A good Scrum Master will give the team the opportunity to remove their own impediments and then learn from the experience. A dysfunctional Scrum Master will allow impediments to linger. If the Scrum Master can't remove the directly impediment, he or she should at least find someone else in the organization who can.

- **Acts as a developer** In a lot of ways, the Scrum Master is like a firefighter. He or she sits, waiting to be called upon to answer a question or remove an impediment. Having the Scrum Master involved in the actual development, taking on tasks, tends to distract from the job of helping the team follow the rules of Scrum. Sometimes this is unavoidable, however, especially for smaller teams, such as startups.

> **Note** Fellow Professional Scrum Developer Jose Luis Soria Teruel also warns us against the "Mom" Scrum Master. This type of dysfunctional Scrum Master deals only with the secretarial and nanny tasks—paperwork, updating the Sprint Backlog and burndowns, running the stopwatch, and so on. New and uneducated Scrum Teams might think that this is what the Scrum Master does. I only hope somebody in the organization is aware of this dysfunction, since the Scrum Master doesn't seem capable of recognizing the impediment.

Changing Scrum

Scrum is just a set of rules put forth in the *Scrum Guide*. This makes it comparable to the game of chess. Chess has rules too. One rule in chess is that a player is allowed to have only one king on the board. Scrum's rules dictate only having one Product Owner. There are many other comparisons, but you get the idea. When you sit down to play chess, you either play by the rules or you don't. Same with Scrum. If you want a short-term win, you can cheat, but you won't learn how to play the game properly or get good at it. Learning how the chess pieces move is fairly easy, just like learning the rules of Scrum, but mastering chess (and Scrum) is difficult and takes a long time and a lot of experience.

> **Note** Fellow Professional Scrum Master Charles Bradley is someone who knows how to play the game of Scrum properly. Because of that, he can easily spot those who cheat. To avoid the embarrassment of being called out by a Professional Scrum practitioner, don't cheat.

The rules of Scrum should be considered immutable and sacred. An organization or team should not change them. You should inspect and adapt your behaviors within those rules and improve accordingly. Every Scrum role, rule, and event is designed to provide the desired benefits and address predictable recurring problems. Feel safe. Scrum will not fail you.

Old waterfall habits

Waterfall development is the name given to a more traditional, sequential design approach to software development where one phase of development is completed before moving to the next. For example, design is done before programming. Programming is done before testing. And so on. Each phase is performed as though you are not coming back to it. Maximum attention is given in getting it right the first time. This approach to developing software is very risky, more costly, and less efficient than Scrum.

Unfortunately, waterfall has been in existence for over 50 years. Many IT professionals, and present-day managers, are familiar with it and have it imprinted in their mental muscle memory. When these people are introduced to Scrum, they may feel compelled to change it, molding it into something they are more familiar with.

Here are some waterfall habits that should not be implemented in Scrum and the reasons why:

- **Longer Sprints (more than one month)** Sprint lengths of one month or less provide focus and reduce risk. Longer Sprints increase risk exponentially.

- **Multiple Product Owners** Having a single Product Owner reduces complexity and conflicts in prioritizing and ordering items in the Product Backlog.

- **Big requirements up front** Time spent defining detailed requirements, and especially how they should be implemented, is wasted when development is delayed or skipped altogether.

- **Separate teams to code and to test** Cross-functional teams are more efficient because they are able to work together with less context switching. Only features that are done (including testing) are potentially releasable. This abates the exponential buildup of work toward the end of the release.

- **Infrastructure and architecture Sprints** Every Sprint must generate an Increment containing business value. This keeps the Development Team focused on what's best for the customer or user. Emergent architecture is a practice that can help maintain this focus.

- **Delay testing until later Sprints** All aspects of development, including testing, must be done during the Sprint. Delaying testing produces technical debt and undone work that accumulates exponentially.

- **Change is bad so we should minimize it** Change is a fact of life in software development. Scrum embraces this fact through the use of shorter Sprints and an ordered Product Backlog maintained by an engaged Product Owner.

- **Project manager plans and assigns work (command and control)** The Development Team is self-organizing and can create and take ownership of their own work. They are also expected to estimate as a team, not rely on a proxy to do the estimation. There are no project managers in Scrum.

- **Must follow the plan and conform to the schedule** In Scrum, the plan is broken up into Sprints of one month or less in length. Beyond that, there is no firm plan, only a Product Backlog with items ordered in a way that represents what the Product Owner would like developed next.

- **No value in the software until the very end** Every Sprint must generate an Increment containing business value. This means that all development activities, including integration with other teams and systems, must be done by the end of the Sprint to realize any value.

- **Always report a bug** The Development Team is self-organizing and can determine if the strange behavior is a bug or not. They are also capable of just fixing the bug rather than creating a work item.

- **Daily Scrums are status meetings** The Daily Scrum is for the Development Team to synchronize and create a plan for the next 24 hours. It's not meant for other purposes, or for others to attend.

- **Work is never re-estimated** Professional Scrum Developers understand that they know more today than they did yesterday. Applying this new knowledge to existing estimates (either PBIs or Sprint Backlog tasks) is a healthy practice that boosts transparency.

- **Quality gets sacrificed** The Definition of "Done," when properly adhered to, protects the quality of the work the Development Team does and keeps undone work, and the ensuing technical debt, out of the Increment.

- **Gold plating** The Development Team only needs to develop what is fits the purpose for a given PBI, and nothing more. In Scrum, the developers no longer have to predict what might eventually be needed. The next Sprint's features will be revealed just in time.

> **Note** This kind of a change, from waterfall to Scrum, is too much for some managers. Ken Schwaber wrote in his book *The Enterprise and Scrum* that up to 20 percent of them might leave as they find that they don't like the new way of working and managing.

ScrumButs

Many organizations have modified Scrum against this guidance. In their minds, they are doing the right thing and adapting Scrum to fit their particular flavor of chaos. This is partly because past software approaches required tailoring in order to succeed. Scrum is the opposite, in that changing Scrum itself can prevent you from succeeding altogether. These changes and tweaks are generally known as "ScrumButs." When a representative is asked if their organization or team is doing Scrum, they say "Yes, but ...."

In fact, a ScrumBut has a particular syntax:

We use Scrum, but (**ScrumBut**) because (**Reason**) so | instead | therefore (**Workaround**).

Here is an example of a ScrumBut:

"We use Scrum, but (we don't have Daily Scrums) because (they are too much overhead), so (we only have them once a week or as needed)."

ScrumButs are excuses why teams can't take full advantage of Scrum to generate business value in the form of working software. ScrumButs mean that Scrum has exposed a dysfunction that is contributing to the problem but is too hard to fix. A ScrumBut retains the problem while modifying Scrum to make it invisible so that the dysfunction is no longer a thorn in the side.

Organizations may make short-term changes to Scrum in order to give them time to correct deficiencies. For example, a team's Definition of "Done" may not initially include regression and performance testing because it will take several months to develop an automated testing framework. For these months, transparency is compromised, but it is restored as quickly as possible. For more information on ScrumButs, visit *http://www.scrum.org/scrumbut*.

Note Several of my Professional Scrum Developer colleagues feel that "ScrumBut" is too negative. While they acknowledge that they exist, they prefer using a softer, more optimistic metaphor, such as an "adoption compromise." This still suggests that there are compromises being made to the rules of Scrum during adoption that will be tracked and removed as soon as possible. Fellow Professional Scrum Developer Simon Reindl has even provided the new regular expression to highlight the transience of the practice and the aspiration to adopt better Scrum: *We have compromised our adoption of Scrum by using* <**Incorrect Scrum Practice**> *as we found that adopting* <**Correct Scrum Practice**> *too challenging to introduce CURRENTLY.*

Improving

No matter where you are in the game of Scrum, you can always improve. Whether you're a part of a new team just getting started and still not sure what a time-box is, or your team has released several Increments of software successfully using Scrum, there are always new things to learn and new ways to enhance your practices.

A Scrum Team should inspect and adapt constantly. This includes the behaviors and practices of the team beyond simply identifying and removing a dysfunction. The absence of a dysfunction is an improvement, but the team can go beyond that. For example, it may take several Sprints for a dysfunctional Scrum Master to stop providing estimates on behalf of the Development Team. It may take even more Sprints for the Development Team to understand how to estimate on their own. It may take several more Sprints for these estimates to normalize.

Improvement can occur only if the culture allows it. The organization and management must allow its teams to experiment, to fail, to inspect, and to adapt. Successful companies yield successful teams because they allow their people the freedom to explore, learn, cross-pollinate, set up practice communities, and implement their retrospective items. Most of all, the culture must understand that improvement takes time.

In this section, we look at ways in which a Scrum Team can continue to improve beyond just knowing Scrum and removing dysfunctions.

Get a coach

I'll start with the best advice on how to improve. There may be times when the Scrum Team needs help improving their game. Just like any sports team, a Scrum Team can also benefit from the help of a coach. A Scrum coach is an expert in Scrum, both in theory and in practice. They have an in-depth understanding of the practices and principles of Scrum, and have real experience on actual Scrum projects. A Scrum coach is somebody who can teach and coach all of the Scrum roles, including the organization itself, effectively. He or she can teach new patterns and behaviors for increased collaboration and high-performance achievement.

Note Don't confuse a Scrum coach with an Agile coach. For teams doing Scrum, they will want a Scrum coach who absolutely knows Scrum. Agile coaches may or may not know Scrum, and even vary on what or how much they know about Agile and related practices. Nobody accidentally becomes a Scrum coach.

A good Scrum coach will also have experience in a variety of organizational settings, which is useful when educating the rest of the organization. A coach can help the organization understand how the changes will affect leadership and team member responsibilities. By mentoring and gradually sharing best practices about Scrum adoption, the organizational change of adopting Scrum won't be so painful.

Tip When searching for a Scrum coach, pay attention to the candidate's background and if he or she has experience playing the various roles. It's hard to find a coach that has played the role of the Product Owner, Scrum Master, *and* developer. At least make sure the candidate has played the role you are most in need of help with.

There is a myth surrounding what a Scrum coach does. People think that coaching is purely a soft-touch approach—only providing guidance and the ability for people to discover problems and solutions for themselves. People also think that coaches do not tell people what to do. Some coaches fit this mold and, in my opinion, are fairly worthless. The truth is, coaches need to have the difficult conversations and these conversations are sometimes not nice and not polite. This is because coaches help people identify and overcome unpleasant things. One minute the coach will need to be compassionate and understanding, and the next minute authoritative and uncompromising.

Build a cross-functional team

The Scrum Development Team is a cross-functional group of people possessing all the different skills required to turn requirements into an Increment of potentially releasable functionality. The Development Team needs to know all the skills necessary to turn the requirements into something that the organization defines as "done." Team members will need to develop the skills of business analyst, designer, tester, programmer, technical writer, and so on.

It may take several Sprints for the Development Team to even know what functionality it has or may need. When Scrum was first adopted in an organization, all of the analysts, programmers, and testers were united on the Development Team. Since each of them played a role in the development of the Increment, they became known as a developer. As self-organization and collective ownership attitudes became established, the backgrounds and titles previously held by the developers became blurred.

Note The opposite of a cross-functional Development Team is a dysfunctional one.

What is a cross-functional Development Team today may not be so tomorrow. Over time, the team, not the management, may determine that additional team members are required. To satisfy this need, new developers may be added, or the current ones trained, in order to support new technologies for domains being considered for the software product. The opposite may become a reality, as less developers are required because they are able to do more with less.

> **Tip** In Scrum, the Product Owner provides the vision for the software product. This should be reflected by the items, and their order, in the Product Backlog. An ordered backlog serves as a roadmap for the planned features. It also serves as a roadmap for the planned technologies and new domains, which can serve as a "heads-up" for what functionality the Development Team will need in the near and distant future.

Making unnecessary changes to the Development Team will cause problems. When the problems that it causes are less than the problems caused by not changing it, then it is worthwhile. You should be aware and prepared for the difficulty that the new team member(s) are going to have being introduced into an existing team. If we refer back to Bruce Tuckman's stages of group development, any changes made to the makeup of the team will cause the team to revert to the *forming* stage of the model. Just think of the problems associated with a child when his or her family moves to a new town and the overhead that has to happen for that child to fit in. Developers are not much different.

> **Note** Don't confuse cross-functional *teams* with cross-functional *individuals*. Scrum demands cross-functional Development Teams. This means that at a minimum, there must be at least one developer that is capable of performing each type of task in the Sprint Backlog. For example, if there are C++ tasks that must be accomplished, there must be at least one developer who can code in C++. High-performance Scrum Development Teams endeavor to have cross-functional individuals as well. This means that if C++ tasks are becoming more prevalent in the upcoming Sprints, one or more developers should pick up that skillset. Having a cross-functional team of cross-functional developers is a recipe for meeting goals and increasing Velocity.

Achieve self-organization

Scrum relies on self-organizing teams to handle the complexity inherent in software development. A self-organizing team will approach a project, and, based on the requirements at hand, decide how best to develop a solution while taking advantage of each team member's various strengths. It takes a certain mindset and aptitude to be able to self-organize. But, compared with traditional practices—such as a chief architect creating the initial design or a project manager assigning work—self-organization is a revolutionary improvement.

Every developer on a self-organizing team will work, independently or in pairs, towards some shared goal. Everyone collaborates to reach the goal, valuing the team's output over individual productivity. Members of the team trust each other and are interested in each other's work, providing constructive feedback where appropriate. Self-organizing teams are able to get work done and develop an Increment of value. They are not blocked by impediments; they communicate any issues appropriately to achieve transparency.

An organization must *allow* its Development Teams to self-organize and self-manage. This comes with time and the storing up of trust. That trust is a direct result of the Development Team being able to deliver increments of business value regularly in the form of working software. Education, provided by the Scrum Master or Scrum coach, can help the organization see that this is a reason to trust the team. Once that trust is in place, the Development Team will be given more leniency to make its own decisions and plans, and then to execute them.

> **Note** Fellow Professional Scrum Developer Mike Vincent recommends that management and other stakeholders of an organization keep their hands off the Scrum Team. The team should be allowed to make mistakes, inspect, adapt, and improve. Newer teams may need some coaching help to become self-organizing, especially within a heavy command-and-control culture.

Improve transparency

Transparency, along with inspection and adaptation, are the three pillars of Scrum, or any empirical process control framework for that matter. The importance of being transparent—as a developer to the rest of your team, or as a Development Team to the Product Owner, or as the Scrum Team to the organization—cannot be overstated. Significant aspects of the development process must be made visible to those responsible for the outcome. Transparency requires those aspects be defined by a common standard so that observers share a common understanding of what is being seen.

In Scrum, being transparent means that all observers should understand the basics of the framework, as well as the artifacts they may be looking at: Product Backlog, Definition of "Done," burndown charts, task boards, the meetings, and so on. The data reflected in these artifacts are like beacons of light. They shine brightly into all corners of the Development Team's activities, leaving nowhere for slackers or other waste to hide.

Some developers might be reluctant, or at least uncomfortable, about this "nowhere to hide" quality of Scrum. Nobody wants to work in a glass house, even though doing so means that a developer will be more productive and exhibit healthier behaviors because they never know who might be watching. Being able to admit mistakes and ask for help will assist everyone in becoming more comfortable with this quality of Scrum. Besides, making mistakes and learning from them are a good way to improve.

Take the task board, for example. Whether we are talking about a physical one, one implemented on a whiteboard, or an electronic one like in Visual Studio, it is a great information radiator and source of transparency. The board reflects the Development Team's current tasks. It shows where they are, what they've done, and what they still have to do. The transparency of tasks on the board is not created for the sake of reporting, but rather for a general awareness. This awareness enables the team to manage themselves.

Swarm

Swarming is a term used in Agile software development where the entire Development Team focuses on one problem (PBI) and voraciously collaborates on it until it's done. Just like a swarm of bees on a mission, there is no commander, controller, or coordinator—just a self-organizing team working as a unit. Swarming in software development is a relatively new practice and may feel alien to some. Swarming is not a part of Scrum.

Swarming is a way of limiting the work in progress (WIP), and experiencing single-piece flow in an effort to deliver the PBIs successfully in the order the Product Owner expects them. Without some degree of swarming, the Development Team might jump around between several PBIs and accomplish none of them. While there are other ways to limit WIP, swarming is a popular practice used by many high-performance Scrum Development Teams.

When a Development Team swarms, they overcome any disadvantage that individual developers might encounter. This is done by dividing the Development Team into one or two smaller *swarms*. The number and size of the swarm depends on the size of the Development Team. The next PBI (in order) is selected from the Sprint Backlog and swarming begins. The Development Team decides, just-in-time, which tasks will need to be done in order to complete the PBI. Members of the swarm collaborate and communicate constantly in order to find the most effective way to finish their solution. When they get to done, they move to the next one in order, and so on. Members of the subswarms may switch with other members as needed.

> **Note** Maybe we should update Bruce Tuckman's group development model. The new model would be forming, storming, norming, performing, *swarming*. O.K. maybe not.

Before a team considers swarming on a PBI, there are a few prerequisites that should be in place. The team should be cross-functional and self-organizing, as should any subswarm teams. A Definition of "Done," understood by all, should be established and referenced by the entire team. Also, the PBIs that the team will swarm on should be large enough that everyone on the team can contribute to its development. Ownership of tasks, when swarming, can be complex. Some tasks might be handled by a single developer, where others are handled by a pair or more. So long as one of the involved developers owns the task and updates the remaining work estimates daily, there won't be an issue. Remember that in TFS, a work item cannot be assigned to multiple users.

Use a Kanban board to limit WIP

Like Scrum, Kanban is a strategy for managing work that involves breaking down a problem into a plan and then visually transitioning that work through a series of states. Kanban makes heavier use of states in order to limit the WIP. This allows the Development Team to control how much work can be in each state. Scrum Teams prefer to use the burndown chart to visualize and manage work through an iteration. Kanban teams prefer to use a Cumulative Flow Diagram to visualize work across the entire backlog. Visualizing the backlog in this manner can help to identify bottlenecks in the process. Scrum Teams can also use a Cumulative Flow Diagram.

At the time of this writing, Microsoft has enabled Kanban support in their hosted Team Foundation Service and, at the same time, announced upcoming support for on-premises TFS. With this feature, Development Teams can now allow you to manage their Scrum Team projects using Kanban to visualize the flow of the items in the Product Backlog.

In the center of this new support is the Kanban board. It can be used with a team project created using the Visual Studio Scrum 2.0 process template. The board is associated with the Product Backlog and is found on the board *tab*, as opposed to the board menu option, as you can see in Figure 9-4.

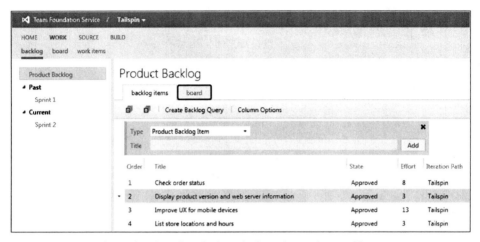

FIGURE 9-4 Access the Kanban board on the board tab on the Product Backlog page.

On the new Kanban board, the Product Backlog items appear by state, in descending order according to the *Backlog Priority* field. Only the top 20 work items are visible in each column. You can see an example of this in Figure 9-5. You can set a limit to the number of items that can be in any particular state, such as Approved or Committed. If you try to drag more than the limit of work items into that column, the color will change to provide visual feedback that you've exceeded a WIP limit.

At any time, you can review progress by looking at the Cumulative Flow Diagram, available on the Kanban board page. The chart shows cumulative flow of progress over time. The start date is the first week there is data, or, if you have more than 30 weeks of data, then the chart will show data for the 31 weeks prior to the current date. Figure 9-6 shows an example of this chart.

Scrum and Kanban are two different approaches to Agile software development. Scrum prescribes cross-functional, self-organizing teams working in fixed-length Sprints. Kanban prescribes visualizing the workflow and limiting WIP by workflow state. Optimization in Scrum comes from continuous inspecting and adapting, whereas in Kanban, it comes from measuring and optimizing lead time (cycle time). Both Scrum and Kanban are just process tools, and aspects of these tools can be mixed and matched.

Tip Be careful mixing Scrum and Kanban. Only high-performance Scrum Teams should consider adopting Kanban practices.

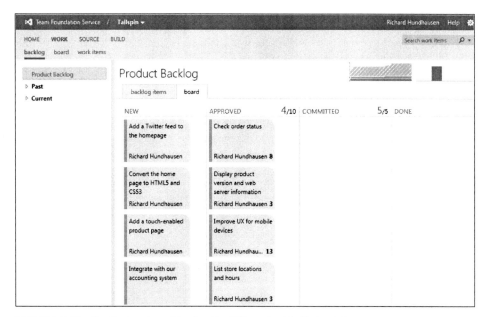

FIGURE 9-5 Use the Kanban board to visualize PBIs and set limits by state.

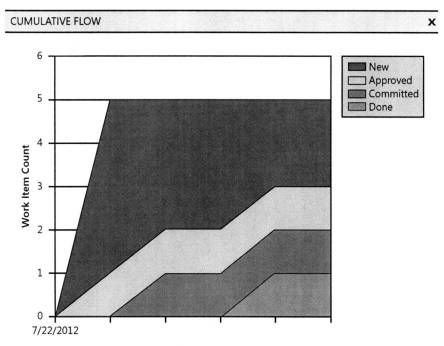

FIGURE 9-6 Use the Cumulative Flow Diagram to see progress over time.

Professional Scrum Developer training

Great software development using Scrum and today's application lifecycle management (ALM) tools requires the seamless integration of the tools, a well-functioning team, and software development best practices. Scrum.org's PSD course is the only course available that teaches how this is done.

The PSD course teaches students how to work in a team, using contemporary software development practices and the ALM tools found in Visual Studio 2012 to develop an Increment of potentially releasable functionality. All of this is done as iterative incremental development within the Scrum framework. This course was developed in partnership with Microsoft.

The PSD course is suitable for any member of a software development team, including architects, programmers, database developers, testers, and others with some technical knowledge. Product Owners, Scrum Masters, and other stakeholders are welcome to attend this class, so long as they keep in mind that all attendees will be expected to participate fully on their development team.

As with all Scrum.org courses, the curriculum and materials are standardized and regularly enhanced through contributions from the Scrum.org network of Professional Scrum Trainers. Only the most qualified instructors are selected to teach the PSD course. These are individuals with top-notch skills in the technologies coupled with excellent knowledge of how to use them within the Scrum framework. Each instructor brings his or her individual experiences and areas of expertise to bear, but all students learn the same core course content. This improves a student's ability to pass the Professional Scrum Developer assessment and apply Scrum in his or her workplace.

For more information on the PSD program and training, visit *http://www.scrum.org/Courses/Professional-Scrum-Developer*.

Assess your knowledge

Scrum.org also provides tools that you can use to examine and enhance your knowledge of Scrum. The primary aim of these assessments is to provide information about an individual's, or a team's, level of knowledge and thereby to enable improvement.

Scrum.org assessments are grounded in the Scrum Body of Knowledge—the *Scrum Guide*, which is written and maintained by Scrum's founders Ken Schwaber and Jeff Sutherland. The *Scrum Guide* is published by and freely available at Scrum.org.

Each of Scrum.org's assessments is developed by Scrum thought leaders with formal input from a wide range of industry experts and then enhanced with input from the larger Scrum community. They are then monitored in an ongoing attempt to ensure their continued integrity and relevance.

Currently, Scrum.org provides four families of assessments:

- **Scrum Open** A freely available assessment of basic Scrum knowledge, available for members of the Scrum.org community.

- **Professional Scrum Master** Two levels of assessment of Scrum knowledge for Scrum Masters.

- **Professional Scrum Developer** An assessment that tests the knowledge of developing software on a Development Team using contemporary development practices. The assessment is tool- and technology-agnostic.

- **Professional Scrum Product Owner** Two levels of assessment of Scrum knowledge for Product Owners.

Those who achieve a minimum passing assessment score receive certification. All Scrum.org assessments use the most recent version of the English *Scrum Guide* as the source for questions regarding the rules, artifacts, events, and roles of Scrum. Reading the *Scrum Guide* alone will not provide enough preparation for someone to pass an assessment. Questions often ask test-takers to interpret information and apply it to challenging situations, so knowledge gained from personal experience of Scrum, as well as other sources, is typically required.

Become a high-performance Scrum Development Team

High-performance Scrum Development Teams are the best of the best. They have mastered the key pillars of Scrum: self-organization, transparency, inspection, and adaptation. They have focus, exhibit courage and openness, believe in and practice commitment, and respect others. They know the rules of Scrum according to the *Scrum Guide*, and are able to deliver Increments of business value regularly in the form of working software.

It's possible to become a high-performance Scrum Development Team through continuous improvement, as you can see in Figure 9-7.

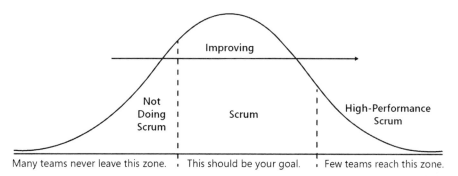

FIGURE 9-7 Teams can progress from not doing Scrum all the way to High-Performance Scrum.

Looking at a distribution curve and contemplating your own situation, you might be wondering, "Is my team doing Scrum?" It turns out that this is a harder question to answer than you might think. One might believe that just reading the *Scrum guide*, filling all the roles, attending all of the event meetings, and using the artifacts correctly would be enough. Even this is not easy to define, however.

Note In November 2011, several Professional Scrum Trainers met in Redmond, WA, prior to the annual ALM Summit. One of the items on the agenda was to create a way to definitively determine if a team was on the left side of the first dotted line in Figure 9-7. Teams wanted to know if they were "doing Scrum." To determine this, the PSTs created a simple, measurable checklist that a team could answer. If all questions were answered in the affirmative, that team was doing Scrum. The measure of "how well" they are doing Scrum and where they are at on their journey to improvement is another story.

- ☐ Does your Scrum Team maintain an ordered Product Backlog?
- ☐ Does your Development Team contain three to nine developers?
- ☐ Does your Product Owner actively manage the Product Backlog?
- ☐ Does your Scrum Master actively manage the process?
- ☐ Do you have fixed-length Sprints of one month or less?
- ☐ Does the Development Team create a Sprint Backlog during Sprint Planning?
- ☐ Can progress be assessed from the Sprint Backlog?
- ☐ Does your Scrum Team hold Sprint Review and Sprint Retrospective meetings?
- ☐ Does your Development Team develop done, potentially releasable software each Sprint?
- ☐ Do your stakeholders inspect the Increment and provide feedback?

Note The above is not an official checklist. It represents a work in progress, drafted by several like-minded Professional Scrum Trainers.

All throughout this book, I have provided patterns to adopt and anti-patterns to avoid when it comes to Professional Scrum development. All of this guidance, in addition to adopting the core principles and values of Scrum, should be consumed and applied in order for you and your fellow developers to become high-performance Professional Scrum Developers.

Chapter burndown

Here are the key concepts we covered in this chapter:

- **Professional Scrum Developers** Know the rules of Scrum and how to overcome its common challenges. They also know that dysfunctions should be identified and removed.

- **High-performance Scrum Developers** Are hungry to do better and take every opportunity to inspect and adapt, remove or mitigate dysfunction, and continuously improve their game of Scrum.

- **Fix bugs, don't manage them** Fix in-Sprint bugs, if possible, rather than creating work items and kicking them around.

- **Remove impediments, don't manage them** Remove your own impediments rather than relying on the Scrum Master to do it for you.

- **Estimate as a team** Help the Product Owner keep the Product Backlog groomed, including estimating the size of the upcoming PBIs.

- **Assess progress** Use burndown charts, work item counts, or passing tests to assess your progress towards a goal.

- **Renegotiating scope** This can happen, and when it does, collaborate with the Product Owner to accommodate the change. Constant changing of scope is a dysfunction.

- **Canceling a Sprint** Only the Product Owner can cancel a Sprint. It is a traumatic event and should be avoided if possible.

- **Undone work** Unfinished PBIs cannot be released. Instead, they should be put back on the Product Backlog for grooming and consideration to be developed in a future Sprint. Visual Studio doesn't offer any tooling support for this.

- **Spikes** Spikes are experiments performed by the Development Team to learn and prove concepts. Larger spikes should be represented in the Product Backlog and Sprint Backlog.

- **Fixed-price contracts** Scrum works as well as any other process when it comes to fixed-price contracts. It works better when a level of trust and shared risks exist between the Scrum Team and the customer.

- **Measuring performance** This should be done at a team level, not an individual level.

- **Done** Every PBI should be done, according to the Development Team's Definition of "Done." Undone work should not be released.

- **Inspect and adapt** Take advantage of the built-in Scrum events to ask yourself and your team how are you are doing with the product, as well as the process. Be sure to act on any of those findings that require it.

- **Don't change Scrum** The framework is already very pluggable, allowing any number of processes and practices to be implemented. Changing Scrum is usually done to hide an underlying dysfunction.

- **Scrum is like chess** You either play it as its rules state, or you don't. Scrum and chess do not fail or succeed. They are either played or not played.

The Scrum Guide is the official Scrum Body of Knowledge and is maintained by Scrum's creators, Ken Schwaber and Jeff Sutherland. It is available in 30 languages. The latest version can be found at *http://www.scrum.org/scrum-guides*.

The Scrum Guide

The Definitive Guide to Scrum: The Rules of the Game

Scrum is a framework for developing and sustaining complex products. This Guide contains the definition of Scrum. This definition consists of Scrum's roles, events, artifacts, and the rules that bind them together. Ken Schwaber and Jeff Sutherland developed Scrum; the Scrum Guide is written and provided by them. Together, they stand behind the Scrum Guide.

Scrum Overview

Scrum (n): A framework within which people can address complex adaptive problems, while productively and creatively delivering products of the highest possible value. Scrum is:

- Lightweight

- Simple to understand

- Extremely difficult to master

Scrum is a process framework that has been used to manage complex product development since the early 1990s. Scrum is not a process or a technique for building products; rather, it is a framework within which you can employ various processes and techniques. Scrum makes clear the relative efficacy of your product management and development practices so that you can improve.

Scrum Framework

The Scrum framework consists of Scrum Teams and their associated roles, events, artifacts, and rules. Each component within the framework serves a specific purpose and is essential to Scrum's success and usage.

Specific strategies for using the Scrum framework vary and are described elsewhere.

The rules of Scrum bind together the events, roles, and artifacts, governing the relationships and interaction between them. The rules of Scrum are described throughout the body of this document.

Scrum Theory

Scrum is founded on empirical process control theory, or empiricism. Empiricism asserts that knowledge comes from experience and making decisions based on what is known. Scrum employs an iterative, incremental approach to optimize predictability and control risk.

Three pillars uphold every implementation of empirical process control: transparency, inspection, and adaptation.

Transparency

Significant aspects of the process must be visible to those responsible for the outcome. Transparency requires those aspects be defined by a common standard so observers share a common understanding of what is being seen.

For example:

- A common language referring to the process must be shared by all participants; and,

- A common definition of "Done"1 must be shared by those performing the work and those accepting the work product.

Inspection

Scrum users must frequently inspect Scrum artifacts and progress toward a goal to detect undesirable variances. Their inspection should not be so frequent that inspection gets in the way of the work. Inspections are most beneficial when diligently performed by skilled inspectors at the point of work.

Adaptation

If an inspector determines that one or more aspects of a process deviate outside acceptable limits, and that the resulting product will be unacceptable, the process or the material being processed must be adjusted. An adjustment must be made as soon as possible to minimize further deviation.

Scrum prescribes four formal opportunities for inspection and adaptation, as described in the Scrum Events section of this document.

- Sprint Planning Meeting

- Daily Scrum

- Sprint Review

- Sprint Retrospective

Scrum

Scrum is a framework structured to support complex product development. Scrum consists of Scrum Teams and their associated roles, events, artifacts, and rules. Each component within the framework serves a specific purpose and is essential to Scrum's success and usage.

The Scrum Team

The Scrum Team consists of a Product Owner, the Development Team, and a Scrum Master. Scrum Teams are self-organizing and cross-functional. Self-organizing teams choose how best to accomplish their work, rather than being directed by others outside the team. Cross-functional teams have all competencies needed to accomplish the work without depending on others not part of the team. The team model in Scrum is designed to optimize flexibility, creativity, and productivity.

Scrum Teams deliver products iteratively and incrementally, maximizing opportunities for feedback. Incremental deliveries of "Done" product ensure a potentially useful version of working product is always available.one is allowed to tell the Development Team to work from a different set of requirements, and the Development Team isn't allowed to act on what anyone else says.

The Product Owner

The Product Owner is responsible for maximizing the value of the product and the work of the Development Team. How this is done may vary widely across organizations, Scrum Teams, and individuals.

The Product Owner is the sole person responsible for managing the Product Backlog. Product Backlog management includes:

- Clearly expressing Product Backlog items;

- Ordering the items in the Product Backlog to best achieve goals and missions;

- Ensuring the value of the work the Development Team performs;

- Ensuring that the Product Backlog is visible, transparent, and clear to all, and shows what the Scrum Team will work on next; and,

- Ensuring the Development Team understands items in the Product Backlog to the level needed.

The Product Owner may do the above work, or have the Development Team do it. However, the Product Owner remains accountable.

The Product Owner is one person, not a committee. The Product Owner may represent the desires of a committee in the Product Backlog, but those wanting to change a backlog item's priority must convince the Product Owner.

For the Product Owner to succeed, the entire organization must respect his or her decisions. The Product Owner's decisions are visible in the content and ordering of the Product Backlog. No one is allowed to tell the Development Team to work from a different set of requirements, and the Development Team isn't allowed to act on what anyone else says.

The Development Team

The Development Team consists of professionals who do the work of delivering a potentially releasable Increment of "Done" product at the end of each Sprint. Only members of the Development Team create the Increment.

Development Teams are structured and empowered by the organization to organize and manage their own work. The resulting synergy optimizes the Development Team's overall efficiency and effectiveness. Development Teams have the following characteristics:

- They are self-organizing. No one (not even the Scrum Master) tells the Development Team how to turn Product Backlog into Increments of potentially releasable functionality;

- Development Teams are cross-functional, with all of the skills as a team necessary to create a product Increment;

- Scrum recognizes no titles for Development Team members other than Developer, regardless of the work being performed by the person; there are no exceptions to this rule;

- Individual Development Team members may have specialized skills and areas of focus, but accountability belongs to the Development Team as a whole; and,

- Development Teams do not contain sub-teams dedicated to particular domains like testing or business analysis.

Development Team Size

Optimal Development Team size is small enough to remain nimble and large enough to complete significant work. Fewer than three Development Team members decreases interaction and results in smaller productivity gains. Smaller Development Teams may encounter skill constraints during the Sprint, causing the Development Team to be unable to deliver a potentially releasable Increment. Having more than nine members requires too much coordination. Large Development Teams generate too much complexity for an empirical process to manage. The Product Owner and Scrum Master roles are not included in this count unless they are also executing the work of the Sprint Backlog.

The Scrum Master

The Scrum Master is responsible for ensuring Scrum is understood and enacted. Scrum Masters do this by ensuring that the Scrum Team adheres to Scrum theory, practices, and rules. The Scrum Master is a servant-leader for the Scrum Team.

The Scrum Master helps those outside the Scrum Team understand which of their interactions with the Scrum Team are helpful and which aren't. The Scrum Master helps everyone change these interactions to maximize the value created by the Scrum Team.

Scrum Master Service to the Product Owner

The Scrum Master serves the Product Owner in several ways, including:

- Finding techniques for effective Product Backlog management;
- Clearly communicating vision, goals, and Product Backlog items to the Development Team;
- Teaching the Scrum Team to create clear and concise Product Backlog items;
- Understanding long-term product planning in an empirical environment;
- Understanding and practicing agility; and,
- Facilitating Scrum events as requested or needed.

Scrum Master Service to the Development Team

The Scrum Master serves the Development Team in several ways, including:

- Coaching the Development Team in self-organization and cross-functionality;
- Teaching and leading the Development Team to create high-value products;
- Removing impediments to the Development Team's progress;
- Facilitating Scrum events as requested or needed; and,
- Coaching the Development Team in organizational environments in which Scrum is not yet fully adopted and understood.

Scrum Master Service to the Organization

The Scrum Master serves the organization in several ways, including:

- Leading and coaching the organization in its Scrum adoption;
- Planning Scrum implementations within the organization;
- Helping employees and stakeholders understand and enact Scrum and empirical product development;
- Causing change that increases the productivity of the Scrum Team; and,
- Working with other Scrum Masters to increase the effectiveness of the application of Scrum in the organization.

Scrum Events

Prescribed events are used in Scrum to create regularity and to minimize the need for meetings not defined in Scrum. Scrum uses time-boxed events, such that every event has a maximum duration. This ensures an appropriate amount of time is spent planning without allowing waste in the planning process.

Other than the Sprint itself, which is a container for all other events, each event in Scrum is a formal opportunity to inspect and adapt something. These events are specifically designed to enable critical transparency and inspection. Failure to include any of these events results in reduced transparency and is a lost opportunity to inspect and adapt.

The Sprint

The heart of Scrum is a Sprint, a time-box of one month or less during which a "Done", useable, and potentially releasable product Increment is created. Sprints have consistent durations throughout a development effort. A new Sprint starts immediately after the conclusion of the previous Sprint.

Sprints contain and consist of the Sprint Planning Meeting, Daily Scrums, the development work, the Sprint Review, and the Sprint Retrospective.

During the Sprint:

- No changes are made that would affect the Sprint Goal;

- Development Team composition remains constant;

- Quality goals do not decrease; and,

- Scope may be clarified and re-negotiated between the Product Owner and Development Team as more is learned.

Each Sprint may be considered a project with no more than a one-month horizon. Like projects, Sprints are used to accomplish something. Each Sprint has a definition of what is to be built, a design and flexible plan that will guide building it, the work, and the resultant product.

Sprints are limited to one calendar month. When a Sprint's horizon is too long the definition of what is being built may change, complexity may rise, and risk may increase. Sprints enable predictability by ensuring inspection and adaptation of progress toward a goal at least every calendar month. Sprints also limit risk to one calendar month of cost.

Cancelling a Sprint

A Sprint can be cancelled before the Sprint time-box is over. Only the Product Owner has the authority to cancel the Sprint, although he or she may do so under influence from the stakeholders, the Development Team, or the Scrum Master.

A Sprint would be cancelled if the Sprint Goal becomes obsolete. This might occur if the company changes direction or if market or technology conditions change. In general, a Sprint should be cancelled if it no longer makes sense given the circumstances. But, due to the short duration of Sprints, cancellation rarely makes sense.

When a Sprint is cancelled, any completed and "Done" Product Backlog Items are reviewed. If part of the work is potentially releasable, the Product Owner typically accepts it. All incomplete Product Backlog Items are re-estimated and put back on the Product Backlog. The work done on them depreciates quickly and must be frequently re-estimated.

Sprint cancellations consume resources, since everyone has to regroup in another Sprint Planning Meeting to start another Sprint. Sprint cancellations are often traumatic to the Scrum Team, and are very uncommon.

Sprint Planning Meeting

The work to be performed in the Sprint is planned at the Sprint Planning Meeting. This plan is created by the collaborative work of the entire Scrum Team.

The Sprint Planning Meeting is time-boxed to eight hours for a one-month Sprint. For shorter Sprints, the event is proportionately shorter. For example, two-week Sprints have four-hour Sprint Planning Meetings.

The Sprint Planning Meeting consists of two parts, each one being a time-box of one half of the Sprint Planning Meeting duration. The two parts of the Sprint Planning Meeting answer the following questions, respectively:

- What will be delivered in the Increment resulting from the upcoming Sprint?

- How will the work needed to deliver the Increment be achieved?

Part One: What will be done this Sprint?

In this part, the Development Team works to forecast the functionality that will be developed during the Sprint. The Product Owner presents ordered Product Backlog items to the Development Team and the entire Scrum Team collaborates on understanding the work of the Sprint.

The input to this meeting is the Product Backlog, the latest product Increment, projected capacity of the Development Team during the Sprint, and past performance of the Development Team. The number of items selected from the Product Backlog for the Sprint is solely up to the Development Team. Only the Development Team can assess what it can accomplish over the upcoming Sprint.

After the Development Team forecasts the Product Backlog items it will deliver in the Sprint, the Scrum Team crafts a Sprint Goal. The Sprint Goal is an objective that will be met within the Sprint through the implementation of the Product Backlog, and it provides guidance to the Development Team on why it is building the Increment.

Part Two: How will the chosen work get done?

Having selected the work of the Sprint, the Development Team decides how it will build this functionality into a "Done" product Increment during the Sprint. The Product Backlog items selected for this Sprint plus the plan for delivering them is called the Sprint Backlog.

The Development Team usually starts by designing the system and the work needed to convert the Product Backlog into a working product Increment. Work may be of varying size, or estimated effort. However, enough work is planned during the Sprint Planning Meeting for the Development Team to forecast what it believes it can do in the upcoming Sprint. Work planned for the first days of the Sprint by the Development Team is decomposed to units of one day or less by the end of this meeting. The Development Team self-organizes to undertake the work in the Sprint Backlog, both during the Sprint Planning Meeting and as needed throughout the Sprint.

The Product Owner may be present during the second part of the Sprint Planning Meeting to clarify the selected Product Backlog items and to help make trade-offs. If the Development Team determines it has too much or too little work, it may renegotiate the Sprint Backlog items with the Product Owner. The Development Team may also invite other people to attend in order to provide technical or domain advice.

By the end of the Sprint Planning Meeting, the Development Team should be able to explain to the Product Owner and Scrum Master how it intends to work as a self-organizing team to accomplish the Sprint Goal and create the anticipated Increment.

Sprint Goal

The Sprint Goal gives the Development Team some flexibility regarding the functionality implemented within the Sprint.

As the Development Team works, it keeps this goal in mind. In order to satisfy the Sprint Goal, it implements the functionality and technology. If the work turns out to be different than the Development Team expected, then they collaborate with the Product Owner to negotiate the scope of Sprint Backlog within the Sprint.

The Sprint Goal may be a milestone in the larger purpose of the product roadmap.

Daily Scrum

The Daily Scrum is a 15-minute time-boxed event for the Development Team to synchronize activities and create a plan for the next 24 hours. This is done by inspecting the work since the last Daily Scrum and forecasting the work that could be done before the next one.

The Daily Scrum is held at the same time and place each day to reduce complexity. During the meeting, each Development Team member explains:

■ What has been accomplished since the last meeting?

- What will be done before the next meeting?

- What obstacles are in the way?

The Development Team uses the Daily Scrum to assess progress toward the Sprint Goal and to assess how progress is trending toward completing the work in the Sprint Backlog. The Daily Scrum optimizes the probability that the Development Team will meet the Sprint Goal. The Development Team often meets immediately after the Daily Scrum to re-plan the rest of the Sprint's work. Every day, the Development Team should be able to explain to the Product Owner and Scrum Master how it intends to work together as a self-organizing team to accomplish the goal and create the anticipated Increment in the remainder of the Sprint.

The Scrum Master ensures that the Development Team has the meeting, but the Development Team is responsible for conducting the Daily Scrum. The Scrum Master teaches the Development Team to keep the Daily Scrum within the 15-minute time-box.

The Scrum Master enforces the rule that only Development Team members participate in the Daily Scrum. The Daily Scrum is not a status meeting, and is for the people transforming the Product Backlog items into an Increment.

Daily Scrums improve communications, eliminate other meetings, identify and remove impediments to development, highlight and promote quick decision-making, and improve the Development Team's level of project knowledge. This is a key inspect and adapt meeting.

Sprint Review

A Sprint Review is held at the end of the Sprint to inspect the Increment and adapt the Product Backlog if needed. During the Sprint Review, the Scrum Team and stakeholders collaborate about what was done in the Sprint. Based on that and any changes to the Product Backlog during the Sprint, attendees collaborate on the next things that could be done. This is an informal meeting, and the presentation of the Increment is intended to elicit feedback and foster collaboration.

This is a four-hour time-boxed meeting for one-month Sprints. Proportionately less time is allocated for shorter Sprints. For example, two week Sprints have two-hour Sprint Reviews.

- The Sprint Review includes the following elements:

- The Product Owner identifies what has been "Done" and what has not been "Done";

- The Development Team discusses what went well during the Sprint, what problems it ran into, and how those problems were solved;

- The Development Team demonstrates the work that it has "Done" and answers questions about the Increment;

- The Product Owner discusses the Product Backlog as it stands. He or she projects likely completion dates based on progress to date; and,

- The entire group collaborates on what to do next, so that the Sprint Review provides valuable input to subsequent Sprint Planning Meetings.

The result of the Sprint Review is a revised Product Backlog that defines the probable Product Backlog items for the next Sprint. The Product Backlog may also be adjusted overall to meet new opportunities.

Sprint Retrospective

The Sprint Retrospective is an opportunity for the Scrum Team to inspect itself and create a plan for improvements to be enacted during the next Sprint.

The Sprint Retrospective occurs after the Sprint Review and prior to the next Sprint Planning Meeting. This is a three-hour time-boxed meeting for one-month Sprints. Proportionately less time is allocated for shorter Sprints.

The purpose of the Sprint Retrospective is to:

- Inspect how the last Sprint went with regards to people, relationships, process, and tools;

- Identify and order the major items that went well and potential improvements; and,

- Create a plan for implementing improvements to the way the Scrum Team does its work.

The Scrum Master encourages the Scrum Team to improve, within the Scrum process framework, its development process and practices to make it more effective and enjoyable for the next Sprint. During each Sprint Retrospective, the Scrum Team plans ways to increase product quality by adapting the Definition of "Done" as appropriate.

By the end of the Sprint Retrospective, the Scrum Team should have identified improvements that it will implement in the next Sprint. Implementing these improvements in the next Sprint is the adaptation to the inspection of the Scrum Team itself. Although improvements may be implemented at any time, the Sprint Retrospective provides a formal opportunity to focus on inspection and adaptation.

Scrum Artifacts

Scrum's artifacts represent work or value in various ways that are useful in providing transparency and opportunities for inspection and adaptation. Artifacts defined by Scrum are specifically designed to maximize transparency of key information needed to ensure Scrum Teams are successful in delivering a "Done" Increment.

Product Backlog

The Product Backlog is an ordered list of everything that might be needed in the product and is the single source of requirements for any changes to be made to the product. The Product Owner is responsible for the Product Backlog, including its content, availability, and ordering.

A Product Backlog is never complete. The earliest development of it only lays out the initially known and best-understood requirements. The Product Backlog evolves as the product and the environment in which it will be used evolves. The Product Backlog is dynamic; it constantly changes to identify what the product needs to be appropriate, competitive, and useful. As long as a product exists, its Product Backlog also exists.

The Product Backlog lists all features, functions, requirements, enhancements, and fixes that constitute the changes to be made to the product in future releases. Product Backlog items have the attributes of a description, order, and estimate.

The Product Backlog is often ordered by value, risk, priority, and necessity. Top-ordered Product Backlog items drive immediate development activities. The higher the order, the more a Product Backlog item has been considered, and the more consensus exists regarding it and its value.

Higher ordered Product Backlog items are clearer and more detailed than lower ordered ones. More precise estimates are made based on the greater clarity and increased detail; the lower the order, the less detail. Product Backlog items that will occupy the Development Team for the upcoming Sprint are fine-grained, having been decomposed so that any one item can be "Done" within the Sprint time-box. Product Backlog items that can be "Done" by the Development Team within one Sprint are deemed "ready" or "actionable" for selection in a Sprint Planning Meeting.

As a product is used and gains value, and the marketplace provides feedback, the Product Backlog becomes a larger and more exhaustive list. Requirements never stop changing, so a Product Backlog is a living artifact. Changes in business requirements, market conditions, or technology may cause changes in the Product Backlog.

Multiple Scrum Teams often work together on the same product. One Product Backlog is used to describe the upcoming work on the product. A Product Backlog attribute that groups items is then employed.

Product Backlog grooming is the act of adding detail, estimates, and order to items in the Product Backlog. This is an ongoing process in which the Product Owner and the Development Team collaborate on the details of Product Backlog items. During Product Backlog grooming, items are reviewed and revised. However, they can be updated at any time by the Product Owner or at the Product Owner's discretion.

Grooming is a part-time activity during a Sprint between the Product Owner and the Development Team. Often the Development Team has the domain knowledge to perform grooming itself. How and when grooming is done is decided by the Scrum Team. Grooming usually consumes no more than 10% of the capacity of the Development Team.

The Development Team is responsible for all estimates. The Product Owner may influence the Development Team by helping understand and select trade-offs, but the people who will perform the work make the final estimate.

Monitoring Progress Toward a Goal

At any point in time, the total work remaining to reach a goal can be summed. The Product Owner tracks this total work remaining at least for every Sprint Review. The Product Owner compares this amount with work remaining at previous Sprint Reviews to assess progress toward completing projected work by the desired time for the goal. This information is made transparent to all stakeholders.

Various trend burndown, burnup and other projective practices have been used to forecast progress. These have proven useful. However, these do not replace the importance of empiricism. In complex environments, what will happen is unknown. Only what has happened may be used for forward-looking decision-making.

Sprint Backlog

The Sprint Backlog is the set of Product Backlog items selected for the Sprint plus a plan for delivering the product Increment and realizing the Sprint Goal. The Sprint Backlog is a forecast by the Development Team about what functionality will be in the next Increment and the work needed to deliver that functionality.

The Sprint Backlog defines the work the Development Team will perform to turn Product Backlog items into a "Done" Increment. The Sprint Backlog makes visible all of the work that the Development Team identifies as necessary to meet the Sprint Goal.

The Sprint Backlog is a plan with enough detail that changes in progress can be understood in the Daily Scrum. The Development Team modifies Sprint Backlog throughout the Sprint, and the Sprint Backlog emerges during the Sprint. This emergence occurs as the Development Team works through the plan and learns more about the work needed to achieve the Sprint Goal.

As new work is required, the Development Team adds it to the Sprint Backlog. As work is performed or completed, the estimated remaining work is updated. When elements of the plan are deemed unnecessary, they are removed. Only the Development Team can change its Sprint Backlog during a Sprint. The Sprint Backlog is a highly visible, real-time picture of the work that the Development Team plans to accomplish during the Sprint, and it belongs solely to the Development Team.

Monitoring Sprint Progress

At any point in time in a Sprint, the total work remaining in the Sprint Backlog items can be summed. The Development Team tracks this total work remaining at least for every Daily Scrum. The Development Team tracks these sums daily and projects the likelihood of achieving the Sprint Goal. By tracking the remaining work throughout the Sprint, the Development Team can manage its progress.

Scrum does not consider the time spent working on Sprint Backlog Items. The work remaining and date are the only variables of interest.

Increment

The Increment is the sum of all the Product Backlog items completed during a Sprint and all previous Sprints. At the end of a Sprint, the new Increment must be "Done," which means it must be in useable condition and meet the Scrum Team's Definition of "Done." It must be in useable condition regardless of whether the Product Owner decides to actually release it.

Definition of "Done"

When the Product Backlog item or an Increment is described as "Done", everyone must understand what "Done" means. Although this varies significantly per Scrum Team, members must have a shared understanding of what it means for work to be complete, to ensure transparency. This is the "Definition of Done" for the Scrum Team and is used to assess when work is complete on the product Increment.

The same definition guides the Development Team in knowing how many Product Backlog items it can select during a Sprint Planning Meeting. The purpose of each Sprint is to deliver Increments of potentially releasable functionality that adhere to the Scrum Team's current Definition of "Done."

Development Teams deliver an Increment of product functionality every Sprint. This Increment is useable, so a Product Owner may choose to immediately release it. Each Increment is additive to all prior Increments and thoroughly tested, ensuring that all Increments work together.

As Scrum Teams mature, it is expected that their Definition of "Done" will expand to include more stringent criteria for higher quality.

Conclusion

Scrum is free and offered in this guide. Scrum's roles, artifacts, events, and rules are immutable and although implementing only parts of Scrum is possible, the result is not Scrum. Scrum exists only in its entirety and functions well as a container for other techniques, methodologies, and practices.

Acknowledgements

People

Of the thousands of people who have contributed to Scrum, we should single out those who were instrumental in its first ten years. First there was Jeff Sutherland, working with Jeff McKenna, and Ken Schwaber, working with Mike Smith and Chris Martin. Many others contributed in the ensuing years and without their help Scrum would not be refined as it is today. David Starr provided key insights and editorial skills in formulating this version of the Scrum Guide.

History

Ken Schwaber and Jeff Sutherland first co-presented Scrum at the OOPSLA conference in 1995. This presentation essentially documented the learning that Ken and Jeff had over the previous few years applying Scrum.

The history of Scrum is already considered long. To honor the first places where it was tried and refined, we recognize Individual, Inc., Fidelity Investments, and IDX (now GE Medical).

The Scrum Guide documents Scrum as developed and sustained for twenty-plus years by Jeff Sutherland and Ken Schwaber. Other sources provide you with patterns, processes, and insights about how the practices, facilitations, and tools that complement the Scrum framework. These optimize productivity, value, creativity, and pride.

Index

Symbols and Numbers

About the author

 RICHARD HUNDHAUSEN is the president of Accentient, a company that helps
software development teams understand and leverage Application Lifecycle
Management and Scrum tools and practices. He has over 30 years of software
development experience and over 20 years of training experience. He is a
Microsoft Regional Director, Visual Studio ALM MVP, and the author of several
books and courses—including the Professional Scrum Developer program from Microsoft.
You can reach Richard via email at *richard@accentient.com*.

What do you think of this book?

We want to hear from you!

To participate in a brief online survey, please visit:

microsoft.com/learning/booksurvey

Tell us how well this book meets your needs—what works effectively, and what we can do better. Your feedback will help us continually improve our books and learning resources for you.

Thank you in advance for your input!

CPSIA information can be obtained at www.ICGtesting.com
Printed in the USA
BVOW001000300413

319463BV00014B/361/P